# The
# Research
# Act

# The
# Research
# Act

A Theoretical Introduction to Sociological Methods

# Norman K. Denzin

## Routledge
Taylor & Francis Group

LONDON AND NEW YORK

First published 2009 by Transaction Publishers

Published 2017 by Routledge
2 Park Square, Milton Park, Abingdon, Oxon OX14 4RN
711 Third Avenue, New York, NY 10017, USA

*Routledge is an imprint of the Taylor & Francis Group, an informa business*

First paperback printing © 2009 by Taylor & Francis.
Originally published copyright © 1970 by Norman K. Denzin.

Library of Congress Catalog Number: 2008055012

Library of Congress Cataloging-in-Publication Data

Denzin, Norman K.
    The research act : a theoretical introduction to sociological methods / Norman K. Denzin.
        p. cm.
    Includes bibliographical references and index.
    ISBN 978-0-202-36248-9 (alk. paper)
        1. Sociology--Methodology. 2. Sociology--Research. I. Title

HM511.D456 2009
301.072--dc22

                                                    2008055012

ISBN 13: 978-0-202-36248-9 (pbk)

# Contents

**PART IV**
**STRATEGIES OF TRIANGULATION AND THE**
**ART OF DOING SOCIOLOGY**

Continuous advance in science has been possible only when analysis of the objects of knowledge has supplied not elements of meanings as the objects have been conceived but elements abstracted from those meanings. That is, scientific advance implies a willingness to remain on terms of tolerant acceptance of the reality of what cannot be stated in the accepted doctrine of the time, but what must be stated in the form of contradiction with those accepted doctrines.

*George Herbert Mead*
In Creative Intelligence: Essays in the Pragmatic Attitude, p. 173.

The most important advice I can give the contemporary sociologist has nothing to do with the validity of my arguments. It is this: you do not have to believe anything about theory and methodology that is told you pretentiously and sanctimoniously by other sociologists—including myself. So much guff has gotten mixed with the truth that, if you cannot tell which is which, you had better reject it all. It will only get in your way. No one will go far wrong theoretically who remains in close touch with and seeks to understand a body of concrete phenomena.

*George Caspar Homans*
In *Handbook of Modern Sociology*, pp. 975–976.

# *Preface*

In this book I present a symbolic interactionist view of sociological theory and methodology. I take the view that theory and method must be brought closer together and that both must be interpreted from a common perspective if sociologists are to narrow the breach that presently exists between their theories and their methods. Accordingly, I have taken one theoretical perspective from the many currently available in the social sciences, and consistently evaluated theory and method from it. Chapter 1 of this book presents the symbolic interactionist and methodological perspective used in my analysis. I develop the case that theories and methods represent different ways of acting on the empirical environment. I indicate the role of symbolic interaction in the conduct of sociology and suggest that there must be a recognition of the "symbolic" before a science called sociology can be systematically built.

Chapters 2 and 3 apply this framework to the process of theory development. Elements of theory are examined and problems of developing theory are discussed. Various views of theorizing are presented, including a perspective consistent with the interactionist point of view, which I feel should be the desired approach to theory development. Chapters 4 and 5 continue the application of this framework to the problems the sociologist confronts as he moves from theory to empirical reality—the selection of sampling or observational units. In Chapter 4 I present a synthesis of statistical and theoretical sampling models. Rather than viewing the sampling problem as resolved either by rigorous statistical procedures or by more loosely conceived theoretical strategies, however, I suggest that all steps in the sampling process must be theoretically guided. When they are, sociologists may sample such theoretically relevant objects as time and its passage, situations and their variations, or persons in different forms of social organization. In addition, theoretical schemes may be sampled just as sociologists currently sample communities, or entire societies.

In Chapter 5 I offer a review of the major measurement and scaling techniques employed by sociologists. Several themes guide my discussion in this chapter. First, measurement is seen as an interaction in which the sociologist attempts to identify reliably observations as instances of theoretical concepts. These identifications are problematic, and in this context I expand the notions of internal and external validity to include the interaction that occurs in "observational encounters." Second, the costs and consequences of selecting one measurement strategy over another are examined as I treat the relevance of measurement decisions for subsequent data analyses. I propose an elaborated view of triangulation, or the combination of measurement strategies, as one strategy for resolving the inherent biases of one measurement technique. Finally, the differences between qualitative and quantitative are discussed, and I suggest that qualitative measurement strategies may serve as well as quantitative strategies in the development and testing of social theory.

Chapter 6 takes up the problems of interviewing and here I propose an interactionist conception, treating the interview as a special type of face-to-face encounter. Strategies of interviewing recalcitrant, deviant, hostile, and silent respondents are presented, as are the validity and reliability problems of such encounters. I indicate the appropriate role of interviews in the total observational process and conclude by suggesting that interviews may be studied for what they reveal about interactions between strangers.

Chapters 7 through 11 present what I regard as the five major methods of the sociologist: experiments, surveys, participant observation, life histories, and unobtrusive measures. These methods are assessed in the interactionist perspective. Validity and causation are treated and I propose that the sociologist has three chief means of formulating causal propositions: the experimental model of control, the survey-multivariate analysis model of design, and analytic induction. The use of these models at once raises and solves in different ways certain problems, which are indicated as I treat the strengths and weaknesses of the five methods.

Chapter 12 presents the logic for "multiple triangulation"—a framework for combining multiple theories, observers, data sources, and methods in single investigations. I take the position that sociologists must move beyond single-method, "atheoretical" investigations; sociological reality is such that no single method, theory, or observer can ever capture all that is relevant and important.

The book concludes with a logical and necessary treatment of the ethical, social, and political contingencies that always make sociological investigations less than ideal. There is more to the "doing of sociology" than the formal methods treated in this or any other methodological manual would suggest. The roles of differing pressure groups, ethics, values, and ideologies in the sociological research process are sketched, with special attention to the interpersonal demands of colleagues, granting agencies, clients, and subjects. A perennial dilemma of the sociologist arises from the fact that humans are studying other humans; hence, values, personalities and social pressures lie at the heart of sociology. The final chapter closes with a treatment of the ethical implications of sociological research. Various positions on this issue are reviewed and, on the grounds that the sociologist's first commitment should be to his discipline, I take a stance that justifies "unannounced," disguised research methods. If we are not permitted to study things that people wish hidden, then sociology will remain a science of public conduct based on evidence and data given us by volunteers, a condition that runs counter to the dominant ethos of the scientific-intellectual enterprise.

Perhaps some readers will feel that I have ignored important recent developments in sociological methods. For instance, I do not treat the use of computers and high-speed data-processing techniques, because of a personal bias against such strategies, which too often become substitutes for the sociological imagination. They are tools that can, and under certain circumstances should, be used, but they are not substitutes for rigorous knowledge and use of sociological methods in the theory process. Nor have I treated recent developments in what some now call the comparative method. The methods treated in this book are well suited to the comparative method—the basic principles of methodology apply to any field setting, a native village in Africa, Cartagena, Colombia, or Chicago. To speak of a comparative method is to speak of all sociological methods. Finally, although I have drawn on materials from ethnomethodology in several of the chapters on the field method, there is no systematic presentation of this point of view, since, with few important exceptions, I see it as a special expression of principles from symbolic interaction theory.

It is my hope that the perspective of and the problems treated in this book will shed new light on old issues and lead the sociologist to better link his vague images of reality with research activities. I am suggesting that theory and method must interact so that each contributes to the growth of the other.

*To Evelyn, Johanna, and Rachel*

# Acknowledgments

I am indebted to my publisher, Alexander J. Morin, for forcing me to revise and for ever reminding me that the act of doing sociology must be seen in symbolic interactionist terms. He has given me a sense of scholarship that I hope someday to attain. Howard S. Becker painfully endured the reading of revision upon revision and his suggestions have kept me mindful that one must learn to defend his positions without being at the same time overly polemical. Richard J. Hill subjected me to the greatest pains; his criticisms forced a major revision. The quality of my presentation owes much to his efforts, and to a reader who remained unidentified. Herbert Blumer's works and remarks have fundamentally shaped my conception of the sociological enterprise; it is my hope that this book does justice to his perspective. My students at the University of Illinois patiently sat through the many drafts of this book. I am grateful for their comments, grimaces and criticisms, as well as the comments of David A. Fabianic and Sheldon Stryker.

For placing the final product in readable form I am indebted to Regan and Lillian Smith. They undertook a rush job at the last moment and admirably performed under the pressures of a tight publication schedule.

I dedicate this book to my wife and two daughters who patiently put up with an absent husband and father. My wife's perspective has indelibly shaped my sociological stance. It is to her and my daughters that I am most deeply indebted.

All books, I suppose, are ultimately personal statements. I am grateful to the above persons for making this book more public in nature.

# The Interactionist Perspective and the Process of Theory Construction

Part I
The Interactionist Perspective
and the Process of Theory
Construction

# A Point of View

Nor is it enough to say that research and theory must be married if sociology is to bear legitimate fruit. They must not only exchange solemn vows —they must know how to carry on from there. Their reciprocal roles must be clearly defined.

*Robert K. Merton,* 1969, p. 171.

We can, and I think must, look upon human life as chiefly a vast interpretative process in which people, singly and collectively, guide themselves by defining the objects, events, and situations which they encounter. . . . Any scheme designed to analyze human group life in its general character has to fit this process of interpretation.

*Herbert Blumer,* 1956, p. 686.

Methodology—that vague word sociologists have come to associate with research—has occupied a peculiar role in the sociological enterprise. There are spokesmen who see little connection between methods, research activities, and the process of theorizing. For example, in a particularly perplexing passage, that contradicts the above quotation, Robert K. Merton states:

At the outset we should distinguish clearly between sociological theory, which has for its subject matter certain aspects and results of the interaction of men and therefore is substantive, and methodology, or the logic of scientific procedure. The problems of methodology transcend those found in any one discipline, dealing either with those common to groups of disciplines, or, in more generalized form, with those common to all scientific inquiry. Methodology is not peculiarly bound up with sociological problems, and though there is a plenitude of methodological discussions in books and journals of sociology, they are not thereby rendered sociological in character. Sociologists, in company with all others who essay sociological work, must be methodologically wise; they must be aware of the design of investigations, the nature of inference, the requirements of a theoretic system. But such knowledge does not contain or imply the particular *content* of sociological theory. There is, in short, a clear and decisive difference between *knowing how to test* a battery of hypotheses and *knowing the theory* from which to derive hypotheses to be tested. It is my impression that current sociological training is more largely designed to make students understand the first than the second [1967, pp. 140–41].

Merton suggests that theory is of greater value than methodology. He further suggests that methods as such have little, if any, substantive-theoretical content. From Merton's perspective, methods are "atheoretical" tools suitable for any knowledgeable and skilled user.

This position, which potentially leads to a wide gap between theory and methodology, contrasts with Blumer's (1931, 1940, 1954, 1956), for as the Blumer quotation beginning this chapter implies, he calls for research and theoretical designs that accurately reflect and capture what he regards as the special features of human interaction. From his perspective the study of methodology demands a consistent theoretical perspective; theory and method must go hand in hand.

Other sociologists have implicitly subscribed to Blumer's position but have tended to use methods with little thought for either their theoretical implications or their differing ability to shed light on theory. Many sociologists now use only one method in their studies—thereby eschewing the potential value of other methodologies. Small-group theorists, for example, rely nearly entirely upon the experiment, while family sociologists primarily utilize the survey technique, and students of organizations overemphasize field strategies such as participant observation. This tendency has given rise to a rather parochial, specialty-bound use of research methods.

Closely related to this position is the tendency to develop within limited boundaries theories resting on special methodologies—what Merton (1967) terms middle-range sociology—and while it brings theory and method closer together, a specific commitment to special areas of inquiry seriously limits the far-ranging value of general or formal theory. To read of a tightly integrated theory of small-group interaction is pleasing because it is theory, but disappointing because it is not developed from a more abstract set of formulations. Small-group theory exists hand in hand with theories of the family, of political sociology, of delinquency, and so on, but seldom do these specialized theories with their localized methods come together in one large and more general theory.

## A Point of View

I hold that methods are indeed of great theoretical relevance—that in fact every method has a different relevance for theory, and that significant advances in substantive sociological theory will occur only after sociologists adopt a consistent and viable framework for the dual analysis of theory and method. Each can best be assessed and evaluated in the same general framework, and to this end—out of personal preference—I have selected symbolic interactionism as my perspective (see Mead, 1934; Blumer, 1962, 1966, 1969; Kuhn, 1964). This selection is deliberate because in my judgment interactionism best fits the empirical nature of the social world. It would have been possible to use another theoretical stance—to apply, say, structural-functional theory to the issues treated in this book—but I am convinced that any other approach would lead to significantly different conclusions, even though it would also, at the same time, lend support to my thesis that methods can no longer be viewed as "atheoretical" tools. It should be apparent that each theory demands a special view of methods.

### The Interrelationship of Theory and Method

The sociological enterprise may be said to rest on these elements: theory, methodology, research activity, and the sociological imagination. The function of *theory*, which I define as an integrated body of propositions, the derivation of which leads to explanation of some social phenomenon, is to give order and insight to research activities. *Methodology*, on the other hand, represents the principal ways the sociologist acts on his environment; his methods, be they experiments, surveys, or life histories, lead to different features of this reality, and it is through his methods that he makes his research public and reproducible by others. As the sociologist moves from his theories to the selection of methods, the emergence of that vague process called *research activity* can be seen. In this process the personal preferences of a scientist for one theory or method emerge. Furthermore, his selection of a given problem area (e.g., delinquency, the family, etc.) often represents a highly personal decision.

Order is given to theory, methodology, and research activity through the use of what Mills termed the *sociological imagination.*

The sociological imagination, I remind you, in considerable part consists of the capacity to shift from one perspective to another, and in the process to build up an adequate view of a total society and its components. It is this imagination, of course, that sets off the social scientist from the mere technician. Adequate technicians can be trained in a few years. The sociological imagination can also be cultivated; certainly it seldom occurs without a great deal of routine work. Yet there is an unexpected quality about it. ... There is a playfulness of mind back of such combining as well as a truly fierce drive to make sense of the world, which the technician as such usually lacks. Perhaps he is too well trained, too precisely trained. Since one can be *trained* only in what is already known, training sometimes incapacitates one from learning new ways; it makes one rebel against what is bound to be at first loose and even sloppy. But you cling to such vague images and notions, if they are yours, and you must work them out. For it is in such forms that original ideas, if any, almost always first appear [1959, pp. 211–12].

The sociological imagination demands variability in the research process. The processes by which sociology is done should not be made too rigorous; an open mind is required. What some regard as doctrinaire will be challenged by others and, therefore, methodological and theoretical principles must always be evaluated in terms of the sociological imagination. Rather than applying just a set of methodological principles to research strategies —which leads to an even greater gap between theory and method—I combine a theoretical perspective with a series of methodological rules, with symbolic interactionism as the theoretical framework and taking certain key principles from the scientific method and applying them to both theory and method. My aim is first to show that each method takes on a different meaning when analyzed in the interactionist framework—and hence can be shown to have different relevance for that theory—and second, by employing notions from the scientific method, I indicate how these methods can best be put to use to fit the demands of interaction theory. Third, and returning to the central thesis, I will suggest that methods are not atheoretical tools, but rather means of acting on the environment and making that environment meaningful. This point of view will, I hope, permit sociologists to overcome what I view as errors of the past, and reduce the gap that presently exists between theory and method. It should also lead sociologists to cease using methods in rote and ritualistic fashion, and enable us to move away from middle-range and small-scope theories to what I will term formal theory (see Simmel, 1950). Finally, I hope that this perspective will assist sociology toward the goal of a mature science of human interaction.

### The Interactionist Perspective

The interactionist's conception of human behavior assumes that behavior is self-directed and observable at two distinct levels—the symbolic and the interactional (or behavioral). By "self-directed," I mean that humans can act toward themselves as they would toward any other object. As Blumer (1966) says, the human may "perceive himself, have conceptions of himself, communicate with himself, and act toward himself [p. 535]." This behavior, which Blumer calls "self-interaction," permits humans to plan and to align their actions with others. Integral to this position is the proposition that man's social world is not constituted of objects that have intrinsic meaning, but that the meaning of objects lies in man's plans of action. Human experience is such that the process of defining objects is ever changing, subject to redefinitions, relocations, and realignments, and for conduct toward any object to be meaningful, the definition of the object must be consensual. That is, if I cannot persuade another sociologist to accept my definition of what a particular research method means, I shall be incapable of discussing my actions with him.

The interactionist assumes that humans are able to act because they have agreed on the meanings they will attach to the relevant objects in their environment. But before such consensus can occur, common symbolic languages must be present, and in sociology it is mandatory that agreement over basic terms be established before serious activity can begin. (Consequently it will be necessary to give precise definitions to the terms *theory, method, experiment, social survey, participant observation* and *validity.* The interactionist additionally assumes that man learns his basic symbols, his conceptions of self, and the definitions he attaches to his social objects through interaction with others. Man simultaneously carries on conversations with himself and with his significant others.

### Methodological Considerations from Interaction Theory

Given these basics of the interactionist perspective, I can now propose a series of principles that this perspective demands of its methodologies. If human behavior is observable at two levels—the symbolic and the behavioral—then central to understanding such behavior are the range and variety of symbols and symbolic meanings shared, communicated, and manipulated by interacting selves in social situations. Society contributes two essential elements that reflect directly on concrete interactions: the symbols, or various languages provided and communicated through the socialization process; and the concrete behavioral settings in which behavior occurs.

An interactionist assumes that a complete analysis of human conduct will capture the symbolic meanings that emerge over time in interaction. But the sociologist must also capture variations in ongoing patterns of behavior that reflect these symbols, images, and conceptions of self. These symbols are manifold and complex, verbal and nonverbal, intended and unintended. Verbal utterance, nonverbal gesture, mode and style of dress, and manner of speech all provide clues to the symbolic meanings that become translated into and emerge out of interaction.

The *first methodological principle* is that symbols and interaction must be brought together before an investigation is complete. To focus only on symbols, as an attitude questionnaire might, fails to record the emergent and novel relationships these symbols have with observable behavior. If I am studying the relationship between marijuana use and the strategies of concealing the drug in the presence of nonusers I will want to show that a marijuana user's attitude toward outsiders is reflected in his behavior in their presence. It would be insufficient to document only the fact that users do not like to get "high" when an outsider is present. Committed to the interactionst position, I must go further and demonstrate how this attitude is influenced by contact with nonusers.

Becker (1953, 1955, 1962) has provided such an analysis. In his interviews (1962, p. 597) it was discovered that among nonregular smokers fear of discovery took two forms: that nonusers would discover marijuana in one's possession; and that one would "be unable to hide the effects of the drug when he is 'high' with nonusers." This type of user adopts deliberate strategies to conceal the effects and presence of marijuana; he may even smoke infrequently because he cannot find a "safe" setting. Among regular users such fears are not present, although Becker indicated that as their interactional contacts change regular users may find it necessary to revert to only occasional use. One regular user who had married a nonuser eventually turned to irregular use. The following excerpt from Becker describes this pattern and demonstrates how the meanings attached to the social object (marijuana) actually emerged in patterns of interaction:

(This man had used marijuana quite intensively but his wife objected to it.) Of course, largely the reason I cut off was my wife. There were a few times when I'd feel like . . . didn't actually crave for it but would just like to have had some. (He was unable to continue using the drug except irregularly on those occasions when he was away from his wife's presence and control [1962, p. 598].)

A *second methodological principle* suggests that because symbols, meanings, and definitions are forged into self-definitions and attitudes, the reflective nature of selfhood must be captured. That is, the investigator must indicate how shifting definitions of self are reflected in ongoing patterns of behavior. He must, therefore, view human conduct from the point of view of those he is studying—"take the role of the acting other in concrete situations"—and this may range from learning the other's language to capturing his salient views of self. Returning to the example of the marijuana user, it would be necessary to learn the language of marijuana subcultures, which, as Becker shows, includes special words for getting "high" and has various categorizations for "outsiders."

Taking the role of the acting other permits the sociologist to escape the *fallacy of objectivism;* that is, the substitution of his own perspective for that of those he is studying. Too often the sociologist enters the field with preconceptions that prevent him from allowing those studies to tell it "as they see it." A student of marijuana use, for example, may incorrectly generalize from his own experiences with it to the group of users he is studying. Often the investigator will find that the meanings he has learned to attach to an object have no relevance for the people he is observing. This error occurs frequently in areas of conduct undergoing rapid change; studies of racial interaction, political activity, fads and fashions, and even analyses of stratification hierarchies in bureaucracies may provide cases where the definitions of the sociologist bear only slight resemblances to the actual situation.

*Everyday and Scientific Conceptions of Reality*

I wish to maintain a distinction between the sociologist's conceptions of his subject's behavior and the motives and definitions that subjects ascribe to their own conduct. The way a subject explains his behavior is likely to differ from the way a sociologist would. Marijuana users, for example, do not employ such terms as "morality," "rationalization," "collusion," "social control," "subculture," "socialization," or "role behavior." Commenting on this fact Becker notes that the sociological view of the world is "abstract, relativistic and generalizing [1964, p. 273]." On the other hand, the everyday conception of reality that guides our subject's conduct is specific, tends not to be generalizing, and is based on special concepts that often lack any scientific validity.

These points suggest that it is insufficient merely to state that the sociologist must take the role of the acting other in his investigations, and that a distinction must be made between everyday conceptions of reality and scientific conceptions of that reality. An adherence to my second principle suggests that the sociologist first learns the everyday conceptions of this reality and then interprets that reality from the stance of his sociological theory. This is the strategy Becker employed in his analysis of the marijuana user. He began with a symbolic interactionist conception of human conduct, and applied it to behavior in the marijuana subculture. His concepts were shaped by the meanings given them by the user, but he retained their sociological meaning. The sociologist must operate between two worlds when he engages in research—the everyday world of his subjects and the world of his own sociological perspective. Sociological explanations ultimately given for a set of behaviors are not likely to be completely understood by those studied; even if they prove understandable, subjects may not agree with or accept them, perhaps because they have been placed in a category they do not like or because elements of their behavior they prefer hidden have been made public. An irreducible conflict will always exist between the sociological perspective and the perspective of everyday life (Becker, 1964). This is a fact the sociologist must recognize. I raise this problem at this point to indicate that a commitment to my second principle goes further than merely taking the role of the other; sociologists must also place their interpretations within a sociological perspective.

Taking the role of the acting other leads to the *third methodological principle:* The investigator must simultaneously link man's symbols and conceptions of self with the social circles and relationships that furnish him with those symbols and conceptions. Too frequently failure to achieve this link leaves studies of human conduct at an individualistic level, and as a consequence the impact of broader social structures on subjects' conduct can be only indirectly inferred. This principle is not unique to the interactionist perspective, but derives ultimately from a conception of sociology that holds that the impact of social structure on groups and individuals must be examined.

Applying this principle to the study of marijuana use suggests that the investigator must demonstrate how an individual user's definitions of the object are related to his group's conceptions. The following excerpt from Becker's interview with a regular user satisfies this principle.

(You don't dig [like] alcohol then?) No, I don't dig it at all. (Why not?) I don't know. I just don't. Well, see, here's the thing. Before I was at the age where kids start drinking I was already getting on (using marijuana) and I saw the advantages of getting on, you know, I mean there was no sickness and it was much cheaper. That was one of the first things I learned, man. Why do you want to drink? Drinking is dumb, you know. It's so much cheaper to get on and you don't get sick, and it's not sloppy and takes less time. And it just grew to be the thing you know. So I got on before I drank, you know. . . .

(What do you mean that's one of the first things you learned?) Well, I mean, as I say, I was just starting to play jobs as a musician when I got on and I was also in a position to drink on the jobs, you know. And these guys just told me it was silly to drink. They didn't drink either [1962, p. 603].

This interview offers an excellent instance of how a person's attitude toward a social object represents a combination of his own attitudes and those of his social groups. My third principle is satisfied when personal and social perspectives are blended in a fashion similar to Becker's analysis. In Chapters 7 through 11 I show that the major methods of the sociologist meet this requirement in different ways.

The *fourth methodological principle* derives from the statement that any society provides its members with a variety of behavior settings within which interaction can occur. Research methods must therefore consider the "situated aspects" of human conduct—that is, whenever sociologists engage in observation, they must record the dynamics of their specific observational situations. Situations vary widely in terms of the norms governing conduct within them, and participants in any behavioral setting both create and interpret the rules that influence normal conduct within that situation. Recording the situationality of human interaction would be less important if it were not that symbols, meanings, conceptions of self, and actions toward social objects all vary because of the situation. As shown by Becker's study of marijuana users, in "safe" situations among regular users, the marijuana smoker is likely to get "high" and feel no restraints in discussing the effects of the object on his conduct; in "unsafe" situations he will go to extremes of secrecy and concealment.

"Situating" an observation or a respondent may require no more than asking the respondent to answer questions in terms of the situations where he normally engages in the behavior under study. Stone (1954) achieved this goal in his study of female shoppers in a large urban locale; he explicitly situated his respondents by symbolically placing them within their favored shopping locale, thus permitting a designation and description of relevant activities on that basis.

Social selves, I am suggesting, are situated objects that reflect ongoing definitions of social situations. For this reason both the meanings attached to these situations and the types of selves and interactions that emerge within them must be examined. Stone's investigation treats the meanings attached to shopping situations and indirectly infers the types of selves that flow from them. Becker's study achieves both goals: the meaning or definitions of the situation and the self-attitudes of marijuana users in varying situations.

Implicit thus far has been the assumption that the forms and processes of interaction must be reflected in sociological methodologies. Since the emergent relationship between self-conceptions, definitions of social objects, and ongoing patterns of interaction must be recorded, analyzed, and explained, the *fifth methodological principle* is that research methods must be capable of reflecting both stable and processual behavioral forms. Speaking of models of causation, Becker makes the following argument for processual analyses of human behavior.

All causes do not operate at the same time, and we need a model which takes into account the fact that patterns of behavior *develop* in orderly sequence. In accounting for an individual's use of marijuana, as we shall see later, we must deal with a sequence of steps, of changes in the individual's behavior and perspectives, in order to understand the phenomenon. Each step requires explanation, and what may operate as a cause at one step in the sequence may be of negligible importance at another step. We need, for example, one kind of explanation of how a person comes to be in a situation where marijuana is easily available to him, and another kind of explanation of why, given the fact of its availability, he is willing to experiment with it in the first place. And we need still another explanation of why, having experimented with it, he continues to use it. In a sense, each explanation constitutes a necessary cause of the behavior. That is, no one could become a confirmed marijuana user without going through each step. He must have the drug available, experiment with it, and continue to use it.

The explanation of each step is thus part of the explanation of the resulting behavior [1963, p. 23].

As I turn to the individual methods of the sociologist it will become apparent that some are better suited than others for the above kinds of analyses, that surveys better measure static and stable forms of behavior while life histories and participant observation more adequately lend themselves to processual analyses.

### The Role of Methods

The *sixth methodological principle* necessarily becomes more abstract and reflects directly on the role of methods in the entire sociological enterprise. It states that the very act of engaging in social research must be seen as a process of symbolic interaction, that being a scientist reflects a continual attempt to lift one's own idiosyncratic experiences to the level of the consensual and the shared meaning. It is in this context that the research method becomes the major means of acting on the symbolic environment and making those actions consensual in the broader community of sociologists.

When a sociologist adopts the surveys as a method of research he does so with the belief that when he reports his results other investigators will understand how he proceeded to gather his observations. The word *survey* designates a social object that has some degree of consensus among other sociologists. But more than this the word implies a vast variety of actions in which one will engage after he has adopted the method. Persons will be sampled, questionnaires will be constructed, responses will be coded, computers will be employed, and some form of statistical analysis will be presented. If, on the other hand, participant observation is chosen as a method, smaller samples will be selected, documents will be collected, informants will be selected, unstructured interviewing wil be done, and descriptive statistical analyses will be presented.

If a situation can be imagined in which two sociologists adopt different methods of study, the impact of symbolic interaction on their conduct can be vividly seen. Suppose that the same empirical situation is selected—for example, a mental hospital. The first investigator adopts the survey as his method; the second, participant observation. Each will make different kinds of observations, engage in different analyses, ask different questions, and— as a result—may reach different conclusions. (Of course the fact that they adopted different methods is not the only reason they will reach different conclusions. Their personalities, their values, and their choices of different theories will also contribute to this result.)

Ultimately the sociologist's actions on the empirical world are achieved by the adoption of specific methodologies. His actions are translated into specific methods through lines of action that reflect his definitions of those methods. At the heart of this interaction is the concept. The concept, in conjunction with the research method, enables the sociologist to carry on an interaction with his environment. Observers indicate to themselves what a concept and a method mean and symbolically act toward the designation of those meanings. Sociologists are continually reassessing their imputed object meanings—assessing them against their relationships to theories, their ability to be observed by others, and their ability to generate understanding and explanation of empirical reality.

This point can be illustrated by again turning to Becker's study of the marijuana user. Beginning with an interactionist conception of human conduct, Becker applied the generic principles from that perspective to the problem of how occupancy of a role in a subculture shapes a person's perceptions and activities. His theory suggested that an intimate knowledge of the subject's perspective must be learned, and to this end he adopted the open-ended interview and participant observation as methodological strategies. Beginning with this conception, Becker's main line of action was to approach marijuana users and to have them present their experiences as they saw them. The final result of his analysis was a series of research findings that modified a role theory and subcultural theory of deviant behavior. In formulating his research observations and conclusions, Becker continually assessed his findings against his conceptual framework; his methods and concepts continuously interacted with observations and theory —that is, symbolic interaction guided the process of his research and theory construction.

The scientist, then, designates units of reality to act upon, formulates definitions of those objects, adopts research methods to implement these lines of action, and assesses the fruitfulness of his activity by his ability to develop, test, or modify existing social theory. Thus, both his concept and his research methodology act as empirical *sensitizers* of scientific observation. Concepts and methods open new realms of observation, but concomitantly close others. Two important consequences follow: If each method leads to different features of empirical reality, then no single method can ever completely capture all the relevant features of that reality; consequently, sociologists must learn to employ multiple methods in the analysis of the same empirical events.

It can of course be argued that all research methods stand in an instrumental relationship to the scientific process. Methods become plans of action employed as sociologists move from theory to reality. They are the major means of organizing creative energy and operational activities toward concepts and theories and, as such, they at once release and direct activity, the success of which is assessed by the ability to satisfy the normal criteria of validity while establishing fruitful ties with theory.

Research methods serve to provide the scientist with data that later may be placed in deductive schemes of thought. By observing several discrete instances of a concept or a series of concepts, scientists are able to move above the single instance to the more common problems that transcend immediate perceptions and observations. A failure to move beyond particularistic observations leaves the sociologist at the level of descriptive empiricism. He must establish articulations between his observations and some variety of theory. To the extent that Becker's investigation was related to a theoretical framework, he satisfied this demand. I can now claim another important role for methods in the scientific process: Methods are one of the major ways by which sociologists gather observations to test, modify, and develop theory.

In this sense, methods go hand in hand with the following less rigorous techniques of theory-work. It is reasonable to argue, I believe, that methods do not do all the relevant work for the sociologist. As stated earlier, underlying the use of methods must be a sociological imagination. It is necessary to recognize that such techniques as introspection, the use of imagined experiments, and the playful combination of contradictory concepts also serve as aids in the development of theory. Methods, because of their more public nature are too frequently given greater attention than these other techniques that are of equal relevance. (In Chapter 2 I will develop further the use of introspection and imagined experiments in the construction of social theory.)

The *seventh methodological principle* indicates that from the interactionist's perspective the proper use of concepts is at first sensitizing and only later operational; further, the proper theory becomes formal; and last, the proper causal proposition becomes universal and not statistical. By *sensitizing concepts* I refer to concepts that are not transformed immediately into *operational definitions* through an attitude scale or check list. An operational definition defines a concept by stating how it will be observed. Thus if I offer an *operational definition* for "intelligence," I might state that intelligence is the score received on an I.Q. test. But if I choose a *sensitizing approach* to measuring intelligence, I will leave it nonoperationalized until I enter the field and learn the processes representing it and the specific meanings attached to it by the persons observed. It might be found, for example, that in some settings intelligence is not measured by scores on a test but rather by knowledge and skills pertaining to important processes in the group under analysis. Among marijuana users intelligence might well be represented by an ability to conceal the effects of the drug in the presence of nonusers. Once I have established the meanings of a concept, I can then employ multiple research methods to measure its characteristics. Thus, closed-ended questions, direct participation in the group being studied, and analysis of written documents might be the main strategies of operationalizing a concept. Ultimately, all concepts must be operationalized—must be measured and observed. The sensitizing approach merely delays the point at which operationalization occurs.

Goffman's treatment of stigma provides an excellent example of what I mean by "sensitizing a concept." He began with a rather vague and loose definition of stigma that he claimed was "an attribute that is deeply discrediting." Three types of this attribute were designated: abominations of the body or physical deformities, blemishes or character (mental disorder, homosexuality, addiction, alcoholism), and last, tribal stigma of race, nation, and religion. Moving beyond classification, he analyzed data collected in such traditional sociological specialities as social problems, ethnic relations, social disorganization, criminology, and deviance. From these areas, relevant commonalities were organized around the stigma theme. In summarizing this analysis he states:

I have argued that stigmatized persons have enough of their situations in life in common to warrant classifying all these persons together for purposes of analysis. An extraction has thus been made from the traditional fields of social problems. . . . These commonalities can be organized on the basis of a very few assumptions regarding human nature. What remains in each one of the traditional fields could then be reexamined for whatever is really special to it, thereby bringing analytical coherence to what is now purely historic and fortuitous unity. Knowing what fields like race relations, aging and mental health share, one could then go on to see, analytically, how they differ. Perhaps in each case the choice would be to retain the old substantive areas, but at least it would be clear that each is merely an area to which one should apply several perspectives, and that the development of any one of these coherent analytic perspectives is not likely to come from those who restrict their interest exclusively to one substantive area [1963, pp. 146–47].

Sensitizing a concept permits the sociologist to discover what is unique about each empirical instance of the concept while he uncovers what it displays in common across many different settings. Such a conception allows, indeed forces, the sociologist to pursue his interactionist view of reality to the empirical extreme.

The notion of formal as opposed to other types of theory will be further developed in chapters 2 and 3. At this point it is only necessary to indicate that such a stance relates directly to the assumption that universal explanations of human behavior can be developed. With Simmel (1950, pp. 3–25), I argue that human conduct presents itself in behavioral forms that differ only in content. The job of sociology is to discover the forms that universally display themselves in slightly different contexts. Simmel termed this the strategy of "formal sociology," an attempt to abstract from generically different phenomenon commonalities or similarities. The synthesis of these common threads into a coherent theoretical framework represents the development of "formal theory."

Society, for Simmel, existed only in forms of interaction:

More specifically, the interactions we have in mind when we talk of "society" are crystallized as definable, consistent structures such as the state and the family, the guild and the church, social classes and organizations based on common interests.

But in addition to these, there exists an immeasurable number of less conscious forms of relationship and kinds of interaction. Taken singly, they may appear negligible. But since in actuality they are inserted into the comprehensive and, as it were, official social formations, they alone produce society as we know it. . . . Without the interspersed effects of countless minor syntheses, society would break up into a multitude of discontinuous systems. Sociation continuously emerges and ceases, emerges again. . . . That people look at one another and are jealous of one another; that they exchange letters or dine together; that irrespective of all tangible interests they strike one another as pleasant or unpleasant; that gratitude for altruistic acts makes for inseparable union; that one asks another man after a certain street, and that people dress and adorn themselves for one another—the whole gamut of relations that play from one person to another and that may be momentary or permanent, conscious or unconscious, ephemeral or of grave consequence (and from which these illustrations are quite causally drawn), all these incessantly tie men together. Here are the interactions among the atoms of society [1950, pp. 9–10].

The sociological task, for Simmel, became the isolation of these forms of interaction.

In its very generality, this method is apt to form a common basis for problem areas that previously, in the absence of their mutual contact, lacked a certain clarity. The universality of sociation, which makes for the reciprocal shaping of the individuals, has its correspondence in the singleness of the sociological way of cognition. The sociological approach yields possibilities of solution or of deeper study which may be derived from fields of knowledge continually quite different (perhaps) from the field of particular problem under investigation [1950, p. 14].

As examples of this strategy Simmel suggests that the student of mass crimes might profitably investigate the psychology of theater audiences. Similarly, the student of religion might examine labor unions for what they reveal about religious devotion, the student of political history, the history of art. The argument, I believe, is clear: A series of concepts and propositions from the interactionist perspective are thought to be sufficient to explain the wide ranges of human behavior—whatever the social or cultural context.

More contemporary spokesmen of this position include Goffman and Homans. Goffman proposes a "formal sociological" stance for the analysis of face-to-face interaction.

Throughout this paper it has been implied that underneath their differences in culture, people everywhere are the same. If persons have a universal human nature, they themselves are not to be looked to for an explanation of it. One must look rather to the fact that societies everywhere, if they are to be societies, must mobilize their members as self-regulating participants in social encounters. One way of mobilizing the individual for this purpose is through ritual; he is taught to be perceptive, to have feelings attached to self and a self expressed through face, to have pride, honor and dignity, to have considerateness, to have tact and a certain amount of poise. . . . If a particular person or group or society seems to have a unique character of its own, it is because its standard set of human-nature elements is pitched and combined in a particular way. Instead of much pride, there may be little. Instead of abiding by rules, there may be much effort to break them safely. But if an encounter or undertaking is to be sustained as a viable system of interaction organized on ritual practices, then these variations must be held within certain bounds and nicely counterbalanced by corresponding modifications in some of the other rules and understandings. Similarly, the human nature of a particular set of persons may be specially designed for the special kind of undertakings in which they participate, but still each of these persons must have within him something of the balance of characteristics required of a usable participant in any ritually organized system of social activity [1967, pp. 44–45].

While the reader need not accept Goffman's theoretical perspective, its thrust is apparent—a small set of very abstract and general principles can explain all human behavior. Statements similar to Goffman's have been made by Homans, who has suggested that principles from economics and behavioral psychology can be employed to explain all of human conduct.

I believe that, in view of the deficiencies of functional theory, the only type of theory in sociology that stands any chance of becoming a general one is a psychological theory, in the sense that the deductive systems by which we explain social behavior would, if completed, contain among their highest-order propositions one or more of those I call psychological. The time may come when they will lose their place at the top, when they in turn will be shown to be derivable from still more general propositions such as those of physiology. But the time has not come yet, and psychological propositions remain our most general ones [1964, p. 968].

In the statements of Simmel, Goffman, and Homans there is an explicit commitment to formal sociological theory. Homans' theory would be based on propositions from psychology, Goffman's from functional theory and certain portions of symbolic interaction. In this context I can now *define* formal theory as any set of interrelated propositions based on a small set of concepts. Furthermore, these concepts will be ordered in such a way that some are more specific than others and hence capable of being derived from higher-order statements. Once this feature is achieved, *explanation* of the behavior indicated by those propositions shall be said to have occurred. A last feature of the formal theory, which distinguishes it from other types of theory, is the fact that it explicitly rests on empirical referents. Goffman's formulations are based on the observation that wherever face to face interaction occurs, participants will be observed employing strategies of tact, pride, defence, honor, and dignity. His highest-order proposition holds that all societies train their member-participants in the rituals of face-to-work because to do otherwise would leave that society without participants who could routinely engage in interaction. His lower-order propositions then include predictions concerning the balance between various types of rituals and their enactment in daily encounters.

While I have not extensively quoted from Homans, his highest-order proposition holds that "The more rewarding men find the results of an action, the more likely they are to take this action" [1964, p. 968]. It is Homans' belief that variations on this proposition will explain historical revolutions, daily interactions in work groups, and conduct within social organizations.

The work of these two spokesmen illustrates the use of formal theory as I have defined it. Contrast their perspective with that of Merton (1967 pp. 39–72), who believes that sociologists should develop middle-range theories of specific problem areas. Merton's formulation is too restrictive for our purposes; it leads to the endless proliferation of small-scope theories. (I shall develop this point in greater detail in the next chapter.) Grand theory represents the other alternative; it suggests that one very abstract and general theory can be developed to explain all of human behavior. Unfortunately, as it is currently practiced, grand theory has few, empirical referents. Formal theory, empirically grounded at all points, is preferable to a grand theory with a few empirical referents, or a series of middle-range theories, each of which have their own methods and specific domains.

Basic to formal theory will be universal interactive propositions that are assumed to apply to all instances of the phenomenon studied—at least until a negative case is discovered. By stating that these propositions will be interactive, I suggest that they will describe interrelationships between processes that mutually influence one another. In Becker's analysis of the marijuana user, an explicit reliance on interactive propositions of universal relevance can be seen.

The analysis is based on fifty intensive interviews with marijuana users from a variety of social backgrounds and present positions in society. The interviews focused on the history of the person's experience with the drug, seeking major changes in his attitude toward it and in his actual use of it and the reasons for these changes. Generalizations stating necessary conditions for the maintenance of use at each level were developed in initial interviews, and tested and revised in the light of each succeeding one. The stated conclusions hold true for all the cases collected and may tentatively be considered as true of all marijuana users in this society, at least until further evidence forces their revisions [1962, p. 592].

Becker's generalizations rest on the assumption that they apply to all persons who have ever used marijuana. More abstractly, his formulations bear a relationship to a formal theory concerning symbolic interaction and the development of self-attitudes in a group setting. The earlier quoted passage describing the marijuana user who altered his using patterns after marrying a nonuser represents a description of an instance of interaction. The user's attitudes toward the object shifted and changed as he was forced to interact daily with a person who did not hold his definitions.

If the fact of human behavior is interaction, then sociological propositions must take an interactional form. In this sense Becker's analysis fits the criterion. The seventh principle, to summarize, is that methods must be constructed so that they contribute to formal theory while at the same time permitting sensitizing concept analysis and the discovery and verification of universal interactive propositions.

## The Interactionist Principles in Review

I have shown that interaction theory suggests seven principles against which methods and sociological activity may be evaluated. These principles state:

1. Symbols and interactions must be combined before an investigation is complete.
2. The investigator must take the perspective or "role of the acting other" and view the world from his subjects' point of view—but in so doing he must maintain the distinction between everyday and scientific conceptions of reality.
3. The investigator must link his subjects' symbols and definitions with the social relationships and groups that provide those conceptions.
4. The behavior settings of interaction and scientific observation must be recorded.
5. Research methods must be capable of reflecting process or change as well as static behavioral forms.
6. Conducting research and being a sociologist is best viewed as an act of symbolic interaction. The personal preferences of the sociologist (e.g., his definitions of methods, his values and ideologies, etc.) serve to shape fundamentally his activity as an investigator, and the major way in which he acts on his environment is through his research methods.
7. The proper use of concepts becomes sensitizing and not operational; the proper theory becomes formal and not grand or middle-range; and the causal proposition more properly becomes interactional and universal in application.

These principles will reappear in my subsequent analysis of theory and method. They are somewhat peculiar to the interactionist perspective, but their use gives sociologists one consistent theoretically grounded point of evaluation. I now turn to salient features from the scientific method which must be combined with the interactionist point of view. By wedding the two, a degree of rigor and precision may be added to the final set of evaluative principles. I assume, then, that any theory, and research methodology must meet the following additional preconditions.


### Considerations of Validity, the Causal Proposition, and the Interactive Context of Observation


All research methods must provide answers to the problem of causal inference. A method must permit its user to gather data concerning time, order and covariance between variables, while allowing the discarding of rival causal factors. When it is claimed that one variable or process caused another, it must be shown that the causal variable occurs before that it is assumed to cause; that is, as the causal variable changes value, so too must the variable being caused. When investigators formulate causal statements they must recognize that other variables—rival causal factors—not directly measured or considered may be causing the variations observed. Before discussing the nature of rival causal factors, it is necessary to describe the causal proposition itself. Becker's analysis of marijuana use provides my illustration, and central to his theory is the point that:

The extent of an individual's use of marijuana is at least partly dependent on the degree to which conventional social controls fail to prevent his engaging in the activity. Apart from other possible necessary conditions, it may be said that marijuana use can occur at the various levels described only when the necessary events and shifts in conception of the activity have removed the individual from the influence of these controls and substituted for them the controls of the subcultural group [1962, p. 606].

This and previous excerpts from Becker's study provide the basis of the following propositions.

Proposition One: A potential marijuana user must have regular access to the drug and must learn the proper means of acting toward it before he will become a regular user.

Proposition Two: An individual will engage in marijuana use to the extent that he symbolically removes the effects of conventional social control mechanisms upon his behavior.

Proposition Three: If a regular user systematically comes in contact with nonusers, he will alter his drug-using patterns to use it only among members of the subculture, or he will adopt strategies of secrecy to conceal his use of the drug when in the presence of nonusers.

Proposition Four: The extent of use among nonusers will vary by the strength of the nonusers' negative attitudes. If these negative attitudes are strong and if the situation does not permit concealment, then nonregular use will occur.

Additional propositions could be developed from Becker's argument, but the above are sufficient to illustrate the essential features of the causal proposition. Becker's primary causal variable is the reduction in effect of normal mechanisms of social control. His basic dependent, or caused variable, is the degree and nature of drug use. Given this dependent variable, he proceeds to establish time order between the variables by showing that the degree of use varies by the attitudes of nonusers with whom the user is in contact; the degree of access to the drug; the attitudes the person develops toward the drug; and the situations available for its use. Regular and systematic use thus occurs when marijuana is available on a routine basis, when the user's interactional partners sanction and reinforce its use, and when the user has learned how to act toward the effects of the drug.

It is important to note that Becker has introduced additional causal factors into his final explanatory network. No single variable is assumed to cause marijuana use. The four factors outlined are his additional causal factors and he carefully points to the situations under which they will have the greatest impact. These propositions meet the normal criteria of the causal proposition: time order, covariance, and the partial consideration of rival, or additional causative factors.

### Rival Causal Factors

While Becker's study treats additional causal factors that influence the extent of marijuana use, it does not give careful consideration to rival factors that may have distorted or, in fact, caused his observed causal relationship. Rival causal factors may emerge from the following: time and its passage; the situations of observation; characteristics of those observed; characteristics of the observer; and interaction among any of the preceding four elements. In short, the generic question asked when an observer focuses upon rival causal factors is whether or not the causal propositions he has formulated accurately represent the events under study, or whether aspects of the process of making those observations caused the differences. If the investigator concludes that rival factors have caused his observed differences, then he is unable to generalize his findings to other situations, and his research has failed to reach the goal of developing sound causal propositions.

Traditionally, rival causal factors have been treated as falling into two broad classes: either factors external to the observations themselves, or factors that arise from or during the observational process. External factors are termed conditions of *external validity* and internal factors are labeled conditions of *internal validity*. External validity asks to what populations, settings, treatment variables, and measurement variables the causal propositions may be generalized (Campbell, 1963a: p. 214). Internal validity asks whether the assumed causal variables made a difference, or whether the observational process caused the difference. Under internal validity Campbell (1963a: p. 215) presents the following eight factors.

1. *History:* the other specific events occurring between the first and second measurement in addition to the experimental variable.
2. *Maturation:* processes within the respondent operating as a function of the passage of time *per se* (not specific to the particular events), including growing older, growing hungrier, growing tired, and the like.
3. *Testing:* the effects of taking a test upon the scores of a second testing.
4. *Instrumentation:* changes in the calibration of a measuring instrument or changes in the observers or scorers which may produce changes in the obtained measurements.
5. *Statistical regression:* regression operating when groups have been selected on the basis of their extreme scores.
6. *Selection:* Biases resulting in differential recruitment of respondents for the comparison groups.
7. *Experimental mortality:* the differential loss of respondents from the comparison groups.
8. *Selection-maturation interaction, etc.:* in certain of the multiple-group quasi-experimental designs, such as the nonequivalent control-group design, such interaction is confounded with (i.e., might be mistaken for) the effect of the experimental variable.

External validity is seen by Campbell (1963a, p. 215) as involving:

9. The *reactive* or *interaction effect* of *testing,* in which a pretest might increase or decrease the respondent's sensitivity or responsiveness to the experimental variable and thus make the results obtained for a pretested population unrepresentative of the effects of the experimental variable for the unpretested universe from which the experimental respondents were selected.
10. *Interaction* effects between *selection* bias and the *experimental variable.*
11. *Reactive effects of experimental arrangements,* which would preclude generalization about the effect of the experimental variable for persons being exposed to it in nonexperimental settings.
12. *Multiple-treatment interference,* a problem wherever multiple treatments are applied to the same respondents, and a particular problem for one-group designs involving equivalent time-samples or equivalent materials samples.

Campbell's concern is clear. Changes in observers, measuring instruments, and subjects during the course of a study can distort the events investigated. The passage of time as seen by subjects' maturation, or as evidenced in historical shifts and events, can introduce distorting influences, as can unique characteristics of respondents.

As far as it goes, this system is fine, but it lacks a theoretically grounded set of criteria for the evaluation of research methods. I turn to interaction theory for such a grounding. My earlier treatment of this theory suggests that for human interaction to occur, the following elements must be present: two or more persons able to take the role of the other; a situation for the interaction to occur in; and time to carry out that interaction. When these factors are present an interactional sequence is observed. Persons dining, making love, listening to a record, or negotiating a purchase are in such sequences.

Placed within this context, it is evident that social research becomes a type of symbolic interaction. Role-taking must occur, meaningful symbols must be present, situations have to be available, and time has to be allocated for the research (filling out a questionnaire, taking part in an experimental task). Any encounter between an investigator and a subject shall be termed an *observational encounter*. The interactants shall be called *observer* and *observed*. The situations will range from laboratories, offices, classrooms, living rooms—even automobiles. The time sequence may be brief, lasting no longer than an hour or two, or may extend into months and years, as it does in long-term field studies.

Every research method represents a special combination of these interactive elements. Some, like the experiment, are relatively short-term, include persons who remain unacquainted, and occur in structured situations. Others, like the life history and participant observation, take the investigator to diversely structured situations, rest on multiple identities, lead to the development of close relationships between observer and observed and, as noted, extend over long periods of time.

Each of the interactive elements (time, situations, characteristics of observers and observed) introduce into any study a special set of potentially distorting factors. Unless the observer is aware of his own characteristics, attends to unique features of time and its passage, and records the nature of the situations where his observations occur, he cannot validly develop sound causal propositions.

*The Observer*    Observers vary by their interactive style, their self-concepts, their interpretations of the research project, and their ability to relate to those observed. I assume that whenever an observer gathers an observation he brings into that observational sequence a series of attributes that make his observations different from any other observer. Some experimenters, for example, are overattentive to the emotions of subjects—others are underattentive. Some survey interviewers insist on using first names—others are more formal. The list of possible variations is endless, yet every stylistic difference can distort the processes under study.

*The Observed*  No respondent is perfectly duplicated by another, so the unique characteristics of respondents and subjects may also introduce distortion into an observation. When it is realized that observers interact with those observed, it can be seen that the interaction between an interviewer and respondent, experimenter and subject, observer and informant, may itself create difference across observational encounters.

*The Situation*  Because all behavior occurs in social situations, the settings of observation may become sources of invalidity. One interview may take place in a living room, another in an office, and still another in an automobile. Each of these settings is different from the other, each has different rules governing permissible, comfortable, and serious interaction. To the extent that there is variation, the behavior that occurs will also vary. Thus, situations of observation must be treated as a class of rival causal factors.

*Time and Its Passage*  Interaction involves an orderly sequence of events that unfold over a temporal period. Every observational encounter must be seen as having its own unique temporal career. Some are long, others short; some are difficult, others flow smoothly. During the passage of time events extraneous to an observation may occur (this is what Campbell means by historical factors jeopardizing internal validity). Yet the passage of time also signals changes in observers and those observed. Self-concepts change, intents of the investigation may shift, and symbols may take on new meanings. The following statement by Geer illustrates the type of change that may occur in the first week of a field study.

Throughout the time the undergraduate study was being planned, I was bored by the thought of studying undergraduates. They looked painfully young to me. I considered their concerns childish and uninformed. I could not imagine becoming interested in their daily affairs—in classes, study, dating, and bull sessions. I had memories of my own college days in which I had appeared as a child: over-emotional, limited in understanding, with an incomprehensible taste for milk shakes and convertibles.

Remembering my attitudes as I began to sort out the thirty-four comments in the field notes on the prefreshmen, I expected to find evidence of this unfavorable adult bias toward adolescents. But on the third day in the field I am already taking the students' side. . . . Perhaps the rapid development of empathy for a disliked group does not surprise old hands at field work, since it seems to happen again and again. But it surprised me; I comment on it seven times in eight days [1964, pp. 328–29].

Campbell's dimensions of mortality, maturation, testing effects, and instrumentation also relate to time. In studies that require repeated observations, the mortality factor becomes crucial. Persons observed at time two may differ from those observed at time one. Loss of subjects, or even observers, can create distortion, and this can also happen with testing effects in which the subject takes on a special attitude because of the interpretation given the first test, interview, or experimental session. Similarly, shifts in measuring instruments over time may occur.

Observers, situations, subjects, and measuring instruments, then, become social objects within the research design. They are objects whose meaning shifts because their meaning is created through the process of interaction. The sociologist must guard against these changes, if only by recording his interpretations of them.

## Treatment of the Rival Factor

In subsequent chapters I shall show how each research method addresses the potential distortion created by the rival factors of time, situations, observers, and observed. Here I want only to indicate the possible strategies for their treatment. In formulating causal propositions the sociologist has three basic strategies of control and design. Under conditions of great rigor, as in experiments, he can explicitly design situations of observation where time order, covariance, and rival causal factors are manipulated. The use of the experimental model of inference is the strongest strategy for formulating the causal proposition and, by implication, is the strongest method of controlling rival causal factors.

Under conditions of less rigor, such as the social survey, the sociologist loses the control given by the experimental model and must resort to a method of analysis termed the multivariate method. Events remain uncontrolled, but the investigator constructs comparisons within his sample that parallel, as nearly as possible, the experimental model. He may compare persons with college education to those completing high school on attitudes toward sexual permissiveness, constructing two comparison groups that vary on the independent variable (education) and measuring the relationship of education to the dependent variable (sexual permissiveness). In his analysis the sociologist will attempt to treat rival causal factors by classifying them as events that were either antecedent to his main variables, or intervening between them. He will maintain the same classification in his attempt to establish covariance and time order for the principle variables.

An important consequence follows from this strategy. Because he lacks control over the temporal occurrence of his variables, the investigator must infer their relationship. He cannot control their occurrence as the experimenter does, and this places him one step below his experimental counterpart. Where the experimenter controls his variables, the survey analyst must infer their relationship.

The last model of inference the sociologist may utilize is analytic induction. Experimental control is again absent, but now the investigator follows the events he is studying through time. This is best represented in studies employing participant observation and life histories. Rather than snapshooting the relationship between variables as the survey method so often does, the user of analytic induction engages in long-term studies that permit the direct identification of time order, covariance, and rival causal factors. Yet he too lacks experimental control. But while experimental and survey models lead to causal propositions that treat proportions of events subsumed under a proposition (e.g., 90 per cent of those college-educated favor permissive sexual attitudes, while only 35 per cent of those high-school educated favor such permissiveness), analytic induction generates propositions that cover every case analyzed; it leads to universal-interactive propositions. The last important feature of analytic induction is its emphasis on negative cases that refute the investigator's propositions. In his search for universal propositions, the user of this method seeks cases that most severely test his theory, and until his propositions cover every case examined, his theory remains incomplete.

These three strategies (experimental method, multivariate analysis, analytic induction) represent the major means the sociologist has for examining causal propositions. They also represent the principal strategies of handling rival causal factors. The experimental model controls them, the survey method infers them, and analytic induction follows their occurrence over time.

Each research method employs one or more of these strategies, and each in its own way treats rival causal factors. Consequently, each method can be evaluated in terms of its ability to construct sound causal propositions. To the extent that one method permits greater control of situations, time, observers, and subjects than another, it is superior to the other.

### The Logic of Triangulation

Unfortunately no single method ever adequately solves the problem of rival causal factors. For example, while experiments can establish valid causal propositions, the problem of observer reactivity (his presence in a laboratory) potentially creates a situation where subjects act as they think the experimenter wants them to. Following Webb, *et al.* (1966), I conclude that no single method will ever permit an investigator to develop causal propositions free of rival interpretations. Similarly, I conclude that no *single* method will ever meet the requirements of interaction theory. While participant observation, for example, permits the careful recording of situations and selves, it does not offer direct data on the wider spheres of influence acting on the self. I earlier stated (p. 13) that because each method reveals different aspects of empirical reality, multiple methods of observations must be employed. This is termed triangulation and I now offer as a final methodological rule the principle that multiple methods must be used in every investigation, since no method is ever free of rival causal factors, (and thus seldom leads to completely sound causal propositions), can ever completely satisfy the demands of interaction theory, or can ever completely reveal all of the relevant features of empirical reality necessary for a theory's test or development. A similar conclusion is reached by Webb, *et al.*:

It is too much to ask of any single class that it eliminate all the rival hypotheses subsumed under the population-, content-, and reactive-effects groupings. As long as the research strategy is based on a single measurement class, some flanks will be exposed. . . . If no single measurement class is perfect, neither is any scientifically useless . . . for the most fertile search for validity comes from a combined series of different measures, each with its idiosyncratic weaknesses, each pointed to a single hypothesis. When a hypothesis can survive the confrontation of a series of complementary methods of testing, it contains a degree of validity unattainable by one tested within the more constricted framework of a single method. . . . There must be multiple operationalism [1966, pp. 173–74].

I will offer a definition of each method that rests on several discrete, but interrelated strategies and techniques. For example, I will show that participant observation is best seen as a method that combines survey data, descriptive statistical analysis, quasi-experimental variations, document analysis, and direct observation.

My last criterion under the category of validity, then, is the triangulation of methodologies. This proposes a new line of action for the sociologist as well as a new set of symbolic meanings for the research process generally. I concur with Webb, *et al.* (1966), who argue that in the present stage of social research it is no longer appropriate to conceive of single-method investigations. The combination of multiple methods—each with their own biases, true—into a single investigation will better enable the sociologist to forge valid propositions that carefully consider relevant rival causal factors.

### Discovery versus Verification

Should the sociologist give more attention to verifying, or to modifying existing theory? Many sociologists have abandoned theory development for a concern with refining their methods and skills of verification; but methods are of value only to the extent that they lead to better social theory—and the basic concern of the sociologist should be the development of theory. My own concern with combining principles from interaction theory and causal analysis represents a dual interest in discovery and verification. Interaction theory tells the sociologist how to approach empirical reality; the principles of causal analysis tell him how to identify valid, correct, and reproducible observations. The two problems are inseparable, and until sociology has a set of criteria that permits discovery and verification, the separation between theory and method will persist.

## Notes

This and subsequent chapters draw heavily upon Glaser and Strauss' (1967) treatment of theory and research in contemporary sociology. In this book the case is made that sociologists have ceased to concern themselves with theory development, and that a concern with theory verification has increased the division between theory and method. Glaser and Strauss offer a series of very useful strategies for generating theory with qualitative research methods.

The symbolic interactionist perspective that guides my interpretation of theory and method is best presented in Mead (1934), Blumer (1969) and is well reviewed in Manis and Meltzer (1966), in Rose (1962), and in Stone and Farberman (1969).

My distinction between everyday and sociological conceptions of reality draws on Cicourel (1964, 1967), Garfinkel (1967), and Schutz (1963). What has recently been termed ethnomethodology by Garfinkel (1967) represents another attempt to maintain this distinction. The terms *phenomenology, ethnomethodology,* and *symbolic interactionism* represent different attempts to confront empirical reality from the perspective of those who are being studied.

Because formal theory occupies a central position in my perspective, the reader is advised to consult criticisms of the strategy. In addition to the Wolff (1950) collection of Simmel's work, the volumes by Coser (1965), Wolff (1959), and Spykman (1966) provide criticisms and comments on Simmel's method. An especially critical review of Simmel's concept of formal theory is contained in Sorokin's essay, which appears in Coser (1965, pp. 142–53).

My treatment of validity and the causal proposition draws on Hirschi and Selvin's (1967) critical review of research methods in the field of delinquency research. The reader should consult this work for an excellent application of the principles of causal analysis to substantive area research. In my attempt to rework Donald T. Campbell's conception of rival causal factors, I have modified the scheme of analysis presented in his 1963 treatment of experimental design (co-authored with Julian Stanley).

For fuller discussions of the three models of inference that may be employed in the resolution of causal problems, consult chapters 7, 8, and 9.

A problem not treated in this chapter, but one that is taken up later, is the use of sampling models in the selection of units of observation. Glaser and Strauss (1967, pp. 45–77) offer a useful but critical review of theoretical and statistical sampling models. My position (see Chapter 4) is that a theoretically directed sampling model that stresses the random selection of observational units provides the most reasonable strategy for selecting units of observation, since it assures the investigator that his subjects accurately represent the populations they are drawn from, and unless the investigator can show that his subjects represent people in the broader population he is restricted in his ability to generalize findings to that population.

My discussion of rival causal factors suggested that Becker's analysis of marijuana users was deficient because it did not carefully treat rival factors. Specifically I suggest that his study fails to report the situations of observation, lacks any concrete description of those observed, gives little description of the measuring instruments employed, and leaves unexamined the temporal features of observation. The additional problems of subject maturation, mortality (loss of subjects), and observer changes are also untreated. Becker attempted to resolve these problems through the use of analytic induction, which dictated the examination of every deviant case. My position is that while analytic induction provides the proper perspective on causal analysis, it is deficient in its ability to treat rival causal factors. Hence, I conclude that Becker's study *may* offer universal propositions concerning marijuana use but we have no clear way of disproving his theory.

My discussion of theory verification versus theory generation draws on Glaser and Strauss (1967) but is heavily influenced by Herbert Blumer (1969), who suggests that sociologists have displaced the goals of their discipline by concerning themselves with methodological refinements at the expense of developing strategies for approaching and interpreting empirical reality. A view that favors verification may be found in Zetterberg (1965), who presents several strategies for testing existing theory. For other views of theory, consult Merton's (1967) discussion of middle-range and general social theory. I slighted middle-range theory in this chapter because I wanted to avoid confusion regarding formal theory. In Chapters 2 and 3 I treat other views of theory development and verification.

# 2

# The Substance of
# Sociological Theory

Contemporary sociologists have been preoccupied with "theory," yet have seldom tried to make clear what a theory *is*.

*George Caspar Homans, 1964, p. 951.*

To speak of a science without concepts suggests all sorts of analogies—a carver without tools, a railroad without tracks, a mammal without bones, a love story without love.

*Herbert Blumer, 1931, p. 515.*

One of the most valuable functions of the research method is its ability to contribute to the growth and refinement of social theory, but to state only this much sidesteps the central question of why sociologists want theory in the first place. To answer this question, I must briefly treat sociology as an institution.

## The Sociological Community

It is instructive to view any science from three perspectives: as a social institution, as a method, and as a body of accumulated knowledge (see Smelser, 1968, pp. 3–44). (A synthesis of these perspectives provides a central theme of subsequent chapters.) Viewing science as a method demands a treatment of current sociological research strategies; viewing it as a body of accumulated knowledge requires discussion of theory construction and verification. But science as an institution is best expressed once it is understood that any scientific community is a human community composed of differing personalities, roles, values, and political pressures. (These human elements are given fuller treatment in Chapter 13.)

From the interactionist perspective, social organization consists of patterned and intertwined lines of action. Common symbolic meanings are attached to social objects and regular styles of acting toward those objects may be observed. A completely formed social organization takes on a life of its own. Fixed patterns of entry and exit stabilize, salient values are agreed upon, and various functions and role positions crystallize. Just so, contemporary sociology has a special form of organization. In other words, it is a viable, changing, shifting unit of social organization that has at its center a small cluster of values and goals.

All of modern science takes as given the existence of a knowable empirical reality (Blumer, 1969). The methods of observing this reality serve to differentiate one science from another (Smelser, 1968). Some sciences, such as psychology, approach the empirical world primarily through the use of experiments; others, such as sociology and anthropology, rely on less rigorous strategies. But the empirical world represents the constant referent, and it is to this reality that theories are applied for their major tests, since its phenomena are assumed to be causally related.

Some sociologists prefer to approach empirical reality through surveys, others through life histories, some through participant observation, and still others attempt to model their activity after the experimental psychologist. The common thread in these diverse perspectives is the belief that the following goals should be pursued: first, that the sociologist be able to describe the phenomena he is studying so that others can repeat his descriptions with a high degree of agreement. Such a description may take the form, as did Becker's, of stating how a marijuana user learns the values of a deviant subculture. Description is essential for the next goal—explanation, probably the most elusive of the sociologist's goals. It involves essentially, as Homans (1964) states, the construction of a system of interrelated propositions that permits the scientist to "make sense" out of the events observed. To say that a set of events has been explained is to argue that their occurrence in the future can be predicted. Thus, prediction is the third goal. It follows and provides a test of the explanation. If a sociologist claims to have explained why a given set of variables occurs together, he must be able to predict their future relationships. However, on occasion, prediction can occur in the absence of an explanatory framework. (Becker's analysis of the marijuana subculture attains these goals. The nature of the subculture is described, patterns of differential use are explained, and a set of propositions predicting future marijuana use is offered.) Explanation assumes resolution of the causality problem. That is, time order, covariance, and the exclusion of rival causal factors must be demonstrated.

The fourth scientific goal of the sociologist is theory construction. Until theory is developed, fully adequate descriptions, explanations and predictions cannot be forthcoming, since it is theory that provides their framework. If it is the job of a scientist to discover and systematize knowledge, then theories become the expression of what is known, what is predicted, and what is assumed. In the construction of theoretical frameworks, then, the full-fledged nature of sociology as a science emerges, for in theory methods take on meaning, observations become organized, and the goals of prediction and explanation are reached.

Another goal that has concerned the sociologist is control. It is often assumed that once explanation and prediction have been achieved, the analyst is in position to control the processes he has explained. But control is an elusive term. To some it may mean that under ideal experimental or statistical conditions the effect of one variable upon another can be controlled; to others, control means manipulation. Thus, in Becker's analysis of marijuana use it might be argued that members of society could use his information to control the spread and use of the drug. Perhaps they might, but the pursuit of control as a goal takes the sociologist out of scientific enterprise and into politics. To recommend how marijuana use may be controlled involves a value decision that the use of marijuana is undesirable. I am not suggesting that sociologists avoid making value decisions, since they cannot. (Indeed, setting theory construction as a goal is a value decision itself.) I do not want to discuss or make control one of the central goals of sociology, however. Instead, I assume that the sociologist is a member of a human community that stresses certain values over others, and I assume a commitment by him to the pursuit of knowledge for its own sake.

## Dysfunctions of the Sociological Reward Structure

The reward structure of contemporary sociology favors the above goals in varying degrees. The valued sociologists are those who can either contribute novel refinements to existing methods, or can construct new social theories (Hill, 1969), both worthy pursuits. Unfortunately, however, rewards are not given for the more mundane and time-consuming features of doing sociology. Replications of existing studies, for example, are seldom rewarded, and this means, in effect, that sociology remains a noncumulative science. Bonjean, Hill, and McLemore (1967, p. 9) have observed that between 1954 and 1965 some 2,080 scales and indices appeared in the *American Journal of Sociology, American Sociological Review, Social Forces,* and *Sociometry.* Of these scales only 47, or 2.26 per cent, were used more than five times. This points to an important feature of current sociology: Apparently many sociologists feel more compelled to construct their own scales and indices than to use those that already exist, almost as if they felt that each new scale developed could build a reputation for its constructor and user.

Neither is the reporting of negative results rewarded. Unless a sociologist can show positive relationships between his variables, his research typically remains unpublished. Yet the obvious value of reporting studies that failed —another way of stating that negative cases should be examined—is clear. Sociologists could certainly benefit by learning what causal propositions, what designs, and what strategies failed for others; at the very least the mistakes of the past might not be repeated.

Nor are studies that take long periods of time usually rewarded. There exists only a handful of studies in the literature that took longer than one or two years to complete—studies such as Lipset, Trow, and Coleman's (1962) of the International Typographical Union, which ranks as a sociological classic in the area of organizational analysis (from inception to publication, some 13 years elapsed), or Becker, Geer, Hughes, and Strauss' (1961) of socialization in medical school, which took nearly five years from inception to publication, and which also ranks as an outstanding investigation. These two studies are cited as representative of the small number of investigations that exceed the normal length of sociological research —yet they are classics and the research reported in them significantly influenced the subsequent careers of the investigators. A paradox must be noted. Sociologists shun long-term studies, yet reward those members of the discipline who carry out such research. There is a great need for long-term field studies, especially if the interactionist perspective is adopted, because events must be followed over time in their natural settings and investigations need to be designed and carried out that have a natural history, a long-term focus. But unless studies of this nature are rewarded, sociology will remain at the one-shot, short-term study level.

My discussion in subsequent chapters represents an attempt to shift the current reward and goal structure of sociology, with theory becoming a major goal and research methods seen as line actions taken toward the empirical world. With such a shift, studies that replicate, and extend over long periods of time, will take on special value.

## The Substance of Sociological Theory

In his indictment of modern sociological theory in 1954, Herbert Blumer traced sociologists' inability to develop sound theory to a misunderstanding of concepts. This charge is still valid and is compounded by a number of other difficulties. Perhaps most basic is a misunderstanding of what theory is and what theory consists of.

## Social Theory Defined

Surely the most voiced concept in modern sociology, the term *theory* has had attached to it multiple levels of meaning and interpretation. Models are called theories, classical sociological criticism passes for theory, and so do conceptual frameworks and interconnected sets of propositions. To paraphrase Homans, theory refers to a set of propositions that are interrelated in an ordered fashion such that some may be deducible from others thus permitting an explanation to be developed for the phenomenon under consideration (1964, p. 951). A theory is a set of propositions that furnish an explanation by means of a deductive system. Theory is explanation. Durkheim's theory of suicide in Spain conforms to the above specifications (see Homans, 1964, p. 951). It states that: (1) In any social grouping, the suicide rate varies directly with the degree of individualism (egoism); (2) the degree of individualism varies with the incidence of Protestantism; (3) therefore, the suicide rate varies with the incidence of Protestantism; (4) the incidence of Protestantism in Spain is low; (5) therefore, the suicide rate in Spain is low.

## General Characteristics of Social Theory

From this example I can now describe the central features of social theory. It consists first of a set of concepts that forms a conceptual scheme. Some of these concepts, as Homans notes, are descriptive and serve to show what the theory is about (individualism, suicide, and Protestantism). Others are operative or relational and specify empirical relationships between other elements in the theory (rate and incidence, when combined with suicide and Protestantism, specify such relationships; Durkheim's theory predicts conditions under which suicide rates would be high and low by specifying the relationship between individualism and religion). But taken alone, "a conceptual scheme is insufficient to constitute a theory [Homans, 1964, p. 952]." A theory must contain a set of propositions or hypotheses that combine descriptive and relational concepts. Propositions state a relationship, such as "suicide rates vary directly with the degree of egoism in a society." Propositions must describe a relationship between two or more elements in a conceptual scheme.

Unfortunately, a set of propositions taken alone does not constitute a theory either. The set must be placed in a deductive scheme. Durkheim achieved this feature by deducing his proposition three from propositions one and two. Proposition five, in turn, is derived from three and four. "When propositions are so derived they are said to be explained and a theory is nothing if it is not explanation [Homans, 1964, p. 952]."

When a deductive system provides explanation, it also permits prediction. That is, while Durkheim explained the low rate of suicide in Spain by his theory, he could also have predicted suicide rates elsewhere.

If, for instance, one did not know what the suicide rate in Eire was, but did know that the incidence of Protestantism was low, this proposition, together with proposition 3, would allow one to predict that the suicide rate there was low too [Homans, 1964, p. 952].

Theory, as I have defined it meets the goals of sociology. It permits the organization of descriptions, leads to explanations, and furnishes the basis for the prediction of events as yet unobserved. Only when all of these features are present will social theory be said to exist; the absence of any element renders the final product something less than theory. Given this position, it is clear that contemporary sociology has few, if any, theories (but see Berger, Zelditch, and Anderson, 1966, for exceptions to this conclusion). There exist, instead, small attempts at theory, many conceptual frameworks, a few propositional systems without deductive schemes, and, more often than not, vague explanations that bear little formal relationship to theory. Before I turn to these misrepresentations, it is necessary to treat each element in a theoretical system

**The Content of Theories**

*Concepts*

As an image of reality, concepts are perhaps the most critical element in any theory. Yet while one function of theory is to identify concepts for examination, the concept itself may turn back on a theory and become the major flaw in an otherwise excellent system. This is often the case in theoretical systems with vague, ill-defined or inappropriately measured concepts.

A concept carries with it what all definitions of social objects contain: It designates and suggests a plan of action toward some social object. For example, the concept of self, which occupies a central position in the interactionist framework, is seen as a series of definitions persons hold toward themselves as social objects. Sociologists interested in observing this object have typically assumed that one strategy is to ask persons who they are. This simple question elicits self-definitions and can be seen as following from the definition given that object in the interactionist perspective.

When placed within a theoretical system, concepts become its major designating units. Concepts *define* the shape and content of theories. In the example from Durkheim, his major descriptive concepts were suicide, individualism, and Protestantism.

In addition to their designating function, concepts perform at least three other functions (Blumer, 1931). First, they introduce a new orientation or point of view into the scientific process. Second, they serve as tools or as means of translating perceptions of the environment into meaningful scientific dialogue and operations. Third, they make possible deductive reasoning and, thus, the anticipation of new experience and perceptions.

As a source of new perspectives, scientific concepts carry a double meaning: as a way of looking at things, and as a way of bringing things into existence. Through scientific conceptualization the perceptual world is given an order and coherence that could not be perceived before conceptualization. The concept enables the sociologist to capture a moment of reality and give it a common quality. While scientific action cannot precede conceptualization, the most critical function of the concept is that it permits the scientist, in a community of other scientists, to lift his own idiosyncratic experiences to the level of consensual meaning. It also enables him to carry on an interaction with his environment; he indicates to himself what a concept means and acts toward the designation of that meaning. Scientists are continually assessing the meanings imputed to concepts—assessing them against their relationships to theories, their ability to be perceived by others, and their abilty to facilitate understanding and explanation. The concept thus acts as a sensitizer of experience and perception, opening new realms of observation, closing others. That is, to conceive and perceive an object in one manner precludes conception from another, and this is the dilemma of the sociologist (and of all sciences in general). To restrict, for example, observations of the social self to answers given to the question "Who am I?" means that the self is perceived and analyzed in terms of this question and not by another. The need for triangulation is again apparent; sociologists must approach the empirical world from as many methodological perspectives as possible.

The second function, that of a *tool,* is best understood when it is recognized that the concept suggests operational activity the scientist undertakes as he gathers observations. When I say the self is measured by answers to the question "Who am I?" I am utilizing a concept in this instrumental fashion—that is, I am directing concrete empirical activity toward that event. The success of the activity is measured by the extent to which concrete observations of the concept can be made. If such observations cannot be made, conception of the object is lacking. The valued concepts in sociology should be those that both release empirical activity and facilitate new sensitizing perceptions of reality.

It is often the case that a concept cannot be directly observed—its existence must be inferred, as when the sociologist attempts to discuss nonbehaviorally observable events such as symbols, attitudes and selves. When the existence of a concept must be inferred, the usual canons of observation must be replaced by the criteria of explanation. The scientist must ask himself, "If I infer this process to occur, can I develop better explanations than if I did not make such an inference?" If the answer is yes, then the scientist is said to be employing hypothetical and noncontingent or nonempirically observable concepts.

It matters little whether sociological concepts designate empirically observable or empirically inferred events. If the product of the inference or observation is better sociological theory, the concept has served a useful purpose. Often in the early phases of a concept's development, inferences, not observations, will be dictated, since conceptualizations typically come before operationalizations and observations. The act of measurement and observation may at first be crude and inexact, but in time methods of observation will develop, and perhaps become standardized. This has been the case with the concept of "self." For many years its existence was inferred, seldom observed. With the development of the "Who am I?" test, a method of observing it was finally available.

Too often, however, strategies of measurement are taken as ends in themselves and the theoretical role of the concept is ignored. Since so many key sociological concepts can be only inferred, many analysts feel that moderate advances can be made by developing empirical tools to measure at least some components of these vague concepts. Unfortunately, as Blumer has argued, this strategy avoids the issue. Commenting on the attempts of sociologists and psychologists to operationalize the concept "attitude," he notes:

The clarification of concepts is not achieved by . . . inventing new technical instruments or by improving the reliability of old techniques—such instruments and techniques are neutral to the concepts on behalf of which they may be used. The clarification of concepts does not come from piling up mountains of research findings. As just one illustration I would point to the hundreds of studies of attitudes and the thousands of items they have yielded; these thousands of items of finding have not contributed one iota of clarification to the concept of attitudes. By the same token, the mere extension of research in scope and direction does not offer in itself assurance of leading to clarification of concepts. These various lines of endeavor, as the results themselves seem abundantly to testify, do not meet the problem of the ambiguous concept [1954, pp. 5–6].

For operationalizations of concepts to be of use, their role as a source of deductive systems must be utilized. By observing several discrete instances of a concept, sociologists are able to move beyond them to problems that transcend them. This was the major achievement of Goffman in his analysis of stigma. As brought out in Chapter 1, he began with a vague definition of the concept (strained interaction) and observed that varieties of this process occurred in such areas as race relationships, crime and delinquency, social disorganization, and mental illness. By combining observations from these other settings, he was able to abstract a series of propositions that explained behavior in more than one situation. As an example, he observed that under conditions of strained interaction the stigmatized person was led to categorize the audiences he would come in contact with. Some audiences were informed of the stigmatizing conditions, some shared the condition, and others were not informed. From this observation a number of propositions were developed to specify the form and shape of interaction taken by the stigmatized person.

Ideally, the sociological concept permits new perceptions of reality by opening previously unexplored avenues of action. Once this occurs the concept will specify lines of empirical activity. If this happens, the sociologist will place his observations into propositional schemes of reasoning—in short, into theory. At each of these steps theory and methodological activity take on increasing importance. Research methods serve to operationalize the concept; theory both stimulates new concepts and provides a framework within which emergent propositions are placed.

## Scientific versus Everyday Concepts

While all concepts propose lines of action toward social objects, scientific concepts must meet certain criteria. They must be consensually defined within the community of scientists. When Durkheim states that suicide rates vary by the degree of egoism, it is assumed that other sociologists know what he means. Everyday concepts seldom possess this quality; often they are not consensually defined and most frequently they refer to what is sensed, not what is analyzed. Furthermore, the everyday concept lacks the development toward systematization that the scientific concept must have. In short, the scientific concept is continually evaluated by the canons of science; the everyday concept is evaluated by its ability to give order to the life of its user—everyday man.

These points can be illustrated by examining the concept "self." For the symbolic interactionist, the self refers to a very special set of events. Within the theoretical system it is accorded high priority and a number of tests and strategies have been developed for its measurement. The "Who am I?" test is but one of many (see Kuhn and McPartland, 1954), in the nearly 80 years symbolic interactionists have struggled with the meaning of this term. Kuhn and McPartland have described the uneven scientific career of this concept as follows:

Although the self has long been the central concept in the symbolic interaction approach to social psychology, little if anything has been done to employ it directly in empirical research. There are several reasons for this, one of the most important of which is that there has been no consensus regarding the class of phenomena to which the self ought to be operationally ordered. The self has been called an image, a conception, a concept, a feeling, an internalization, a self looking at oneself, and most commonly simply the self (with perhaps the most ambiguous implications of all) [1954, p. 68].

The self as a concept has had a career, even if it has been uneven. Everyday concepts seldom have a life of this order. Blumer notes:

To my mind, the chief difference is that the abstraction embodied in the common-sense concept is just accepted and is not made the subject of special analysis and study. Consequently abstraction is soon arrested and not pushed to the length that is true in the case of scientific concepts. . . . The common-sense concepts are sufficient for the crude demands of ordinary experience. Minor elements of inconsistency within experiences and a fringe of uncertainty can be ignored and are ignored. Hence experiences that might be productive of more refined abstractions do not arise as problems. With such a background it is to be expected that "common sense," as the term strongly suggests, refers to what is sensed, instead of what is acutely analyzed [1931, pp. 522–23].

That Blumer's position is correct, is documented when a sociologist proposes to ask an ordinary individual what he means by a common-sense term. The individual takes its meaning for granted, and if pressed for an explanation, is likely to point to the reference of his designation. He is not likely to show how that term relates to several others in a deductive scheme —as a scientist properly would. Hence, while persons daily make references to themselves and in so doing employ the concept self, they do so without the heightened criticalness of the scientist.

But while the scientific concept has a career and is subject to special demands, it still has a great deal in common with everyday concepts. This is so because ultimately the subject matter of sociology is: ". . . precisely the matter about which people have convictions, prejudices, hates, the things about which they praise or blame another." Hence, ". . . it would be rather too much to expect our concepts to be as free of popular feeling and distortion as are most names in chemistry or physics [Hughes, 1952, p. 131]." This points to one of the major problems of sociological concepts— that they are ultimately derived from everyday actions (see Rose, 1960). On the one hand, sociological concepts must have an everyday relevance; on the other hand, they must have a meaning that is strictly and totally sociological. If they do not, they become subject to the same ambiguities of the everyday term.

Concepts, then, are the most important element in a theoretical system. They provide the basis for a theory's operationalizations, open unexplored avenues of analysis, and lead the way to new deductive schemes. Scientific concepts must point clearly to instances of the classes of objects they designate, distinguish the conceptualized objects from other classes of objects, and permit the development of cumulative knowledge that pertains to the class of objects conceptualized (see Blumer, 1955, p. 59). In contrast to everyday common-sense terms, scientific concepts have careers, demand consensual, scientific definition, and are assessed by their ability to fit into and generate theory. They open the way for new perspectives, while common-sense terms only validate and reinforce what is known.


## The Definition

Behind most concepts is a definition that permits the sociologist to move from the concept to a single case or instance of it. Definitions intervene between the perception of an instance of a concept and the operational process of acting on that instance. Thus, definitions attached to concepts become critical links in the theory process; they assist in the movement toward the second function of the concept—to facilitate observation. Returning to the example of the self, it can be seen that by defining the self as answers to the "Who Am I?" test the sociologist has moved from his conception of the object to its observation.

Because definitions occupy such an important role in the total structure of a theory, a series of ideal standards or norms are associated with their use. Definitions must be exact and state what they do and do not apply to. To state that the self is measured by answers to the "Who am I?" test precisely designates an empirical referent of that concept. Negative definitions ("The self is not the sum total of the attitudes a person holds") do not provide direct specifications for observation; they only tell what not to look for.

In addition to being exact and positive, definitions should be phrased in precise scientific terminology, not in everyday, common-sense terms. (The scientific definition is subject to the norms of consistency, precision and criticalness.) Finally, definitions should not contain the term they propose to define. A tautological definition defines by naming and serves no designating function. If, for example, the self is defined as "self-attitudes held toward the self," no external referent for its observation is given.

The sociologist may employ three types of definitions as he moves from concepts to observations. First are nominal definitions, which "are declarations of intention to use a certain word or phrase as a substitute for another word or phrase [Bierstedt, 1959, p. 126]." One might, for example, define the concept self by the symbol $S$ and use only that symbol when referring to the self. Nominal definitions have three characteristics. As the example indicates, the concept defined has "literally no meaning than that given arbitrarily to it [Bierstedt, 1959, p. 126]." Second, the definition has no claim to empirical verification—it cannot be proven true or false, because by definition it is as it is defined. Third, because nominal definitions are true by definition, they cannot serve as a basis for inference or systematic theory construction. Nominal definitions, while not contributing to empirical verifications of theory, do serve several functions for the sociologist. They represent a way of introducing new terms and concepts into a scientific terminology; they indicate a way by which the sociologist can give special recognition to his concepts; and they "permit us to economize space, time and attention in the same way that abbreviations do [Bierstedt, 1959, p. 131]." In this sense they act as symbols and permit the analyst to state his theory with terms that have precise meaning and brevity. Finally, nominal definitions allow the sociologist to "substitute new concepts for familiar words or ordinary speech that have emotional or other nonlogical connotations [Bierstedt, 1959, p. 131]."

A word of qualification must be inserted regarding this last function, for—as Hughes (1952, p. 131) notes—the act of renaming a social object does not eliminate the fact that it may still carry the same qualities. Still, the chief function and justification of the nominal definition is its ability to provide precise designations of concepts—even if these designations lack a concrete empirical base.

The second major type of definition is the real definition. It differs from the nominal definition because it "operates not only on the symbolic or linguistic level but also on the referential level [Bierstedt, 1959, p. 126]." A real definition gives meaning to a concept by resolving it into its constituent elements. For example, a social group might be defined as a number of persons called members who interact with one another. In this case, the concept is broken into sub-elements (person, member, action). By combining these elements, symbolic meaning is given the term. In addition, specifications for its observation are offered. Real definitions take the form of propositions because they place a number of elements together in a relational system.

The ultimate test of these two types of definitions is quite different. Nominal definitions are tested by their ability to give precise meaning to concepts; real definitions are examined in terms of the empirical observations they generate.

The last major type of definition is operational. This relates a concept to the process by which it will be measured. An operational definition of the self could be responses to the "Who Am I?" test. The concept is defined by a statement that specifies how it will be observed. Like the real definition, the operational definition is tested by its ability to generate concrete observations. It does not contain elements of the proposition, however. The operational form becomes the major way of translating real definitions into empirical units; the stress is once again on the second function of concepts (as tools).

*Careers of Concepts and Types of Definitions*

It is useful to reconsider the point that scientific concepts have careers and to illustrate the role of definitions at various points in their careers. I suggested earlier that theories contain two basic types of concepts: descriptive and relational or empirical. Descriptive concepts point to the domain of the theory; empirical concepts indicate how it is to be put into propositional form. I also suggested that the best concepts are those that specify new propositions with empirical referents. In the career of a concept it can be seen that the three types of definitions will be of varying value. In its early phase a concept is likely to be defined nominally. This will be the case, for example, when the theorist is struggling to give new meaning to an old concept. (Under other circumstances he may be striving for a precise definition of his concepts and might also turn to the nominal definition.) As the theorist attains greater conceptual clarification, he is likely to move toward real and operational definitions; by this point his concepts will have begun to bear scientific fruit, as demonstrated by his ability to state them in propositions, and as he strives toward this goal, the necessity of empirical observations will become apparent. The concept thus begins its movement into the operational phase. Various tests, questions, and methods of observation will be adopted, as tentative forms of data are brought to bear upon his propositions. In this phase of a theory's development, a relatively balanced proportion of real and operational definitions will be incorporated. An excess of any of the three types hampers a theory's ability to achieve the goals of explanation and prediction. Nominal definitions keep the theory too far from empirical reality; real definitions lack the precise empirical specifications a theory demands; operational definitions alone do not provide the base for theory. There must be a continual interaction between conceptualizations, propositions, and the empirical world.

Since a theory becomes an ongoing form of interaction the scientist carries on between his conceptualizations and his observations of empirical reality, at no point in its career can it be said that conceptualizations end and observations begin. The two processes go hand-in-hand—each contributing equally to the other's growth. Blumer has described this relationship as follows:

Theory, inquiry and empirical fact are interwoven in a texture of operation with theory guiding inquiry, inquiry seeking and isolating facts, and facts affecting theory. The fruitfulness of their interplay is the means by which an empirical science develops [1954, p. 1].

If a sociologist forgets that the major goal of his discipline is the development of theory, a process of goal-displacement can occur such that operational definitions and empirical observations become ends in themselves. Placing empirical inquiry above theoretical development represents an undue emphasis on definitive-empirical concepts, with a corresponding de-emphasis on sensitizing-generic concepts. By relying solely on concepts that can be easily translated into operational definitions, the sociologist too quickly leaves the world of theory and enters the world of empirical fact.

The better strategy is to work slowly and carefully from emergent conceptualizations to empirical observations (the sensitizing approach discussed in Chapter 1). The sociologist who adopts this method does not ignore empirical observations—he simply moves more cautiously in his collection and interpretation of them.

## The Hypothesis and Proposition

The next element of theory that must be considered is the hypothesis. A hypothesis, or proposition (I view them as identical), is defined as a statement of relationship between two or more concepts. Durkheim's statement that "In any social grouping, the suicide rate varies with the degree of egoism" is a proposition. It expresses an interrelationship between more than one concept. Fundamentally, propositions rest upon the definition and the concept because, as I have just shown, they combine concepts in an explanatory and predictive manner. A proposition can be no better than the elements that comprise it (concepts and definitions). In turn, concepts can be of no greater utility than the plans of action derived from them. And, last, definitions are of little value unless the concepts they define are ordered in a propositional system. There is a complex interdependence between all the elements of theory thus far discussed. A weak concept, definition, or proposition weakens any theory.

Because concepts represent tentative ways of looking at reality, propositions become tentative statements concerning the occurrence and interrelationship of events in the empirical world. Thus, propositions, occupy the same tentative and processual position in theory as concepts and definitions. Durkheim's propositions regarding suicide represent the cardinal feature of all propositions: It states a relationship between two or more concepts where one element in the proposition is assumed to be the cause of another. In Durkheim's first proposition, egoism is assumed to be the cause of suicide. That concept seen as causal is termed a causal, determinant, or independent factor; that concept which is caused is the resultant, caused, or dependent variable. When a proposition states an empirically observable event, the concepts it combines are variables. In some cases these variables will have two values (e.g., present or not present); in other cases they will take values of degree (e.g., greater or less); in still other cases, differences in degree can be expressed in terms of a unit of measurement.

Propositions must meet the following criteria. First, the status of the related concepts must be so clearly defined that it is apparent which is caused and which is causal. Unless a reader can unequivocally determine this, it is difficult for him to work with the proposition. Zetterberg illustrated this rule in his discussion of Max Weber's *The Protestant Ethic and the Spirit of Capitalism*. He noted (1965, p. 67) that Weber's work has been misunderstood because it fails to precisely state its key proposition.

Its proposition is hinted in its very title: the Protestant ethic is the determinant and the spirit of capitalism is the result. There are, however, at least four different ways of specifying the determinant and the result in this proposition. If the terms in italics stand for the variates that may be related, we have these possibilities:

1. The *Protestant* Ethic and the Spirit of *Capitalism*
2. The Protestant *Ethic* and the Spirit of *Capitalism*
3. The *Protestant* Ethic and the *Spirit* of Capitalism
4. The Protestant *Ethic* and the *Spirit* of Capitalism

There are four possible propositions stated in Weber's title. The first suggests a comparison of persons who are Protestants and become capitalists with non-Protestants who become capitalists. The fourth assumes "that some ethical precepts in Protestantism lead to a particular spirit which is manifested in a concern for one's material wealth and prestige [Zetterberg, 1965, p. 68]." Zetterberg suggests that

All four ways of interpreting the thesis are in varying degrees present in Weber. Also, Weber's critics often touch upon some of these ways of interpreting the thesis in a haphazard way. Thus, claims by his critics that Weber has been proved right or wrong are usually restricted to one or two of these possibilities. Much confusion could have been avoided if the determinant and the result of the proposition had been more clearly specified [1965, p. 68].

Second, propositions must be so stated that they can be tested. In general, the more varied the tests of a proposition, the greater its power. This rule suggests that propositions may be tested in more than one way, which is in fact the case, although sociologists commonly assume that empirical verification is the only true test. This is an erroneous assumption, for many propositions combine concepts that have no empirical referents. When propositions combine concepts that have empirically inferred referents, the test of logical consistency may be employed. This test asks whether or not the proposition contains contradictory elements that if logically analyzed could lead to its disproof, a test that is commonly used in purely deductive theory formulations. It will be remembered that Durkheim's theory contains five propositions, two of which are deducible from others. Had Durkheim made an illogical deduction within this system, the proposition so derived could have been immediately disproven. In this sense, "the prime test is that no contradictory inferences can be or are drawn from the theory [Schrag, 1967, p. 250]."

If propositions combine empirical concepts, the test of operational adequacy may be utilized. Unless concepts can be related to observations, the proposition, and ultimately the theory, remain untested (Schrag, 1967, p. 250).

Another test is empirical adequacy. This deals with the degree of congruence between the proposition and empirical evidence. A subsidiary test is the general predictive and explanatory power of the proposition. Not only must it fit the data, but it should cover as many different empirical situations as possible, be as abstract and powerful as possible.

Ideally every proposition should pass each of these tests. The third rule states that propositions should be combined with other propositions so that a deductive theoretical system may be developed. Unless this combination is achieved, the explanatory power of any proposition is greatly reduced. Fourth, propositions should be stated so that they predict and explain the domain specified by the concepts. If they do not, they remain at the level of description and do little to move the sociologist closer toward theory. Fifth, some theoretical propositions must contain higher-order concepts. It is quite easy to formulate propositions of an ordinary nature. These are likely to contain few, if any, higher-order concepts and therefore contribute little to theory development. In Durkheim's theory the proposition that "Spain has a low suicide rate because the incidence of Protestantism is low" is relatively ordinary, although it does permit a body of data to be organized. Durkheim's higher-order proposition concerning rates of suicide and degree of egoism is much more powerful and more adequately meets this test.

Sixth, propositions must be stated in terms of the normal rules of concepts and definitions. They must be positive and not negative; must be precise and stated in scientific terms; must not be tautological; and must be capable of test, be that logical, empirical, or operational. Seventh, propositions must be capable of reflecting both process and stability. The most common propositions in sociology take the form of direct relationships that assume that one variable simply causes variations in another (see Homans, 1964, p. 956–59). Durkheim's proposition concerning variations in suicide rates represents this kind of proposition. It is argued that as rates of egoism change, so too does the rate of suicide. There is nothing inherently wrong with these propositions—the problem is that virtually all of the propositions in contemporary sociology are stated in this form; it is commonly ignored that a large proportion of human behavior involves situations where variables interact and that as one changes value, so too does the other. But this is not a one-way change, as Durkheim assumed in his analysis of suicide. In cases of interaction, variables mutually influence one another.

This rule was discussed in Chapter 1 when I stated that interaction theory demands propositions of interaction. Becker's analysis of the marijuana user illustrates this type of proposition. The third proposition from his analysis met this rule. It indicated how the attitudes and actions of a marijuana user changed depending on who his interactional partners were. This proposition is a lower-order statement of the prediction that "the actual responses of others toward the individual will effect the behavior of the individual [Kinch, 1963, p. 482]." Remaining consistent with interaction theory it can be predicted that: (1) The reactions of Person A to Person B's definitions of him will alter the definitions of B toward A.

On the concrete level: (2) Nonusers of marijuana will change their attitudes toward the drug and toward users to the extent that they meet users who act favorably in their presence.

Similarly: (3) Marijuana users who favorably influence nonusers are likely to change their definitions of the nonuser and begin to smoke and use the drug with greater frequency in the presence of nonusers.

These three propositions illustrate how interaction may be treated propositionally. They represent interactive propositions and are to be contrasted to the directional statements of Durkheim discussed earlier. Had I confined the above predictions to the directional form I might have stated: (4) The more favorable the attitudes of nonusers of marijuana to the drug, the more frequently users will smoke in the presence of nonusers—a proposition that merely states that as the independent variable (attitudes of nonusers) takes on positive values, the dependent variable (smoking in the presence of nonusers) increases in frequency. Propositions 1–3 significantly differ from 4 because they posit reciprocal changes in each variable such that the value of the independent and dependent variables at any point in time is a function of this interaction.

As these examples suggest, interactive propositions cannot be adequately stated in the language of independent and dependent variable analysis. At one point in time, that which is caused is also causal, and vice versa. This raises the general problem of causal analysis and interactive models and is more fully treated in Chapter 9. It is mentioned at this point to suggest as another criterion of the proposition its ability to handle forms of interaction.

Eighth, some propositions should be stated so that they express the temporal and situational context under explanation—even though propositions should be made as abstract as possible—because to understand any relationship it is necessary to understand the context in which it exists. This of course was achieved by Durkheim's lower-order proposition concerning suicide rates in Spain. While his highest-order prediction contained no specific time-place reference, his lower-order ones did. The necessity of expressing these references in the proposition derives from the fundamental fact that the social events sociologists analyze are embedded in ongoing units of social organization, and unless statements concerning the social nexus of these events can be made, propositions are reduced in explanatory power. Blumer has illustrated this point:

A variable relation states that reasonably staunch Erie County Republicans become confirmed in their attachment to their candidate as a result of listening to the campaign materials of the rival party. This bare and interesting finding gives us no picture of them as human beings in their particular world. We do not know the run of their experiences which induced an organization of their sentiments and views, nor do we know what this organization is; we do not know the special atmosphere or codes of their social circles; we do not know the reinforcements and rationalizations that come from their fellows. . . . In short, we do not have the picture to size up and understand what their confirmed attachment to a political candidate means in terms of their experience and social context. This fuller picture of the "here and now" context is not given in variable relations. . . . Yet, as I think logicians would agree, to understand adequately the "here and now" relation it is necessary to understand the "here and now" context. The variable relation is a single relation, necessarily stripped bare of the complex of things that sustain it in a "here and now" context. Accordingly, our understanding of it as a "here and now" matter suffers [1956, p. 685].

Blumer's point is clear—for a proposition to be understood it must contain specifications regarding the situations explained. Becker's analysis of the marijuana user satisfies this rule. At several points his material points to the situated context of marijuana smoking and describes a sequential model for its use. By specifying the time and place of this activity he was able to give substance to his propositions that a user takes on shifting attitudes toward the drug as he moves through the subculture. His situational specifications concerning interaction in "safe" and "unsafe" settings illustrates this feature of the proposition.

Some propositions, because of their abstract nature, will not contain time-place references. These references will appear in the exposition of higher-order propositions and in the derivation of concrete predictions.

I have stated eight rules for the proposition:

1. The causal status of all elements in the proposition must be established unequivocally.

2. The proposition must be stated so that it is testable in more than one way. Common tests include logical consistency, operational, and empirical adequacy.

3. Propositions should be placed within a deductive system.

4. Propositions must predict and explain the domain under analysis.

5. Some propositions must contain at least some concepts of high theoretical value.

6. Propositions must be stated in terms of the normal rules of concepts and definitions.

7. Propositions must be capable of reflecting both process and stability.

8. Some propositions should be expressed in a manner that permits temporal and spatial specifications.

*Properties and Types of Propositions*

Propositions give theory its quality of explanation. They represent an advance beyond concept development and permit the construction of deductive schemes. The sociologist has at his disposal a number of different types of propositions. Propositions may be categorized in terms of: the number of concepts combined; their causal breadth (e.g., the number of cases explained); the relationship between concepts (e.g., interactive, direct, etc.); the causal status assigned the independent variable (e.g., interchangeable with other independent variables, etc.).

Propositions that combine only two concepts are termed bivariate (as distinguished from multivariate propositions, which combine three or more concepts in a sequential pattern). It might be predicted, for example, that as education increases, upward mobility is enhanced, which increases the probability that one's life style will also change. A sequential explanation is implied in this statement. Education itself is insufficient to explain change in life style; upward mobility must also occur. In general, analysts should strive for multivariate predictions, even while recognizing these could be formulated as a series of bivariate relationships, because (as the earlier discussion of causal propositions indicated) variables other than those explicitly contained in a causal system may be creating the differences observed. Multivariate predictions permit the consideration of additional causal factors.

Propositions may be formed to cover all of the cases analyzed, in which case they are universal, or they may apply to just a proportion of those cases. This is the distinction between universal and conditional predictions. The interactionist favors universal predictions. Blumer offers an example of such a prediction. Paraphrased it reads:

Objects in the symbolic environment never carry their own meanings—meaning is always conferred upon them through the process of interpretation, definition and interaction [1966, pp. 539–40].

Becker's analysis of the marijuana user also furnishes a universal prediction:

A potential user must have regular access to the drug and must learn the proper means of acting towards it before he will become a regular user [Becker, 1962].

Conditional predictions cover some sub-class of the events observed. Thus it might be predicted that for males, those exposed to marijuana on a regular basis become regular users of the drug.

The basic flaw with this type of prediction is the question of the remaining females. In the prediction they represent deviant cases. Analysis of such cases can serve two important functions (Kendall and Wolf, 1955, pp. 167–70). First, through deviant-case analysis the researcher is able to uncover additional and relevant factors that could lead to needed theoretical revision. Kendall and Wolf state:

Through careful analysis of the cases which do not exhibit the expected behavior, the researcher recognizes the oversimplification of his theoretical structure and becomes aware of the need for incorporating further variables into his predictive scheme [1955, p. 168].

Kendall and Wolf offer the example of an investigation directed to the impact of Orson Welles' "War of the Worlds" broadcast. It was predicted that listeners who heard the entire program would understand that Welles was presenting a play. An analysis of cases revealed that 15 per cent of those who heard the entire program considered it to be news. Investigation of these cases uncovered the fact that for those listeners interruptions of radio programs with news bulletins was so taken for granted that they did not "hear" Welles' statements describing his report as a play. The final proposition was revised on the basis of these cases to include the listeners' expectation for radio listening, as well as whether or not the entire program was heard.

A second function of deviant case analysis is to refine the measurement of statistical variables used to locate the deviant cases (Kendall and Wolf, 1956, p. 169). Virtually all of modern social research assumes that scales and indices can be constructed to measure complex social events. Many times, however, these scales blur the very distinctions the investigator wishes to establish through his analysis. By analyzing deviant cases, weaknesses of the measurement process can be uncovered. Merton's (1946, pp. 125–30) study of responses to Kate Smith's war bond broadcast illustrates this function of the deviant case. He predicted that listeners who had close relatives in the armed forces would be more likely to buy war bonds. His analysis compared listeners with close relatives in the armed forces with those who did not. While his prediction was largely confirmed, a number of listeners who had brothers, sons, and husbands in the armed forces were not persuaded by the broadcast. Investigation of these deviant cases revealed that his index had misclassified them: The close kin of deviant cases were stationed in the United States and were not seen as in immediate danger. A reclassification confirmed Merton's general prediction. In his study, analysis of deviant cases led to revisions of the measurement index and then to confirmation of the hypothesis.

If the researcher seriously strives for universal propositions, then, his probabilistic predictions can be made universal by analysis of deviant cases. As a general rule I propose analysis of every case initially not covered by a proposition. The functions of deviant-case analysis for subsequent research and theory justify this rule.

Earlier I illustrated the difference between interactive and directional propositions. If the interactionist perspective is only partially adopted, I believe there is sufficient justification for constructing propositions that describe interaction or interdependence between social events. Clearly both types of propositions are needed. Currently, however, there is an under-representation of interactive propositions in the literature (Homans, 1964, pp. 958–59).

Many multivariate propositions will assign equal causal status to independent variables. For example, both upward mobility and higher education may, under certain conditions, cause changes in life style. In universal propositions, the investigator assumes that he has isolated the necessary causal variables. When deviant cases are ignored this assurance is often lacking in conditional predictions. The distinction under consideration is the extent to which sociologists can discover necessary and sufficient causes for the social events examined. Necessary conditions predict that whenever a certain event occurs, that which it is assumed to cause will also follow. Sufficient conditions are those that will only cause the event studied. Becker's study of the marijuana user represents an attempt to uncover a series of necessary conditions that led to marijuana use. Regular access to the drug, learning to perceive the drug's effect, and interaction with other users were seen as necessary conditions that cumulatively produced regular drug use; no single condition was sufficient. Seldom will the sociologist find such conditions, because few social events are the product of only one cause.

Given this view of causation, I propose that sociologists need sequential propositions that describe the events necessary for the production of any social process. These must be sequential in the simple sense that all human interaction occurs over time, and they must discover necessary events, because few events are the product of one condition.


### The Ordering of Theories


Ordering propositions into a theoretical scheme is conventionally seen as the logical outcome of concept formation, construction of definitions, and the collection of data. In this conventional view, the axiomatic method of ordering propositions has become a major strategy. With it, certain propositions are treated as axioms and from them theorems, or lower-order predictions, are derived. Concepts are viewed as either basic or derived. Basic concepts are introduced without definition and derived concepts are constructed from them. The ordering of propositions then follows the simple rules of syllogistic logic, as Durkheim's theory of suicide illustrated; that is, certain propositions are logically deduced from other, higher-order, predictions. Durkheim's fifth proposition, for example, is deduced from his propositions three and four.

Zetterberg (1956, pp. 533–40) has argued that the axiomatic method has the virtues of organizing previously unconceptualized data, permitting the location of strategic research areas; and allowing the construction of explanatory schemes through deduction. I do not quarrel with these points

—any theory should do exactly what Zetterberg says the axiomatic theory does. The basic problem with the axiomatic method—as Costner and Leik (1964, pp. 819–35) indicate—is that empirical reality seldom conforms to such. Specifically, the axiomatic method as it currently stands does not adequately handle propositions with asymmetrically correlated variables. Nor does it satisfactorily treat situations of interactive causation. In the ideal axiomatic system, sufficient causes have been located to permit the direct deduction of propositions. I have suggested that empirical reality seldom conforms to single causal models where sufficient conditions can be located. For these reasons I choose to view the axiomatic method as of only limited value. Its chief virtue is its ability to serve as a check for the theorist as he formulates propositions. By following the rules of logical deduction, implicit or overlooked propositions may be formalized. I suggest that theorists employ a far looser and imprecise model of theory construction, included in this activity is the method of insight, or introspection, as Cooley (1926) termed it.

## Theory Work and the Method of Insight

The assumption that significant sociological work does not occur within the confines of rigorous models of inference is best stated by Weber:

Ideas occur to us when they please, and not when it pleases us. The best ideas do indeed occur to one's mind in the way in which Ihering describes it: when smoking a cigar on the sofa; or as Helmholz states of himself with scientific exactitude: when taking a walk on a slowly ascending street; or in a similar way. In any case, ideas come when we do not expect them, and not when we are brooding and searching at our desks. Yet ideas would certainly not come to mind had we not brooded at our desks and searched for answers with passionate devotion [1958, p. 136].

Once this view of the creative process is accepted, a major problem confronting any scientist is the stimulation of a psychological state in which new ideas can appear. In this sense no scientist can ever separate his personal and public lives. He is continually thinking, puzzling over, and troubled about unsolved issues. As Weber states: "In the field of science only he who is devoted *solely* to the work at hand has 'personality' [1958, p. 137]." The scientist, like all humans, is forever conversing with himself, checking out plans of action, experimenting with new formulations, combining contradictory events, and judging future action against what has succeeded and failed in the past. It is in the arena of private conversations with the self that new ideas appear, that propositions are constructed, and that predictions take place. Only after these ideas are transferred to the written page, or communicated verbally to others, does the scientific process become public. It seems to me that Zetterberg's axiomatic method leaps too rapidly from the private to the public arena of discourse.

Several features of this private side of science may be noted. First, the scientist must accept the fact that his own experiences probably provide the most important sources of data for his theory. Blumer has described the role of personal experiences in Mead's theory of interaction as follows:

Mead was intensely preoccupied with cardinal matters which are present in every human society. He was concerned with such fundamental questions as how do human beings fit their lines of activity to another, what is the nature of communication, what is the nature of objects, how do objects come into being, how does the human being become an object to himself, . . . how is human action constructed. Mead worked out his answers to these fundamental questions not by postulating an ideal society, but by close and persistent observation of those around him and of himself. Where is there a more directly presented and ever accessible area of empirical happening for inquiry into the nature of human communication than the daily conversations one has with one's fellows? Where does one have a richer body of recurring instances of human beings fitting their lines of action to one another than that which takes place under one's nose? . . . The natural happenings which set the cardinal problems of human action occur continuously in the area of immediate experience and observation. It was such natural happenings that constructed the empirical matters that Mead studied with care, with persistence, and with his unusual gifts of originality [1964, p. 121].

Blumer's description suggests that a closely related source of data are the experiences one shares with other acquaintances—whether they are friends closely observed, or fellow colleagues. Indeed, theories of deviance, of labeling, or of socialization, may be empirically grounded (initially at least) through observations of one's friends. Cooley (1922), for example, developed his theory of self and socialization through systematic observations of his own children. Gross and Stone (1964) expanded a theory of interaction and the functions of embarrassment partially in terms of experiences of embarrassment furnished by friends and colleagues. And while introspective moments of insight may suffer from biases of observation, it is the function of rules of inference and design to give them scientific rigor.

Few sociologists have attempted to formalize this process; Glaser and Strauss (1967, pp. 251–57) are exceptions. They offer the following rules (which parallel the observations of Weber and Blumer): Significant insights may come from one's own experience, from those of others, and from existing social theory. The inquiring mind, they suggest, always pushes beyond that which is known or formalized. This rests on Mead's (1917) description of the scientific method which, in essence, involves the challenging of previous perspectives. Two rather contradictory directives follow from this suggestion. First, the creative thinker may initially choose to ignore that which has preceded him, on the assumption that his own insights will be hampered by other's formulations. Thus, some investigators prefer not to review the literature in a given area before beginning research. On the other hand, an equally valid principle suggests that repetitions of other's efforts will occur unless one is thoroughly familiar with previous work. My own suggestion lies somewhere in the middle. I prefer to develop a loose sense of previous research, together with specific knowledge about concrete research or theoretical activity. With this perspective the sociologist is able to relate his own research to that of others but, at the same time, feel unconstrained by any specific hypothesis or theoretical system.

C. Wright Mills (1959, pp. 195–226) has given perhaps the most complete statement on the creative frame of reference. His suggestions call for continuous note-taking and introspection. Files and complex cross-referencing systems can be constructed and whenever a new idea, reference, or finding is discovered it is placed in the appropriate file. In Mills' system the scientist is often involved in several projects simultaneously—thus all of his creative energies can be relevant to at least one of those projects. Mills also suggests the deliberate confrontation of contradictory elements, echoing Hughes' (1956, pp. 42–55) directive that a fundamental principle of social inquiry is the study of contradictory social types—for example, prostitutes and psychiatrists, physicians and plumbers. This raises the related principle that one continually think in a comparative manner. For example, the experiences of patients in mental hospitals might be profitably highlighted by studying college students, since they also occupy positions in a total institution.

These suggestions of Weber, Mead, Blumer, Hughes, Glaser, Strauss, and Mills leave unanswered the basic question of how a researcher moves from his insights to social theory. No pat answer can be given. Every scientist works somewhat differently. Some prefer complex filing systems, others never make so much as a marginal note in a book. I have employed the following strategies in my own work. I continually make notes to myself. They are typically organized around problems I am still working on, and range from incorrectly memorized quotations from works I have found useful, to a sheer imaginary bibliography for a given area. In the course of preparing this book, for example, I prepared a complex file of reprints and xerox copies of articles, bibliographic references, and notes on the problems to be treated under each problem that now represents the major chapters and problems I have written on.

When I begin a work I attempt a rough outline to insure that I cover all the points considered relevant. During the process of writing, this outline is often discarded or drastically revised. It is impossible to predict what is going to be written once paper is inserted in the typewriter, because the process of self-interaction is explosive and emergent; references are thought of, quotations come to mind that trigger new problems, and even the selection of words leads to the modification of sentences—which, in turn, often creates or forces revision. When writing I find that I am continuously editing (not always successfully) my selection of words. This self-editing represents an attempt to find a series of statements that sounds correct, and it represents an attempt to take the role of others who will read what is written.

But beyond putting ideas on paper is the problem of stimulating the sociological imagination; for this, continual immersion in sociological work is required. Even while viewing television, the perusal of a sociological journal or the rereading of a favorite novel may stimulate thoughts that will later be of worth.

It has also proven useful to interpret social experiences from the sociological perspective. Notes to the self, predictions of forthcoming interactions, and after-the-fact explanations of what has just occurred become valuable ways of developing emerging theory. I find it useful to test different social theories against the same body of experiences. Goffman's dramaturgical theory of interaction can be loosely tested by bringing Homans' exchange perspective or Parsons' functional theory to bear upon the same empirical event. The researcher can test the utility of each of these perspectives by forcing each to explain and predict what has just happened.

If such a stance toward social experience is taken, the sociological imagination is stimulated, and when an investigator attempts to fit propositions together into a theoretical system all of his past experiences, predictions, and observations can be channeled toward the problem at hand. It no longer becomes necessary to check out unstated propositions; these should all be present in one's mind, in some form or another.

I find Mead's suggestion that the scientist never accept at face value prior interpretations valuable. It demands that one's own achievement be measured by the degree to which new theory has been formulated. Each sociologist becomes his own theorist and methodologist. But above all, a critical view of all other work must permeate sociological activity; every sociologist is thus accountable for knowing, if only roughly, all that has been done before. At some point, then, literature reviews must be conducted, and every sociologist must become a miniature, self-contained representation of the total discipline. Colleagues become sounding boards for new ideas, but their suggestions and interpretations are not taken for granted. A dialectic of respect and disrespect underlies this view of the sociological imagination: on the one hand, knowledge of the past is required; on the other, as Mead suggests, nothing is taken for granted.

The true test of insight, I suggest, is whether or not the researcher is troubled about his work. If it is impossible to relax, if problems keep appearing in one's consciousness, it is safe to assume that the imagination is at work. The sociological self is in process, but is a self troubled over the development of new ideas and the resolution of problems.

A work schedule is important. Time must be set aside for thinking, for writing, and for reading. Time must also be allocated for interactions with other sociologists—whether in the class room, the office, or a bar. It is useful to set a work and writing schedule; the activity of a day can be measured by the number of words written, the number of pages read, or the number of new ideas that have been developed. Unfortunately, the researcher must be prepared for nonproductive periods; schedules will be interrupted, or be set aside. New ideas, as Weber suggests, do not come at specified times during the day. The best that can be hoped for is the creation of conditions conducive to work and insight.

The movement from insights to propositions and ultimately to theory follows from the continual focus on a core problem or set of issues. Problems and questions, not theory, create new perspectives.

At some point in the reflective process a series of tentative solutions, often expressed as propositions, begins to emerge. The examination of these leads to other predictions, new concepts, and renewed empirical activity. As observations in the empirical world confirm tentative predictions, additional scope is added, and relationships with previous research are discovered. At this point the theorist begins to consider the public nature of his formulations. When he moves from self-conversations to public discourse, the medium of scientific communication forces alterations in his perspective; his presentation becomes formal. Propositions move from imprecision to precise statements; rules of evidence and inference are adopted; standard styles of exposition are utilized. Variations in the use of inference, propositions, and exposition give each scientist a personal style, but similarity will be present.

If this process reaches completion, what began as an attempt to answer a specific question becomes a fully developed theory. Even if theory in the precise sense is not developed, interrelated propositions, clearly defined hypotheses, and bodies of data will be present. At no point in this process will the sociological imagination cease work and give way to formal rules of inference and design, but unless rules of method are employed, insight suffers from a lack of direction. Conversely, theory does not arise from a knowledge of theory construction or data analysis, from the presence of typewriters, comfortable desks, and well-intentioned colleagues. Interaction must exist between all of these elements.

### On the Verification of Theories: An Additional Function of Methods

How is it that the theorist knows that his actions are valid? This is the question of theory verification, and several different criteria can be employed to test or verify a theory. The first, and most basic test is a theory's ability to generate valid causal propositions; if it cannot do this, it is not a theory. In Chapter 1 it was suggested that all causal propositions contain three elements: demonstration of time order, covariance, and the exclusion of rival hypotheses. Theories must also meet these criteria.

A second verificational test is logic. Once a system is constructed, then the first test is that of logic. Third, the power of theory to illuminate or make more understandable an area that has not been examined before, or has been examined by another theory should be checked. If the theory cannot do as well as a theory that already exists, it fails this test.

But all of these tests are of little value until it is realized that research methods provide the fundamental test of all theories. It is through their use that the data necessary to test any theory are gathered. Through the use of research methods elements of the causal proposition are brought together, and new observations are brought forth to modify, verify, and change the theory under examination. Methods, then, work hand in hand with theories in the verificational process.

### The Functions of Theory

It is appropriate to conclude with a summary statement on the functions of theory for the sociologist. Theory must, of course, provide explanations of the phenomenon under analysis—if it fails to do this, it is not a theory. It must also generate new images of reality, new hypotheses, and new propositions; it must move sociologists toward the goals of explanation and prediction.

Theories serve as critical guides to future thought, research, and conceptualization. This of course implies a close working relationship with the research method and the research finding. Theories set problems for research, stake out new objects for examination, and direct empirical inquiry (Blumer, 1954). In turn, methods and research findings suggest new problems for theory (e.g., the negative case), invite new theoretical formulations, and lead to the ultimate refinement and verification of theories themselves. Theory, conceptualization, and empirical activity are interwoven in a contextual operation such that theory guides research while research guides theory.

### Notes

In my discussion of the foundations of science I have drawn heavily from Herbert Blumer's "The Methodological Position of Symbolic Interactionism" (1969), which clearly establishes that all sciences must assume the existence of a knowable empirical reality. Symbolic interaction's contribution to modern sociology is its ability to provide techniques for approaching and interpreting this reality from the perspective of the acting individual. The reader should also consult Harold Garfinkel's (1967, pp. 262–83) treatment of everyday and scientific perspectives of the empirical world. Garfinkel offers a stance at variance with interactionism, but he suggests some important distinctions between the scientific and everyday points of view.

The discussion of sociology's current reward structure borrows from Richard J. Hill's "The Relevance of Methodology" (1969). Hill offers a devastating critique of the division between methodologists and general theorists and suggests that the reward structure of sociology maintains this false separation.

In my estimation two of the best spokesmen on theory in contemporary sociology are Homans and Blumer. Homans' "Contemporary Theory in Sociology" (1964) is an excellent discussion of what theory consists. It also provides an insightful review of the current theories of sociology. Blumer's "What Is Wrong with Social Theory?" (1954) offers a severe criticism of attempts to improve theory by the method of variable analysis, and also offers an illuminating treatment of sensitizing concepts. Arthur Stinchcomb's *Constructing Social Theories* (1967) presents an excellent discussion of how one moves from theory to the construction of propositions and causal analysis. Hans Zetterberg's *On Theory and Verification in Sociology* (1965) should be examined in the context of theory verification. Zetterberg proposes a model that stands in opposition to Glaser and Strauss' (1967, pp. 1–43) view of theory generation. The contrast between Glaser and Strauss and Zetterberg is informative for the sound arguments supporting the value of theory generation as well as theory verification. I favor Glaser and Strauss' endorsement of theory generation.

My treatment of propositions draws on Zetterberg's (1965, pp. 63–100) typology, and he should be reviewed in this context. Many theorists have maintained a distinction between propositions and hypotheses (e.g., Zetterberg, 1965); I choose to view them as interchangeable. The argument for making a distinction rests on the assumption that propositions are further removed from empirical observations; hypotheses are seen as specific empirical predictions. While there is value in this position, it seems of little use to sociologists. There are too few propositions in the first place, and even when the distinction is made, it is seldom followed through in theoretical or empirical activity.

Any discussion of insight and the scientific method must treat Weber's 1922 essay, "Science as a Vocation," which is reprinted in Gerth and Mills (1958) translation of Weber's work. The essay also presents a review of the problem of science and values. Weber's position that scientists should be free to study what they want to study has stimulated the modern sociological controversy over values and scientific activity (see Gouldner, 1962, 1968). Weber argued for the separation of values and science, feeling that the scientist should not bring values, or politics, into his work.

Because I have extensively drawn on C. Wright Mills' (1959, pp. 195–226) essay "On Intellectual Craftsmanship," I recommend a thorough examination of his proposals, and of his entire book *The Sociological Imagination* (1959). Glaser and Strauss' (1967, pp. 251–57) chapter on "Insight and Theory Development" extends Mills' discussion and gives specific examples from their own research. It also provides a useful review of studies on insight. George Herbert Mead's (1917, pp. 176–227) "Scientific Method and the Individual Thinker" should be read for the excellent review of perspectives and the mind of the scientist. This essay also offers glimpses of Mead's views on the scientific method and analytic induction.

# 3

# Difficulties of Theory Construction

Theory has not often been designed with research operations in mind. Theory as we have it in social science serves indispensably as a very broad frame of reference or general orientation. Thus modern theories of culture tell us that it is usually more profitable to focus on the learning process and the control of what is learned rather than on the innate or hereditary traits. But they do not provide us with sets of interrelated propositions which can be put in the form: If $x_1$, given $x_2$ and $x_3$, then there is a strong probability that we get $x_4$. Most of our propositions of that form, sometimes called "theory," are likely to be *ad hoc* common-sense observations which are not deducible from more general considerations and which are of the same quality as the observation, "If you stick your hand in a fire and hold it there, you will get burned."

*Samuel A. Stouffer, 1950, p. 359.*

Nearly every observer of modern sociology has developed his own criticism concerning the present status of theory in the discipline. In some instances this has taken the form of a belief that sociologists misunderstand what theory is (Homans, 1964). Other critics feel that too wide a gap exists between theories, methods, and data. Thus Merton (1957, 1967) feels justified in calling for theories of the middle range that stay close to empirical observations, and Glaser and Strauss (1967) propose solidly grounded theories of the formal and substantive variety. Spokesmen such as Furfey (1959), Mills (1959), and Gouldner (1962, 1968) call for greater attention to the problems of metatheory.

All of these criticisms are valid and not contradictory. If, for example, a sociologist misunderstands what a theory is, he is hard put to make the appropriate links between conceptualizations and empirical data. Unfortunately, to some degree, each of the critics has been parochial in his vision of how sociological theory might be better developed; he has taken his own favored biases and excluded other positions and alternative lines of action. Thus Glaser and Strauss (1967), in their reactions against verification and middle-range theories, have excessively focused on grounded theory.

It is my belief that sociologists make significant theoretical advances when they recognize the symbolic elements that permeate their conduct. Sociologists are in certain important respects no different from the persons and objects they study, and a full awareness of these symbolic processes will better permit the development of viable and realistic images of social man. This stance leads to my second bias, which is the belief that sociologists must turn away from what has appeared to be a futile and fruitless emulation of other sciences and disciplines. There must be a turn inward to sociology's own subject matter, which is human interaction, and metaphors and analogies that reflect the distinctive nature of this subject must be developed (Homans, 1950, pp. 1–23). Instead of viewing social systems as computers, or biological organisms, an analysis based on the unique features of the behavior under study is needed.

These are my biases, or value positions. Their validity cannot be established by empirical fact, but I feel that the strategies employed up till now by sociologists have not yielded sufficient rewards to justify their continued use.

### Metasociological Considerations: The Problem of Metaphors, Role Models, Values and Ideologies

Broadly speaking, metasociology concerns itself with "the methodological considerations necessary for carrying out sociological research, constructing sociological systems and criticizing such research and systems after they have been completed [Furfey, 1959, p. 510]." The domain of metasociology extends beyond methodological considerations, or standards for appropriate theory. The use of one set of methodological or theoretical directives ultimately represents an involvement in value decisions, and metasociology directs attention to the study of value decisions as they become embedded in the sociological enterprise. A value decision refers to a declaration of preference, such as "sociology is a science," or "sociologists should concern themselves with problems of theory," or "a goal of sociology should be better theory." Each of these statements declares an intent, a desired condition, an "ought" world. Value decisions cannot be analyzed and empirically proven or disproven, but they can be studied for their logical nature, and the study of values becomes axiology. Scientific declarations are statements of "what is," such as "the rate of suicide in Spain is low." Ultimately all sociological statements rest on a series of values taken on faith. Their acceptance rests on the belief that they are correct lines of action for the sociologist.

Sociologists have long debated the relevance of models of science taken from physics and chemistry. The proponents of the physical science model claim that if it worked for physics, it should work for sociology (Lundberg, 1955, 1960). Other spokesmen claim that the subject matter of sociology is so different from that of the physical sciences that physical models are inappropriate for sociological analysis. This position is well stated by MacIver:

Sociology has been plagued all through its history by its tendency to seek for models in the fields of other sciences. At one time the fashion was to think of a society as a kind of organism, to make sociology a pale reflection of biology. Now the attitude changes and the first article of the creed has become the formula that sociology is a "natural science". . . .
The trouble is that the social sciences suffer from certain embarrassments from which the "natural sciences" are more or less free. They have to deal with phenomena which involve a kind of causation unknown in the purely physical world, since they are "motivated," in fact brought into being, by that elusive complex, but undeniable, reality, the mentality of man. Not a single object which the social sciences study would exist at all were it not for the creative imagination of social beings. . . . I conclude that the great need of sociology is not ready-made methods nor ready-made models but the trained and disciplined imagination. . . . Our aim is to understand and to convey to others the understanding of the intricate and often baffling web of social relationships, which, being created by man, must be understood by a similar creative capacity in ourselves [1931, pp. 25–27, 35].

MacIver's statement reflects the central problem of metasociology: what are the assumptions, beliefs, metaphors and role models necessary for sociologists to adopt in their quest to be scientific? His answer is to reject models and metaphors taken from the physical sciences, but he fails to offer a satisfactory alternative. It is insufficient to say, that one model does not work. If it does not, then what should be adopted in its place? (Part III of this book represents an attempt to provide a solution to MacIver's unanswered question.)

*Alternative Metasociological Positions*

At least four alternative metasociological stances have been offered. The first is the biological model; the second is the natural science model; the third, never systematically articulated, is the social science model; and the fourth is a model taken from the humanities. Each model has its own bundle of metaphors and values, and each represents differing role models the sociologist may emulate. If the natural science model is followed, logico-deductive theories, and rigorous quantified measurement strategies are likely to be employed. Methods such as surveys and experiments will be used to a greater extent than life histories and participant observation. When findings are presented, the model will be the scientific article. Methods, hypotheses, and findings will be clearly spelled out. Terms will be precisely defined and prose style will be free of ambiguous and evocative images (see Merton, 1967, pp. 1–37).

An additional consequence of adopting the natural science model will be a selective use of metaphors in the process of theorizing. Every sociological theory, Stone and Farberman (1967, pp. 149–64) suggest, "implies some image of man, communication, society and their interrelations." In the presentation of these interrelationships the theorist is likely to employ some form of the metaphor that is:

an implied comparison between things essentially unlike one another. . . . One image is superimposed upon another in order to provide a better perspective and understanding of the subject at hand. . . . The major metaphors in the social sciences have been drawn from the physical and organic worlds. Social and psychological analysis of human behavior are replete with terms borrowed from the physical world such as structure, forces, system, etc., and terms borrowed from the organic world such as evolution, differentiation, integration, etc. [Bruyn, 1966, p. 133].

Thus, Lundberg, a spokesman for the natural science model, heavily used terms such as "force," "vector," and "velocity."

If the social science model is adopted, the metaphors of the physical sciences are dropped, the theorist uses phrases such as "drift," "rebellion," "anomie," "strain," "love" and "hate" (see Matza, 1964), evocative words that stand in marked contrast to the more precise "vector," or "velocity." The social science model, which has been heavily influenced by the humanities perspective, directs the analyst's attention to what is unique about human conduct. The ideal is one of "holding man up and seeing him for what he is," which immediately turns attention to the arts, literature, and drama, where the panorama of human emotional experiences are vividly portrayed (Redfield, 1948; Homans, 1950).

An important consequence of the social science-humanities' position is the mode of scientific presentation. Commenting on this, Merton states:

Through the generations, most sociological writing . . . has been in the style of the scientific essay. Unlike the long-established format of papers in the physical and biological sciences, it has only recently become established practice for papers in sociology to set out a compact statement of the problem, the procedures and the instruments of investigation, the empirical findings, a discussion of these, and the theoretical implications of what was found. Past sociological papers and particularly books were written in a style in which the basic concepts were seldom strictly defined, while the logic of procedure and the relationships between variables and the specific theory being developed remained largely implicit, in keeping with the long-established humanist tradition [1967, p. 14].

This latter style has had two important consequences for the sociologist. First, underlying concepts, propositions and definitions are vaguely stated: consequently, their role in cumulative sociological knowledge remains underdeveloped. Second, sociologists are continually rediscovering theories and insights in older works. Since so many theorists have adopted the essay form, sociologists must reread their work to discover exactly what was said. Merton states:

The predilection in the nineteenth century and, in some quarters, today for sociologists to develop their own "systems of sociology," means that these are typically laid out as competing systems of thought rather than into a cumulative product [1967, p. 23].

Not only do many sociologists attempt to develop their own systems of thought, which strikes against a cumulative nature of the discipline, but the essay form makes the goal of cumulative growth even more difficult. The contemporary sociologist is caught in a struggle between role models. In one sense, he bows in the direction of the physical sciences and attempts to be precise in his style of presentation, but

in another way, sociology retains its kinship with the humanities. It is reluctant to abandon a firsthand acquaintance with the classical works of sociology and pre-sociology as an integral part of the experience of the sociologist *qua* sociologist. Every contemporary sociologist with a claim to sociological literacy has had direct and repeated encounters with the works of the founding fathers: Comte, Marx and Spencer, Durkheim, Weber, Simmel and Pareto, Sumner, Cooley and Veblen, and the rest of the short list of talented men who have left their indelible stamp on sociology today [Merton, 1967, p. 29].

It is important to distinguish between the humanities and social science models. Homans has offered the following analysis:

The men of letters, novelists and poets, may be, as some tokens suggest, resentful of the social scientists. They see the latter moving into their territory. But they have no reason to be afraid. If the social scientists are to do their job, they must follow a rigorous code, and it could not be better calculated to make their books and articles hard reading. The rules of theory-building contradict the rules of art at every point. Thus the obvious, or what looks like it, is the thing the writer is most careful to avoid. Since most efforts at serious conversation show that it hurts people to think about one thing at a time, a writer uses words that refer to several things at once. He also uses different words for the same thing, or he will be told he lacks variety. For the same reason, he must not repeat himself, whereas systematic discussion is notoriously repetitious, because the same things must be considered in several different connections. Finally, a writer, in a novel or poem, is always concerned with evoking a vivid and integrated sense of concrete reality, either physical or psychological, and his success in doing so is the measure of his charm. A theory begins by breaking up concrete reality and ends by leaving out most of it. The social scientists are not competing, and cannot compete, with the literary artists. They are doing a different job [1950, p. 17].

In my judgment Homans has reversed the source of resentment. Sociologists have long been resentful of physical scientists and this accounts, I believe, for their continuing attempt to emulate those sciences. Perhaps the discipline would have advanced more rapidly had sociologists emulated novelists and artists. At the very least, the concern for a subject matter that reflected human events would have been cultivated; a sensitivity to human emotions and relationships most evident in literature, is quite lacking in current sociological theory. If sociologists set for themselves the goal of understanding patterned forms of human behavior, then a valuable source of data for secondary analysis are the poems, novels, paintings, and musical compositions of artists in various historical periods (see Coser, 1963). I am proposing a dual interest in the humanities perspective—as a source of data and as a stimulation for the sociological imagination.

These models—humanities, biological, social, and physical science—represent three different ways of going about the job of theory construction. Each poses a different set of metaphors, lays out a different mode of scientific presentation, and stakes out only certain problems for analysis. It would seem apparent that the answer for social theory lies in a combination of these perspectives. If sociology is to remain close to its subject matter, metaphors must be adopted that reflect this subject. But if sociologists are to move closer to the goal of rigorous theory, some variant of the natural science model is needed. It should be remembered that an interest in the form of theory (e.g., logico-deductive theory) must not replace a concern for the content (e.g., what it is about—social systems, interaction). The metaphorical thrust of the humanities perspective furnishes the needed emphasis on content. This is not to say that the necessary substantive leads will invariably come from the humanities; they certainly will not, although the "art of social science," as Redfield termed it, is broadened by an exposure to the humanities.

If the social scientist is to apprehend, deeply and widely and correctly, persons and societies and cultures, then he needs experience, direct or vicarious, with persons, societies and cultures. This experience is partly had through acquaintances with history, literature, biography and ethnography [Redfield, 1948, p. 189].

## The Choice of Metaphors, Role Models, and Values

The career of a sociologist reflects a wide variety of personal choices and decisions. For example an undergraduate major in the humanities who enters sociology in graduate school is more likely to adopt the stance I have just proposed, than one who was an undergraduate in mathematics. The very choice of sociology, as opposed to another discipline, reflects a value-laden line of action, as does the choice to be a particular type of sociologist (e.g., functionalist, interactionist, family specialist). Every sociologist approaches his profession from a spatial and temporal perspective that will never be fully replicated in the experiences of another sociologist. Only in an abstract sense is the common identity of sociologists shared. It is this fact that leads each researcher as he enters the field of research, selects thesis topics, or prepares lectures to take a peculiar line of action. In the final analysis, the selection of metaphors and models of scientific-theoretical conduct is personal. Yet, within the sociological community this selection must be consensual—if only in degree. The position I am advocating calls for a movement away from metaphors and models that are alien to the subject matter of sociology.

## The Use of Metaphors

The metaphor is chiefly a tool for revealing special properties of an object or event. Frequently theorists forget this and make their metaphors a real entity in the empirical world. It is legitimate, for example, to say that a social system is like an organism, but this does not mean that a social system *is* an organism. When metaphors, or concepts, are reified, they lose their explanatory value and become tautologies. A careful line must be followed in the use of metaphors so that they remain a powerful strategy of illumination.

## Theory Misunderstood

A second deficiency of modern sociology theory is a misunderstanding of what theory is. Some theorists suggest that theories are interrelated sets of concepts, or logico-deductive schemes, or images of reality, or even conceptual frameworks. Others refer to sociological classics as theory, while still others distinguish grand theory from middle-range, formal, and/or substantive theory. These designations refer both to form and content. For example, grand theory is taken to mean one abstract system that covers all matters of importance to the sociologist, while middle-range theory designates formulations that are closely tied to empirical reality (and is thus quite close to substantive theory). Formal theory, as discussed in Chapter 1, refers to a small set of propositions and concepts that are believed sufficient to explain some significant segment of human conduct.

What often passes for theory in sociology, however, is not theory. Instead there are various types of theory-work ranging from ad hoc classificatory systems to categorical systems, taxonomies, and vaguely interrelated conceptual schemes. In the following section the most common designations of theory will be discussed. Distinct levels of theory-work will be discussed, as will types of theory.

### What Theory Is Not: Levels of Theory-Work Recognized

There are at least five levels of theory-work: (1) ad hoc classificatory systems; (2) categorical systems or taxonomies; (3) conceptual frameworks; (4) theoretical systems; and (5) empirical-theoretical systems. (Parsons and Shils, 1959, pp. 47–52).

The ad hoc classificatory system consists of more or less arbitrary classes constructed for the sake of summarizing data. No attempt is made to fit classes to data so that relations between variables and dimensions can be summarized; the classes are independent of one another. This is basically a method of organizing observations so that the more sophisticated theory development can follow. Examples include such schemes of analysis as Gordon's (1968, pp. 115–36) proposal for the treatment of responses to the "Who am I?" test, which proposes 30 categories for answers. These answers range from an uncodable category to statements reflecting interpersonal style, situational references, material references, and statements describing ascriptive characteristics (e.g., age, sex, name). Gordon's scheme is ad hoc in nature because a large proportion of his categories are not theoretically derived; they have been constructed to fit the data. To the extent that they are later placed within a theoretical scheme, they serve their function for theory-work, but ad hoc classificatory schemes are not theory.

The *categorical system,* or taxonomy, is a movement beyond the ad hoc classification. It consists of a system of classes constructed to fit the subject matter so that relationships among classes can be described. There is often an interdependence between classes so that classification into one category demands treatment in another. The system should bear a close relationship to empirical reality, and in this sense the categories mirror the reality described. Parsons' analysis of social action is this type of theory-work. He suggests that behavior has four characteristics: It is goal oriented; occurs in situations; is normatively regulated; and involves an expenditure of energy. When behavior is so organized it is said to constitute a social system. Social systems take three forms: personality systems, cultural systems, and social systems (Parsons and Shils, 1959, pp. 47–275). This formulation fits the taxonomy as I have defined it; categories are formed to fit the data and there are interrelationships between categories.

Taxonomies perform several functions for the sociologist. First, they specify a unit of reality (in Parsons' use, social systems) to be analyzed and indicate how that unit may be described (Zetterberg, 1965, pp. 24–28). Such definitions tell the sociologist what to look for, but they are primarily descriptions, not analytical explanations. Thus, the second function (Zetterberg, 1965, p. 26) of the taxonomy is to "summarize and inspire *descriptive studies.*" Commenting on Parsons' framework, Zetterberg notes that his taxonomy of the pattern variables guided Stouffer and Toby "to a descriptive study which presented the distribution of some college students on the variable 'particularism-universalism' [1965, p. 26]." The taxonomy does not offer explanations; it only describes behavior by fitting it into a series of classes or categories. As indicated in Chapter 2, however, one of the basic goals of the sociologist is the development of viable descriptive schemes that anticipate explanatory and predictive theories; this is the chief contribution of the taxonomy.

*Conceptual frameworks* stand above the taxonomy. Here descriptive categories are placed within a broad structure of both explicit and assumed propositions. The theory of symbolic interaction is best termed a conceptual framework. Concepts such as "self," "object," "act," "interaction" and "socialization" are used to analyze the data, and a systematic image of the empirical world is assumed. The framework is yet too imprecise to permit the systematic derivation of propositions, but deductions are possible. The empirical verifications in the framework are of varying quality, yet there is a continuous interaction between the framework and empirical observations. Versions of conceptual frameworks include Scheff's (1966) propositional summary of labeling theory and mental illness, and Goffman's (1963) statements on stigma. In Scheff's case, nine different propositions are offered to explain how certain persons are labeled and treated as mentally ill. The system stands above a taxonomy because its propositions summarize and propose explanations for vast amounts of data. It is not a theory, however, because the propositions are not systematically derived in a deductive fashion.

Much of what now passes as theory in sociology are conceptual frameworks that systematically direct empirical and theoretical activity around a core set of problems (e.g., interaction, mental illness, stigma). Because of this directive function, the conceptual framework offers the best hope for development of systematic theory.

*Theoretical systems* move closer to ideal theory. They represent combinations of taxonomies and conceptual schemes, but now descriptions and predictions are combined in a deductive fashion. Zetterberg's (1955, pp. 533–40) axiomatic presentation of Durkheim's theory of the division of labor is an instance of a theoretical system. Kinch's (1963) axiomatic theory of the self in interaction and my integration of Becker's analysis of the marijuana user with Kinch's theory are other examples. Theoretical systems are distinguished, somewhat arbitrarily, from *empirical-theoretical systems* by their lack of a precise empirical base. The empirical-theoretical represents the highest level of theory development. With it sociologists can move with ease direclty from theory to empirical propositions and observations. This level of theory-work contains all of the elements theory should have—but there are few clear representations of this type of theory in contemporary sociology.

## Levels of Theory in Review

A major hindrance to theory construction has been a failure to note the five varieties of theory-work. A clear understanding of the varieties should lead sociologists to become more precise in their use of the term. Additionally, a recognition of the functions played by ad hoc systems, taxonomies, and conceptual frameworks should aid analysis and criticism of what now passes for theory. And because conceptual schemes and taxonomies are closest to formal theory, their development should be encouraged.

## The Content of Sociological Theory: Types of Theory Recognized

Four distinct types of social theory may be noted. The first is a grand, or general, social systems theory that proposes "a master conceptual scheme for deriving all subsidiary theories [Merton, 1967, p. 51]." The second is middle-range theory, which is

applicable to limited conceptual ranges—theories, for example, of deviant behavior, the unanticipated consequences of purposive action, social perception, reference groups, social control, the interdependence of social institutions—rather than to seek immediately the total conceptual structure that is adequate to derive these and other theories of the middle range [Merton, 1967, p. 51].

Middle-range theory may be given another, and nearly equivalent meaning, which is substantive theory. This represents theory developed for a "substantive, or empirical area of sociological inquiry, such as patient care, race relations, professional education, delinquency, or research organizations [Glaser and Strauss, 1967, p. 32]." Substantive theory is here distinguished from middle-range theory, as Merton defines the term, by virtue of its focus on a particular problem area. A theory of patient care, of race relations, or of professional education is considerably different from a theory of reference groups that draws on the area of race relations or patient care. Both are similar because "they fall between the 'minor working hypotheses' of everyday life and the 'all inclusive' grand theories [Glaser and Strauss, 1967, p. 33]."

While middle-range and substantive theories work primarily with one focus of inquiry in examining a variety of different areas, (e.g., reference groups as seen in race relations), the fourth type of theory works with a series of interrelated concepts and applies these to several distinct substantive areas. This is formal theory; it was illustrated by excerpts in Chapter 1 from the work of Simmel, Goffman, and Homans. The unique contribution of formal theory is its wide relevance to more than one area and its use of many different, yet interrelated concepts and propositions.

*Advantages and Disadvantages of Each Approach to Theory*

Unless theory fits the data it is constructed to explain, it is of little scientific value. In this sense all theory must be grounded in the firm empirical sense stressed by Glaser and Strauss (1967). If it can be assumed that all that passes as theory meets the requirements so far outlined, then all that remains is to review the advantages and disadvantages of grand, middle-range, substantive, and formal theory.

*Grand, or Social Systems Theory* The chief advantage of this strategy is best stated by its major proponent, Talcott Parsons. Commenting on the status of sociological theory in the 1950's Parsons states:

At the end of this road of increasing frequency and specificity of the islands of theoretical knowledge lies the ideal state, scientifically speaking, where most actual operational hypotheses of empirical research are directly derived from a general system of theory. On any broad front . . . only in physics has this state been attained in any science. We cannot expect to be anywhere nearly in sight of it. But it does not follow that, distant as we are from the goal, steps in the direction are futile. Quite the contrary, any real step in that direction is an advance. Only at the end point do the islands merge into a continental land mass.

At the very least, then, general theory, can provide a broadly orienting framework. . . . It can also serve to codify, interrelate and make available a vast amount of existing empirical knowledge. It also serves to call attention to gaps in our knowledge, and to provide canons for the criticism of theories and empirical generalizations. Finally, if they cannot be systematically derived, it is indispensable to the systematic clarification of problems and the fruitful formulation of hypotheses [1950, p. 7].

Significantly Parsons, a general theorist himself, recognizes that general theory seldom provides the basis for specific hypotheses. His scheme, or any other general social systems theory, must be seen not as a theory, but as a formulation lying between a taxonomy and a conceptual framework. General theory, then, is not theory. Thus Parsons acknowledges that it provides only a general orientation to specific problems. At its best, however, it does provide a basis for codifying empirical generalizations and specific theories (see Johnson, 1960).

These latter features are best seen in Parsons' attempt to integrate theories of personality and culture into his more general framework for the analysis of social systems. To give just one example, on several occasions Parsons has indicated how the Freudian theory of socialization may be articulated into his social systems model. If the interest is in formulating a total theory that integrates all features of all social systems (e.g., biological through social), then there is value in the Parsonian taxonomy. But it must be realized that this is only theory-work; the overwhelming implication of the evidence thus far gathered indicates that general theory, as it now stands, is of limited empirical value because of the abstract nature of the perspective and the rather deliberate avoidance of specific empirical issues by its major proponents (for exceptions see Johnson, 1960; Smelser, 1968). The earlier evaluation of taxonomies seems to fit general theory—it is fine for descriptive purposes, but its use in explanatory and predictive schemes is very restricted.

*Middle-Range, or Substantive Theory*   Because of the failures of general theory, the strategy of middle-range theory has gained wide acceptance. Merton, the major spokesman for this kind of theorizing, argues that "sociology will advance insofar as its major (but not exclusive) concern is with developing theories of the middle-range, and it will be retarded if its primary attention is focused on developing total sociological systems [1967, p. 50]."

Middle-range theory focuses on the development of special theories empirically grounded at strategic points. Hence, Merton envisions theories of deviant behavior, of reference groups, of social perception, and so on. These special theories would be tested and grounded in widely varying areas. He states:

The essential point is that these are empirically grounded theories—involving sets of confirmed hypotheses—and not merely organized descriptive data or empirical generalizations or hypotheses which remain logically disparate and unconnected. A cumulative set of such theories has emerged in investigations of bureacracies; notably by Selznick, Gouldner, Blau, Lipset-Trow-and-Coleman, Crozier, Kahn and Katz, and a long list of other investigators [1967, p. 61].

Work of this kind, Merton suggests, will ultimately permit sociologists to develop more general conceptual schemes that consolidate groups of special theories. Thus it might be presumed that a theory of bureaucracy would eventually merge with theories of deviance, social perception, and reference groups to form one large, empirical-theoretical system.

The chief virtue of middle-range theory is its close tie to empirical observations and its emphasis on a small set of concepts. Its disadvantages take many forms. Bierstedt, for example, has criticized it for its restrictive and limited aims.

We have been invited to forego those larger problems of human society that occupied our ancestors in the history of social thought and to seek instead what T. H. Marshall called, in his inaugural lecture at the University of London, "stepping stones of the middle range," and other sociologists since, "theories of the middle range." But what an anemic ambition this is! Shall we strive for half victory? Where are the visions that enticed us into the world of learning in the first place? I had always thought that sociologists too knew how to dream and that they believed with Browning that a man's reach should exceed his grasp [1960, p. 6].

Bierstedt's criticism rests on a vision of the sociological enterprise that sees it striving for an analysis of significant human issues and problems, but it is not clear how general theory, which he appears to hold up as the alternative, can do this. His argument appears to rest on the metaphorical stance of the humanities. As such it challenges the metasociological basis of middle-range theory, which is more squarely based on a blend of the natural science and social science models.

Another criticism of middle-range theory holds that it leads to an inevitable splintering of the discipline; it is felt that tendencies toward fragmentation are accelerated because each specialist develops his own middle-range theory. Seldom are these separate perspectives integrated into one framework, or summarized as one concept. Merton rejects this criticism by claiming that

On the contrary theories of the middle range *consolidate,* not fragment, empirical findings. I have tried to show this, for example, with reference group theory, which draws together findings from such disparate fields of human behavior as military life, race and ethnic relations, social mobility, delinquency, politics, education, and revolutionary activity [1967, p. 65].

This claim is partially true, as can be seen in the wide applicability of reference group theory. Yet it seems that few practitioners of this mode of theorizing have taken the integrative strategy. Quite often, in fact, there is no attempt by the middle-range theorist to show the relevance of his theory for other areas. This was the criticism lodged by Goffman against specialists in the various areas of deviance. (See p. 15, Chapter 1.)

Goffman's position is quite clear. The persistent pursuit of theory within special substantive areas leads to a parochialism that blinds the investigator to the commonalities apparent in other areas of analysis. Unless middle-range theory is conceived in this broad fashion, I am led to accept the argument that it in fact does lead to a splintering of the discipline.

Another potential flaw of middle-range theory has been an overemphasis by its practitioners on strategies of verification as opposed to strategies of generation. This bias, at times, stems from the belief that the significant theories have already been developed and that the major task now confronting sociology is their verification. Glaser and Strauss fear that too many sociologists have wedded themselves to a particular middle-range theory and have ceased to examine critically those theories in a way that would lead to the generation of new perspectives.

We contend . . . that the masters have not provided enough theories to cover all the areas of social life that sociologists have only begun to explore. Further, some theories of our predecessors, because of their lack of grounding in data, do not fit, or do not work, or are not sufficiently understandable to be used and are therefore useless in research, theoretical advance and practical understanding. On the other hand, the great theories have indeed given us models and guidelines for generating theory, so that with recent advances in data collection, conceptual systematization and analytic procedures, many of us can follow in their paths: from social research we can generate new theories for new areas, as well as better theories for areas where previous ones do not work [Glaser and Strauss, 1967, p. 11].

This criticism is not confined to middle-range strategy; it can be lodged against any type of theorizing. To the extent, however, that persons adopting the middle-range approach restrict their interests to verification, their work represents a flaw of the method.

*Formal Theory* With the formal theory—which is middle-range theory— the theorist ceases to focus on one or a handful of substantive areas and moves to many different areas in a simultaneous-comparative fashion. For example, a researcher may develop a specific low-level theory to account for the trajectory of patients who die in hospitals. Having developed and verified this theory, his interest becomes comparative and formal, for he now wishes to apply the theory to as many different areas as possible. Glaser and Strauss (1966, 1968) provide an example of this. They first generated an empirically grounded theory of dying in the hospital. A major concept in their theory was status passage, referring to the fact that patients are seen by hospital staff as passing through a number of differentiated statuses or positions on their way to death. Commenting on their attempt to make this low-level theory formal they state:

If the focus were on formal theory, then the comparative analysis would be made among different kinds of substantive cases which fall within the formal area, without relating them to any one substantive area. The focus of comparisons is now on generating a theory of status passage, not on generating a theory about a single substantive case of status passage [Glaser and Strauss, 1967, p. 43].

Substantive (middle-range) theory, then, takes a given area as its domain; formal theory takes a conceptual area of analysis (e.g., status passage, strained interaction, deviance) as its domain.

While these strategies remain distinct, it should be a goal of all investigators to work toward formal theory. Indeed, any given investigation should be working on both levels at once. By generating a theory of dying, for instance, a researcher might compare other types of status passages (e.g., marriage, birth, promotions, demotions, etc.) to illuminate what is unique about dying. In addition, a variety of different instances of dying might be analyzed comparatively. For example, dying could be studied as it occurs outside of hospitals, in suicides, or as it appears in different areas of the same setting (e.g., wards of the same hospital). To illustrate the uniqueness of dying as an instance of status passing, this substantive focus on different dying situations could be compared to a formal analysis of other types of status passage, in which case the theorist would be combining middle-range and formal approaches in the same study. In so doing the principles of empirical grounding and the general method of formally applying one perspective across many different areas would be maintained.

Glaser and Strauss (1967), for example, have offered what they call a formal theory of status passage prompted by their substantive theory of status passages during death in the hospital. Their formal theory begins by delineating several properties of the concept (and event) "status passage." First, a status may be unscheduled, as in dying, or scheduled, as in a job promotion. Second, a status passage may "follow an institutionally prescribed sequence of transitional statuses [1967, p. 86]." That is, any given social structure may keep its members in between two given statuses for a specified or unspecified length of time. A civilian, for example, is made into a soldier by spending a certain number of weeks as a basic trainee. A person becomes an adult, however, only after a lengthy presence in the status called adolescent. Third, status passages may be analyzed by the degree to which they are regulated or nonregulated. Dying, which is a nonscheduled status passage, is marked by varying elements of regulation [but see Sudnow, 1967]. For patients it appears to be nonregulated (e.g., they are seldom informed of their impending death, though relatives are; in this case it is regulated for one party and not another).

A fourth dimension is the extent to which the passage is seen as desirable. Dying is undesirable, marriage desirable, and so on. Last, it may be asked to what degree the passage is inevitable. Dying is inevitable, marriage is not.

Given these properties of the status passage, dying in the hospital is seen as nonscheduled, nonprescribed, undesirable, and—after a point—inevitable. Having made this substantive analysis of dying as a status passage,

the next step is to study different types of status passage in order to begin generating a formal theory. Various combinations of the above dimensions provide ways of typing different status passages as well as some of the conditions under which the passage is managed. Differences between two sets of these conditions will, therefore, tend to explain why two types of status passages are managed differently [Glaser and Strauss, 1967, p. 87].

Glaser and Strauss proceed to apply this theory to engagement, mental illness, polio recovery, and failure at work. Thus, by beginning with the generic proposition that all status passages will be regulated in different ways, they are led to a formal yet substantive analysis of a variety of different areas.

Several characteristics of this process must be noted. First, once a researcher has generated his own substantive theory, his efforts at formal theory may depart—at least momentarily—from additional empirical research. That is, any analyst may take other substantive theories and extract his own formal theory from them. In this instance a great deal of empirical legwork is saved by drawing on published materials (Glaser and Strauss, 1967, p. 90).

### The Multiple-Paths Approach to Formal Theory

A second feature of the formal theory approach should be the use of a sensitizing-triangulated methodology. This is what I call the multiple-paths-to-theory approach. If it is appropriately employed, it will yield firmly grounded formal theory of wide relevance. Instead of formulating single empirical definitions of key concepts, the investigator works with several different empirical definitions of his central concepts. Rather than operationalizing status passage as the movement between two clearly defined positions in a social structure, the investigator might define it as movement through a social structure in which the statuses may or may not be clearly defined. Furthermore, it might be noted that during the passage process definitions of who has and who has not passed will vary by position in the structure. This rather vague, yet sensitizing definition immediately permits a comparative analysis of dying and marriage that the more operational definition would overlook. Thus, in dying, definitions of whether or not a patient has passed from one position to another will vary by the awareness context and the position of the definer. Medical personnel, for example, will have quite precise definitions of a dying patient's status, while the patient and his relatives will be viewing it from another stance.

By defining key concepts and propositions in this sensitizing fashion, investigators are led to adopt specific triangulated methodologies that capture the relevant features of their concepts. Combining all of these methods and their resulting empirical observations places researchers in a much better position to state what is unique about dying as a status passage than if they used only a single method. A strategy of utilizing different methods will reveal that each instance of a concept is better examined from one method than another. Thus, the definitions held by physicians regarding a given status passage might be gleaned from their records on the patient; for nurses it might be best revealed by their patterns of care for the patient; for relatives it might be evidenced by the frequency and duration of their visits. In each instance a slightly different method is taken to measure key concepts and propositions.

Armed with a triangulated set of observations, researchers can begin analysis of status passages in other contexts. That is, once a well-grounded and triangulated substantive theory has been developed, investigators can move with ease and confidence to unstudied areas, a strategy that has the advantage of maintaining a firmly grounded empirical approach that is comparative in nature. The analysis of dying, for example, is grounded comparatively by the analysis of all relevant perspectives. Not only have the commonalities of the concept been uncovered in one area, but it is possible to show how the concept varies by position and points of view. This is the invariant strategy of the sensitizing approach and when lifted to the formal level it permits the kind of theory stressed by Homans and exemplified by Goffman.

The use of this sensitizing approach does not lead the researcher into a situation where his concepts remain nonoperationalized; the point of operationalization is only delayed. Once the distinctive nature of concepts are uncovered, analysts can rapidly move to the use of triangulated strategies. It may be argued that sociologists are led to the use of this sensitizing-triangulated approach because of the distinctive nature of the empirical world. That is, in studying the empirical, sociologists cannot confine their considerations to what is covered by the empirical definitions of concepts; they must seek out the distinctive features of their concepts and propositions. It would be an error to assume that different kinds of support of propositions across situations reflects faulty measurement or instances of a negative case. The distinct, the unique, and the unusual aspects of concepts must be accepted, because empirical reality presents itself in forms that vary by time, place, and point of observation. A heavy emphasis on single methods of observation and precise empirical definitions that miss the unique instances of concepts only takes sociologists further away from firmly grounded empirical theory. The sensitizing-triangulated perspective is offered as a method of theory-building that both stays close to empirical reality and demands a commitment to tightly integrated theory.

*Single versus Multifocused Formal Theory*

Formal theory as I have defined it is close to middle-range theory, as is evident in Glaser and Strauss' theory of status passage. Like Merton's theory of reference groups, the theory of status passage is based on a single dimension or concept. At this point I wish to propose as an additional strategy formal theory that combines and applies more than one concept to several different substantive areas. This is multifocused formal theory and is illustrated by Homan's theory of social exchange, which he believes will explain behavior in such differing areas as contemporary small groups and during the industrial revolution in England. At one point his theory (1950) was built around the concepts of interaction, sentiment, and activity. He supplemented these with terms describing the external and internal social systems of interaction and derived a series of concepts that describe status and role systems within these systems. This conceptual framework was articulated into a formal-propositional theory and subsequently applied to a series of case studies ranging from a friendship clique, a primitive tribe, and, finally, to a small community in New England.

This is multifocused formal theory. The analyst moves beyond a single-concept-based theory (e.g., status passage or reference groups) to a theory that cross-cuts as many different conceptual sectors of human behavior as possible.

### Strategies for Developing Multifocused Formal Theory

In general, the sociologist committed to multifocused theory proceeds just as if a middle-range and single-based formal theory was under construction. Work begins by empirically grounding an instance of the theory that furnishes a series of interrelated concepts and propositions that can be applied to other areas. Homans, for example, first generated and verified his theory in a work group. Then he formally stated his propositions and proposed that his system would explain interaction in a variety of other situations. He then selected existing case studies that offered strategic tests. The next step was to apply the theory to each case and begin revisions as the data demanded. The ultimate product was an empirically revised and grounded formal theory.

This type of formal theory has the advantage of consolidating smaller substantive theories. It differs from grand or general theory because of the grounded element. While sociologists may never develop a theory that encompasses all levels and forms of human conduct, multifocused formal theory is a strategy that moves beyond middle-range statements to a more abstract level.

Before sociologists can reasonably pursue such a line of theoretical attack, however, they must have confidence in their concepts and propositions. Hence, as an analyst works in this direction, the rules of concepts and propositions stated in Chapter 2 must be remembered. Unless concepts and propositions can generate observations and be fitted into theory, they are of little value. This is why work must begin with one grounded area. Having achieved satisfactory verification, researchers can then confidently and legitimately move to the multifocused level.

A final word of preference: Multifocused theorizing offers the greatest potential, I believe, for the ultimate consolidation of sociology into a systematic perspective that uniformly progresses toward the status of a mature science. Sociologists must discard the polarized stances they now take toward the form and content of theory. They must learn to apply one set of standards to all theory, and they must give up the critical stereotyping and rejection that characterizes their evaluation of the theories and points of view of others. Ideology must be replace by consensual standards of evaluation.

One last point: In this and the previous chapter, many prescriptions have been presented. These were stated as preferred lines of action that, if adopted, would give all sociologists one set of consensual standards against which theory can be evaluated. These rules, of course, must not be taken as ends in themselves, for in the final analysis the sociological imagination is the true source of all social theory.

## Notes

A convenient review of the major criticisms lodged against modern social theory is Hans L. Zetterberg's *On Theory and Verification in Sociology* (1965, pp. 1–29). In my estimation the single best treatment of values and sociology is Paul H. Furfey's "Sociological Science and the Problem of Values," (1959, pp. 509–30). Furfey anticipates many of the points made in Gouldner's (1962) analysis of the value-free myth in sociology, and also offers a useful extension of the Weberian perspective discussed in Chapter 2.

An insightful analysis of metaphors may be found in Severyn T. Bruyn's *The Human Perspective in Sociology* (1966, pp. 125–59). Bruyn draws upon Kenneth Burke's *Permanence and Change* (1965), which presents a more complete analysis of literary forms of exposition. A very good illustration of how metaphors may become reified is Theodore R. Sarbin's "On the Futility of the Proposition that some People are Labeled 'Mentally Ill' " (1967, pp. 447–53).

Robert K. Merton (1967, pp. 1–37) presents the single best analysis of role models and varieties in the sociological enterprise. His essay should be examined for the insights it offers into the discovery process and the problems of analyzing differing sociological schemes of thought.

Glaser and Strauss' (1967) analysis of grounded theory provided the theme for my discussion of formal theory. They use the term multiarea formal theory to describe what I have called multifocused formal theory. Their treatment of various types of theorizing (1967, pp. 1–99) should be read for additional examples and procedures in the construction of formal theory.

# Part II
# Theory to Method: Sampling and Measurement Problems

# 4

# *Problems of Sampling: The Merger of Theory and Method*

In my judgment the inherent deficiency of public opinion polling, certainly as currently done, is contained in its sampling procedure. Its current sampling procedure forces a treatment of society as if society were only an aggregation of disparate individuals.

*Herbert Blumer, 1948, p. 546.*

Two fundamental problems confront the sociologist as he moves from theory to observations. First, observations with direct relevance for theory must be collected. If they are not, theoretical revisions, modifications, and verifications are restricted, and subsequent research activities become after-the-fact attempts to establish what should have been initially present—theoretically relevant observations. Second, the researcher must have confidence in his observations so that generalizations to other groups and situations not explicitly examined can be made. These two problems restate the issue of discovery and verification in the scientific enterprise. Their resolution is partially solved through the use of theoretically directed sampling models.

It must be stressed again that every activity of the sociologist—including the movement from theory to relevant empirical data—represents a form of symbolic interaction. The use of sampling models implies that the sociologist will be conceiving and acting on the empirical world in terms of certain specific rules.

## What May Be Observed?

I assume that the sociologist may observe one, or any combination, of the following elements: concepts or propositions from a theory; social situations; time and its passage; persons aggregately distributed through time and space; and interactive collectivities of persons distributed through time and space as seen in encounters, social relationships, small groups, organizations, communities, and entire societies.

By making concepts and propositions special observational units, I reverse the conventional view that empirical events are studied to test features of a theory. I do this because too often empirical events bear little relationship to the content of a theory. By specifically focusing on features of theory, concrete empirical leads are given for subsequent observations. Thus I am proposing as one observational strategy the arraying of concepts and propositions from a theory and then the location of empirical events that directly reflect on those theoretical properties.

Social situations may be taken as sampling units; in the past this has been the assumption underlying the sampling of persons from communities. Yet I wish to make situations of interaction specific sampling units. Time and its passage may be taken as an observational unit in the simple sense that behavior varies by historical period, time of day, and so on.

Special emphasis must be given to the observation of persons. Too often sociologists forget that a major aim of their discipline is the analysis of persons in varying forms of social organization. An exclusive focus on aggregately distributed persons restricts such generalizations, whereas a major aim of any study should be the observation of persons in natural interactive units. Hence my emphasis on encounters, relationships, groups and organizations. I assume that each of these interactional forms represents differing degrees of social organization. The investigator must be clear as to the interactional unit under analysis and take pains to insure that the appropriate units are observed.

Problems of access to the elements being studied, or restrictions of time and personnel, impose limitations on a researcher no matter how careful his planning. For example, when testing a theory, an analyst is likely to assume that by examining a small number of hypotheses, general conclusions concerning the total theory can be made (see Zetterberg, 1955, pp. 533–40); or perhaps when studying a social organization, only a portion of organizational members can be observed (see Coleman, 1958). Observing only a portion of a total set of events is termed sampling.

### Elements of Theoretically Directed Sampling

In sampling, a theoretically relevant set of events is located and enumerated. This may go no further then specifying a series of hypotheses from a theory, or it may involve the listing of all members of an organization or community. From the total set of events used, conventionally termed a population, a sample of subunits must be drawn, and this sample must be representative in the sense that all sampled units are members of the broader population and have characteristics which do not significantly differ from that population. (It is assumed that differences between the sampled units and the total population can be estimated; this is necessary for any generalizations to that population.) A desirable sample is one that mirrors as nearly as possible the total population (Upshaw, 1968, p. 69), but it is important that the degree of variation between the two is determinable.

Sampling does not end until a completely grounded theory is constructed. A logic of ongoing inclusion (Glaser and Strauss, 1967, p. 50) that dictates progressive sampling from relevant events must be employed. If such a logic is absent, the investigator runs the risk of prematurely ending his observations. A fluid, interactive relationship must exist between theory and sampling.

Attention must be given to the selection of natural data outcroppings (Webb, 1966, p. 37) that bear directly on theory. Studies of social groups might, for example, sample athletic teams (Fiedler, 1967), street corner gangs (Whyte, 1955; Liebow, 1967), or even natural work groups (Roy, 1952). Under many circumstances the natural interactional unit parallels the theoretical unit (this would be so in the study of organizations). Frequently, however, investigators fail to achieve a satisfactory correspondence between theory and data, as has happened in experimental study of social groups (McGrath and Altman, 1966).

The logic of ongoing inclusion suggests that triangulated sampling procedures should be utilized. Rather than restricting observations to one data source, the investigator must attempt to locate as many data sources as possible, thus increasing the probability that his theory will be fully tested. All data outcroppings have restrictions, and seldom will one body of data offer all the necessary observations for a theory. Webb terms this *multiple sampling.*

We might also profitably explore the possibility of using multiple samples. Again, this is different from the usual definition of multiple samples. In addition to sampling a number of different classrooms, or groups of students or cities, one may ask if there are different types or categories of samples available for the variable under study. Is there a group of natural outcroppings among occupations, already formed social and interest groups, or people who have common experiences? Can we economically exploit for research purposes the broad spectrum of already formed groups which may be organized along some principle of direct substantive applicability to the investigation? [1966, p. 37]

Webb suggests another principle. Where possible, investigators should go beyond samples that are merely convenient. Instead of restricting observations to college classrooms, local communities, friends, or captive populations of prisoners, sociologists might move to samples that have been studied less frequently and that are probably of greater theoretical utility. This is merely an extension of the natural outcropping principle.

Last, theoretically directed sampling assumes that wherever possible observations will be made in terms of temporal and situational variations as well as by the relevant natural unit of interaction. Unless situational and temporal variations are captured, problems of data restrictions arise. The study of bars, for example, illustrates the importance of time and space as restrictive dimensions. Cavan (1966) has shown that behavior in the same bar will vary by time of day and by physical location within the bar.

### Steps and Problems in Theoretically Directed Sampling

The above assumptions can now be specified by indicating steps in the sampling process. First, a population of theoretical relevance must be located and enumerated. Several procedures are available for the enumeration process. If large interactive collectivities are sampled, as might be the case with organizations or communities, office or city directories, telephone books, recent censuses, or utility listings may be employed. (Few listings of a population are ever fully accurate, however. Some degree of bias will always be present simply because people move away, die, or do not avail themselves of the services recorded by the listing agency.)

Enumeration of smaller interactive units is much easier. If the unit is a social relationship, then typically any member of the relationship can specify the other members. This is also the case with social groups. What are termed snowball and sociometric sampling procedures offer precise techniques for these enumerations.

The study of face to face encounters presents special problems. By definition, an encounter is a gathering of two or more persons who maintain visual and cognitive coorientation during the period of interaction (Goffman, 1961, p. 7–8). Yet the encounter lasts only as long as persons are in one another's physical presence. Consequently, encounters can seldom be enumerated before their occurrence, although they can be easily established after the fact, as the experimental study of small groups demonstrates.

Two procedures can be employed to overcome this limitation. First, persons can be asked who they routinely interact with over a specified period of time. This may provide no more than a list of statuses and roles such as bartenders, clerks, secretaries, or graduate students. By temporally and spatially specifying the unit of interaction, the investigator can enumerate situations for observation (e.g., classrooms, bars, offices) and then sample from those situations. This becomes the second procedure—enumeration of situations or interaction wherein encounters routinely occur.

After the population is selected and enumerated, the problem of selecting a sound inferential and theoretical sample must be solved. By inferentially sound I mean that observations must permit generalizations to the population; by theoretically sound I mean that a sample must permit empirical reflections for the theory. A sound inferential sample should mirror as perfectly as possible the population. This raises the question of sample size. How does an investigator know when a sample adequately mirrors a population? Lazerwitz (1968, pp. 285–87) has suggested that an adequate rule of thumb is to select a sample that does not vary on relevant dimensions by more then 5 per cent from the population. For example, if a population has 300 white collar and 200 blue collar workers, a representative sample would have a proportion of white and blue collar workers that varied by no more than 5 per cent from that in the percentage for the total of such workers (If a sample of 100 workers were drawn, a perfect mirror of the total population, with respect to occupation, would yield 60 white collar and 40 blue collar workers.)

To maximize the possibilities of drawing a representative sample, randomization is employed. The basic assumption of randomization is that every element, or some combination of elements, in the population has a specified chance of being included in the sample. Additionally it is assumed that by drawing a random sample any differences between the sample and the population will be randomly, or normally distributed. The population elements are consecutively assigned a number from 1 to N (where N represents the total number of elements in the population). Then the sample size is determined and by using a table of random numbers "$n$ different random numbers that fall between 1 and N are selected" (Lazerwitz, 1968, p. 280). Those elements in the population that have been assigned those random numbers constitute the final sample. (Randomization assumes that the population can be clearly defined and enumerated.)

But these procedures do not automatically insure an adequate theoretical sample. While a sample may be representative of a broader population, the techniques of drawing the sample may not permit data of theoretical relevance to be gathered. In essence this is Blumer's (1948) criticism of public opinion theory. He suggests that although sound inferential samples have been drawn by students of public opinion, the sampling procedures have failed to capture the essence of the opinion process. Blumer's point, later elaborated by Coleman (1958), suggests that samples of aggregately distributed persons do not reflect processes of organization and interaction. Public opinion arises out of such interaction, yet sampling procedures do not reflect it. This of course raises the problem of sampling from interactive units; this will be discussed later, but at this point I wish to note that to draw a sample of theoretical relevance a firm grasp of the theory under investigation is necessary. If a theory contains propositions concerning leadership patterns at the community level, for example, then the sampling procedure must yield data on such patterns; samples of persons aggregately distributed within a community seldom provide such data.

The following steps appear necessary. First, the investigator must array all of the situations that could potentially be relevant to his theory. Second, those situations must be enumerated, and their representativeness in the total population of events must be determined. A modification of Glaser and Strauss' (1964; 1968) study of dying illustrates these steps. Their theory rested on the proposition that reactions to death as a status passage varied by the awareness context, or who knew what about the event at any given point in time. The concept of awareness context points to the fact that in any given encounter persons will have different degrees of knowledge about the events at hand. To test this notion, reactions to dying were examined by position in the awareness context, type of death, and location in the hospital social structure. The sampling procedure was theoretically directed to the extent that only those events deemed relevant to the awareness context concept were examined.

A combination of the principles thus far given would add the following procedures to Glaser and Strauss' investigation. First, as earlier indicated, the total population of relevant empirical events would have been defined and enumerated. This would have involved specifying the number of deaths that occurred by ward location, time of day, personnel present, and the knowledge each participant possessed about the event. The enumeration would have permitted the determination of how representative each type of death and awareness context was. Given this information, the theory would have been critically examined for empirical sampling leads. This would have revealed that some propositions and empirical situations had to be examined, others could be ignored. The critical propositions would then be linked to their empirical representations and sampling would have proceeded on a proportionate basis. Those propositions demanding greatest test would have been linked to the greatest number of empirical situations, and so on. As critical propositions were verified or modified, additional situations that maximized comparisons would have been sought. Empirical examination of any given situation would continue until no additional data were forthcoming. Saturation of natural empirical outcroppings would thus go hand in hand with the process of propositional verification. Sampling and observation would cease when the theory was fully grounded (Glaser and Strauss, 1967, p. 45).

These revisions of Glaser and Strauss' research maintain their theoretical rigor, but add the use of inferential sampling rules as a measure of a theory's ability to be generalized. Additionally, the use of enumeration, randomization, and proportionate sampling would have increased the ability of future investigators to build upon the study. Unless precise information is given on the empirical distribution of theoretically sampled units, replication is hampered. This is also the case for generalization, because a researcher must have confidence in the fact that the events observed are characteristic of the population being generalized to.

## Interactive and Noninteractive Models of Sampling

Two basic types and models of sampling may be distinguished: noninteractive and interactive. Noninteractive models fail to establish directly patterns of relationship between natural social units. In the past these have been termed variations on the simple random sample. Interactive sampling models recognize the fact of interrelationship between natural units and attempt to reflect those patterns accurately and directly. These have been termed relational or contextual sampling models (Coleman, 1958; Lazarsfeld and Menzel, 1962, pp. 422–40).

### Noninteractive Sampling Models

Noninteractive models typically sample on the basis of position in the social structure, as in samples drawn on the basis of social class position, age, sex, occupational or educational status, or position in the life cycle or some combination of these variables. By treating persons in terms of these structural dimensions, patterns of interaction are overlooked; while these samples are inferentially sound, their relevance for social theory is obviously restricted.

The generic noninteractive sampling model is the simple random sample. Lazerwitz describes its assumptions and limitations as follows:

It requires a clear definition of a population to be sampled, a complete listing of all its elements, and the assumption that all such elements are statistically independent of one another. For social scientists, the requirement of statistical independence means that the elements can engage in only a very small amount of interaction. The variables being measured must relate to each other very much like the successive outcomes obtained by flipping a coin.

The two basic assumptions of complete listing and little or no interaction seriously restrict the opportunities for the use of simple random sampling. Much of the time, complete listing is prohibitively expensive, and the groups under investigation have large amounts of interaction among all or some of their component parts [1968, p. 279].

The technique of randomization furnishes a simple random sample. While the restrictions of complete enumeration and independence between population elements are well recognized, the simple random sample persists as one of the most popular models among sociologists. Its deficiencies are partially overcome by the use of stratified sampling models that move from aggregately distributed population elements to strata and clusters of such elements.

The basic model for a stratified sample requires the division of a population into separate, more or less homogeneous units, strata, or clusters (Lazerwitz, 1968, p. 288). Clear criteria for forming strata must be developed and the population is divided into the appropriate strata. These commonly represent such social structural dimensions as occupational or educational status, position in the life cycle, or religious preference. Typically, no interaction is assumed between elements of the population. In order to successfully stratify, however, prior knowledge about the population is necessary, as is some theoretical rigor concerning stratification criteria. These last two features of the stratified model mark its improvement over the simple random sample—though once the population is stratified, some form of random sampling is utilized to select the sample from each stratum.

In general, researchers may employ one of two stratified techniques. The first calls for proportionate random sampling within each stratum. Elements from each stratum are randomly sampled at a rate proportionate to their distribution in the population. Thus, if a community of 1,000 members is divided into five social class strata and it is found that each class represents one-fifth of the total community, then a proportionate random sample would include one-fifth from each class. If a 10 per cent community sample was drawn, there would be 20 members from each of the five social classes.

Under certain conditions the researcher will randomly sample at a disproportionate rate from each stratum. This would be the case if the sample varied between strata (Kish, 1953, p. 191–92) such that one strata represented individuals and another clusters of individuals in work groups. Geographical distribution of the strata might demand that some be more heavily sampled than others for reasons of convenience, economy, or time. If a theory points to certain strata as critical test cases, it would be reasonable to oversample those strata, even if they were unevenly distributed in the population. In this case, theory takes precedence over procedure, but the rules for a sound sample are still employed.

A technique that often utilizes the principles of stratification is cluster sampling. This is the name given "to methods of selection in which the sampling unit, or unit of selection, contains more than one population element; the sampling unit is a cluster of elements [Kish, 1953, p. 203]." Such units might include city blocks, counties, entire cities, classrooms, or work groups. Here the sampling procedure varies from the simple random and stratified techniques, because now the population elements are not listed one at a time (Lazerwitz, 1968, p. 298), but are clustered together, often into natural units, as the examples above suggest. Once the clusters are listed, a random sample of clusters is drawn on either a proportionate, or disproportionate basis.

After the initial clusters are sampled (Lazerwitz, 1968, p. 298), it is possible to divide them into secondary sampling units. Within each cluster or primary sampling unit, a sample can be selected. "Such a process of continuous sampling is called *multistage cluster sampling* [Lazerwitz, 1968, p. 298]." Lazerwitz offers the following example of this procedure:

1. Divide the United States into counties and select a sample of counties. This is the first sampling stage, and the counties are the primary sampling units.
2. Within each p.s.u. (sampled counties), let three strata be formed. Stratum 1 consists of all large cities, stratum 2 consists of all small cities and villages, and stratum 3 contains the remainder of the county divided into clusters through use of the U. S. Bureau of the Census enumeration districts. Within each of the three strata, select samples of the large cities, small cities and villages and enumeration districts. This obtains the secondary selection units.
3. Divide each secondary unit into blocks or other small geographic areas. Then select a sample of them to obtain the third stage of sampling.
4. Within each of the third-stage clusters, select a sample of housing units for the fourth stage of sampling.
5. Finally, within each sampled housing unit select one adult to be interviewed. This is the fifth and final sampling stage [1968, p. 298].

It is possible to stratify within each cluster, for any phase of the sampling process. When this is done, "the sample design is called a *multistage, stratified cluster sample* [Lazerwitz, 1968, p. 299]."

As a technique, cluster sampling has the advantage of overcoming the problem of population enumeration. If a researcher wanted a probability sample of adults in the United States, it would be impossible to construct a listing of all adults in order to employ a simple random or stratified random sample design (Lazerwitz, 1968, p. 299), but the cluster method would permit the use of county listings as a means of enumeration, and thus a multistage sampling procedure that ultimately selected on a random basis could be developed.

This technical advantage overlooks the fact that the final sampling units are not clusters of interacting persons, however; the unit remains aggregately distributed persons within clusters. The cluster method does not lead to the direct sampling of natural interacting social units.

*Interactive Sampling Models*

Five types of interactive sampling units may be distinguished, each corresponding to a level or form of interaction between natural social units. At the first level are social relationships, or dyadic structures. These are commonly represented by marriages, engaged couples, friends, work partners, colleagues, or acquaintances. A relationship shall be said to exist between two or more persons when those persons engage in recurrent forms of symbolic interaction. For a relationship to exist, the parties involved must share the same, or a similar set of reciprocal definitions about the other. These definitions extend through time such that the influence of the other does not disappear when out of his co-presence. Relationships may be purely symbolic as seen in the conversations a wife might have with a deceased husband, or they may be both symbolic and co-present, as seen in marriage.

The second type of interactive sampling unit involves the study of face to face encounters that represent situations of intereaction where definitions and symbols do not extend beyond the point of co-presence. Encounters are represented by all situations of interaction in which the participants maintain

a single visual and cognitive focus of attention; a mutual and preferential openness to verbal communication; a heightened mutual relevance of acts; an eye-to-eye ecological huddle that maximizes each participant's opportunity to perceive the other participant's monitoring him [Goffman, 1961, p. 18].

Examples of encounters include jury deliberations, a game of cards, couples dancing, or subjects brought together in a small groups laboratory for the purpose of solving a common problem. Encounters are clearly different from relationships, because their influence on the interactant may last only during the period of interaction or co-presence. Encounters may be unfocused and simply arise because persons are in one another's physical presence. People crowded into elevators or two people acknowledging each other's presence in a bar are examples. In such situations little coorientation of action is present and little, if any, joint action occurs. Some encounters are focused and represent interactions where a joint action is formed, where a common task is pursued, and where the mutual openness of interactants is obligatory. Purchasing a product in a store, paying a fine, answering a phone, or opening a door for another are instances of the focused encounter. In the focused encounter it is often possible to observe simultaneous interactions. While one task may be agreed upon, many side or subordinate activities will also be sanctioned. Interactions at cocktail parties, eating a dinner, or driving an automobile while smoking and conversing with a passenger represent the multifocused encounter (see Goffman, 1961; 1963).

Analytically, encounters have no prior or after life. Their existence lasts only as long as persons are in each other's symbolic and physical presence. But there are many encounters whose significance extends beyond the point of co-presence, and these are termed encounters of significance. It is out of such engagements that the stuff of interactional life is made. Job interviews, marriages, witnessing a birth, or taking an examination represent this class of encounter.

The next interactive form is the social group. Here the study of relationships and encounters merges, for groups are characterized by recurrent interactions among two or more persons where a symbolic after effect can be located. Groups, like relationships, take on a life of their own and begin to exist beyond the lifetime of any given member. Groups may be analyzed by their focal activity, their places of interaction, and the nature of involvement among participants. Some are shortlived, lasting only for a few months, as in certain work groups, while others last a lifetime, as in marriages and families.

Above groups stand social organizations or bureaucracies, which represent situations of interaction among large numbers of like-situated persons who are engaging in legitimated, cooriented action. Organizations have specified territorial locales, often legally defined, and within this territory relationships, encounters, and groups may be observed. Indeed, the life of organizations rests on the existence of relationships and groups.

Last, it is possible to distinguish communities and entire societies as units of analysis. Conceptually they share a great deal in common with organizations (e.g., territorial legitimation, setting for other interactional forms). The empirical examination of communities, societies, or even organizations cannot escape the fact that in the final analysis observational units become persons in interaction. Sampling models must be capable of reflecting this fact.

These five levels of interaction become units for interactive sampling activity. Before any interactive sampling model can be implemented, the following rules must be recognized. First, a clear theoretical definition of the unit must be given, and the unit must be a natural interactive form, or empirical outcropping. Second, this outcropping must conform as perfectly as possible with the concept as it is theoretically defined. Third, a triangulated-comparative sampling perspective must be adopted. Sampling should not be restricted to one class of empirical outcroppings; the researcher must attempt to locate as many comparison groups as possible. If studying encounters, sampling could easily include unfocused, focused, multifocused, and encounters of significance. Use of a triangulated perspective insures that sampling will proceed on the basis of temporal and situational variations. Thus, unfocused encounters in elevators, bars, sidewalks, and office corridors could be sampled. This would involve within-class triangulation —to be distinguished from between-class triangulation, which would dictate comparing types of encounters.

Fourth, a continual interaction with theory must be involved. It may be found that certain data outcroppings are inappropriate for comparison, or some may be inaccessible or even empirically unidentifiable. In such cases the sampling model must be flexible enough to permit new selections and samples. Last, the rules for an inferentially sound sample must be included in the interactive model. None of these rules, however, should be permitted to stand in the way of a sound theoretical sample (see Glaser and Strauss, 1967, p. 51).

When theory takes precedence in the sampling process, certain inferential rules have to be relaxed; for instance, the rule that statistical independence exists between sampling units. Indeed, Lazerwitz (1968, p. 279) recognized this fact in his analysis of the simple random sample. Cluster sampling relaxes this rule, because while clusters may be randomly selected, secondary sampling units within the cluster may not be independent of one another. For example, persons seldom distribute themselves randomly through a city block. The assumption of complete enumeration is often inappropriate for interactive sampling. As I indicated earlier, it is difficult to develop a complete listing of all encounters within an organization.

For these reasons, interactive sampling models combine probability or random sampling principles with nonprobability or purposive assumptions. This combination often occurs in the study of social relationships. The researcher may begin with a random sample of persons within a community and then have each person designate a number of significant others who are friends, relatives, or acquaintances (see Katz and Lazarsfeld, 1955). The designation of significant others is certainly nonrandom, and any observations of those significant others depart from the rules of independence and randomness, although it might be possible to select a pool of significant others randomly. Unfortunately, the location of such persons seldom permits random selection.

*Sampling Social Relationships*   At least a two-step process is involved in the sampling of social relationships. A theoretically relevant population is first selected, defined, and enumerated, and then a random sample of persons is drawn and these persons are asked to list the names, addresses of, and their relationship to, a specified number of significant others. In this sense a "significant other" is defined as any person of importance to the person (see Kuhn, 1964, pp. 5–24). Significant others may be of two types: those important to the person in his occupancy of specific roles and statuses and those of general importance to him as a person. The first type are termed role-specific significant others; the second, orientational others (see Denzin, 1966, pp. 298–310). One empirical procedure for operationalizing samples of significant others has been to ask the following question: "Would you please give me a list of those persons or groups of people whose evaluation of you as a *person* concern you the *most* [Denzin, 1966, p. 300]?" This question elicits the names of orientational others and with slight modification can be used to obtain role-specific others. The substitution of the relevant role for the word *person,* and the location of that other in a concrete situation furnishes this category of other. By asking the respondent to give the addresses of those persons, a ready made population of significant others for each respondent is given. The sampling and interviewing of those others moves the investigation to the level of the social relationship. Sampling of significant others can include a complete saturation of those listed—in which case everyone listed is interviewed and a population, not a sample, is observed. Occasionally it is more feasible to have the respondent rank-order his significant others from most to least important, and then the most important other is observed. The choice of saturation versus sampling should be determined by theory, although demands of time, access, and personnel are likely to dictate the sampling procedure.

This has been termed the snowball technique (Coleman, 1958, p. 29) and is a variation on the general sociometric method of having persons list the persons they feel closest to within a specified social structure. I prefer to term it the "significant other" method, because this more accurately reflects the rationale for examining social relationships.

*Sampling Encounters* Because encounters represent situated units of social organization, their sampling may be situational in nature. The study of encounters within organizations could certainly proceed on this basis. Through empirical examination the potential situations for interaction could be located and enumerated, then a sample of those situations could be drawn at a rate proportionate to the probability that an encounter would occur within them. Often little field work is necessary to isolate the relevant situations of interaction for any set of persons; our society is so organized that such situations are conveniently labeled for sampling purposes, (offices, lounges, libraries, waiting rooms, bars, corridors, and beaches are examples). Observations by time of day, week, and month will quickly reveal prime periods of interaction, and sampling can then follow on a temporal basis.

This strategy suffers from the "wait and see" problem. An investigator may station himself in a situation where few encounters occur. A strategy that combines the situational method with the significant other method is the encounter question. Here respondents within a specified social structure are asked to list the situations they most frequently interact in, and to give the times of those interactions, the task involved, and the persons met. Such a question might read as follows:

In the following space please list the situations you are most likely to enter and interact in on an average work day. Please locate those situations within your organization by an office number and indicate the time of day and length of time you are likely to be in this situation. Last, please list the persons or groups you are most likely to meet or see in this situation.

Answers to this question can be structured on the following format:

### Encounter Test

| Situation (Rm./Office number) | Time Enter | Time Leave | What Is Done | Persons Seen | Their Relationship to You |
|---|---|---|---|---|---|
| 1. | | | | | |
| 2. | | | | | |
| 3., etc. | | | | | |

The number of lines can vary with the demands of the theory. The question is given to members of certain floors within an organization, members of social, or work groups, and so on. Answers furnish a near complete enumeration of potential encounters for any given day or longer period of time. Because respondents list the task involved in each situation and their relationship to persons met, this method has the additional advantage of isolating forms of the encounter for comparative purposes.

Because encounters are acting units of social organization, their sampling must include analysis of those involved. In this sense the sampling of encounters permits direct movement between persons and a form of social organization. This is also the case for samples of relationships, groups, organizations, and communities. In one sense I have adopted the principles of cluster sampling for the study of natural interactional forms—yet I am proposing simultaneous sampling of persons and their relationships to these interactional forms. Hence, a study could be designed that sampled encounters and saturated participants, or the opposite could be done, depending on theoretical necessity. In either case, inferential rules are relaxed to fit a theoretical model.

*Sampling Social Groups*  Because groups exist on both symbolic and interactional levels, techniques for sampling relationships and encounters easily fit their analysis. That is, members of any social structure can be asked to list and locate persons who share membership with them in a social group. The situations of interaction for the group can be elicited with the encounter question. By combining the results of both questions, membership in the group is immediately identified. Sampling could proceed from member to member, or situation to situation. Ideally, both dimensions would be included so that the interactional structure could be examined. Variations on the significant other or sociometric question will permit isolation of attraction, communication, and power patterns in the group.

*Sampling Organizations and Communities*  In the past, organizations and communities have either been sampled randomly, in which case patterns of interaction were ignored, or dense or saturation samples were employed to obtain a more complete picture of the setting under analysis (Coleman, 1958). Saturation sampling (drawing complete samples) is certainly satisfactory, as are dense samples, which may include half the membership of any collectivity. Yet a model of sampling is needed that firmly relates to levels of interaction. The models for sampling relationships, groups, and encounters are designed to meet this.

Three techniques may be employed to locate membership in the interactional forms: the reputational, subjective, and objective methods. The reputational method selects a small sample of leaders within any social structure and asks them to list the names of important or influential persons. These leaders may also be asked to place persons in appropriate social strata, classes, or situations. The subjective method goes to each person and asks him to locate himself in the social structure on the basis of certain criteria such as class position. The objective method proceeds on the basis of variables that are known to correlate with such dimensions as prestige, social class, or leadership. All of these methods have inherent weaknesses. The reputational approach may suffer from subject bias; the subjective approach relies totally on the respondent's judgment; and the objective approach may rest on variables that are irrelevant to members of the social structure (see Svalastoga, 1964, pp. 536–44).

I offer a proposal that is not new, but has merit: the merger of the objective, subjective, and reputational methods in the determination of a sampling frame for the study of social organizations, communities, or entire societies. Further elaboration of Glaser and Strauss' (1965, 1967, 1968) investigations of dying will illustrate how this may be done. Suppose the theory dictates analysis of as many different awareness contexts as possible within the hospital. Since dying is the focal activity under analysis, only those awareness contexts that had dying as a concern would be sampled. Similarly, only those persons who had a direct relationship with an instance of dying would be sampled. This immediately restricts sampling to those situations in the hospital where death routinely occurs. It also restricts analysis to family members and relevant persons in the hospital social structure who routinely handle or observe death. If an awareness context is defined as an encounter of significance, then one sampling unit will be death encounters. Because family members occupy a position in relation to persons dying, the social relationship becomes another unit. Since most hospital personnel routinely involved in death form social groups, or teams, the social group becomes an additional sampling unit. Last, the hospital as an organization becomes the global sampling unit. Any generalizations about reactions to death will ultimately refer to the hospital.

Thus far I have broken the sampling process into interactional forms. A satisfactory theoretical sample would incorporate all levels. By combining the reputational, objective, and subjective methods, each population and sample can be defined. Nurses, physicians, aides, and attendants can be approached concerning where death encounters routinely exist. A modification of the encounter test would provide these data. The significant other test would reveal groups and relationships within the hospital and would supplement reports by experts, as well as objective evaluations by the researcher. The objective approach would be relevant to the extent that past research suggested certain areas of personnel for study.

Once the population of death encounters was located, sampling would proceed on a sequential-comparative basis that recognized temporal variations. Sampling would be proportionate within classes of encounters, and as subjective reports by respondents yielded new situations, they would be sought out.

It is hoped that the merger of these three techniques would uncover the relevant empirical universe for the awareness-context theory. There is no reason why this procedure cannot be adopted to the study of communities, or even of total societies. The sampling and enumeration problems would certainly be greater, but the goal of sampling natural interactive units with a theoretically and inferentially sound model would be achieved.

The concept of sample size changes when interactional forms are studied. While several hundred discrete encounters, relationships, or groups may be observed within an organization, in the final analysis the sample size is one. In this sense, sample size is determined by the largest interactional form and not by the number of observations within that form. This of course raises perplexing problems as to how many organizations or communities have to be sampled before generalizations can be made? I propose that to the extent that any given organization or community represents a general class of similar events, generalizations to that broader class are justified. To insure this it is important to approximate random selection of the primary sampling unit. If random selection is impossible, or theoretically indefensible, then the researcher must clearly specify what is unique about the setting studied. If he does not, his generalizations will be difficult to defend. This argument also holds for generalizations to other units of interaction within communities or organizations. The investigator is obligated to report the representation of every interactional unit examined. Similarly, the procedures for defining and sampling those units must be given.

## The Sampling Process as Symbolic Interaction

Noninteractive models of sampling, as lines of symbolic interaction, make the following assumptions: first, the objects observed mirror those objects not observed; second, it is assumed that those objects do not interact with one another—that they are independent objects selected from an aggregate cluster of like-situated objects, third, noninteractive sampling models often lead to a sense of impersonality between the investigator and the object observed (that is, they are treated as anonymous units).

Interactive sampling models, on the other hand, demand a great deal of acquaintance on the part of the observer with those observed. Objects are assumed to interact with one another, although the principle of representation is maintained. These models flow from a particular view of the scientific process. The scientist explicitly sets out to formulate universal-interactive propositions and to do so he searches for critical or negative cases that will challenge his theory.

The choice to adopt one or another of these two models ultimately rests on the scientist's conception of the empirical world. In my judgment, interactive sampling models best fit the nature of this world because they permit a direct and open form of interaction between the observer and those objects he examines.

**Notes**

I have drawn heavily on Glaser and Strauss' (1967, pp. 45–77) analysis of theoretical sampling. My attempt to integrate their perspective with the more statistical presentation of Kish (1967) and Lazerwitz (1968, pp. 278–328) is represented in the notions of theoretically directed sampling and interactive models of sampling. I have taken the concept of theoretically directed sampling from Richard J. Hill (1969). The reader should examine the Kish and Lazerwitz sources, and certainly Glaser and Strauss must be read.

# 5

# Problems of
# Measurement
# and Instrumentation

The research techniques and measurement scales of any science can be viewed as a problem in the sociology of knowledge.

*Aaron V. Cicourel*, 1964, p. 7.

Once an adequate sampling model has been adopted, the problem of how to observe or measure the sampling units must be resolved. My intent here is to review the major techniques of measurement currently available to the sociological researcher, and to detail the assumptions underlying the measurement process. Scales and instrumentation procedures will be reviewed, but for a thorough review of scaling and measurement strategies available to the sociologist, consult Stevens (1951, pp. 1–49), Togerson (1958), Edwards (1957b), Miller (1964), Upshaw (1968, pp. 60–111), Bradley (1968), and Bonjean, Hill, and McLemore (1968). I will elaborate Cicourel's (1964, pp. 7–38) position that strategies of measurement represent symbolic acts carried on between the sociologist and the empirical world.

In several senses the measurement problem represents the most fundamental dilemma confronting the sociologist. If theories are to stand on empirical observations, then valid and reliable observations must be gathered. Thus theories of measurement must be made to fit theories of social interaction. If they do not, measurement occurs by fiat (see Togerson, 1958, pp. 21–22; Cicourel, 1964). Too frequently, sociologists develop measurement strategies that fail to yield empirical observations of high theoretical relevance, and many researchers have placed more emphasis on justifying than on discovering theoretically relevant observations. I advocate a synthesis of these two processes, and to this end measurement strategies will be evaluated by the traditional standards of reliability and validity; in addition, the principles of triangulation and theoretical relevance will be applied, for unless a research instrument permits triangulated observations of theoretical relevance, validity and reliability are of limited interest. Consequently, instruments will be evaluated by their ability to reflect and capture salient features of natural interactional units. A great proportion of current measurement instruments are well suited for the study of isolated individuals, but there are few measurement strategies for the analysis of natural forms of interaction. Thus, if a researcher wishes to analyze patterns of group interaction, say, or variations in social relationships, he finds few scales and instruments explicitly constructed for his problem (for exceptions, see Boyle, 1969, pp. 99–119; Cronbach, 1957, pp. 353–79).

## Elements of the Measurement Process

The act of measurement assumes that observations of concepts may be transformed into statements concerning the degree to which they are present in a given empirical instance. Because concepts are typically observed in degree only, and because they are seldom observed in their original theoretical form, the term *variable* is employed to describe empirical observations of concepts. "Any object or event which can vary in successive observations either in quantity or quality may be termed a *variable* [Mueller and Schuessler, 1961, p. 12]." A *quantitative variable* represents a concept that may take on various values of greater or less; these would include age, income, degree of social prestige, or size of family. Variables that differ in degree or quality and not in quantity are qualitative in nature and are commonly termed *attributes* (Mueller and Schuessler, 1961, p. 12). A person's marital status may be single, married, divorced, widowed; his nationality may be English, French, or Italian. "Such attributes cannot be scaled, or arranged in order of magnitude; that is, one sex or nationality cannot be considered greater or less than another" (Mueller and Schuessler, 1961, p. 13).

Levels of measurement may be distinguished, and corresponding to each level are statistical measures appropriate for quantitative analysis (see Siegel, 1956; Blalock, 1960; Bradley, 1968); these are commonly termed *scales*. At the simplest level is the *nominal scale* (Stevens, 1951), in which objects are placed in mutually exclusive categories and there is no necessary order among the categories (Green, 1954, p. 337). Numbers assigned to the objects in a category act only as labels; they serve no quantitative purpose. Thus a person is either male or female, black or white, Catholic or Protestant. When objects can be placed in a rank order with respect to some variable, they form an *ordinal scale* (Green, 1954, p. 337). Numbers corresponding to the rank order can then be assigned to the objects. If persons are classified on a scale measuring liberalism and conservatism, for example, five categories might be constructed describing the degree of liberalism-conservatism, with the higher numbers, say, representing greater liberalism (Upshaw, 1968, p. 62). In this case a variable is measured in quantity. The restrictions for an ordinal scale include those of the nominal scale—namely, that all observations receiving the same number must be alike in terms of the same scale quality. Additionally, the ordinal scale requires that numerical assignments reflect the order of classes on the scale (Upshaw, 1968, p. 62).

When the distance or intervals between objects on a scale can be measured, an *interval scale* exists (Green, 1954, p. 337). An interval scale is like an ordinal scale except that

its numerical assignments reflect not only the order of the observations, but in addition, the magnitude of the differences in the scale property between pairs of observations [Upshaw, 1968, p. 62].

With interval measurement the degree of difference between categories can be described so that a difference between pairs of numbers on the scale reflects the amount of difference between the empirical events measured (Upshaw, 1968, p. 63). In this case, the difference between scores 1 and 2 and 4 and 5 on a liberalism-conservatism scale could be interpreted.

A *ratio scale* exists "when there is some way of showing how many *times* greater one object is than another [Green, 1954, p. 337]." Numbers are assigned to categories in the same ratio as the ratios between objects in the empirical world. A ratio scale implies "a fixed zero point, so that the only admissible transformation is multiplication by a constant ($y = \text{A}x$) [Green, 1954, p. 337]." Weight forms a ratio scale because "we can show that four pounds is four times as heavy as one pound, and similarly for all pairs of weights [Green, 1954, p. 337]."

Nominal, ordinal, interval and ratio scales represent the most common types employed by the sociologist. While others could be discussed (see, for example, Coombs, 1952), they typically represent transformations of these four. Whatever its form, developing a scale involves considering the following: an empirical event that is classified; a number; and a rule or set of rules that links that event to the number (Upshaw, 1968, p. 61). Nominal, ordinal, interval, and ratio scales display these features and the rules specifying how numbers will be applied to empirical events distinguishes each of them.

*What May Be Measured?*

Scales may be constructed to measure attributes or characteristics of any sampling unit. These variables typically take the form of either attitudes or behavior patterns. Consequently, instruments may be applied to the attitudes or behaviors of individuals in various forms of interaction. Additionally, elements of time or social situations may be taken as empirical events to be measured. If this is the case, there will commonly be an intersection of measured and sampled units such that what people think or do in various situations will be studied. It can now be seen that there is a direct relationship between sampling decisions and measurement strategies. Unless the sampling model designates appropriate empirical units for observations, measuring instruments will fail to provide the data needed for a theory.

As a researcher moves from theory to observations, a variety of interrelated acts must be organized. Some sense of the concepts and hypotheses to be tested must be present, and specific aspects of those theoretical elements must then be designated so that concepts can be translated into variables. Then a series of empirical indicators, measuring instruments, or scales must be developed. These instruments must meet certain rules, and after they are applied to the empirical world, everything must be put back together; that is, the investigator must be able to piece his observations and measurements into a coherent framework that permits theoretical analysis (Lazarsfeld, 1958; Lazarsfeld and Barton, 1955).

## Standards of Evaluation for the Measurement Process

Every act in the measurement process may be assessed by the following criteria. First, do the designated and collected observations permit theoretical analysis? If they do not, resolutions of all other criteria are of limited use. Second, because no single measurement class is likely to yield all the relevant data for a theory, a combined or triangulated measurement perspective must be adopted (see Webb, *et al.*, 1966) if sociological research is to become better suited for the analysis of social events; research instruments must be constructed with an eye to their combination with other techniques. This can involve within-class triangulation so that multiple scales or indices are employed to measure the same empirical event, or it may involve between-class triangulation, in which case several different methods and measurement strategies are combined in the same empirical analysis (see Campbell and Fiske, 1959, p. 81–105). Because within-class triangulation represents variations on the same measurement technique, the between-class method is recommended. Ideally, both would be combined. Thus a study of alienation could be designed that combined several of the existing alienation scales with other research techniques. Seeman (1967, pp. 105–23) has reported a study that triangulated alienation scales in the replication of his earlier studies of alienation in hospitals, reformatories, and work settings. By adding such methods as unobtrusive analysis, life histories, and participant observation, Seeman's study would have achieved a more complete form of methodological triangulation.

Third, techniques of measurement must be assessed in terms of their ability to be employed in natural settings. If theories and sampling models dictate the study of natural interactional forms, then sociologists must have scales and instruments that can be employed in such settings. This need often imposes severe restrictions, for many populations cannot be brought into a classroom and given a three hour paper and pencil test. Nor will complicated interaction rating forms be usable in all field settings. Thus, while a scale may meet the rigorous rules of measurement theory, a researcher will find that it is inappropriate for natural field analysis. This lends even greater support to the triangulation argument: If one measurement class is weakened because of field contingencies, perhaps another can be found to remedy the flaws of the major instruments—the researcher may have to forsake rigorous techniques for less precise but more appropriate methods.

This rule raises the related point made by Cicourel (1964; 1968) that many sociological research instruments imply—indeed demand—an explicit correspondence between the sociologist's frame of reference and those he studies. Unfortunately, the culture and language of the sociological researcher may not correspond to those studied, or it may correspond only on a superficial level. Becker and Geer elaborate this point:

Any social group, to the extent that it is a distinctive unit, will have to some degree a culture differing from that of other groups, a somewhat different set of common understandings around which action is organized, and these differences will find expression in a language whose nuances are peculiar to that group and fully understood only by its members. . . . In interviewing members of groups other than our own, then, we are in somewhat the same position as an anthropologist who must learn a primitive language, with the important difference that, as Icheiser, has put it, we often do not understand that we do not understand and are thus likely to make errors in interpreting what is said to us. . . . In speaking American English with an interviewee who is, after all, much like us, we may mistakenly assume that we have understood him and the error be small enough that it will not disrupt communication to the point where a correction will be in order [1956, p. 29].

There may be a cultural restriction inherent in a research instrument, and even though respondents may sit quietly for hours during an interview this restriction will be hidden from the sociologist. If multiple methods are employed such a possibility is less likely. Instruments, then, must be phrased in the language of those studied, otherwise we run the risk of committing the fallacy of objectivism.

To be reliable, a measuring instrument must yield stable responses under conditions of repeated observation. "The reliability of a scale is an index of the extent to which repeated measurements yield similiar results [Green, 1954, p. 338]." Perfect reliability for any instrument would be represented by respondents giving the same answers at two different times. Few instruments attain perfect reliability, since the instrument may change from time one to time two—that is, the order or pattern of questions may be changed by the investigator—the investigator may introduce changes in his application of the instrument (his interpretations of a scale may change, as may his presentation of self); the subject may change from time one to time two (maturation and historical or situational factors may lead him to view the instruments differently, or his attitudes may change); or the measuring instrument may create changes in the subject. What Webb, *et al.* (1966, pp. 13–16), term the "guinea pig" or "reactive effect" of testing points to the fact that many scales and instruments create the very attitudes and changes the investigator is attempting to measure. In a study of the careers of mental patients (Spitzer and Denzin, in process) focused on the changes in attitudes undergone during the various phases of movement in and out of hospitals, one aspect of the measuring instrument examined the patient's attitudes toward mental illness and psychiatric treatment. Another section asked the patient to give answers to the "Who Am I?" test. Pilot applications of the instrument revealed that patients would vary in their self-descriptions depending on whether they received the questions on psychiatric treatment before or after the "Who am I?" test.

A further cause of imperfect reliability is that interaction between researcher and subject may create changes between measurements. If the application of any measuring instrument is viewed interactionally, it is possible to locate variations within the interaction process, within the observer, within the subject, and in the situations of observation; this suggests that the interpretations given measuring instruments will vary also. Since the human observer is imperfect, and sensitive to the demands of others, it may be expected that changes will arise from the interaction process; the instrument may be reliable, the person applying it is unreliable. Yet instruments have to be applied in interactional encounters and thus reliability is as much a property of those interactions as it is of instruments; reliability cannot be separated from interaction.

"The reliability of an instrument is commonly assessed by correlating the instrument with itself [Upshaw, 1968, p. 65]." There are three basic approaches to the determination of reliability. The first is the test-retest method. "This means that the scale is applied twice to the same population and the results compared [Goode and Hatt, 1952, p. 235]." A high correlation between the two measurements must be established before reliability can be assumed. This method suffers from the problems of testing effects. That is, the first application of the instrument may influence responses on the second measurement.

A second technique is to construct multiple forms of the same instrument. "The alternate forms are administered successively to the same sample [Goode and Hatt, 1952, pp. 235–236]." This method also presents the problems of testing effects, and again high reliability is judged by a high correlation between the two applications.

A third method removes the problem of testing effects. This is the split-half technique and is a modification of the multiple-forms method. Now the scale, or instrument, is randomly divided into halves. Each of the halves is treated as a separate scale. "The two subscales are then correlated and this is taken as a measure of reliability" (Goode and Hatt, 1952, p. 236; see also Cronbach, 1960, pp. 126–142; Anastasi, 1961, pp. 105–134).

The question of validity of an instrument asks to what extent the event being measured corresponds to what is intended to be measured. That is, if the investigator is testing hypotheses about the alienation process, he must ask whether his instruments measure alienation as he has defined it theoretically. One technique for establishing validity is to link the empirical measurement of a concept directly with its theoretical definition. This method asks to what extent the measurement process complements and draws upon the theoretical perspective under analysis. In developing the "Who Am I?" test, Kuhn and McPartland employed this method of validation:

We do not have space here to discuss the theoretical clarification which results from the conscious conceptualization of the self as a set of attitudes except to point out that this conceptualization is most consistent with Mead's view of the self as an object which is in most respects like all other objects, and with his further view that an object is a plan of action (an attitude) [1954, p. 68].

The test is justified because it derives directly from Mead's theory of the self and interaction.

A second way of conceptualizing validity is to focus on the predictive ability of an instrument. Thus, if a scale measuring alienation exists and if that scale has been shown to predict patterns of alienation, the investigator constructing a new scale would correlate his findings with the earlier scale. If the two highly correlate, he can assume predictive validity for his new scale.

A variation on predictive validity is to select as a criterion variable known groups that display the behavior being investigated. If a new scale for measuring alienation is developed, the researcher locates a group of people who by consensus are defined as alienated and gives the instrument to them. If they fail to score high on the instrument, its validity is in doubt. The use of known groups, or judges, as a validity test is another way of saying that instruments should predict concrete patterns of behavior. Instruments may be reliable and valid on one level, but they may fail to predict concrete behavior patterns. The classic demonstration is La Piere's (1934, pp. 230–37) study of the attitudes of managers of hotels, restaurants, and auto camps toward the serving of racial minorities. When La Piere accompanied a Chinese couple on their travels, only one of 251 establishments refused to serve them. When he sent the same establishments a questionnaire, more than 90 per cent replied they would deny service. The implications are clear and have been elaborated by Deutscher (1969, pp. 35–41) and La Piere (1969, pp. 41–42): Investigators must look beyond technical tests of validity to the problem of whether or not their instruments predict what is of theoretical interest. Instruments that elicit only predispositions to act, and fail to follow the unfolding trajectory of action through time, run the risk of leaving analysis at a superficial level. Deutscher makes the following point by drawing on Herbert Blumer's conception of the social act:

Herbert Blumer has argued repeatedly that prediction of a latter phase of a social act is not possible on the basis of knowledge of an earlier phase. As Blumer points out, the act is a process of constant development: it is being constructed. The earlier dimension tapped (for example, attitudes toward Dingbats) does not determine any latter dimension that may be tapped (for example, overt action toward a Dingbat). The determination is made during the course of the intervening period and may be heavily influenced by factors in the immediate situation in which the act or attitude is called forth [1969, p. 36].

These comments are not intended to disparage efforts to establish the validity of any research instrument, but relate to the earlier argument for the triangulation of research methods. The validity of any instrument must be established—but multiple approaches combining behavioral and attitudinal dimensions should be employed. Attempts to establish validity should not end with a single test or demonstration; instruments must be validated at both the theoretical and behavioral level.

If it can be shown that an instrument correlates highly with similar measures of the same event, and if that instrument discriminates between conceptually distinct events, then a satisfactory demonstration of validity has been made—what Campbell and Fiske (1959, pp. 81–105) term convergent and discriminant validation has been achieved.

The problems of reliability and validity return the investigator to the interactional nature of his research. Theory dictates a sampling model, which in turn demands certain empirical observations. Those observations must be reliable and valid and they must flow from the theory. At every point in the cycle the world is seen through the eyes of the scientist, for his definitions dictate his activities. A test's reliability rests on the interactions directed toward it. Validity, as I have conceptualized it, arises out of the interactions between a researcher's definition of a theory and his attempts to translate that theory into concrete empirical activity.

In many ways the measurement act represents the cardinal feature of all sociological activity—indeed, of all human activity. Like everyone else, the sociologist inhabits a world of socially defined objects. Actions directed towards those objects are dictated by the definitions attached to them. The meaning of an object, be it an instance of alienation or the confrontation of another person, arises out of the concrete activity directed toward it. Consequently, a flavor of the "self-fulfilling prophecy" is part of all sociological activity. Measuring instruments, empirical events, theories, sampling units, and even research methods represent what they are defined as representing; action toward them tends to confirm those meanings. As a result, the ultimate validation of any sociological activity becomes a symbolic validation based on the degree of consensus attached to the objects and events under consideration. Rules for establishing a sound sample, a reliable test, or a valid scale are only symbolic—they have no meaning other than that given by the community of scientists.

Unless scientific activity fits the empirical world and permits the development of theories, it fails. For this reason rules of sociological research cannot be separated from theories and data. The ultimate test is empirical and all rules must be adjusted to fit the empirical world. It is because of this that I advocate occasional relaxation of the formal rules of the sociological method to meet what I regard as the demands of the empirical world as viewed interactionally.

### Types of Scales

Scales may be distinguished by their level of measurement. Many common scales corresponding to interval measurement are based on some variation of the Thurstone method (see Green, 1954, pp. 344–51; Upshaw, 1968, pp. 80–94), which is primarily a judgmental technique requiring the use of items representing a certain degree of favorableness toward a set of social objects. Examples of such items would include the following (Droba, 1930; also cited by Green, 1954, p. 344):

All nations should disarm immediately. Wars are justifiable only when waged in defense of weaker nations. The benefits of war outweigh its attendant evils.

There are several techniques for determining the scale value of an item. If only a few are scaled, the method of paired-comparison is appropriate (Green, 1954, p. 345; Thurstone, 1927; also Hill, 1953, pp. 564–66). Each of several judges—Green (1954, p. 345) suggests 25 or more—is presented with every possible pair of items and is asked which of the pair is more favorable to the issue in question. For each pair of items, the proportion of times one statement is judged more favorable than the other is determined (Green, 1954, p. 345). Hill describes the method as follows:

The method of paired comparision is used to obtain a set of relative scale values for a given set of objects. The set of objects, arranged in all possible pairs, is presented to a panel of judges. Each member of the panel records his preference for one member of each of the possible pairs [1953, pp. 564–65].

Assuming that an adequate sample of items appropriate to the needed analysis can be constructed, the paired-comparison method provides one technique of scaling. When a large number of items must be evaluated, the paired-comparison method becomes cumbersome, for as Green shows, for "$k$ items there are $\frac{1}{2}(k)$ $(k\text{-}l)$ pairs; for 25 items the number of pairs becomes $(12.5)$ $(24)$ or 300 [1954, p. 347]." Obviously the judgmental task becomes enormous for a large sample of pairs.

Hill (1953, pp. 565–66) has shown that inconsistencies in judge's ratings may also create a problem for the paired-comparison. He makes the following argument:

Inconsistencies in judgment occur when A is preferred to B, B preferred to C, and C preferred to A. Such inconsistencies, here called *circular triads*, are to be considered errors of judgment. As errors, inconsistencies decrease the reliability of the scale values computed from the comparative judgment of the objects [1953, p. 565].

He suggests that if the rationale underlying the paired-comparison method is valid, the occurrence of inconsistent judgments should "increase as the difference between those objects on the underlying continuum decreases [1953, p. 565]." That is, the greater the difference between the objects being rated, the lower the probability of inconsistent ratings. Hill reports data that also indicate that individuals who make inconsistent judgments in one situation are likely to do so in a second situation.

These findings point to a problem of the Thurstone Method—the interpretations of the judges cannot on face value be taken as free of bias or inconsistency (see also Hovland and Sherif, 1952, pp. 822–32), although Thurstone submitted that

If the scale is to be regarded as valid, the scale values of the statements should not be affected by the opinions of the people who help to construct it. This may be a severe test in practice, but the scaling method must stand such a test before it can be accepted as being more than a description of the people who construct the scale. At any rate, to the extent that the present method of scale construction is affected by the opinions of the readers who help to sort out the original statements into a scale, to that extent the validity or universality of the scale may be challenged [1929, p. 92].

Thurstone also offered other methods for determining the scale value of items. These are generally regarded as shortcuts in the paired-comparison technique and include the methods of rank order, of equal-appearing intervals, and of successive intervals (Green, 1954, p. 347).

The method of equal-appearing intervals is the most widely used of the judgment methods (Green, 1954, p. 347). It is simpler than the paired-comparison technique because it requires only one judgment per item. "Each judge is required to sort the items into a fixed number of categories (usually 7, 9, or 11) that are arranged in order of favorableness [Green, 1954, p. 347]." The judge is asked to place the items into categories so that the intervals between them are subjectively equal. "That is, it should appear to him that the difference in degree of favorableness between the statements of any two adjacent categories is equivalent to the difference in favorableness between any other two adjacent categories [Green, 1954, p. 347]." This method suffers, however, from the fact that there is no way of determining whether in fact the distance between intervals *is* equal; the perspective of the judges may influence their placement of items.

The method of successive intervals overcomes some of the problems of the equal-appearing technique. With it judges sort the items into fixed categories (usually 7, 9, or 11) spaced along a continuum of favorableness. The categories (Green, 1954, p. 347) have a rank order on the continuum, but they are not necessarily equally spaced. The items in any category are simply judged to be less favorable than those in the adjacent category to the left, and more favorable than those in the adjacent category to the right (Green, 1954, p. 347). After a number of judges have sorted the items, a value for each can be determined based on the proportion of judges who placed it into each category.

Once a scale of items has been constructed by one of these judgmental techniques, a procedure for scoring respondents must be adopted. "The usual scoring procedure is to give each person a score which is the median of the scale values of the items which he endorses [Green, 1954, p. 350]." The mean scale value could also be used, but by either scoring method respondents are placed on a scale of favorableness toward the issue being studied (Green, 1954, p. 350).

In selecting items to include on the Thurstone scales, the following rules have been proposed (Thurstone and Chave, 1929; Green, 1954, p. 350; Upshaw, 1968, pp. 90–94). First, ambiguous items should be discarded. Ambiguous items are those that generate widely varying evaluations. Second, irrelevant items should be avoided. To determine the operating consistency or endorsement pattern for any given item, the investigator may compare the popularity of an item with its scale value. If an item is frequently endorsed, other items close to it on the scale should also be endorsed, while items far from it should have a low popularity (Green, 1954, p. 350). If the popularities of any item are independent of the scale values, then some "factor other than the latent attitude variable is determining the responses to it [Green, 1954, p. 350]." Items that generate such response patterns are judged irrelevant and are taken out of the final scale.

The major criticism of the Thurstone scaling techniques has been mentioned: The opinions of judges influence their ratings of items and thus it becomes difficult to meet Thurstone's requirement that item judgments be free of bias. The general operating rule proposed by Green (1954, p. 350) is that every investigator employing a Thurstone scale must determine for his scale the degree of bias introduced by judges. The method of summated ratings, or the Likert scaling technique offers an alternative to the Thurstone method.

In Likert's method of summated ratings, five categories of response are provided for each item: *strongly approve, approve, undecided, disapprove,* and *strongly disapprove.* These categories are scored 5, 4, 3, 2, and 1 respectively [Green, 1954, p. 350].

The score for any individual is the sum of his scores on the items. The items for a Likert scale should reflect the underlying attitude dimension being measured; the more favorable a person's attitude, the higher his expected score for the item. To select items for inclusion on the Likert scale, respondents are asked to indicate their attitudes on the proposed items, and then items with the highest discriminating power are included. A common method of determining the discriminatory power of an item is to select those items endorsed by the upper and lower 25 per cents of the sample.

The Likert technique primarily rests on the assumption that an underlying or latent attitude variable is being measured. The scores for any respondent are assumed to represent his position on the latent dimension and the items are assumed to reflect that dimension. The investigator makes this assumption after he has tested his items for internal consistency—that is, "respondents must respond to all tests in terms of the same pattern of regularity, and the test must as a whole be checked for split-half reliability [Hickman and Kuhn, 1956, pp. 227–28]."

The Likert method differs from the Thurstone technique primarily because with the former there is no need to collect the evaluations of judges before the items are placed on the final scale. "The statements, once collected are administered directly to respondents rather than given to 'judges' [Hickman and Kuhn, 1956, p. 227]."

Guttman (1944, pp. 139–50; 1947, pp. 247–78; 1950a, pp. 46–59; 1950b, pp. 60–69; 1950c, pp. 312–61) has proposed a method of scale construction termed scalogram analysis. The product of this form of analysis is commonly termed a Guttman scale. The basic objective is to select a group of items or questions so that all persons who answer a given question affirmatively, will have higher ranks than those who answer it negatively (Hickman and Kuhn, 1956, p. 230; Green, 1954, p. 353). A set of items that achieves this result 90 or more times out of a hundred is designated a unidimensional scale. "This characteristic of the Guttman scale makes it possible to infer from a respondent's score not only how many but also which questions he has answered positively and negatively [Hickman and Kuhn, 1956, p. 230]."

As with the Likert method, scalogram analysis does not require judges in the selection and placement of items on the final scale. "Provided that the investigator has exercised proper care in his choice of items, his first use of the test may be his final application of it [Hickman and Kuhn, 1956, p. 230]." The manipulations sufficient to produce an acceptable Guttman scale may be made after the data have been gathered. That is, the investigator discards items that do not scale and proceeds to manipulate the remaining items in order to produce the final ranking procedure.

The items on a Guttman scale must be cumulative, so that positive answers to one question also yield positive answers to all questions below that item on the scale. Hickman and Kuhn offer the following example:

1. Have you finished fourth grade?
   yes        no
2. Have you finished eighth grade?
   yes        no
3. Have you finished twelfth grade?
   yes        no
4. Have you finished college?
   yes        no

In analyzing this example they note:

A respondent answering the fourth item affirmatively will have properly answered the other three affirmatively also. We may note, parenthetically, that some respondents may have "skipped" one or another of the lower grades mentioned. Hence, even from a measure as simple as this and with such seemingly clean-cut gradations, we can derive only a somewhat imperfect scale. We cannot predict with 100 per cent accuracy from an individual's score alone which questions he answered affirmatively [1956, p. 231].

Two basic features underlie the Guttman model: it permits the transformation of nominal data into an ordinal scale of greater- or less-than properties; and the scalogram technique provides a test of whether or not the investigator is measuring a unidimensional variable. That is, if the scale yields a 90 per cent or better approximation of a perfect rank-ordering of responses, the investigator can infer the measurement of a single, as opposed to a multidimensional, variable.

Additional criteria of the Guttman scale include the following: first, if the final scale contains dichotomous responses, there must be ten or more items; second, all errors in response to the scale must be random ("If any particular error occurs much more frequently than others, it is evidence of a *nonscale type* [Green, 1954, p. 356]"); third, the distribution of respondents by "scale type" for any sizable population must be more or less even (Hickman and Kuhn, 1956, p. 233); fourth, each response category should have more non-error than error (if it does not, the category does not correlate highly with the total scale score). Several modifications of the scalogram model have been offered and the reader will find excellent discussions of these in Green (1954, pp. 353–58) and Upshaw (1968, pp. 98–106). One variation that should be mentioned here is Coombs (1950, 1952) unfolding technique. Primarily this involves each respondent locating himself on a scale and then designating his order of preference for a series of items or questions. "The respondent's order of preference is determined by the relative distance of the items from his location [Green, 1954, p. 358]."

A scaling technique that has received a great deal of use is the semantic differential (see Osgood, Suci, and Tannenbaum, 1957). This method rests on Osgood's studies in the measurement of meaning which revealed that a recurrent feature of all semantic statements was an evaluative component. Upshaw describes the technique as follows:

Among the polar adjectives found to have high loadings on the evaluative factor, regardless of the concept that was rated, were good-bad, optimistic-pessimistic, positive-negative. To measure the status of a group of subjects on an affective variable, Osgood *et al.*, suggest that each respondent be asked to rate the attitude object on a set of properties which have been shown to have high loadings on the evaluative factor. The respondent's score is taken as the sum (or the average) of his ratings of the object on the evaluative properties.

According to the model underlying the semantic differential, every pair of evaluative, polar adjectives approximates in meaning a hypothetical pair of adjectives which defines a pro-anti variable, exactly [1968, p. 97].

The particular set of adjectives selected are assumed to be representatives of any other set of adjectives. Additionally it is assumed that the pairs selected will approximate the evaluative component of attitudes for any population. The format for the semantic differential typically offers the respondent a 5- or 7-point scale arranged by degree of favorableness and unfavorableness. The scale has been applied to deviant, cross-cultural, and American samples and has repeatedly demonstrated the presence of the evaluative component of meanings.

*Forced versus Open-Ended Measurement Strategies*

The Thurstone, Coombs, Likert, Guttman, and semantic differential scaling techniques represent closed, or forced-choice measurement strategies; subjects are given a finite set of categories, the logic for this resting on the assumption "that respondents have a sufficiently common vocabulary so that it is possible to construct questions that have the same meaning for each of them [Richardson, Dohrenwend, Klein, 1965, p. 40]." It is additionally assumed that a uniform wording for all questions on the scale can be constructed. As our discussion indicated, the choice of questions and their wording varies by the scaling technique. The Thurstone method employs a judgmental strategy, the Likert and Guttman measures rely more on the perspective of the investigator.

It is an empirical question, however, whether the investigator's interpretation of a subject's perspective is correct. As criticisms of the Thurstone method indicate, the judge's and respondent's perspectives may vary, as may the investigator's interpretations of the respondent's position. A second, and related, difficulty of the closed-ended strategy is that it may not permit the subject to express his own point of view adequately. A subject may, for example, find that he does not have an attitude toward the dimension being scaled, or he may find that his position does not directly correspond to a point on the scale. Or, he may find the question uninterpretable.

For these reasons, an alternative measurement technique is the use of open-ended questions. With this less standardized strategy, subjects are typically asked a question and then given a blank space for their answers. No check points, scale positions, or alternative categories are offered. The subject frames his answer in terms of his definition of the question and the situation. Newcomb offers an additional assumption of the unstructured measurement strategy:

It seems reasonable to assume that a very salient attitude—one expressed with great spontaneity—has more importance for the person expressing it than does an attitude which he expresses only after a good deal of prodding or questioning. The weakness of direct questions is that they provide no way of measuring the salience of an attitude; we never know whether the attitude would have been expressed at all, or in the same way, apart from the direct question [1950, p. 151].

Kuhn and McPartland related Newcomb's position to the rationale underlying the "Who am I?" test.

Thus when a respondent in reply to the "Who am I?" question on the "Twenty Statements" test, writes "I am a man," "I am a student," "I am a football player," it is reasonable to believe that we have far more solid knowledge of the attitudes which organize and direct his behavior than if, on a checklist and among other questions, we had asked "Do you think of yourself as a man?" "Do you think of yourself as a student?" and "Do you think of yourself as an athlete?" [1954, pp. 72–73].

In several senses the logic of open-ended measurement strategies reflects a commitment to the delayed operationalization position developed in Chapters 1, 2, and 3. It will be remembered that a major strategy of symbolic interactionism is the use of sensitizing methods. Rather than formulating questions before entry into the field, the sensitizing approach directs the observer first to determine the positions and definitions of those studied. With this knowledge, more rigorous and precise questions and scales can be constructed.

My own position favors a combination of both methods. There will certainly be many questions in any study that have to be asked in the same structured way of all respondents, and these will often be questions that elicit a great deal of consensual meaning among respondents (examples would include level of education, age, annual income, and perhaps mobility patterns). On the other hand, attitudes toward the self, feelings of stigma, and other more subjective attitudes often resist consensual interpretation. Under such circumstances the ability of structured methods to yield an accurate and complete analysis must be doubted. At the very least it becomes an empirical question that is best answered with a triangulation of methods. A study of self-attitudes could easily test this argument by giving respondents both types of questions (see, for example, Spitzer, *et al.*, 1966, pp. 265–80). The comparison of answers would indicate the extent to which the unstructured method yielded more nonconsensual statements. If no difference between the instruments was observed, then such criteria as economy of effort, ease of replication, and standardization of coding procedures would favor the structured method. As a summary rule I offer the following principle: To the extent that an attribute or concept is conceived as theoretically stable, and to the extent that empirical observations support this conception, stable measures of observation are justified. But if a concept is viewed in a processual manner, subject to shifting definitions, open-ended, unstructured methods should be employed.

*Index Construction*

Often the investigator will want to measure several aspects of the same concept or attribute. This is necessary if the concept is not unidimensional. Thus, attitudes toward the self, for instance, involve more than the dimension of favorableness; they include such factors as salience, consensuality, social locus, and preferences (see Kuhn and McPartland, 1954). As Lazarsfeld (1958, pp. 105–9) has shown, for example, the attitude of conservatism involves such factors as personal preference, political location, and legal stances. In such circumstances a scale consisting of several highly interrelated questions would be inappropriate; only one aspect of the property being measured would be revealed. Because so many sociological concepts are multidimensional, indices combining several questions into one measure are needed (Lazarsfeld and Rosenberg, 1955, p. 16; Bonjean, Hill, and McLemore, 1967, p. 2). A scale may now be seen as a type of index "designed to reflect only a single dimension of a concept [Bonjean, Hill, and McLemore, 1967, p. 2]."

At the heart of the measurement process are empirical indicators of the concepts under analysis. Within their own limits, these indicators must reflect what is being measured and conceptualized. In general, sociologists may employ only two broad classes of empirical indicators: those that point to what people think or believe, and those that point to what they do. The combination of attitudes and behavior must be achieved for an ultimate link between interactional theories and the empirical world. With this in mind, our concern is with the construction of appropriate empirical indicators and with their combination into indices.

Two questions are involved in this process: the development of appropriate indicators, and the selection of certain of these indicators for the final index and analysis. This process, which represents the generic attempt to translate a concept into an empirical observation, involves at least four steps: "an initial imagery of the concept, the specification of dimensions, the selection of observable indicators, and the combination of indicators into indices [Lazarsfeld, 1958, p. 101]."

It can be argued that all measurement begins with some vague sense of what a concept means. Observations of social relationships might begin, for example, with reflections on one's own personal experiences in relationships and, on this basis, specifications of the concept follow. Thus, if a relationship is conceived as involving regular forms of symbolic and behavioral interactions between two or more persons, it can be argued that some relationships are purely symbolic in nature: the love of a wife for a deceased husband, for example. Others combine symbolic and behavioral interaction: the marriage or work relationship, for example. In this sense, aspects or dimensions of the original concept are specified. The concept, then, consists of "a complex combination of phenomena, rather than a simple and directly observable item [Lazarsfeld, 1958, p. 101]." Relationships are of this nature and can be further specified by the nature of involvement, whether long- or short-term; by the nature of the reciprocation between the members; by the rules that members observe, and so on. Each dimension leads to additional specifications, and suggests specific empirical indicators and instances that might be examined. Once a set of specifications for a concept are settled upon, even if only tentatively, the problem becomes one of locating and developing indicators, or measures. Realizing that no single measurement or indicator class will cover all the dimensions of a concept, the investigator develops multiple strategies. Lazarsfeld phrases this as follows:

The fact that each indicator has not an absolute but only a probability relation to our underlying concept requires us to consider a great many possible indicators. The case of intelligence tests furnishes an example. First, intelligence is divided into dimensions of manual intelligence, verbal intelligence, and so on. But even then there is just not one indicator by which imaginativeness can be measured. We must use many indicators to get at it [1958, p. 103].

No firm rule can be given for the development of empirical indicators. All that can be hoped is that careful field work and observation reveal relevant measures and instances of the concept being analyzed. In this process the investigator must adhere to the same rules that underlie scale construction—the construction of indicators, or questions, that can be adapted to the field setting, that derive from theory, that can be triangulated with other indicators, and that are valid in a predictive sense and as reliable as the situation permits.

Those indicators that predict best, are most valid, best suited to the field setting, and easiest to triangulate should represent the final set of indicators. It is useful to distinguish those indicators that are part of the concept from those external to it. External indicators can furnish useful predictive criteria for checks against the central-component indicators of the concept. Lazarsfeld offers the following example.

If we start listing indicators of the "integration" of a community, is the crime rate a part of the conception of integration, or is it an external factor which we might try to predict from our measure of integration? Here again, as with the problem of projective indices, knowing the laws which relate indicators to one another is of great importance. Even if we exclude crime rates from our image of the "integrated" city, they might be so highly correlated, as a matter of empirical generalization, that we would use them as a measure of integration in situations where we could not get data on the indicators which we "really" want to call integration. To do this, of course, we must first have "validating studies" where we correlate crime rate with the other indicators of integration and establish that it is generally closely related. We should also know whether there are other factors besides integration influencing crime rate which might confuse our measurements if we used it alone to measure integration, so that we can check if we used other factors, or add enough other factors, or add enough indicators so as to cancel out their influence [1958, pp. 103–4].

Once a set of indicators has been developed and applied, a final index must be developed. Not only is it inefficient to work with ten different measures of a given concept, each of the ten may only reflect certain aspects of the concept. An index offers a way of fitting several, oftentimes discrete, indicators into one measure that combines the strengths of each while minimizing their inherent weaknesses. I cite Lazarsfeld:

For some situations we have to make one over-all index out of them [the indicators]. If I have six students and only one fellowship to give, then I must make an over-all rating of the six. To do this I must in some way combine all the information I have about each student into an index. At another time we may be interested in how each of several dimensions is related to outside variables. But, even so, we must find a way of combining the indicators, since by their nature the indicators are many, and their relations to outside variables are usually both weaker and more unstable than the underlying characteristics which we would like to measure.

To put it in more formal language, each individual indicator has only a probability relation to what we really want to know. A man might maintain his basic position, but by chance, shift on an individual indicator; or he might change his basic position. But if we have many such indicators in an index, it is highly unlikely that a large number of them will all change in one direction, if the man we are studying has in fact not changed his basic position [1958, p. 104].

To illustrate this process of index construction I again draw upon Lazarsfeld (1958, pp. 105–9), who has suggested that as the investigator selects a relatively small number of indicators for an index, the problem of the interchangeability of indices must be considered. That is,

It is one of the notable features of such indices that their correlation with outside variables will usually be about the same, regardless of the specific "sampling" of items which goes into them from the broader group associated with the concept. This rather startling phenomenon has been labeled "the interchangeability of indices" [Lazarsfeld, 1958, p. 105].

In his discussion of this problem, Lazarsfeld offers the example of his study of conservatism among social science professors during the McCarthy period. The problem was to select a series of indicators that would locate conservative professors within the sample. Each respondent was given a series of rights and prohibitions relating to the academic life and asked whether they were for or against them. Out of the answers an index of conservatism was developed, and assessed in the following manner:

Two questions had to do with the respondent's attitudes towards student activities. "If there are students who want to join it, do you think that a Socialist League ought to be allowed on this campus, or not?" The attitude toward Socialists seemed a good indicator because whether they classified with communists or not is an issue on which educated conservatives and their opponents are likely to disagree. Fourteen per cent, or 355 professors, reported that they would be definitely against such a policy. Characteristically enough, the second question, also pertaining to student activities, gave almost the same number of conservative replies. We asked respondents to suppose that they were faculty advisors to a student organization on the campus that "proposed inviting Owen Lattimore, Far Eastern expert (now under indictment in Washington) to speak at a public meeting here." Again, about 14 per cent of the sample, in this case 342 professors, put themselves on record that this "ought not to be allowed" [Lazarsfeld, 1958, p. 106].

While both questions yielded about the same number of conservative answers, analysis revealed that the Lattimore questions reflected answers of some respondents who disliked Lattimore personally—the attitude of conservatism involved more than the question appeared to measure. The Socialist League question involved an element of ambiguity, because respondents tended to merge their own attitudes with those of their college or uni-versity. Neither measure was pure, as Lazarsfeld notes, and the problem now involved whether analysis would be greatly affected by interchanging the two indices.

To answer this, an "outside" or "external" variable was needed to enable analysis of the discriminatory power of the two indices. The following question was chosen:

If you had to make a choice, in a case in which a member of the faculty is accused of being subversive or of engaging in un-American activities, which do you think is *more* important for the college (university) administration to protect—the reputation of the college (university) or the rights of the faculty members? [Lazarsfeld, 1958, p. 107].

This question relates conservatism to the concern for human rights, and this concern represents the outside variable for the evaluation of the Lattimore and Socialist League indices. Analysis revealed that both indices discrim-inated about equally. The Lattimore question located 46 per cent conserva-tive responses and the Socialist League question yielded 43 per cent conser-vative responses. The trend produced by each index was about the same. Lazarsfeld offered the following conclusion:

In actual research practice, a larger number of items rather than one item alone is used for the purposes of classification. This has a variety of rea-sons. For example, indices based on more items permit finer distinctions, and they tend to cancel out the peculiarities of any single item. . . . Even if we use several items for classificatory purposes, we have always a selec-tion out of a much larger pool of reasonable possibilities [1958, p. 108].

When the investigator chooses his indicators he will commonly find that although they are related, they will not classify respondents in the same way, as the discussion of the Lattimore and Socialist League questions showed. But when the two indices are correlated with a third variable, they will usually lead to very "similar empirical results [Lazarsfeld, 1958, p. 109]." This is both the problem and advantage of indices that are inter-changeable. Neither measure is perfect, yet economy of effort is achieved by employing only one of them.

To the extent that any set of indices similarly correlate with an outside variable, convergent validity is established. To the extent that each discrim-inates between different events, discriminate validity is established. Ideally, both types of validity should be met by an index.

Index construction is one strategy of triangulation, then. While confined to the measurement level, the assessment of indices internally and against outside variables represents a technique for combining different measures in the analysis of the same empirical event.

*The Measurement of Natural Social Units*

The scales and indices thus far presented primarily focus on what people think, but the link between subjective states and overt acts must be established. Similarly, the relationship between thoughts and actions and interactional forms must be made. That is, the question of how a man's attitude draws upon the perspectives of his friends, co-workers, or associates cannot be ignored. Nor can the tie between his actions and those of others. What are the relevant strategies? Unfortunately there are few, and this absence reflects, I believe, the immature state of sociological analysis of social organization. One major strategy is to combine the sampling implications of a sociometric model with appropriate questions. This method, which asks persons to list friends, co-workers, or associates within a specified group, has been adapted to the analysis of organizations (Weiss and Jacobsen, 1955, pp. 661–68; Boyle, 1969, pp. 99–119). It basically involves the location of interactional relationships between like-situated persons in a social organization at a given point in time. Weiss and Jacobsen describe their use of the sociometric method as follows:

To obtain the basic information about attitudes and patterns of interaction, each of the 196 members of the professional and administrative staff of the agency was interviewed privately in sessions that lasted from one to three hours. When the interview was about two-thirds completed, each respondent was asked to fill out a "Personal Contact Checklist" form. Instructions were:

Now go back over the past two or three months and think of the people (in the organization) with whom you have worked most closely. We would like to get the names of the people with whom you work most closely. Write their names in here. You will notice that we want some who are higher than you in the organization, some lower than you, and some at the same level [1955, pp. 662–63].

This question produced 2400 work relationships for the 196 respondents. Of these, 44 per cent were reciprocated in the sense that if Individual A reported that he worked with B, B also reported that he worked with A. These contacts formed the bulk of the analysis for their study that focused upon natural groups of interactants within the organization. To establish these groups, a work group was defined as "a set of individuals whose relationships were with each other and not with members of other work groups (except for contacts with liaison persons or between groups) [Weiss and Jacobsen, 1955, p. 663]."

A liaison person was defined as a person who worked with at least two persons who were not members of his group. "A contact between groups was defined as a single working relationship between members of sets of individuals who would otherwise be classified as separate work groups

[Weiss and Jacobsen, 1955, p. 664]." By removing liaison and contact persons, natural interactive groups were located.

This use of the sociometric method represents one strategy for locating and measuring natural units of interaction. Once natural work groups have been located, the scales discussed earlier can be applied, or a variety of indices can be constructed. In either event, the actual measurement process proceeds on the basis of natural units.

In a study referred to earlier (Spitzer and Denzin, in process), a modified sociometric method combined with open- and closed-ended measurement strategies was adopted for the analysis of the mental patient's career. The basic unit of analysis was the social relationship between a patient and his major significant other. Once significant others were located, they were interviewed with the same measures as the patient. Measurements focused primarily on the self-attitudes of the patient, on his important social objects, and on his conception of how his significant other viewed him. To this end the "Who am I?" test was first given to patients and then in a modified form it was given to significant others. That is, significant others were asked "I think he is—". In addition, significant others were asked to list what they thought were important social objects for the patient. Through this process of reciprocating tests for each sample, the congruence in attitudes and symbols between the patient and his significant other was located. This use of the sociometric method is mentioned because it represents one strategy for analyzing social relationships with open- and closed-ended methods.

Other examples of measuring natural social units might include "mass observations" (Reiss, 1968, pp. 351–67), and unobtrusive observations (Webb, *et al.*, 1966). The unobtrusive method will be discussed in a subsequent chapter. Here the point is that the measurement of natural units involves at least a two-step process. First, the location of the unit, which is a problem of sampling, and second, the actual observation of that unit (the measurement problem).

*The Functions of Qualitative and Quantitative Measurements*

It is commonly assumed that qualitative observations can only serve an exploratory, or pilot, function for theory. The belief is that because of their loose and rather vague nature such data cannot permit the precise tests theories demand. Consequently, when the problem of theory verification arises, many analysts turn to some form of quantitative data. Drawing upon Glaser and Strauss (1967), I wish to discuss this issue and to indicate that a false dichotomy exists between these two types of data. Theories may be verified with qualitative observations, as Glaser and Strauss' own studies of dying (1964, 1968) indicate, but what are the verificational strategies of qualitative analysis?

It can be argued, I believe, that all data, whether qualitative, or quantitative, serve four basic functions for theory (Merton, 1967, p. 171). They can initiate new theory, or reformulate, refocus, and clarify existing theory. Data can illustrate theory, as Lazarsfeld and Barton's (1955, pp. 356–61) analysis of historical-trend theories suggests, and in this sense, all data stand in an instrumental relationship to theory, and the distinction between qualitative and quantitative data becomes meaningless. To the extent that any body of data is theoretically directed, triangulated, reflects the circumstances of a natural field setting, and is valid and reliable, it can be admitted into the research process. To disparage qualitative data because they are not rigorously scaled, or because they do not permit complicated statistical analysis, avoids the issue. Many field circumstances will not permit quantitative measurements, and frequently theories are so imprecise that quantitative data cannot be specified. Under adverse conditions the researcher must collect what he can. If the just-mentioned rules are kept in mind, however, he can feel confident that at least some level of theory-work will come from his observations.

### Notes

An excellent review of assumptions underlying the measurement process may be found in Green (1954, pp. 335–69), and, more recently, Upshaw (1968, pp. 60–111). For a trenchant critique of these assumptions, Cicourel (1964, 1968) should be examined. His position calls for serious and critical analysis of current theories of measurement. A useful review of the major scales and indices currently employed by sociologists is Bonjean, Hill, and McLemore (1967). The most valuable sources on index construction, in my opinion, are Lazarsfeld and Barton (1955, pp. 321–61) and Lazarsfeld (1958, pp. 99–130). A valuable collection of studies employing the use of indices is contained in Lazarsfeld and Rosenberg (1955, pp. 15–108). The Lazarsfeld and Barton essay also provides an excellent review of the functions and strategies of qualitative data analysis. Their perspective is elaborated and specifically applied to participant observation in Howard S. Becker's "Problems of Inference and Proof in Participant Observation," (1958), and in Becker and Geer's (1960), "Participant Observation: The Analysis of Qualitative Field Data." These specific strategies will be developed in Chapter 9. Glaser and Strauss' (1967) analysis of grounded theory should once again be examined, also. It represents the most recent synthesis of qualitative data strategies and methods.

A useful review of open-ended and projective tests is presented in Anastasi (1961) and Cronbach (1960). The interested reader should consult these sources.

A problem not explicitly discussed in this chapter, but one that was raised earlier, is the continuity in the use of measurement techniques. Bonjean, Hill, and McLemore (1967) present interesting data that indicate that there is a low degree of continuity between such techniques as currently used by the sociologist.

This chapter has drawn on Herbert Blumer's (1969) essay "The Methodological Position of Symbolic Interactionism." In this paper Blumer clearly establishes the role of theory in the selection and development of measurement techniques. He also indicates the interactive nature of the research process and points out that theories and methods are developed for one reason only—explanations of the empirical world. With his heavy emphasis on the empirical side of sociology, Blumer carefully develops a synthesis of the discovery and verification processes. A notable feature of his essay is the position that contemporary sociologists have ignored the process of discovery in their attempts to develop valid measurement instruments.

# 6

# The Sociological Interview

The interview, far from being a kind of snapshot or tape-recording—a simple report either of fact or of emotional response—in which the interviewer is a neutral agent who simply trips the shutter or triggers the response, is instead inevitably an interactional situation.

*Manford H. Kuhn, 1962, p. 194.*

But the interview is still more than tool and object of study. It is the art of sociological sociability, the game which we play for the pleasure of savoring its subtleties. It is our flirtation with life, our eternal affair, played hard and to win, but played with that detachment and amusement which give us, win or lose, the spirit to rise up and interview again and again.

*Mark Benney and Everett C. Hughes, 1956, p. 138.*

It is in the sociological interview—a peculiar form of interaction between observers and subjects—that the act of measurement comes to life. The interview represents, as Benney and Hughes (1956, p. 137) suggest, the favorite "digging tool" of the sociologist. As the favorite tool, it is beset with certain very special problems, the problems of an encounter that must simultaneously rest on polite rules of etiquette while, at the same time, eliciting intimate and private perspectives. There are also problems simply because the rules for such transactions vary from interviewer to interviewee.

**Forms of the Interview**

An interview is "a face to face verbal interchange in which one person, the interviewer, attempts to elicit information or expressions of opinions or belief from another person or persons [Maccoby and Maccoby, 1954, p. 499]." Interviews may be classified by their degree of structuring, or standardization (Richardson, Dohrenwend, and Klein, 1965, pp. 32–55). At the most structured level is the schedule standardized interview in which the wording and order of all questions is exactly the same for every respondent, the purpose being to develop an instrument that can be given in the same way to all respondents. All questions must be comparable, so that when variations between respondents appear they can be attributed to actual differences in response, not to the instrument.

The rationale for this form of the interview rests on the belief that for any study "the respondents have a sufficiently common vocabulary so that it is possible to formulate questions which have the same meaning for each of them [Richardson, Dohrenwend, and Klein, 1965, p. 40]." In other words, it is assumed that each respondent will be presented with the same stimuli and that it will elicit the same range of meanings for each. Benney and Hughes have called this assumption into question.

Interviews are of many kinds. Some sociologists like them standardized and so formulated that they can be administered to large groups of people. This can be done only among large homogeneous populations not too unlike the investigator himself in culture. Where languages are too diverse, where common values are too few, where the fear of talking to strangers is too great, there the interview based on a standardized questionnaire calling for a few standardized answers may not be applicable. Those who venture into such situations may have to invent new modes of interviewing [1956, p. 137].

A second assumption of the standardized form suggests that it is possible to find a uniform wording for all questions equally meaningful to every respondent. The Benney and Hughes' critique indicates that this assumption is best realized in a homogeneous sample. Typically, I would add, only in middle-class samples. That is,

Probably the most intensive presocialization of respondents runs in roughly the social strata from which the interviewers themselves are drawn—the middle, urban, higher-educated groups, while at the top and bottom— though for different reasons—the appropriate role of the informant is apparently much less known [Benney and Hughes, 1956, p. 139].

Third, it is assumed that if the "meaning of each question is to be identical for each respondent, its context must be identical and, since all preceding questions constitute part of the context, the sequence of the questions must be identical [Richardson, Dohrenwend, and Klein, 1965, p. 43]." This assumes an order in which questions can be placed to best capture the interest and mood of the respondent. Typically questions are ordered as follows: those that elicit the interest of the respondent come first; once interest has been obtained, less interesting questions follow; highly emotional questions are embedded in the interview, often near the end. Placing the most threatening questions near the end assures that should the respondent "break off," a major portion of the interview will have been completed.

Whether this outline for questions can be followed depends largely on the needs and intents of the investigation. In our study of mental patients (Spitzer and Denzin, in process) it was necessary to depart from this order. Because we wanted only first-admission patients, it was necessary to begin the interview with questions concerning prior treatment. For some patients, this was a highly emotionally toned question—particularly for those attempting to "pass" in the outside world. Furthermore, we wanted answers to the "Who Am I?" question that were not influenced by other questions. For this reason, we followed the questions about prior treatment with the "Who Am I?" test.

The last assumption of the standard schedule interview suggests that "careful pilot investigation, development, and pretesting will provide a final schedule of questions that meets the requirements of assumptions (1), (2), and (3) [Richardson, Dohrenwend, and Klein, 1965, p. 44]." The pretest phase of the study consists of selecting a group of persons comparable to those who will be interviewed in the final study, but using these persons only to test hypotheses about the interview. In our mental patient study, we engaged in over a year of pilot investigations with the interview schedule. On the basis of these investigations we decided to depart from the normal interview schedule by placing highly emotional items first. Furthermore, from this pretest phase we learned that if you can get respondents to reveal highly emotional feelings early in the interview, nearly any other type of question can follow. Apparently respondents, realizing they could trust us, had no reservations about giving private information after initial trust had been secured.

These four assumptions of the schedule standardized interview are largely untested articles of faith. They appear to be justified when the sample to be interviewed has similar characteristics and experiences. Even this must be challenged, however, for while all the mental patients we interviewed had been in treatment at some time, not all could easily interpret our questions. Certainly when the sample is heterogeneous, the use of the schedule standardized form must be questioned.

The nonschedule standardized interview represents the second basic type of interview. The "nonschedule standardized interviewer works with a list of the information required from each respondent [Richardson, Dohrenwend, and Klein, 1965, p. 45]." This form most closely approximates what has been called the focused interview (Merton and Kendall, 1946, p. 541–52), in which certain types of information are desired from all respondents but the particular phrasing of questions and their order is redefined to fit the characteristics of each respondent. This form of the interview requires that each interviewer be highly trained in the meaning of the desired information and in the skills of phrasing questions for each person interviewed.

Becker, *et al.*, describe their use of this interview form as follows:

The student interviews, following as they did a great deal of "exploratory" work, were much more structured, being designed to get information on particular points for systematic analysis. . . . We used an interview guide, asking each student 138 questions. . . . But we left room for the free expression of all kinds of ideas and did not force the student to stick to the original list of questions or to answer in predetermined categories [1961, p. 29].

The assumptions underlying the nonschedule standardized interview are suggested by this quotation. First, if the meaning of a question is to be standardized, it must be formulated in words familiar to those interviewed. Medical students, for example, do not speak of patients as uniform types of persons. Some are "crocks," some are "good" patients, and so on. Lower-class people do not become mentally ill and suffer from anxiety syndromes; they "get nervous" or "go mental." The nonstandardized schedule indicates an awareness that individuals have unique ways of defining their world. To meaningfully understand that world, researchers must approach it from the subject's perspective. Second, this interview strategy assumes that no "fixed sequence of questions is satisfactory to all respondents; the most effective sequence for any respondent is determined by his readiness and willingness to take up a topic as it comes up [Richardson, Dohrenwend, and Klein, 1965, p. 51]." This assumption was reflected by Becker and his associates when they permitted each medical student to choose his own order of answering their questions. In our study of the mental patient, interviewers were instructed to depart from the formal interview schedule when they felt that patients were becoming too nervous or emotional.

With this approach the interviewer will often find that interviewees will raise important issues not contained in the schedule, or will even summarize entire sections of the schedule in one long sequence of statements. In a study I am currently conducting on the retail druggist, a series of questions are asked all respondents concerning drugs, drug abuses, and the nature and extent of drug addiction in the local community. These issues are covered by some twelve specific questions, but on several occasions it has been useful merely to raise the question of drugs and then allow the druggist to talk. He will often cover all the relevant issues as well as raise topics not included on the list.

A last, although unverified, assumption underlying the nonschedule strategy suggests that

Through careful study of respondents and selection and training of interviewers, the necessary skills can be achieved to tailor the questions and their sequence so that equivalence of meaning is obtained for all respondents [Richardson, Dohrenwend, and Klein, 1965, p. 51].

Not only will all respondents be given the same set of questions, as in the Becker, *et al.*, sample, but it is assumed that each respondent has been exposed to the same uniform set of stimuli (i.e., questions). This suggests a parallel to the schedule standardized approach, which also attempts to place all questions in a uniform context, the basic difference, of course, being that here questions and order are changed for each respondent.

The nonstandardized interview represents the other major interview type. In it, no prespecified set of questions is employed, nor are questions asked in a specified order. Furthermore, a schedule is not employed. This gives the interviewer a great deal of freedom to probe various areas, and to raise and test specific hypotheses during the course of the interview. Lindesmith (1947, p. 6) who employed the nonstandardized approach in his study of opiate addiction, described his interviews as "informal friendly conversations." Similarly, Becker described his interviews with marijuana users as follows:

The interviews focused on the history of the person's experience with the drug, seeking major changes in his attitude toward it and in his actual use of it and the reasons for these changes. Generalizations stating necessary conditions for the maintenance of use at each level were developed in initial interviews, and tested against and revised in the light of each succeeding one [1962, p. 592].

The nonstandardized interview represents the logical extension of the nonschedule standardized interview and rests on essentially the same assumptions. It is clear, however, that there is no attempt to standardize either the interview setting or the format of the interview so that each respondent is presented with the same set of stimuli.

## A Comparison of the Three Types of Interviews

These three approaches to the interview rest on assumptions that are largely unverified. For example, the extent to which it is necessary to present all respondents with common questions in the same order is unclear. It is apparent, however, that each type of interview answers particular types of problems and that each may be most appropriate for certain types of studies. Before turning to comparisons, it is important to note that in virtually every case, each type of interview allows the investigator to gather observations on the following: personal-social data from each respondent, including such dimensions as age, sex, marital status, educational and work history; attitude and opinion data on whatever might be the concern of the investigation (e.g., attitudes toward drugs, political issues, mental hospitals); life-history data on past social and personal experiences (see Chapter 10) such as experiences with law enforcement agencies, or mental hospitals; situational or social setting data concerning such things as the nature of the neighborhood where the respondent lives. Armed with this information it is possible to locate the respondent(s) in a specific time-space locale (e.g., all mental patients interviewed during the summer of 1965 in the eastern half of the state of Iowa), and to associate the typical response patterns of the subject to situational and behavioral factors. Persons who have been released from mental hospitals over one year, for example, tend not to view themselves as mentally ill, while persons released for less than three months still regard themselves as mentally ill.

Maccoby and Maccoby suggest (1954, p. 499) that the unstructured, nonstandardized interview is best suited for exploratory studies, while the structured, schedule standardized interview is best suited for hypothesis testing and rigorous qualification of results. While it is certainly the case that the nonstandardized interview restricts rigorous quantification of data, it is neither obvious, or even necessarily the case, that this form cannot be employed to develop explanatory hypotheses. Both Lindesmith and Becker, for example, concluded that on the basis of data gathered from their unstandardized interviews, their conclusions held for all cases of opiate addiction and marijuana use they observed. In short, they pursued their observations beyond the point of exploration and moved into the realm assumed to be that of the scheduled interview (i.e., hypothesis testing).

If the criterion of ascertaining respondent meanings and definitions is considered, the less structured interviews are more suitable. If, however, it is desired to obtain the same set of information from all persons, then the schedule standardized form is necessary. It is ridiculous, for example, to imagine the U. S. Census being conducted in the form of the nonstructured interview.

If large samples of persons are to be interviewed over wide geographical areas, it is frequently impossible to employ anything except the schedule standardized interview. Furthermore, if the cost factor is considered, once the schedule standarized interview has been pretested and developed, relatively untrained interviewers can be employed to administer it.

Often it is possible to combine the three approaches so that certain standard information is obtained from all respondents, while nonscheduled items and even portions of the nonstandardized interview are included. In the retail druggist study mentioned earlier, I have attempted to combine these three approaches; first by ascertaining such standard information as age, places of training and work, and then by altering the order in which drug abuse questions were raised. Furthermore, when the druggist indicated a varied work history, questions were raised that fit his particular set of work experiences, in an attempt to ascertain his changing conceptions of client and self.

## The Question and the Interview

Up to this point I have considered types of interviews in terms of their underlying assumptions. To complete the comparisons of these approaches it is necessary to return to the very basis of all interviews—the question. Cannell and Kahn (1954, p. 664) have suggested that the questionnaire or interview must serve two broad purposes: it must translate research objectives into specific questions, the answers to which will provide data necessary for hypothesis testing, and it must assist the interviewer in motivating the respondent so that the necessary information is given.

It is to these two ends that the question becomes the major unit around which the interview is constructed. Hyman (1954, pp. 665–74) has argued that all questions should be comprehensive enough to cover all areas of the research, and should elicit responses that can be validly and reliably quantified—that is, the questions should measure the areas intended to be measured by the investigation.

Lazarsfeld (1954, pp. 675–86) has argued that all questions should conform to three principles. The first is what he calls the principle of division, which states that questions in the interview should fit the experiences of those interviewed. This means that the question should be fixed in its meaning and not its wording. If researchers are interviewing mental patients about their experiences with psychiatrists, it is more important to phrase the term "psychiatrist" and the question about "experiences with psychiatrists" in terms of the specific experiences each patient has had with psychiatrists, not in terms of a rigid question format like the following: "Do you think that a psychiatrist would be very successful in helping you with a problem you might have?—(1) possibly, (2) very unlikely, (3) very likely."

This question contains a series of problematic words that are likely to convey different meanings to each patient. What, for example, does "successful in helping you" mean? Or what does "very likely" mean? By Lazarsfeld's criterion, the interviewer should rephrase the question to fit the interpretation of each patient interviewed.

Lazarsfeld's second principle is ascertaining what the respondent's answer means—or the principle of tacit assumption. When a lower-class patient says he thinks seeing a psychiatrist would be very likely to help him, does this mean the same thing as when a middle-class patient says it? The response of the patient provides no clear answer; the interviewer must go beyond responses to a question and probe the specific meanings suggested by each person in his answers.

Added to the problem of tacit assumption is the issue raised by Edwards (1957a) in his research on the social desirability factor. Noting that frequently in the interview-questionnaire situation respondents tend to reply to questions in terms of what they perceive to be the most socially desirable response, Edwards cautions that questions should take this dimension into account. In the study of mental patients cited earlier, we found recurrent instances of the social desirability variable, particularly when ex-patients were presented with a series of questions that concerned their willingness to interact with other ex-patients. One respondent, when asked if she "would be against a daughter of hers marrying a man who had been to see a psychiatrist about a mental problem," answered, "I know I shouldn't say this but I don't want any daughter of mine marrying a man who has been through what I have been." Notwithstanding this, when the question was repeated, the woman replied, "No, I guess I wouldn't be against this!"

These criteria (comprehensiveness, measurability, specificity, pinpointing meaning, and social desirability awareness) suggest the following: questions should accurately convey meaning to the respondent; they should motivate him to become involved and to communicate clearly his attitudes and opinions; they should be clear enough so that the interviewer can easily convey meaning to the respondent; they should be precise enough to exactly convey what is expected of the respondent (a question such as "What are your feelings toward the Vietnam War?" is so broad that a respondent could range far and wide in his answer); any specific question should have as a goal the discerning of a response pattern that clearly fits the broad intents of the investigation (this implies that the respondent should be led through the questions in a logical and "realistic" fashion so that to him they make sense); if questions raise the possibility of the respondent's lying or fabricating (which is always a possibility), care should be taken to include questions that catch him up, or reveal to him and the interviewer that his previous answers have been incorrect.

## The Three Types of Interviews Reassessed

Conveying meaning in the schedule standardized interview (SSI) is difficult to achieve, because respondents are from different backgrounds and settings and frequently a phrase or question does not elicit common meaning. With the unstructured schedule interview (USI), questions can be rephrased and reordered to convey meaning, and in the unstructured interview (UI), of course this is even more the case.

When the problem of respondent motivation is considered, the SSI form again raises problems, but if extensive pretesting has been done, many of these problems can be avoided. When the USI and the UI forms are employed, it is up to the interviewer to reorder and rephrase questions so that they motivate a reply. The third criterion, clarity to interviewer, is less of a problem with the SSI because this has presumably been resolved before the interviewer is sent into the field; with the SSI form there should only be predetermined interviewer rephrasing or reordering of questions. With the USI and UI forms, however, untrained interviewers will often reinterpret questions and restate them in a manner quite different from that intended by the investigator. Precision of intent, the fourth criterion, should not be a problem with the most structured interview form, the SSI—but unfortunately it often is, and the problem of interpretation again falls on the interviewer, just as ideally all three forms should present no problems when set against the fifth criterion, that of each question relating to the overall research intents, but often do.

Last, the problem of fabrication looms largest with the SSI, for too frequently the interviewer has no specific set of questions with which to challenge the respondent's reply. In our study of the mental patient, this was an important factor jeopardizing the validity of many of the questions that probed particularly emotion-laden or socially desirable dimensions. With the USI and UI, it is relatively easy to challenge the respondent, and to check his replies.

### Common Deficiencies of All Interview Types

In their incisive comparison of interviewing with participant observation, Becker and Geer (1957, pp. 28–32) noted the following difficulties of all interview forms. First, there is the difficulty of penetrating a group's language and mechanisms of symbolization (treated in Chapter 5 of this book). In interviewing group members, sociologists are placed in the position of having at once to penetrate and understand the meanings and symbols of the group. While most Americans speak English, they do not all employ the language in the same way. This often leads to the first error in an interview—tacit assumption of understanding. All interview forms are susceptible to this error and unless the investigator can become firmly entrenched in a group's way of life, he has no assurance that he fully understands what is communicated.

The second possible error of the interview is that people do not always tell the interviewer what he wants to know. Women are often reluctant to discuss their sexual relationships, for instance; drug addicts are not likely to reveal to a stranger their sources of drugs; mental patients will not readily tell why they dislike other mental patients. This resistance to telling "all" may reveal insecurity in the interviewer's presence, may indicate a commitment to a sense of propriety unknown to the interviewer, may indicate mis-understanding of the question, or may be deliberate resistance (see Paul, 1953, pp. 430–51). While it is easier to broach difficult "conversational topics" with the USI and UI interview forms, even with them that may sometimes be impossible.

Becker (1954, pp. 31–32) has suggested as one tactic "playing dumb" and forcing the respondent to become concrete when he appears unwilling to answer questions directly. This tactic, which forces the respondent to make clear what he only alludes to, works best in the unstructured inter-view. Becker describes it as follows:

The interview ordinarily started with questions at a high level of generality: "What are the problems of being a school teacher?" . . . Most teachers were able to talk about these relationships at this abstract level of discus-sion. . . . When a number of such statements had been made and we were well-launched on our conversation, I would assume a skeptical air and ask the teacher if she could give me any evidence for these statements. . . . This somewhat put the interviewee in the position of having to put up or shut up. . . . Once the interview area had been shifted in this way to personal experience, I used another strategy to elicit further information that was being withheld. I played dumb and pretended not to understand certain relationships and attitudes which were implicit in the description the teacher gave, but which she preferred not to state openly [1954, p. 31].

The last source of potential error for all interviews relates again back to the fact that groups create their own rules and symbols, a factor immedi-ately complicated when it is realized that persons occupy different positions within their own groups, and hence have their own interpretations and even distortions of what the group's values are. For this reason, interviews must be combined with other methods of observation.

To summarize, each form of the interview represents a "tentatively" formulated plan of action the investigator may employ as he moves to the level of observation. Reality "out there" is present only to the extent that it is so defined. The interview represents one way by which observers may both define that reality (e.g., its presence as revealed in answers to ques-tions) and act toward it. Employing for a moment the model of the social act, it can be seen that in the interview researchers have a microcosmic picture of the entire theory-research process. Social acts have, as Kuhn (1962, pp. 193–206) argues, three distinct phases: a beginning in which persons imagine how they are going to act, and initially begin to move toward an object; a middle phase in which they actually act toward that object; and a consummation phase in which they agree to terminate their actions. Each of the three interview forms (SSI, USI, UI) represent impor-tant variations of the social act model. With the SSI (and, to a certain degree, with the USI) the social act breaks into three quite clearly discernible phases. In phase one, researchers formulate and pretest questions; in phase two the questions are administered; in phase three the act terminates when all the persons selected in the sampling design have been interviewed.

The UI is different, however, because with it the investigator is continually acting toward his object (i.e., the respondent and his subject matter). He can make no clear distinction between the formulation of the interview and its administration, and interviewing ceases only when all the information needed to test and/or verify hypotheses has been gathered.

The interview represents one of the basic modes by which the investigator carries on an "interaction with" his empirical world. Each interview implies a different plan of action toward that world, and as such must be assessed in terms of the implications that plan of action has for the overall research. Each type of interview has strengths and weaknesses. As a general rule for selecting one as opposed to another, the evaluation by Lazarsfeld (1954, p. 699) seems appropriate. Slightly rephrased, Lazarsfeld says that a structured interview because of its rigidity will hardly be as good as an unstructured interview under its best conditions but hardly lets us down as much as the unstructured interview sometimes does.

In the hands of a skilled interviewer, the USI and UI can hardly be surpassed. In the hands of the unskilled, they can be disastrous, and in such situations it is better to employ the more structured forms. However, interviewers can be trained, and even skilled interviewers make mistakes, so there is no hard and fast rule. The issue resolves largely into personal preferences of the investigator, the intent of the investigation, the available resources, and the investigator's decision concerning what "type of interaction" he desires.

## The Interview as an Observational Encounter: Sources of Invalidity

Whether the interview rests on complex interconnected sets of questions in the form of scales, or relies on open-ended, unstructured questions, the investigator is obligated to report the reliability and validity of his items. Chapter 5 established the centrality of these two problems for the measurement process. Validity, with its concern for what is being measured, and reliability, which points to the stability of observations over time, are directly relevant to the interview. The investigator must show the extent to which his questions measure what is intended, as well as demonstrate the reliability of his instrument. I have suggested that these two problems are interactional in nature. To further extend this proposition, I wish to treat the interview as an observational encounter.

An encounter (Goffman, 1961) represents the coming together of two or more persons for the purposes of focused interaction. An encounter, then, is a form of the joint action and is represented in such divergent contexts as eating a dinner, making a purchase in a store, encountering another person in an elevator, or filling out an interview form. As interactions, all encounters are composed of two or more interacting persons; a situation for interaction; a series of rules or standards of conduct that direct the behavior observed.

These rules may take three basic forms. They may be civil-legal in nature and find their expression in law, official morality, or codes of ethics. They may be ceremonial, as seen in rules of etiquette; such rules govern polite, face-to-face interaction among persons when they are in public or private behavior settings. They can range from statements on proper dress to how one introduces himself to a stranger or takes leave from a party. Third, rules may be relational in form, as seen in long-term social relationships among lovers, co-workers, or friends. These rules redefine civil-legal and ceremonial standards, since participants have constructed their own meaning for what is right and proper. Thus the rules of polite conversation may be greatly relaxed in long-term relationships; profanity, speaking in a loud voice, and even the use of silence may be common in such situations.

The importance of relational rules for the analysis of face to face interaction derives from the fact that they represent a synthesis of civil-legal and ceremonial standards. Consequently, all persons view the world of interaction from the peculiar moral complexion of their own relational standards. These standards go so far as to specify how selves are defined, how knowledge about the self is communicated, and how joint actions with others are organized. These rules do not exist on an abstract level, as is often the case with civil-legal and ceremonial standards—that is, they seldom find expression in law books or catalogues of etiquette—they are observed only through the process of interaction. Their relevance for the observational encounter should be apparent. Interviewers must work within the boundaries of polite etiquette as they probe into the relational rules and moralities of respondents. The problem arises when respondents either possess a different set of interactional rules than the interviewer, or refuse to permit penetration into their relational worlds. In either case, the aim of the interview, which is focused interaction around the content of theoretically relevant questions, may be sidetracked, or even disrupted. The interviewer may also believe that he has penetrated the respondent's perspective and unwittingly be led astray by fabrication or response set.

If the interview, as an observational encounter, is analyzed by its constituent elements (observer, respondent, situation, and rules) the following sources of potential invalidity can be noted. Beginning first with the interviewer, it must be asked "What rules of conduct direct his activity?" "Is he playing by polite rules of etiquette, or is he attempting to bring his relational rules to bear upon the perspective of the subject?" It appears that many middle-class interviewers attempt a synthesis. They assume that all subjects will have a common perspective on such matters as annual income, patterns of sexual behavior, attitudes toward the war, and so on, and they translate their stance on those issues into the interaction process, seldom questioning the legitimacy of that decision.

This is basically the problem of self-presentation. The rules one plays by structure the nature of his presented self. Because the role of interviewer is relatively new and undefined, interviewers seldom have firm guidelines for selecting the proper set of rules and selves to present. Benney and Hughes offer the following comment:

The role of the interviewer, then, is one governed by conventions, rather than by standards, rules or laws; it is a role that is relatively lightly held, even by professionals, and may be abandoned in favor of certain alternative roles if the occasion arises. *What* alternative roles is another matter. The interview is a relatively new kind of encounter in the history of human relations, and the older models of encounter—parent-child, male-female, rich-poor, foolish-wise—carry role definitions much better articulated and more exigent. The interviewer will be constantly tempted, if the other party falls back on one of those older models, to reciprocate—tempted and excused. For, unlike most encounters, the interview is a role-playing situation in which one person is much more an expert than the other, and, while the conventions governing the interviewer's behavior are already beginning, in some professional circles, to harden into standards, the conventions governing the informant's behavior are much less clearly articulated and known [1956, p. 139].

Paradoxically, I would suggest that interview schedules rest on multiple conflicting roles, selves, and rules. The self established in the early phase of the encounter, when names are exchanged, is considerably different from the self that asks about a woman's belief in a higher being, or about her sexual relationships. These selves may be in conflict, and the attendant data must be analyzed in that light.

The interview must be seen as a very special relationship, one often freely entered, and one in which information is exchanged. It is commonly assumed that information is more valid if it is freely given and this assumption stresses

the voluntary character of the interview as a relationship freely and willingly entered into by the respondent; it suggests a certain promissory or contractual element. But if the interview is thought of as a kind of implicit contract between the two parties, it is obvious that the interviewer gains the respondent's time, attention and whatever information he has to offer, but what the respondent gets is less apparent [Benney and Hughes, 1956, p. 139].

There are two additional aspects of this relationship that warrant discussion. First, this is a relationship between two persons who meet as strangers and, except for the life of their encounter, remain strangers. There is nothing intrinsic in this fleeting relationship that will force the respondent to behave as he is supposed to. Observers have it on faith that respondents are telling the truth, that their opinions are well thought out, and that they are sincere. Yet encounters with strangers challenge these assumptions. Indeed, as Simmel (1950) has suggested, such relationships are often characterized by a strong sense of alienation, and fiction. A participant can fabricate "tales of self" that belie the actual facts, and the other party lacks objective evidence to counter such tales. If the probability of future encounters is low, which is usually the case with interviews, the problem is amplified. Interviewers may not be able to penetrate private worlds of experience in such encounters. (This would be especially so with tightly structured interview schedules.)

Second, because interviewers are often forced to try to penetrate private worlds of experience—worlds characterized by a great deal of emotion and affect—a constant interactional tension is likely to be present in the encounter. The interviewer must encourage the expression of affect, not suppress it. If the fiction of equality and open exchange of information cannot be maintained, then the respondent is less likely to express attitudes on emotional issues.

It is these two features of the interview relationship that give it a volatile and emergent nature. Suddenly when questions become personal the respondent may "break off" and force the interviewer to leave. Or, even worse, "flooding out" or embarrassment may occur (Goffman, 1961). The respondent comes to a question that raises long-forgotten or even repressed attitudes, and finds that he cannot go on, and the interviewer may be ill-equipped to move on to other topics, or even to control the sudden appearance of affect. The life of the fleeting relationship drains away, and the interviewer leaves with an incomplete schedule.

This brings us back to the subject and his motivation. Benney and Hughes (1956, p. 140) suggest that the motives for participation in interviews are diverse, and I would add that this diversity contributes to a certain lack of comparability between all interviews. Some respondents talk for the sake of self-expression in a relatively free atmosphere, as they might to their lawyer, physician, or psychiatrist. No reprisal is forthcoming, and so statements can go unmonitored. Others talk for money (this is not uncommon in many studies). Yet the interview remains a medium of self-expression between two parties, a medium where one listens and the other talks.

In this sense, then, the interview is an understanding between the two parties that, in return, for allowing the interviewer to direct their communication, the informant is assured that he will not meet with denial, contradiction, competition, or other harassment (Benney and Hughes, 1956, p. 140).

A degree of muted equality permeates the interview. Even if the interviewer feels superior to the respondent he must not express it; the transaction must be seen as equal. Yet this sense of perfect equality seldom fits any interview. High-status respondents may, as Benney and Hughes (1956, p. 140) suggest, talk past the interviewer (whom they view as lower-status) to a study director, or a total discipline. And interviewers who contact lower-class persons may either force their morality upon the respondent, or talk down to him. Thus if the fiction of equality is to be realized, a fit in backgrounds and status between interviewer and subject must be maximized. If it is not, the investigator runs the risk of having his interviews conducted between selves talking past one another.

The problem of equality suggests that the interaction between an interviewer and subject may itself create sources of invalidity. Yet most if not all standardized interviews rest on what Benney and Hughes call the "convention of comparability":

> Regarded as an information-gathering tool, the interview is designed to minimize the local, concrete, immediate circumstances of the particular encounter—including the respective personalities of the participants—and to emphasize only those aspects that can be kept general enough and demonstrable enough to be counted. As an encounter between these two people the typical interview has no meaning; it is conceived in a framework of other, comparable meetings between other couples, each recorded in such fashion that elements of communication in common can be easily isolated from more idiosyncratic qualities. However vaguely this is conceived by the actual participants, it is the needs of the statistician rather than of the people involved directly that determine much, not only the content of communication but its form as well [1956, p. 141].

This assumption justifies the use of standardized interviews, yet it ignores the interactional features of the interview encounter. If selves are multiply defined, if meaning is not consensual, and if the fiction of equality cannot be maintained, then the assumption of comparability is better seen as a hypothesis to be tested than as an assumption accepted on *a priori* grounds.

The situations of interviewing must also be treated as potential sources of invalidity. Just as selves are defined through the process of interaction, and the interpretation of rules, so too are situations. It is the combination of selves and rules that give situations their definition and it may be assumed that few interviews occur in situations defined in exactly the same manner. Indeed, situations within the same class—such as homes, or offices, or laboratories—seldom share precisely the same interpretations. If it could be assumed that interviews always occurred within the same class of situations, the problem would be somewhat reduced. That is, the normative standards for behaving in homes, offices, or laboratories could be examined. Few studies succeed in locating interviews within the same situational class. Indeed, interviews may range from household settings to automobiles, to the steps of a building, to jail cells, and so on. This raises the problem of between-class situational variance, and if the presence of divergent selves is added to the picture, it becomes difficult to justify the convention of comparability across interviews. I see no suitable solution to the problem other than the systematic recording by interviewers of their situations of observation. This at least gives other investigators some basis for evaluation and replication.

The act of making an observation must also be treated. It is axiomatic, I believe, that the process of interaction creates attitudes and behaviors that did not exist before the interaction. Or, if new attitudes are not created, old attitudes are reshaped. Applied to the interview, this suggests that all observations have some reactive effect on what is being observed (Webb, et al., 1966). In Chapter 5 this was termed the reactive effect of measurement. It suggests that respondents may change attitudes, or even develop new ones, simply because they are being interviewed.

The reactive effects of observations raises the problem of demand characteristic effects within the interview (see Orne, 1962, pp. 776–83), and suggests once again that the respective selves of interviewer and respondent cannot be ignored. That is, the knowledge that one is being observed, or interviewed, leads to a deliberate monitoring of the self so that only certain selves are presented. Because many interviews convey implicit demands to the respondent (e.g., social desirability) there is often an attempt to present a self that meets these demands. This has the potential of creating a built-in, self-fulfilling prophecy within the interview: the subject may tell the interviewer what he thinks the interviewer wants to hear.

It is possible also to speak of reverse-demand characteristic effects within the interview situation: Interviewers may develop their own interpretation of the research instrument and attempt to convey that interpretation to the subject. This often occurs among interviewers who want either to please their study director, or confirm his major hypotheses. By so doing, they destroy whatever reliability and validity an instrument has.

It becomes necessary, then, to strive for a close fit between the selves of the interviewer and the subject. Ideally, this fit will involve focused interaction around the main themes of the interview schedule. The difficulty of achieving this fit derives from the fact that interviewers and subjects are able to enact a wide variety of roles at a moment's notice, ranging perhaps from husband, to student, parent, intellectual, sociologist, enemy, and even interviewer or respondent. The following excerpt is from my field notes in the mental patient study. Interviewers were instructed to force the respondent into the role of either pre-patient, in-patient, or ex-patient. The fact that I, at least, was frequently unsuccessful in this attempt is illustrated by this excerpt.

I entered Mr. and Mrs._____second-story apartment at 6:30 P.M. to interview Mr._____. I had contacted his wife earlier to set up the appointment and at that time she expressed extreme reluctance in having her husband (who had been hospitalized for acute alcoholism) interviewed by anyone, let alone a sociologist. I was successful in establishing an appointment and when I arrived they were still seated at the supper table, Mr._____ having just finished a bottle of beer. When I entered he immediately offered me a drink and insisted I join them at the table. It was some ten minutes later before I successfully established my identity as an interviewer and had communicated to him my desire to interview him about his hospital experiences. At this point in our encounter he had cast me in the role of the sympathetic listener and was presenting to me the role of factory worker. When the interview began he denied his hospital experiences and challenged me for knowing that he had been treated. I was finally able, after again proving my status and my intent, to get him to begin answering my questions as an ex-patient from_____ hospital. When the interview was complete he immediately again offered me a drink and returned to our initial conversation at the supper table.

This summary suggests the problematic interactional nature of the interview and points to the fact that the interviewer may have trouble forcing the respondent to present the role and view of self upon which the entire interview schedule is based. Success in this endeavor will, of course, vary by characteristics of the respondent and interviewer. Those respondents who have been interviewed before, or who are familiar with the specific intent of the interview, are more likely to meet these demands.

Frequently the term *rapport* is employed to describe the degree to which interviewers and respondents are able to accurately take one another's role. Kuhn suggests:

Rapport is probably by no means the intangible, mysterious thing it has been characterized as being. It involves, at the bottom, simply the sharing of a common language, so that through shared frames of reference each person in what he has to say, or in each posture he takes, calls out in himself, incipiently, the response that those gestures, postures and symbols call out in the other [1962, p. 201].

Rapport varies by class background, perceived social status, degree of consensual meaning conveyed by the interview, perceptions of the interview situation, and interpretations given the respective roles of interviewer and respondent. The closer the fit between these dimensions, the greater the rapport.

Rapport can work to the disadvantage of the interviewer, however. Miller (1954, pp. 97–99) has reported a study in which over-rapport between himself and members of a local union leadership hampered his ability to be both objective and to obtain certain types of data. He comments:

Many personal things were told to me in a friend-to-friend relationship;

undoubtedly I gained information because of this relationship which would not have been available to me in any other way.

On the other hand, once I had developed a close friendship to the union leaders I was committed to continuing it, and some penetrating lines of inquiry had to be dropped. . . . Friendship connotes an all-accepting attitude; to probe beneath the surface of long-believed values would break the friend-to-friend relationship. It may also be that development of a friend-to-friend relationship between the leaders and the participant observer was a means used by the former to limit the observer's investigations and criticisms. In a sense, the observer may be co-opted into friendship, a situation which may have prevailed in some studies of management-worker interaction [1954, p. 98].

Miller's second problem was that he became so attuned to the feelings and perceptions of the union leaders that he deemphasized the sentiments of the rank and file members.

Strictly speaking, Miller's observations go beyond the interview situation, for his problems developed in a long-term participant observation study. They do indicate, however, that rapport can be developed too far; the observer must be on guard against cooptation and loss of objectivity.

The problems of over-rapport, and reverse-demand characteristic effects point to what I believe must be present in every observational act—a profound sense of self-cynicism. The observer can never take himself and his own actions for granted, or too seriously. The possibilities of being taken in, duped, or lied to are ever present, as is the potential for thinking that one fully understands the problem, or interview, under analysis.

## The Interview as Interaction: A Summary

Thus far I have suggested that the interview must be seen as a special form of face to face interaction, subject to very peculiar problems because of the lack of consensus surrounding the roles of interviewer and respondent. Sources of invalidity arise from this lack, from variations in the presentation of self, and from differing interpretations of interactional rules.

These difficulties are not unique—interaction seldom flows on the basis of complete consensus. This, of course, means that any interactional experience will be variable, subject to change and perhaps misinterpretation. The process of establishing meaning and purpose in the interview situation involves the following (Strauss, 1959, p. 59): First, each party must determine what the other's purpose in the situation is. Clearly, the interviewer should communicate his intent to interview, but what should the respondent indicate? Second, both must determine how the other defines the situation. Is the interviewee friendly? Is he willing to be interviewed? Will he refuse? What *will* he do and how does he define the situation? Third, each person must ascertain how the other is responding to him—in short, he has to identify the other's view of self as well as the self the other is imputing to him. Does he think I am friendly? Does he trust me? Does he like me? What does he feel and think about me?

These questions (identification of purpose, definition of self, and definition of other) must be resolved by all persons when they engage in interaction. Strauss and Schatzman (1955, pp. 28–31) have shown that the status of the respondent influences interview encounters. Lower-class persons are more likely to misperceive the intent of the interview, to wander during the course of the interview, and to give indirect answers to questions. Middle-class persons, on the other hand, are readily able to define the role of interviewer and interviewee, and quite often readily conform to the demands of the interview.

Basic to the communication of interviewer meaning is the problem of appearance and mood (Stone, 1962, pp. 88–93). Clothes often tell more about a person than his conversation and, in the interview, it is necessary for the interviewer immediately to establish his intent and purpose. In our study of the mental patient, all female interviewers were instructed to dress in the style of the average middle-class female (e.g., heels, skirt or dress, hair well combed, etc.); males were told to wear suits, ties, white shirt, etc. The intent was to have each interviewer communicate immediately to those being interviewed that he was not lower-class but a professional interviewer, skilled in his job. This strategy worked well with nearly all respondents except those from the extreme lower class, who resented the neat appearance. The choice of style of dress, as a prerequisite for establishing meaning and purpose in the interview, is illustrated in the following excerpt—journalists of *Time* magazine had been instructed to interview members of the "hippie" subculture:

Most members of *Time* staff consider themselves reasonably hip, but writing and reporting the hippie cover presented problems. One involved clothes. To put her subjects at ease during interviews, Researcher _____ decided to disguise herself as a hippie wearing, in various combinations, faded old Nebraska Levi's, a red miniskirt and an unwashed London Fog raincoat. . . . Another correspondent managed to get by in ordinary sports clothes, but he found reporting difficult [*Time*, 1967, p. 11].

This offers a basic dictum of the interviewer: dress in the mode of dress most acceptable to those being interviewed but employ a style that communicates who *you* are with respect to *them*.

Gestures also play an important role in the interview. The shrug, the smile, the use of the cigarette, and the handshake are cues that may contribute as much to the communication of purpose as appearance (Stone, 1962, pp. 88–93). In an interview of an upper-class ex-mental patient, I quickly learned the important role of the gesture and the handling of "body equipment." Approaching the interview with a great deal of nervousness, I was directed to her living room, which was expensively furnished, and at once violated the first role of propriety by lighting a cigarette—no ashtrays were present. This caused a feeling of uneasiness, especially since the respondent did not want to be interviewed in the first place. I next dropped my cigarette and spilled the drink I had been given, both on the respondent's expensive coffee table. The woman nearly refused to begin the interview.

The next important aspect of the interview encounter is conversation. Goffman (1957, pp. 47–60) has argued that when persons are in one another's presence, they are obligated to demonstrate a sense of involvement in and commitment to the task at hand. In the interview, the task at hand is a conversation in which one person asks questions, the other responds to them. But what about the woman who insists on fixing dinner or feeding her child during the course of the interview? These represent, from the interviewer's perspective, illegitimate involvement activities that detract from the dominant activity—the interview. The respondent may deliberately, or unconsciously, choose to alienate himself from the on-going interaction, thus communicating his disinterest and noninvolvement. The housewife feeding her child is one example, the casual offer of a cup of coffee is another, for here again the respondent can direct activities away from the interview.

Extreme self-consciousness with one's own stream of interaction represents another activity that can detract from the interview. The respondent who asks, "Am I answering your questions right?" or the housewife who focuses on her sex life at the expense of other interview items are examples. Another respondent tactic is that of bringing into the interview small talk about affairs that have no relationship to the interview. Many respondents will turn the interview into a confession of their problems simply because they have a sympathetic listener.

All of these dimensions of the interview serve to give it a variable and, at times, zigzag career. The respondent will begin the interview, be interrupted, and never return with the vigor of his initial involvement. Add to this the fact that each person is continuously presenting different social selves and the researcher has a situation which, at best, challenges the information elicited from the interview schedule.

### Strategies of Interviewing

If the interview is accepted as a basic tool of the social sciences—as a tool that implements the measurement act—strategies for resolving the validity issue must be considered. The essential features of the interview have been discussed. It is a special type of social relationship that rests on multiple selves, and flows through the process of conversation. It is the conversational feature of the interview that creates special problems. That is, while the interviewer is the expert in asking the questions, the respondent is the expert as far as answers are concerned. The two interactors enter the encounter with different perspectives. Because they do, the interview is not a conversation in the usual sense. Normal conversations give each interactor freedom to choose topics and to range widely in his discussion; interview conversations violate both of these assumptions. The respondent is not free to choose what will be discussed, nor is he free to carry a topic through to completion; the interviewer controls what will be discussed.

This raises special problems for the interviewer for the respondent may not talk, may refuse to stay within the boundaries of the interview, or may be so abstract as to avoid specific questions. Certain strategies can be employed to overcome these problems, however. Silent respondents can be jogged out of their reserve by remarks that openly challenge the respondent's self, or that contradict his known perspectives. If the respondent has any sense of self-esteem, such statements will force open, and perhaps prevent hostile, interaction. Once the respondent is forced to talk, he can then be led back to the interview. Another strategy is to employ small talk to make the respondent feel more at ease. Thus questions about family, job, home, or hobbies can be offered that take respondents back to their home territories of interaction.

Respondents who wander can be brought back with statements concerning the interviewer's demands. Constraints of time can be mentioned, or laudatory remarks concerning the respondent's breadth of perspective can be made. The interviewer can suggest that the respondent's experiences are so varied and interesting that another interview should be scheduled, but at the moment some very pressing questions must be answered. In this case, polite rules of etiquette are employed to bring another into line.

Respondents who speak in abstractions can be brought to specifics by "playing dumb," the interviewer either contradicting a position of the respondent or acting like a novice. Because all persons tend to consider themselves experts on highly valued activities, most respondents will delight in elaborating an abstract point. If the interviewer remembers that he is engaging in a certain type of encounter, he can bring his conversational experiences from the past to bear upon the interview at hand. Such an awareness, if self-consciously directed, can increase the validity of interview interactions.

I have argued that the interview is a peculiar type of human interaction because it represents the coming together of two persons who are strangers. This gives the interviewer the large task of taking control of the situation and defining it so that the questions he has will be answered by the time he departs. While I am fully aware that interviews take place every day between strangers, and further realize that those directing these interviews are by and large satisfied with their results, I wish to call attention to the tremendous variability in the interview situation. If, as Benney and Hughes (1956) argue, sociology is the science of the interview, then I suggest that sociologists as yet know very little about it. I have no firm solutions to the problems raised in this chapter, but I suggest that persons employing the interview be alert to them.

## Notes

There are several excellent sources on interviewing and interview construction; these include the entire issue of the *American Journal of Sociology*, 62 (September, 1956) edited by Mark Benney and Everett C. Hughes. Kahn and Cannell's *The Dynamics of Interviewing* (1962) reviews interview strategies, and Richardson, Dohrenwend, and Klein's *Interviewing: Its Forms and Functions* (1965) provides data on interviewer and respondent effects. Hyman's *Interviewing in Social Research* (1954) offers an earlier, but useful analysis and review of the same problems treated by Richardson, Dohrenwend, and Klein.

Peter Manning's (1967) article, "Problems in Interpreting Interview Data," reviews many of the interactional contingencies in the interview and provides a useful supplement to Kuhn's (1962, pp. 193–206) "The Interview and the Professional Relationship" and Benney and Hughes' (1962, 137–42) "Of Sociology and Interview." These three pieces offer an excellent interactionist perspective.

More recently the interactionist view of interviewing has been supplemented by work of ethnomethodologists. Cicourel, for example, (1964, 1967) has criticized the assumptions underlying standardized interview schedules because of the implicit assumption that meaning is easily conveyed.

A critique of interviewing as the major tool of social scientists is provided by Webb, *et al.* (1966), who call for greater triangulation of research techniques, as well as for more use of unobtrusive methods. This argument will be amplified in Chapters 11 and 12.

Part III
# Theory to Method: Research Strategies

# 7

# The Experiment and its Variations

Experimental results have no built-in validity. This means that some of the disdain with which psychological researchers customarily treat data obtained by sociologists and anthropologists working in the field is inappropriate. It might be profitably replaced by the study and application of their considerable literature on participant-observation methodology. For, whereas the ideal psychological experimenter is an immaculate perceiver of an objective reality, the real psychological experimenter is, to a far greater extent than he has expected, very much like his counterparts in the other social sciences. He too is a *participant observer.*

*Neil J. Friedman,* 1967, p. 179.

In a fundamental sense the experiment is the point of departure for all other methods. It offers the most rigorous solution to the causality problem because the investigator can directly control the three features of the causal proposition: time order between variables, covariance, and the exclusion of rival causal factors. The other four methods—the social survey, participant observation, life histories, and unobtrusive measures—are situations of decreasing control over these factors and are better seen as strategies of analysis.

## The Causality Problem: Alternative Models

In Chapter 1 it was stated that the sociologist has three means of resolving the causality problem: the experimental model, multivariate analysis, and analytic induction. Each of these has come to be associated with particular methods, especially analytic induction, which provides the basic model of inference for participant observation and life histories. Similarly, multivariate analysis is most commonly employed with the survey method and unobtrusive observations.

The strength of a research method is a function of its model of proof. Each model of proof has strengths and weaknesses, and its best use will always require a sensitive ability to apply it. Every research method must permit the investigator to forge a three-way link between covariance, time order, and rival causal factors, or his resultant proposition will be unsatisfactory. A causal proposition is always a tentative formulation, one subject to disconfirmation by future observations or by the failure of any one of its components to withstand empirical test (see Hirschi and Selvin, 1967). The sociologist must infer the existence of a causal relationship, since it is seldom (if ever) possible to demonstrate that one variable or event will invariantly cause changes in another. For this reason, the analyst must give careful consideration to alternative causal conditions, to *test variables*. They can logically occur before the primary independent variable, in which case they are antecedent, or they may be contingent and occur either after the independent variable or simultaneously with the independent and dependent variables.

Test variables may also be classified in terms of their intrinsic or extrinsic nature. *Intrinsic test variables* are events present in the act of research; *extrinsic test variables* represent alternative substantive events that could be causing the observed variations. For example, both education and class background can determine patterns of upward social mobility, but neither may be factors intrinsic to the research process. By such factors I refer to Campbell's (1957) analysis of internal validity, which includes reactive effects of observation, changes in the measuring instrument, and changes in the subject. Intrinsic test factors are events that reside in the observational act. From an interactionist perspective they may be seen as falling into the following categories: features of the observer, including how he presents himself, and how he interprets his research task; aspects of the subject, which parallel the features of the observer; situational variations in the observational act (how the unique aspects of the concrete interview, experimental, or observational setting can influence the nature of the data); the interaction between the observer, the subject, and the situation that can produce jeopardizing data for the causal proposition—that is, the observer and subject may create situationally specific interpretations of the research problem that preclude comparisons with any other set of observations, and if this occurs, each observational act becomes unique (the extent of this uniqueness must be treated as a rival test factor). Extrinsic and intrinsic test factors may either destroy a causal relationship between two variables, in which case they make that relationship spurious, or they may have a contributory effect. That is, their presence may increase or decrease the magnitude of the relationship between an independent and dependent variable. Determining the nature of this effect will be termed specification of a causal relationship (see Lazarsfeld, 1955, pp. 115–25).

There may be specification by either an intrinsic or extrinsic test variable, making it possible to speak, then, of intrinsic and extrinsic specification. This is similarly the case with the spurious relationship, which can be produced by either intrinsic or extrinsic factors. The most damaging attack to a causal proposition is to show spuriousness by intrinsic factors, or intrinsic specification. That is, if a causal relationship is destroyed because of variations in the observational act, the investigator has failed to control his own reactivity and generalizations become impossible because the substantive-extrinsic nature of the causal proposition is now contingent on the research act, and no claim for substantive causality can be made—another reason for triangulating research methods. If one method is overly reactive, a non-obtrusive strategy can be employed to test the relationship between extrinsic variables.

*Alternative Solutions to the Causality Problem*

In its generic form the experiment represents a situation in which the investigator controls some variables while he manipulates the effects of others. This permits him to observe the effects of the manipulated variables upon the dependent variable in a situation where the effect of other relevant factors is believed to have been removed, typically by randomization. The generic experiment may be diagramed thus:

**The Pre-Test—Post-Test One Control Group Design**

|  | Observed | Exposed to Independent Variable | Observed |
|---|---|---|---|
| Experimental Group | *Yes* | *Yes* | *Yes* |
| Control Group | *Yes* | *No* | *Yes* |

This design involves two sets of measurements, one before and one after exposure to the independent variable. Two groups are observed, one exposed to the independent variable and one not exposed. The differences between the scores of the two groups at time two (second measurement) can be attributed to the independent variable if other factors are controlled. In this way evidence relevant to the causal hypothesis is directly gathered. Concomitant variation is established by examining the scores of the subjects in the experimental group; time order between the dependent and independent is established with the first measurement. Both groups should score the same, because neither has yet been exposed to the experimental treatment. In order to insure that no differences exist between the experimental and control groups before the experimental treatment, the typical strategy is to randomly assign subjects to one or another of the two groups. It will be remembered from the discussion in Chapter 4 that randomization serves to distribute any differences between subjects normally, so that valid comparisons can be made. Randomization is an essential feature of experimental design simply because the investigator can neither know nor adequately control all the relevant factors that could influence his causal analysis (Camilleri, 1962, p. 173).

The problem of alternative causal factors cannot be ignored, however, simply because randomization has been employed, since if the same observer and same set of subjects are employed throughout the experiment, changes they undergo may produce the differences observed between the first and last measurement. Thus maturation, instrument change, and subject-observer interaction can emerge as jeopardizing, intrinsic test factors. Randomization offers a basic strategy for controlling the effect of alternative extrinsic test factors, but it cannot directly control the effect of intrinsic variables, events that arise from the observation process. Their effects can be partially controlled by random selection of observers at time one and time two, but the same set of subjects will typically have to be employed at both times. (Designs that minimize the effects of intrinsic variables will be discussed later.)

A simple logic underlies the experimental model. The experimental group is constructed in terms of the method of agreement that assumes:

When two or more cases of a given phenomenon have one and only one condition in common, that condition may be regarded as the cause (or effect) of the phenomenon. More simply, if we can make observation Z in every case that we find condition C, we can conclude that they are causally related [Goode and Hatt, 1952, p. 74].

The negative canon of agreement provides the logic for the control group. It states:

When condition non-C is found to be associated with observation non-Z, we may assert a causal relationship between C and Z. An example would be: Lack of social experience with ethnic stereotypes in childhood is followed by lack of ethnic prejudice in adulthood. In general this proposition, whether accurate or not, states that whenever, throughout all variations of other factors, an absence of factor C is associated with an absence of Z, it is possible to accept a causal relationship between C and Z [Goode and Hatt, 1952, pp. 75–76].

The classical experimental design (outlined above) contains two observational groups observed at two points in time. The logic for this combination is termed the method of difference:

If there are two or more cases, and in one of them observation Z can be made, while in the other it cannot; and if factor C occurs when observation Z is made, and does not occur when observation Z is made; then it can be asserted that there is a causal relationship between C and Z [Goode and Hatt, 1952, p. 76].

The control group represents the combination of non-C and non-Z, while the experimental group represents the combination of C and Z. The logic is clear—a relationship cannot be established between two variables if they do not occur together.

The experimental model has certain weaknesses that are partially overcome with the use of randomization, but the method of agreement provides no evidence that other factors could not have caused the variations observed; it only provides a basis of inferring such a conclusion. Another problem is that the dependent variable may have been causing the independent variable. The method of agreement cannot clearly refute this claim, although if the first observation contains measurements on both variables, this could be established.

This is the underlying logic of the experimental model. The multivariate-survey model attempts to simulate as nearly as possible this strategy, but unfortunately the investigator cannot control the relationship between his independent and dependent variables—simply because he is making observations in a natural setting where control is not possible. His strategy is to construct after-the-fact comparison groups that parallel experimental and control groups. Because two sets of observations are typically not possible, the ability to determine the time order between variables is more difficult. Consequently, greater attention is given to extrinsic test factors. Multivariate analysis becomes a method of sorting out causal relationships—it is not a method of directly controlling causal relationships.

Analytic induction is the third model of causal inference (Chapter 9 treats this). It differs from the above models in the following ways: first, events are studied over time in a natural setting; second, repeated observations are made, often extending over a lengthy period of time; third, explicit attention is given to negative cases—that is, to cases that disconfirm the hypotheses guiding the investigation, the attempt being to formulate hypotheses that have as universal a relevance as possible. In this sense analytic induction pushes the issue of causal inference to its logical extreme: The investigator hopes to conclude with a set of propositions that explains every case he has examined.

Each of the three major strategies of constructing a causal hypothesis gives central attention to rival causal factors; each varies in its ability to control those factors. The experimental model, because of its built-in control, represents the most rigorous approach.

## Experimental Designs

As noted earlier, the true experimental design contains at least one control and one experimental group. Two sets of observations are made, and most typically subjects are randomly assigned to the observational groups. It is possible to classify experimental designs into three groups. Those that fail to meet one or more of the above characteristics are nonexperimental. Designs in this category would include situations with no control groups; those with no before observations; and those which fail to place subjects randomly. These will be treated in Chapter 8, as will the second major category of designs—the quasi-experimental formulations. Quasi-experiments conform to the survey model of research where repeated observations are often made under conditions of decreasing observer control.

Two basic variations on the true experimental design can be noted. The first is the Solomon four-group design. This represents the addition of more than one control group to the pre-test-post-test design. Its analysis will indicate the logic of employing more than one control group in any experimental design. It may be diagramed thus:

### The Solomon Four-Group Design

|                        | Observed | Exposed to Independent Variable | Observed |
| ---------------------- | -------- | ------------------------------- | -------- |
| Experimental Group 1   | *Yes*    | *Yes*                           | *Yes*    |
| Control Group 1        | *Yes*    | *No*                            | *Yes*    |
| Experimental Group 2   | *No*     | *Yes*                           | *Yes*    |
| Control Group 2        | *No*     | *No*                            | *Yes*    |

The first two groups parallel the traditional pre-test-post-test one-control group design. The addition of the second control group allows the investigator to assess the reactive effects of the first measurement, as well as the effect of nonexposure to the experimental treatment. The second experimental group provides assessment of exposure to the first measurement upon a group that has received the experimental treatment.

The Solomon four-group design represents the purest of the experimental models. By stripping away, in a design fashion, as many of the possible threats to internal validity as possible, it permits the most accurate inference of causality. The investigator can directly answer the problem of temporal order between his independent and dependent variables by examining each control group in comparison with the experimental group. The exclusion of rival threats to internal validity is solved by the additional groups, and covariance of variables is solved by the before-after measurements on the first experimental group.

While I have defined a true experiment as one in which before and after measurements are taken, after measurements on randomly assigned groups will often suffice as a control for the before observation. This is the solution proposed by the *post-test-only control group design*. Often it is not possible to take before measurements on the subjects under analysis. While this design offers no data on what the before attitudes were, the fact that subjects are randomly assigned assures that whatever differences did exist were distributed between the two groups in a random fashion. The factor of reactivity of initial measurements is removed, as are the problems of history, maturation, subject bias, differential subject mortality, and changes in the measurement instrument or the experimenter. These factors become irrelevant because initial measurements are not taken—thus removing the time period over which such factors as history, maturation, and experimenter variations could occur. Also, the factor of randomization removes the possibility of initial subject bias.

This design combines certain of the strengths of the *before-after one-control group design* and the Solomon four-group design, its use is recommended only when they cannot be employed. The investigator must still be sensitive to the fact that there is no substitute for before measures when the true and complete effects of experimental treatments are to be determined —still, this design provides the minimal information on causal inference. The time order on variables can be determined by comparing the experimental and control groups. Covariance of variables should appear in the experimental treatment group, and the exclusion of other rival causal factors is minimized because of randomization and the use of two groups.

## Steps in Experimental Design

The first step in designing an experiment is the development of a set of theoretically significant expectations. There must be some reason for conducting an experiment and that reason must be theoretical. A conception of theory that produces hypotheses to be tested resolves the second step, which is determining the actual form of the experiment. A design will be selected, and experimental and control group variations will be developed. The theory will also specify the third step—selection of a population from which a sample will be drawn. The sample should be statistically rigorous and theoretically guided. If it is not, inferences to the broader population will be restricted, as will any theoretical analysis. Fourth, a procedure for randomly assigning subjects to the observational groups must be employed. Fifth, techniques for obtaining before and after measurements must be developed.

Last, given the resolution of above conditions, the actual execution of the experiment follows. In this phase, the experiment will be conceived as a series of encounters between experimenter and subject. Introductions will have to be made, a setting for the experiment will have to be selected, and a scheduling of subjects for the experiment made. Such interactional considerations as style of dress, mode of conversation, and experimenter-subject conduct must be considered, since the experiment represents the coming together of persons with diverse backgrounds, interests and expectations. The ensuing interactions represent attempts to develop consensual meaning regarding the experimental task. The job of the experimenter is to create consensus, and this leads to the consideration of interaction in the social experiment.

## On the Social Psychology of Experiments

Conduct in the experimental setting represents a blend of that behavior Goffman (1963) has termed "behavior in public places," with a very special form of dyadic interaction subject to its own rules of etiquette and propriety. Recent research by Rosenthal (1966), Friedman (1967), and Orne (1962) suggests that interaction in this context is influenced by the nature of eye contact between subject and experimenter, the mode of dress of the experimenter, and the definitions subject and observer bring into the situation.

Orne (1962) has pointed to what he terms the demand characteristic effects of experiment, referring to the fact that subjects cannot be viewed as passive objects upon whom the experimenter performs some operation and then observes the outcome. Orne notes that experimental subjects will perform tasks such as the following for more than five hours:

One task was to perform serial additions of each adjacent two numbers on sheets filled with rows of random digits. In order to complete just one sheet, the subject would be required to perform 224 additions! A stack of some 2,000 sheets was presented to each subject—clearly an impossible task to complete. After the instructions were given, the subject was deprived of his watch and told, "Continue to work; I will return eventually." Five and one-half hours later, the *experimenter* gave up! In general subjects tended to continue this task for several hours, usually with little decrement in performance [1962, p. 777].

In an attempt to find a task the subjects would refuse to do, Orne increased the difficulty of the instructions. Subjects were instructed to compute additions for one page, tear that page up, take a set of instructions from a large pile (which also told them to do the same task), all as rapidly as possible. Again subjects persisted in the assignment. Explanations of this conduct emerged in a post-experimental inquiry period. Subjects invariably interpreted their performance as a meaningful part of an experiment on subject endurance, indicating that entry into the experimental setting may have effects manifestly different from those intended by the experimenter. In fact the latent consequences of such interpretations indicate that an experiment can easily get out of hand. Subjects may have their own interpretations of the encounter and proceed in a manner quite divergent from that intended by the experimenter. Regardless of the direction this interaction takes, however, it is clear that a subject's conduct has reference only in the context of an interpretation that calls for him to "take part in an experiment."

Given the norms of the average experimental subject (e.g., the college sophomore), taking part in an experiment typically represents a belief that the experiment will contribute to science and perhaps to human welfare in general. It appears that regardless of the motive for participation, (e.g., a course assignment, money) both subject and experimenter share the belief that the experimental assignment is important (Orne, 1962, p. 778). Given his belief, it is not unusual to hear subjects asking experimenters: "How did I do?" or "Did I ruin anything?" The norm of the subject role is to be a good subject; to be a good subject demands that one interpret ambiguous meanings and assignments in a context that values participation.

It is appropriate, then, to view behavior in an experiment as problem-solving behavior. The subject attempts to determine what the experimenter is up to and performs in a way that will best satisfy this interpretation. If he interprets the assignment as one in which his attitudes are supposed to change (e.g., the typical before-after design), then he may see to it that his attitudes *do* change—and change in the way he thinks they are supposed to [See Sherman, 1967]. It is in this context that Orne posits the assumption that subject's behavior in any experimental situation "will be determined by two sets of variables: (a) those which are traditionally defined as experimental variables and (b) the perceived demand characteristics of the experimental situation [1962, p. 779]." The extent to which an experiment can be replicated is contingent upon the degree that the subject's behavior is determined by demand characteristics, and not by experimental variables. The greater the influence of demand characteristics, the less the generalizability and the less likely replication can occur.

*Solutions to the Problem of Demand Characteristics*

Orne suggests that demand characteristics can never be removed from the experimental setting. It is an empirical question as to with what kinds of experimental settings, and with what kinds of subjects, this variable becomes important. It is plausible, for example, that in those experimental settings where subject instructions are unclear and highly ambiguous the direction that subject behavior will take will also be unclear. On the other hand, if instructions are quite explicit, subjects are more likely to be consensual in their interpretations of the demand characteristics, thus at least reducing the number and diversity of misinterpretations of the actual intent (Orne, 1962, p. 780).

It is clear, then, that experimenters must be sensitized to this feature of the experiment and take steps to ascertain the diverse meanings subjects impute to the situation. Orne suggests the possibility of post-experimental inquiry wherein subjects are asked an open-ended question such as "What did you think this experiment was about?" Another strategy is to present subjects with the instructions of an experiment and then, before they have been exposed to the actual experiment, ask them questions "as if they had been subjects." The experimenter might ask: "If I had asked you to do all these things, what do you think the experiment would be about?" or "What would you have done?" These questions could then be given to a random sample of subjects in a pre-experimental inquiry period and on the basis of their responses an experiment could be designed that took their interpretations into account—only now on a new pool of subjects. The investigator should be aware, as Orne cautions, that even pre- and post-experimental inquiry sessions have their own demand effect characteristics; therefore, it is suggested that an investigator not acquainted or associated with the actual experiment conduct the sessions.

## Phases of the Experiment

Friedman (1967, p. 40) has shown that experimenter-subject interaction falls naturally into three phases: a face-sheet phase, an instructions phase, and the data collection phase. It is appropriate to argue that the demand characteristics of the experiment will vary in each phase. The face-sheet phase consists of prefatory introductions between subjects and experimenter, as well as attempts by the experimenter to collect certain standardized information from subjects such as age, marital status, major in college, or other salient personal and social characteristics. Friedman has shown quite conclusively that the stance taken by the experimenter in this phase influences subsequent reactions of the subject. This phase consists, as Friedman argues, of a brief give and take of information, the subject giving and the experimenter taking. The interaction is strictly one-way—the experimenter asks questions and the subject answers. The forms this interaction takes varies from strict, ritualistic curtness, to the extremes of informality. I excerpt the following from Friedman (1967, pp. 80–81) to indicate these two extremes.

*Curtness*

E: (never looking at the subject): Last name?
S: Ashton.
E: First name?
S: Carol.
E: Age?
S: Twenty.
E: Married?
S: No.

*Informality*

E: Have a chair.
S: Thank you.
E: How are you?
S: Fine, thank you.
E: Your name?
S: Joyce Dicholson.
E: Joyce, spell the last, please.
S: D-i-c-h-o-l-s-o-n. It's a Scotch spelling.
E: (looking up at her): Dicholson?
S: Yes, Dicholson.
E: Oh! Dicholson! Uh-huh.
S: Hm-hm.
E: Age?
S: (pause, then coyly): Ah-ah. . . . (E looks up.)
    Thirty-four. (E and S laugh.)
E: Marital status?
S: Single.
E: (who is single too): Single, huh. Major field?

That there is a wide degree of variation between these two ways of beginning an interview cannot be denied. The interest expressed by the second
interviewer in his subject suggests a movement out of the experimenter
role and into a role more closely linked to marital status (e.g., bachelor-
hood). The impact of this informal stance upon the subsequent interactions
of the experiment can only be surmised, but no doubt the second subject
approached the experiment with quite a different definition of the experimenter and the task than did the first.

Friedman also calls attention to the influence of such nonverbal gestures
as smiles, eye conduct, shrugs, and nods in setting an initial mood for subsequent interactions in the experiment. The data indicate that it is misleading to assume all experimenters uniformly present the same self to subjects.
Just as subjects approach the experiment with a conception of its demand
characteristics, so too do experimenters. Some "play by the book" and
refuse to depart from the printed instructions, while others introduce their
own personalities into the encounter—thereby lending their own definitions
of what an experiment is and what an experimenter does. Both experimen-

ters and subjects bring to the first phase of the experiment a variety of definitions and meanings that become translated into the ongoing flow of conduct; the sum of these interpretations and behaviors constitutes the behavior called experimental.

In the instructions period, the give and take between subject and interviewer has presumably ended. The experimenter reads a standard set of instructions and the subject listens. In formulating his experimental design, the experimenter has presumably composed a set of instructions to which all subjects will be exposed before they enter the actual data collection phase of the study. It is this set of instructions that sets the stage for subsequent behavior—in a sense, this is the script for the future performance of experimenter and subject. If the experiment flows as it should, all subjects should receive the same instructions. However, as Friedman (1967, p. 91) observes, two contingencies may arise: experimenters may not read the exact instructions (they may add, omit, or even change words), or it is possible that while the instructions are read as they stand, they are read in a way peculiar to the experimenter (differential emphasis on certain words, slurring over of others, and the use of smiles and winks to emphasize certain phrases).

The last period of the experiment, the task or instrumental (data collection) phase, is also influenced by the interactions and selective presentation of selves by both subject and experimenter. Friedman (1967, p. 47) found support for the following conclusions from his observations of experiments in which subjects were asked to make ratings of the success or failure of persons who had been photographed doing a task: the more glances exchanged between experimenter and subject in the instructions period, the more likely the subject was to perceive success in neutral photos; the greater the number of glances directed by the experimenter to the subject (in all phases), the more likely the subject was to perceive success in neutral photos; the longer the duration of the instructions period, the more likely the subject was to perceive success in the photos; the longer the duration of the data collection phase, the more likely the subject was to perceive success in the photos; the longer the duration of the face-sheet period, the greater the number of perceived successes; and the longer the duration of the experiment, the more perceived successes.

The experiment, then, is a face to face encounter, and simple variations in the temporal sequencing of action can produce significant behavioral differences, as can variations in non-verbal gestures. In this sense, interaction creates its own demand characteristic effect.

## The Experiment as an Encounter

The ideal experiment is one in which subject and experimenter respond exactly as the instructions read. Subjects do what they are told—they do not reinterpret instructions. Experimenters are supposed to act as experimenters and not as persons who have other roles and selves. In the closed interaction of the experiment, subject and experimenter are to assume only those roles dictated by the experimental design.

Of course in actuality experiments do *not* flow as they should. Subjects and experimenters respond in terms of their perceptions of the demand characteristics of the experiment. Each reinterprets, adds to, detracts from, and in general acts in a manner that represents his definition of the situation, and, as I have shown, these definitions may not always conform with those held by the person who has designed the experiment.

The relevant question becomes: "What accounts for experimenter-subject behavior if it is not the instructions on which the experiment is based?" Friedman provides an answer when he argues that the ideal experimenter (and, I add, ideal subject) "is . . . supposed to be a wooden soldier who thoroughly disciplines any nonrelevant role behavior (e.g., smiling at pretty girls) [1967, p. 107]."

But, Goffman warns:

Perhaps there are times when an individual does march up and down like a wooden soldier, tightly rolled up in a particular role. It is true that here and there we can pounce on a moment when an individual sits fully astride a single role, head erect, eyes front, but the next moment the picture is shattered into many pieces and the individual divides into different persons holding the ties of different spheres of life by his hands, by his teeth, and by his grimaces [1961, p. 143].

Applied to the experiment, this analogy suggests the falseness of assuming that subjects and experimenters will respond in uniform manners during the course of an experiment. It is more appropriate to view the experimenter-subject dyad as

a tight little island of social interaction cut off from the mainland of everyday social gatherings, it is an island to which the population of two carries its entire interpersonal repertoire [Friedman, 1967, p. 108].

The experiment is then what Goffman terms an encounter or a face engagement in which

two or more participants in a situation join each other openly in maintaining a single focus of cognitive and visual attention—what is sensed as a single *mutual activity* entailing preferential communication rights. . . . Mutual activities and the face engagements in which they are embedded comprise instances of small talk, commensalism, lovemaking, gaming, formal discussion and personal servicing [1963, p. 89].

There is in the encounter a mutual awareness of the other's ongoing action, an attempt to maintain commitment and involvement, and an attempt to close the encounter to intruders. This is clearly the case with experiments. Each in his own way, experimenter and subject are involved in attempts to maintain (for a moment) that fleeting experience that has been transformed into a social gathering. The experimenter probes, reveals aspects of himself, cajoles the subject, punishes him, and even offers rewards in an attempt to carry out the instructions as he has defined them. Conversely (and simultaneously), the subject is defining these actions, attempting to bring a little bit of himself into the setting, and generally acting in a manner he thinks will make this encounter the best possible for the experimenter. The persons in this setting transform the sheer mechanical instructions of the experiment into a little world that represents (during the length of time they are together) their definitions of what the experiment should be.

## The Relevance and Advantages of the Experiment for Sociology

The discussion of threats to internal validity and the detailed treatment of interaction in the experiment indicate the kinds of problems experimenters must be alert to. But such considerations are not reasons for not conducting experiments. My own position in this respect is that of Campbell and Stanley:

The average student or potential teacher reading the previous section of this chapter probably ends up with more things to worry about in designing an experiment than he had in mind to begin with. This is all to the good if it leads to the design and execution of better experiments and to more circumspection in drawing inferences from results. It is, however, an unwanted side effect if it creates a feeling of hopelessness with regard to achieving experimental control and leads to the abandonment of such efforts in favor of even more informal methods of investigation [1963, p. 34].

The formidable list of threats to validity of the experiment only attests to the large amount of research psychologists have directed to the method. It is incumbent upon sociologists to inquire into the usefulness of the method for their purposes and to assess it against the criteria here presented.

The discussion of the causality problem and the experiment pointed to three factors that must be established before an acceptable causal inference can be made: the establishment of covariation between the independent and dependent variables; proof that the independent variables occurred before the dependent variables; and the exclusion of rival causal hypotheses and variables. The experiment, I argued, has become the model for causal inference from which all other inferential strategies are either derived or to which they are compared. While open to criticisms, the experiment provides one of the best methods that can be employed to answer questions of causal inference. What better way to establish time order between variables than to control the presence of the dependent variable? Further, how more accurately can one show covariance than to control the presence or absence of those variables being observed?

In addition, the experiment provides the one research method that allows the investigator to be both a participant and an observer of the behavior he is studying. By directing his own experiment, he has at his disposal information on such factors as experimental demand characteristics as well as the influence of his own gestures and interpretations on the experiment itself. The data that he collects are typically free from the distortions of memory and recollection that so frequently occur with the survey. Schwartz and Skolnick phrase this as follows:

In the field experiment, it was possible to see behavior directly, i.e., to determine how employees act when confronted with what appears to them to be a realistic opportunity to hire. Responses are therefore not distorted by the memory of the respondent [1962, p. 139].

In the experiment it is possible to remove those filters that too frequently come between observers and that which they observe. The behavior is there to be recorded. The use of tape recorders and films of experimental sessions increases this ability to directly observe that which occurs.

A criticism that has frequently been lodged against the experiment is that of its artificiality (see Drabek and Haas, 1967, pp. 337–46). It is held that because real life does not occur in the experimental setting, important sociological issues cannot be brought there for analysis. But as an interactional situation the experiment represents a closed behavioral setting, a setting from which certain persons are restricted entry, and further a setting in which only certain kinds of conduct are permitted. This suggests that the dynamics of face to face interaction as they occur in such a situation could become the focus of serious sociological analysis. Within this situation the investigator can observe the transformation of a four-walled room into a setting for meaningful social conduct. The mechanisms by which selves are defined, projected, and alienated from one another becomes another topic of research in the laboratory. One of the recurring aspects of human conduct is the fact that when brought into another's physical presence people interact. While the laboratory may not be a recurrent situation in the social arena, it is a situation which has enough in common with other behavior settings of its own class that it becomes worthy of investigation in its own right. Just as physicians' offices have waiting rooms, so too do experimental laboratories. Just as patients leave a waiting room and enter an examination room, so too do subjects in experiments. The office of the physician is only one behavior setting that has similarities with the laboratory, and I am suggesting that society is replete with situations that have enough in common with the laboratory to justify the extensive study of conduct in laboratories.

In a sense, the laboratory becomes an interactional theatre. I have shown how experiments flow along a continuum that often deviates widely from the script laid down by instruction sheets. The laboratory is a behavior setting with its own rules and props for conduct. It is, then, a small stage on and in which the drama of interaction is presented. Sociologists must ask how it is that experimenters are able to stage performances in laboratories that manage to stay so close to the actual demands of the experiment. This suggests that the use of appointment rooms, the presentation of self in the guise of the scientist, and the communication of symbols that have meaning within the realm of science represent dramaturgical symbols and strategies employed by scientists as they conduct experiments. To conduct an experiment implies that one is engaging in a performance termed scientific in a situation that can have imputed to it scientific meaning.

## Notes

Two excellent discussions of the causality problem and research design are Hirschi and Selvin's *Delinquency Research: An Appraisal of Analytic Methods* (1967) and Camilleri's (1962) "Theory, Probability, and Induction in Social Research." My treatment of the causal proposition draws heavily upon the Hirschi and Selvin discussion. Another very good analysis of this problem, especially with relevance to the experiment, is Goode and Hatt (1952, pp. 74–91).

The best review of experimental designs is Campbell and Stanley (1963b). Others include French (1953, pp. 98–135), Festinger (1953, pp. 136–72), and Selltiz, *et al.* (1959, Chap. 4). Campbell and Stanley's review provides the basis for my discussion. It represents the most complete analysis of validity problems and experimental design. Additional discussions of experimental designs may be found in Ross and Smith (1965), Wuebben (1968), and Blalock (1967).

Friedman's *The Social Nature of Psychological Research* (1967) provides a very good review of existing studies on experimenters and subject effect and offers a framework for viewing experiments as a form of interaction. It should be read in conjunction with Orne's (1962) analysis of demand characteristic effects. A study that amplifies and further specifies Orne's hypothesis is Sherman (1967), where subjects are classified according to their readiness to respond to the demands of the experimenter. Leik's

(1965) study of stooges in the experimental situation should also be examined for material relevant to experimenter effect, as should Rosenthal (1966).

A very good treatment of the artificiality criticism of laboratory experiments is Drabek and Haas (1967). They present data that indicate that realistic and relevant behavior can be created in the laboratory.

There is a second strategy for placing subjects in observational groups: matching; Selltiz, *et al.* (1959, pp. 98–108), present its logic. I have not treated this method because in my judgment random assignment must still be employed.

# 8

# The Social Survey and its Variations

From our point of view, the essence of a survey is that it is confined to, but can completely exhaust, all the possibilities inherent in a variable language.

The central problem . . . is thus the following: how does one translate ideas of social matters into variables, and how does one analyze the interrelations between these variables so that new ideas can be derived from them? It is not claimed, of course, that the procedures of variable language . . . cover all that the social scientist has to say or wants to say. It is not even clear whether all empirical research, let alone more general reflections, can be carried on in this kind of discourse. What additional "languages" are needed for well-rounded social science must be left to future methodological investigations. But such efforts will undoubtedly be helped if at least one such system has been clarified as far as possible.

*Paul Lazarsfeld, 1955, pp. xii–xiv.*

But throughout all this [the history of survey research] one fact remained, a very disturbing one to the student of social organization. The *individual* remained the unit of analysis. No matter how complex the analysis, how numerous the correlations, the studies focused on individuals as separate and independent units. The very techniques mirrored this as well: samples were random, never including (except by accident) two persons who were friends; interviews were with one individual, as an atomistic entity, and responses were coded onto separate IBM cards, one for each person. As a result, the kinds of substantive problems on which such research focused tended to be problems of "aggregate psychology," that is, *within* individual problems, and never problems concerned with relations between people.

*James S. Coleman, 1958, p. 28.*

This chapter presents the basic rationales for the use of the social survey, which—because of its wide popularity among contemporary sociologists—deserves special attention. The discussion draws upon my earlier treatments of sampling, measurement, interviewing, and causal analysis. Like the experiment the survey may be viewed both as a method of research and as a situation worthy of social psychological analysis.

## The Survey Defined and Its Relationship to the Experimental Model

The survey may be defined as a methodological technique that requires the systematic collection of data from populations or samples through the use of the interview or the self-administered questionnaire. The investigator approaches a sample of persons who have been exposed to a set of events or experiences and interviews them with respect to these experiences. As such, the survey parallels the pre-experimental design defined as the one-shot case study (Campbell and Stanley, 1963, pp. 6–7). Observations are typically collected at one point in time—no before observations are made, no control is exercised over experimental variables, and no control groups are explicitly constructed; a group of persons are observed at one point in time and questioned about their behaviors, attitudes, and beliefs with respect to a series of issues.

This extended definition is not intended to suggest that the survey analyst makes no attempt to simulate the true experimental design. He in fact does and he accomplishes this through the use of multivariate analysis. After having collected his observations, he divides his sample into subgroups that differ on the variables or processes being analyzed. For example, if he is studying attitudes toward sexual relationships in marriage, the analyst might subdivide the sample into three groups: those never married, those currently married, and those married previously but now divorced or widowed. Such a division parallels an experimental design with two experimental groups and one control group. The two groups that were or had been married constitute those subjects exposed to the experimental variable, while the never married group constitutes the control group. It is this strategy—the subdivision of a sample into contrasting control and experimental groups—that shows a general commitment to the experimental model of research and analysis.

### The Survey's Solution to the Causal Inference Problem

Chapter 7 presented multivariate analysis as the basic model of inference underlying the survey. After data are gathered on those variables viewed as relevant to the development of causal propositions, multivariate analysis involves the following steps: cross-classifying two variables, one independent and one dependent; measuring the degree of association between them; and introducing a third variable to assess its affect upon the original association. The third variable becomes the test factor; it may be intrinsic or extrinsic in nature, and temporally may be antecedent or contingent. The repeated introduction of test factors into covariant relationships becomes the major strategy of survey analysis.

It should be clear that even before the analyst can begin these operations he must first demonstrate covariance between his primary variables. He must also have anticipated the causal status of his variables; that is, as either test, independent, or dependent. This anticipation must be theoretically directed, although there is an emergent quality to the analytic process that cannot be ignored. That is, relationships may not appear when they are supposed to, or they may disappear under the effect of unanticipated variables—for example, intrinsic factors. For these reasons the survey process takes on a flavor of continuing analysis and emergence that the experiment lacks. In the experiment the investigator has at his control those variables judged to be relevant; the survey analyst lacks this control. Multivariate analysis, then, is best seen as a strategy of analysis and not of design.

Both the survey and the experiment are strategies for uncovering causal relationships, but the survey takes the researcher to a natural field setting— the experiment typically does not. Additionally, the experiment is based on the assumption that behavior is studied at two points in time in situations controlled by the investigator. The survey, in its most popular forms lacks both of these qualities; therefore, the greater concern with the tentative nature of causal relationships.

A second similarity lies in the survey analyst's attempts to construct ad hoc experimental and control groups. This strategy permits the analysis of causal relationships in situations or groups that share one characteristic in common—at least for the purposes of analysis.

An appropriate question is the suitability of multivariate analysis for resolving the problems of rival causal factors. Traditionally, survey researchers have given greatest consideration to extrinsic test factors in their causal analyses. This concern must be broadened to include the treatment of intrinsic variables that flow from the research process. Every researcher is obligated to report the effects of the following variables upon his causal propositions: the situations of observation; the attitudes and definitions of his interviewers as these pertain to the interview process; variations in definitions and meanings observed among respondents or subjects concerning the research act; unique aspects of subject-observer interaction; time and its passage.

In a conventional sense, the survey analyst must treat internal validity as a basic feature of the research process. Because the survey method requires data collection in widely varying situations among dissimilar persons at different points in time, factors intrinsic to the data collection process cannot be ignored. The survey researcher must become as rigorous in his analysis of rival causal factors as the experimenter.

As a point of strategy, multivariate analysis can be easily adopted to these problems. The investigator need only expand his conception of rival causal factors to include the problems mentioned. Thus interviewers could be classified in terms of their styles of presentation (e.g., formal or informal), and this dimension could be treated as an intervening test variable. This could also be the case for variations in subject presentation, for situational contingencies, and for the effects of temporal, or historical events.

## Types of Survey Designs, the Statistical Sampling Model, and Experimental Variations

It is possible to distinguish several different types of survey designs, each of which varies in some degree from the definition given earlier. Before turning to these variations, it should be noted that as a methodological strategy the survey rests heavily on the sampling considerations presented in Chapter 4. In addition, any classification of survey designs must consider approximations to the experimental model.

### Surveys and Sampling Models

The survey begins with the assumption that a sample of theoretically relevant objects from a population will be studied. The choice of a sampling model (e.g., interactive or noninteractive) becomes a prerequisite in the determination of what objects to include in the study design. Given the distinction between interactive and noninteractive sampling models, it is possible to differentiate survey designs that employ one or the other of these two models. These models seldom make assumptions about recurrent or repeated observations, however (though certain survey designs do employ repeated observations). For this reason investigators must also consider the time base on which survey designs rest.

### Surveys and the Experimental Model

It will be recalled that there are four key elements to the classical experimental model: investigator control over the treatment conditions; repeated observations; construction of two or more comparison groups, (e.g., experimental and control); and the use of randomization as a technique for assignment to experimental and control groups. Nonexperimental or preexperimental designs may include any of these assumptions, but will not combine all four. (The one-shot case study lacks these features, for example.) *Quasi-experimental designs* employ certain combinations of these elements but typically lack the important ability to control exposure or nonexposure to the experimental treatment condition.

Surveys approximate the experimental model through the use of multivariate analysis. The generic definition given the term earlier, however, makes no assumptions about repeated observations or the use of random selection and assignment. In addition to the sampling model underlying the survey, I add to my classification those designs that in no way approximate the experimental model because of any of the following: failure to employ the principle of randomization; failure to construct comparison groups; failure to have repeated observations. Survey designs that fail to meet these criteria are called *nonexperimental*. Second, I distinguish those survey designs that attempt in some systematic fashion to approximate the true experimental model but because of their nonlaboratory nature are necessarily quasi-experimental. Those designs termed *quasi-experimental* are recognizable by: the use of repeated observations; the probable use of comparison groups; the use of randomization.

It can be seen, then, that those survey designs not employing randomization are necessarily nonexperimental, even though they may permit repeated observations and the construction of comparison groups. Conversely, even though the design rests on probability sampling assumptions, it is not quasi-experimental if it lacks repeated observations or comparisons. In making a decision concerning which type of survey design to employ, the investigator should attempt to approximate the quasi-experimental model. The use of multivariate analysis to add experimental dimensions to the design is less desirable than employing a quasi-experimental model initially. (The reader will recall that the discussion of experimental designs distinguished three forms: nonexperimental, true experimental, and quasi-experimental.)

## Types of Survey Designs

### Survey Designs I: Nonexperimental Designs

The following designs are distinguishable because they represent the most popular forms of the survey in use and they fail to incorporate one or more of the critical features of the experimental model (randomization, control groups, repeated observations, investigator control over experimental variable[s].) The first such design is the *one-shot case study*. The survey analyst randomly samples from a larger population a group of subjects who have been exposed to a series of critical events that can be causally analyzed via multivariate analysis. The sample will be theoretically relevant and representative. The sampling model must be random, and may be either interactive, or noninteractive. It may be stratified, or proportionate, in which case it would be termed a weighted one-shot survey design. If no weighting procedures are employed it would be a nonweighted one-shot survey. It should rest on an interactive base so that natural social units are sampled.

These two variations constitute the bulk of modern survey research (Stouffer, 1950). They represent valid strategies for formulating causal propositions to the extent that theoretical guidance and randomization procedures are utilized. They are weakened to the extent that relevant comparison groups are excluded. Also because before measures are not taken, inferences concerning time order are difficult, but because only one set of observations is gathered, problems of reactivity, time, and subject-observer changes are reduced. Still, these two variations represent the weakest form of the survey design.

The second nonexperimental survey design is the *one-group pre-test-post-test design*. Here the investigator makes two sets of observation on the same group. This of course parallels the before-after true experimental model. It lacks a control group, however, and this restricts inference because the investigator has no way of knowing what would have occurred had his sample not been exposed to the critical event. It also suffers from problems of observer and subject loss between observations—that is differential mortality rates. Reactive effects of repeated observation are also present, as are changes in the subject and observer. Last, changes in the measuring instrument can also distort the causal analysis. This design is superior to the one-shot case study because of repeated observations—but repeated observations raise problems that are best resolved by adding at least one comparison group.

The *static-group comparison* survey is the third nonexperimental survey design. Two groups are chosen for study (either randomly or nonrandomly) and each is observed at only one point. In the past (Greenwood, 1945) this has been termed the *ex post facto* survey, or the after-only pre-experimental design. Its essential feature is an attempt to explain events that have occurred in the target sample by comparing them to the control sample. Unfortunately there are no before observations, therefore the analyst must infer what occurred before he made his observations, and valid comparisons and interpretations between the two samples become contingent on the demonstration that they differ only in that one group was exposed to a critical event and the other was not. There are two ways to treat this factor of subject selection and bias. The first is to select the two samples randomly. With respect to the target sample (the one exposed to the critical event), however, the investigator may lack sufficient information about the larger population to gain a sufficiently representative and random sample. Goode (1965) encountered this difficulty in the exploratory phases of his study of divorced women. While he did not employ a complete static group survey design, he did sample women from one geographical area who had been exposed to the experience of divorce during a specified time period. Analysis of the first sample revealed that he had oversampled from the upper class. Comparison of the women in his first sample with the national distribution of divorcee rates by social class indicated that national divorce rates were concentrated to a greater degree in the lower classes. These observations led Goode to shift his final sampling base so that it better approximated the national average.

The second method of treating subject bias is matching respondents in the target and control sample on presumed relevant personal-social factors. Matching, whether by precision or frequency distribution control (Selltiz, *et al.*, 1959, pp. 98–108), assumes that the relevant matching factors are known—but this may not always be the case. Furthermore, when matching target and control samples the investigator may soon run out of cases because he is forced to reject those persons who do not meet his criteria; this may lead to biasing in the final samples, a factor magnified when the target population is so small that rejection of unmatched cases may decrease the target sample to a ridiculously low size. Another difficulty arises when the investigator selects small matched samples. Freedman (1950, pp. 485–87) has shown that when matching occurs on samples of a very small size (in his case 83 matched subjects) as opposed to a large size (more than 150) significant differences appear because the small sample increases the probability that uncontrolled factors are operating. The smaller the matched samples, the greater the likelihood that uncontrolled factors will invalidate meaningful comparisons.

After the investigator has considered subject bias, he must be sensitive to the impact of maturational and historical factors. Because the static group design focuses on events that *have* occurred, as opposed to the prediction of events yet to occur, investigators replicating a static group design may find significant variations because historical events after the initial study have altered the nature of the processes under analysis. While Goode in 1948 could say his sample was not significantly different from the national distribution, an investigator in 1970 might uncover significant variations. (This is a problem that applies to all research, however.)

Of the three nonexperimental survey designs presented, the static-group comparison design is preferred because it involves the use of comparison groups. I have pointed to the deficiencies in those designs that do not have before observations, however. Causal inference is always problematic and the static group comparison design is weakened because of the absence of before measures.

*Survey Designs II: Quasi-Experimental Designs*

The essence of the quasi-experimental survey design is its emphasis on repeated observations, randomization, a focus on naturally induced experimental treatments, and the optional use of comparison groups. The first such design is the *same-group recurrent-time-series survey without comparison groups*. The same group of persons are observed repeatedly in a before-after experimental fashion. No control groups are present. The initial sample of persons is randomly selected on either a weighted or unweighted basis. This design may take the form of a participant observational study where the investigator locates himself within a group for an extended period of time. It is different from the one-group pre-test–post-test survey because more than two sets of observations are made; in this respect it is superior to that design. Repeated observations raise the familiar problems of intrinsic test factors, however. If the study lasts over an extended period of time (one year or more), subjects may drop out at a differential rate, thus making the last set of observations considerably different from the first. Historical factors operating through the period of observations may have impacts greater than the exposure to an experimental treatment condition and, unless the investigator gathers data on such variables, he may not present a realistic picture. Despite the potentially distorting impact of intrinsic factors, this design is favored because attempts are made to continually observe the same group of persons, increasing the investigator's ability to adopt the perspective of those studied, an ability that nonexperimental surveys restrict.

This design is stronger than the *different-group recurrent-time series survey without comparison groups* simply because of this feature. In this latter design recurrent observations are made on a population through the continual random selection of samples from it. The same people are not re-observed as in the previous design; instead, the investigator takes care to sample persons in each wave who are similar to those contained in the first sample. This strategy controls the effect of intrinsic factors, but presents other problems. The Gallup and Harris public opinion polls are examples of this design; they trace, for example, voter attitudes toward political figures or public issues over a specified time period. The essence of the design is to uncover changes in attitudes or behavior by repeated observations.

A recent study reported by Erskine (1967, pp. 116–28) on public attitudes toward morality and sex presented a comparison of a 1965 poll conducted by Gallup with a poll taken by *Look* magazine in 1936. While the time between these two polls may be greater than in the usual survey of this type, it points to the problems; without going into specifics, it can be seen that problems of validity again emerge and that geographical and temporal variations could challenge any meaningful comparisons between the two surveys. The United States was emerging from a depression in 1936, entering a world war in 1941, going through a cold war in the 1950's, and entering into another full-scale war in 1967; a discussion of the causes of attitude change over this period is meaningless without a consideration of these factors. When the time period between the first and last set of observations is great, the investigator must gather data on historical factors that occur between the beginning and end of his study.

In the time series study, the variables of maturation, mortality, instrument change, subject-observer interaction, and observation effects all become important. While recurrent observations reduce the problems of causal inference, the focus on events over time has the potential of introducing reactive factors that exist alongside the events assumed to be causing the change under analysis. The very fact that an investigator repeatedly presents himself before a group of persons introduces a dimension not ordinarily present in their lives, and this must be assessed. Whyte (1955) in his study of Cornerville reports that at one point in his study he was offered the position of secretary in the group he was studying. Fully aware that he would have not been offered this position had he not been accepted in the group, he was reluctant to accept it for fear that it would jeopardize further field relations. His subsequent acceptance of the position permitted him to study another feature of the group's interaction, and he recorded his perceived impact on the group in that position. While this reactive problem arose in a participant observation study, it is representative of the type of problem that arises in any long-term investigation. That is, repeated observations produce new behaviors. The observation of different groups at each point in time, however, reduces these reactive factors.

With the *same-group recurrent-time series survey with comparison groups design,* the investigator creates a comparison group each time he makes observations on the target sample. The design begins with the random selection of a group of persons who will be observed over a long period of time. Prior to observations on the target sample the investigator randomly selects a comparison (control) sample whose responses are employed as checks for the reactive effect of repeated observations on the target sample. This feature of the design, which is often termed the panel design, builds in control for those internal validity factors that other designs are most susceptible to (e.g., interview effects, maturation, history, etc.). If the investigator identifies differences in response patterns between his comparison and focal samples at any point in time he asks, "Are these differences due to my re–interviewing of the target sample, or are they differences arising from the natural events I am studying?" If he concludes that differences are arising from the interviewing-observation process, then a potential source of error in all surveys has been located and can be controlled by retraining interviewers, making sure the interview schedule has not changed, or more closely recording the interactions that do occur when the target sample is interviewed. It might be the case, for example, that certain interviewers are systematically eliciting unfavorable responses from certain types of subjects. If the same types of subjects in the comparison sample do not also give unfavorable responses, then it becomes a reasonable hypothesis that the interviewers are introducing the error. Without the use of comparison sample, which is compared at each point of observation with the target sample, this could not be determined.

The general analytic strategy of this design is to locate specific patterns of social change from the first to the last observation. If the unit of change is voter attitudes, as it was in the Lazarsfeld Elmira study of 1948, then the investigator could focus on the impact of the mass media on voter intentions from the beginning of the presidential campaign to the day of actual vote (see Lazarsfeld, Berelson, and Gaudet, 1955, pp. 231–42). On the first interview party preference and vote choice could be determined, and then during the days of the campaign subjects could be repeatedly observed concerning changes in their attitudes. The final set of observations would be the actual vote, and in this case the investigator has successfully linked attitudes to behavior patterns. The basic goal with this design is by recurrent observations to uncover patterns of change (from the first to the last observation) and to explain this change.

In distinction to the previous designs, this strategy allows the investigator to measure the reactive effects of observation, construct comparison groups so that meaningful causal inferences can be made, and more adequately locate the effect of specific stimuli or experimental conditions (because factors of internal validity can be controlled). For these reasons *the same-group, recurrent-time series survey with comparison groups* is the most sophisticated survey design. Of all the designs presented, it allows the investigator most fruitfully to combine multivariate analysis with the broad intent of the survey as a methodological strategy. It has its problems, however. A first obvious difficulty is recruiting persons who will agree to be re–interviewed. Glock (1955, pp. 242–50) has noted that persons who agree initially to be re–interviewed often differ from those who do not; there are also those who, after having given their permission, later refuse. The extent of this difference must be identified, for it points to the issue of differential subject bias and self-selection. The reactive effect of re–interviewing must be assessed, and this of course is one rationale for employing multiple comparison groups. Participation in an ongoing investigation may, as in the experiment, create a demand characteristic effect.

While this design is superior to those previously discussed, the analyst must be aware that any changes observed may arise from processes other than those he has observed. Historical, interactional, and maturational factors cannot be ignored. Glock (1955, pp. 242–50), for example, has reported a design of this variety in which it was concluded that exposure to a certain film reduced anti-Semitic attitudes. No data were presented on respondent reading habits, contacts with friends, or newspaper stories on the issue, all of which could have occurred between the first and last observation and could have created the attitude changes attributed to viewing a film. Despite its advantages, then, this design has the weaknesses of all studies that rely on repeated observations.


## Survey Designs in Review and Some Recurrent Problems


All six basic types of survey designs share the following features: the use of interviewing and/or questionnaires as the major mode of data collection; collection of data from large numbers of persons; and the use of multivariate analysis as the major method of data analysis. They vary by the presence or absence of the following: randomization; comparison groups created before or after data collection; repeated observations of the same or equivalent groups. Two broad types of survey designs were presented: nonexperimental and quasi-experimental. I have suggested that the survey analyst attempts to approximate the experimental model by using multivariate analysis. No survey is free from flaws, but when possible the same-group recurrent-time series survey with comparison groups should be employed.

The discussion of sampling models and the survey made only brief reference to the relevance of interactive and theoretically directed sampling procedures, however, and it is clear that if the survey is to become a tool that permits the analysis of natural social units, interactive sampling models must be adopted. Thus the suggestions in Chapter 4 concerning the sampling of social relationships, social groups, encounters, and organizations take on central relevance for the survey analyst. By relaxing the formal rules of statistical sampling theory to permit greater theoretical guidance, the survey can become a powerful tool for the large scale study of natural interactive units.

A second problem (and one not peculiar to the survey) is that few investigators think beyond their own work to future studies, a shortsightedness that often leads the analyst to conclude that his survey has raised more problems than can be answered—and unfortunately, the person who builds upon an earlier study seldom replicates it. The survey is one of the most widely used methods in sociology, but paradoxically is seldom used for replication purposes. As I indicated in Chapter 2, this is a reflection of the reward structure in sociology: Replication is not rewarded. As an alternative I propose the following strategy (which would apply to all research endeavors): Each person who chooses to use the survey (or any other method) should regard his study as only one in a long series of interrelated investigations that may not be concluded in his lifetime.

A third problem with the survey is the frequent inability of the analyst to make statements about collectivities of individuals. Reliance on statistical sampling models that do not consider the sampling of groups leaves the investigator with observations only of individuals. In Chapter 4, group sampling models were considered involving snowball, dense, and saturation strategies, methods that may broadly be considered techniques of relational analysis and as such represent one way to raise observation from the atomistic to the group level. Unless the survey is raised to this level, only statements about individuals can be made. This is acceptable if the goal is individual description, but if the survey is to be placed in the mainstream of modern sociological theory, relational methods of survey analysis must be made integral to the method.

These are three recurrent—but soluble—problems of the survey. A fourth problem is one more difficult to solve; it is the question of whether or not the survey is appropriate for the analysis of complex forms of human interaction. While the survey can make statements about large aggregates of individuals clustered in social units, it is not necessarily so that it can provide clues to interaction (see Blumer, 1956, pp. 683–90). Human interaction is continually shifting and establishing new forms, as participants confront one another in concrete situations. Survey methodology, which relies on structured questionnaires is ill-equipped to capture this aspect of interaction. Certain interactional questions can be answered; when the sociologist finds himself in a setting where the meanings and forms of interaction are relatively ritualized it is quite probable that his structured methods will satisfactorily record elements of the interaction. But in situations where symbolic meanings are in flux and where interactional forms are continually being redefined, the survey method will be found lacking because of its structured and relatively inflexible nature.

**Steps in Survey Design and the Resolution of Recurrent Problems**

The first step in carrying out a survey design is designation of the problem to be considered. The problem may involve the test of one or two hypotheses; it may be descriptive (as in the U. S. Census); or it may be explanatory and predictive. Its formulation dictates subsequent decisions—most notably those concerning whom to observe and what type of questions to include in the interview schedule. Having determined the parameters of the problem, the researcher then formulates the specifics of his research so that his concepts can be translated into measurable variables and his observations will be made on a sample of persons who provide the most feasible and logical source of information. Choice of survey design represents the third decision and this of course will be contingent on the broad purposes of the investigation. That is, the specification of the research problem should dictate whether or not repeated observations are needed, whether control groups are necessary, and so on. Fourth, the investigator must formulate the exact nature of his research instrument (care must be taken to anticipate future analyses). Fifth, the exact form of data analysis must be anticipated, the choice of independent, dependent, and control variables must be made, and care must be taken that information on these dimensions will be gathered (if clusters of questions are to be combined into scales or indices, this must be anticipated). Sixth, recognition must be made of the fact that data on the questionnaires themselves will be of direct use. The data must be transferred either to IBM cards or into some form of uniform tabulation sheet to facilitate analysis. The investigator must anticipate the form this analysis will take and if possible precode his questions and items on the questionnaires so that they can be easily transferred to other forms for analysis.

When the survey investigator enters the field, interviewers must be located and trained and respondents must be designated from the total population and then located in the area of their residence. (While the listing of addresses, and perhaps even the designation on city-county maps of general areas may appear relatively simple, it may lead to a serious problem in the survey that rests on a statistical sampling model. Rejection for interviews, or inability to locate certain respondents, builds in an element of error that serves to bias the final sample.)

Once respondents have been located and the interviews conducted, the process of analysis awaits the investigator. A first question that must be answered concerns the degree to which the final sample conforms to the specifications of the initial sample. If the investigator is employing a statistical sampling model, he should first assess the general representativeness of his sample by comparing it to what he originally planned to observe, and the broader population from which he sampled. The refusal rate during the interview process should also be computed. In general all refusals raise questions about the research. The characteristics of those who refused should be determined so that the sample bias in this direction can be assessed.

After the specifics of the final sample have been determined, the investigator can begin testing the initial hypotheses that guided his investigation. This testing will take the general form of multivariate procedures. The broad problem of establishing causal links should be attacked, and with it the investigator will be concerned with establishing covariance between his variables; showing temporal priority; and excluding rival hypotheses and explanations. When the analytic process is completed the investigator is ready to return to his original hypotheses and conclude whether or not his data allowed a sufficient test of his hypotheses, and whether they supported or failed to support them.

These steps are ideal norms that are seldom followed in the precise order listed—and they omitted reference as to how the survey could be constructed to handle the four problems phrased earlier (interaction, temporality, sampling models, aggregate vs. group analysis).

Union Democracy: *Solutions to the Problems of Survey Design*

The survey to be summarized here involved the collaborative efforts of three authors to answer the question of why it was that only one labor union in North America had remained democratic while all others had turned to an oligarchical form of government. The International Typographical Union represented the single deviant case to the general pattern of oligarchy and it was selected by Lipset, Trow and Coleman (1962; 1964, pp. 96–120) for intensive survey analysis; their study is virtually the first to collect sophisticated data on social organizations via the survey method. It also combined an historical case study approach with survey methodology, and was conceived by the senior author (Lipset) as a long-term investigation, one that began as early as 1943 when Lipset wrote his first paper on the union and was not completed until 1954. It took nearly thirteen years, and the final product is the most complete and thorough case study of a single large organization yet reported in the sociological literature.

*Phase One:* Each of the investigation's four phases was marked by different concerns and based on different research methods. Lipset states that the study first took shape in 1949 when he began systematically to study the International Typographical Union (ITU) in the San Francisco area, but it actually began with a paper he wrote in 1943 on the historical roots of the union system and on the failure of then current sociological theories to explain the structure of the union at that time. In early 1950 exploratory interviews were held with informed members of the ITU locals in the San Francisco area. Lipset writes:

It was in this period that the basic problems of the study crystallized: on the one hand, to explain the unique characteristics of the ITU's internal politics, as they appeared in sharp contrast to other trade unions here and abroad; and on the other hand, to consider these democratic internal processes in the ITU as a crucial deviant case challenging the powerful body of organizational theory stemming from Michel's development of his "iron law" of oligarchy in private organization [1962, p. xii].

During this phase, then, the relevant research literature was reviewed and a series of hypotheses were formulated on the basis of a qualitative analysis of union documents and preliminary interviews.

*Phase Two:* From the fall of 1950 to the fall of 1951, Lipset extended his exploratory research from San Francisco to New York City. A systematic study of the history of the ITU was begun and further exploratory interviews were conducted with active and informed ITU members. Members of the research team began to familiarize themselves with the operations of the union by attending meetings and observing local union operations. This led to a reformulation of hypotheses and was summarized in the second article resulting from the investigation. The ideas formulated in this phase provided the basis for the subsequent survey design, for it was decided that certain crucial elements of the ITU could best be studied with survey methods. A study proposal was written outlining the nature of the actual survey and research money was obtained.

*Phase Three:* In the fall of 1951 consent of the New York ITU local was gained, and an interview schedule embodying the major theoretical and substantive formulations was constructed, tested, revised, tested again, again revised, and finally administered to a sample of the New York local. The authors describe their interview schedule as follows:

This schedule had built into it questions designed to produce substantive data bearing on most of the factors and variables the preceding years of preliminary and exploratory work had suggested might be relevant to an understanding of the nature and processes of the union's unique political system. Thus we asked questions not only about the respondent's sentiments and loyalties in union politics but also about his attitudes toward a variety of extra-union social and political issues. We asked questions not only about his activities and participation in union political affairs but also about his involvement in all other kinds of union-connected activities and his relations with other printers' organizations. And we asked about his relations with other printers in his shop as well as whether he spent time with them during his leisure hours away from work.

At the time the schedule was designed we did not by any means anticipate all of the implications and findings that would flow from the data we were aiming to collect.

. . . While the interview schedule was being constructed we decided on a stratified random sampling method, with shop size defining the several strata. . . . At the same time it was decided to interview an additional sample of shop chairmen, in order to have for analysis comparative data on a larger number of those especially important men than would be included in a wholly representative sample [1962, p. xv].

The interviews were collected during the winter of 1951–52 and separate, intensive, "focused" interviews were conducted with leaders in the New York Big Six Union. These included all party and nonparty men in and out of office—35 in all, each interview taking from two to five hours.

The general strategy of the study was to sample the following units: ITU as a whole, locals, shops, and men in shops. Thus data were collected at all levels of the union, from individual aggregate attitudes to collective shop opinions and policy. Coleman describes the sampling strategy:

The primary source of data in this study was a random sample selected from the population of working New York printers. This random sample was supplemented by sixty-six interviews with chapel chairmen, to make a total of five hundred interviews. These interviews were about an hour and a quarter to an hour and a half in length, and were conducted in the shop (sometimes during working hours, sometimes before or after) or at the printer's home. . . .

The sample was a two-stage stratified random sample in which first shops were selected, then men within shops. Shops were stratified into three size groups, those from 3 to 20 men, those with 21 to 99 men and those of 100 or more. Of the last group, all chapels were selected, of the intermediate size group a 1/3 random sample was selected, and of the one and two-man shops a 1/6 random sample was selected. Within the large shops, a 1/8 random sample of men was selected, within the 21–99 shops a 1/16 random sample was selected, and within the 3–20 men shops a 1/3 random sample of men. For those who, through refusals, retirement, or transferral to another shop, could not be interviewed, alternates from the same shop were randomly selected and interviewed [Lipset, Trow, Coleman, 1962, 485–86].

With this sampling strategy, the authors were able to make generalizations about individual shop workers and their career experiences, individual shops themselves, locals, and finally the ITU taken as a total organization.

*Phase Four:* The last phase of the study involved the collection of interviews, coding, and analysis. Preliminary IBM analysis began in the spring of 1952. At that time the forthcoming election of ITU international officers in May suggested the conversion of the study into a time-series survey, but re–interviewing of the earlier sample was not possible. A short mail questionnaire with two followups aimed at learning how the respondents voted was sent out and elicited over a 70 per cent response from the original sample. These data were transferred to IBM cards in the summer of 1952 and analysis continued. In November of 1952 the national presidential election of ITU occurred and another mail-questionnaire was sent out, this time eliciting a 55 per cent response from the original sample. The period from the fall of 1952 to the spring of 1954 was devoted to intensive data analysis. The final product of the survey is contained in the monograph *Union Democracy*.

## Union Democracy *in Review*

The study reported in *Union Democracy* is instructive because it represents the general problems all analysts confront when they propose to carry out a social survey. As Lipset's remarks indicated, the actual survey was not conducted until several years after the problem was conceived. The early phases of the study indicate the importance of field research before a survey questionnaire can be formulated. The importance of this field work was demonstrated in phrasing of questions in the interview schedule. I present the items that were later combined into an index to measure printer participation in the social organizations of ITU. (See Lipset, Trow, and Coleman, 1962, p. 490.)

*Index of Participation in Printer's Formal Social Organizations*
Items: Q. 67 (a)   Have you ever participated in any union
                   clubs, benefit societies, teams, or
                   organizations composed mostly of
                   printers? What about the:
         (1)   Benefit societies?
         (2)   VFW Big Six Post?
         (3)   Bronx or Brooklyn Type Club?
         (4)   Printers' bowling organizations?
         (5)   Other printers' sports groups?
(For each mentioned)
         (b)   When did you first join?
         (c)   Do you still belong?
         (d)   (If answer is no) When did you stop?
         (e)   Do you attend meetings regularly,
               occasionally, or seldom?
         (f)   Do you consider yourself very active,
               moderately active, or quite inactive?
         (g)   Have you ever held office in the group?
               (coded for *present membership, number* of
               organizations, *meeting attendance,* and
               *activity:* coded $+1$ through $+5$)
Q. 68 (a)   Have you ever attended any printers'
               social affairs?
         (b)   (If answer is yes) In the last five years?
         (c)   Which ones?
               (Coded $+\frac{1}{2}$ if respondent attended any
               printers' social affair within the last
               five years)

The fieldwork also sensitized the investigators to the necessity of sampling clusters of individuals in workshops as well as individuals taken singly. Continual contact with ITU informed the authors about the forthcoming elections and allowed resampling the simulation of a time-series survey.

Because the basic concepts and interpretations of ITU were elaborated before survey data were available, a question may be raised concerning the contribution of the survey to the final monograph. Lipset defended the function of the survey as follows:

. . . the role of quantitative analysis was not one of discovering the major relationships, as it would have been if we had begun without such knowledge. Instead, it was a role of uncovering mechanisms, through looking at the line structure of the occupation and the union [1964, p. 111].

The value of the survey was that it uncovered causal relationships and pointed up the limitations of the hypotheses earlier derived in the more qualitative field research. The survey enabled the authors to indicate what elements of the occupation created the occupational community (e.g., size of printshop, nightwork, etc.); the importance of the occupational community for the two-party system in ITU; the importance of religion on the occupational community participation of members; the social-psychological process through which the history and structural characteristics of the union had their effects on the attitudes and behavior of the members.

Without the survey, which permitted precise quantifiable specifications of causal relationships, the authors would have been left with their earlier, more qualitative generalizations. In one sense the survey functioned more to verify and specify those hypotheses than it did to uncover new relationships. A further limitation of the earlier research was its impressionistic generalizations regarding the actual workings of local unions and shops. The survey gathered much more data—and from far more people—than participant observation and document analysis.

*Analytic Strategies in* Union Democracy

*1. Use of Theoretical Sampling*   This investigation employed a form of theoretical sampling, at least in the formative stages. Attempts to gather data from multiple sources, varying geographical areas, and from shops of differing size enabled the investigators to build into their study a sense of comparison that the ordinary survey lacks. The attempt to simulate the longitudinal, time-series study in the latter election surveys added a time dimension to the study that further attested to its commitment to a theoretical sampling model. Last, it can be contended that the authors did not leave the field until they felt they had verified, or dispensed with, the early, yet continually emergent hypotheses that guided their study.

*2. Use of Multivariate and Contextual Analysis: Union Democracy* represents one of the first surveys to use a form of contextual analysis. This strategy (Coleman, 1958, pp. 28–36) may be defined as the process whereby the investigator relates a characteristic of the respondent's social context to a characteristic of the respondent himself. This strategy can be seen in attempts to take individual attitudes and leisure activities and relate these to size of workshop. In shops of high political consensus, men are more politically active than in shops with low consensus. Whatever the explanation offered for the relationship, it can be seen that an attribute of an individual is related to an attribute of his social situation, and this is one form that contextual analysis can take.

A second form of contextual analysis, but one not employed in *Union Democracy,* is to establish *the boundaries of homogeneity* within a social group. Coleman [1958, p. 31] summarizes this technique with data from a study of doctors in four communities who adopted a new drug for medical practice. The question addressed was: "At each point in time after the drug was marketed, were cliques more or less homogeneous with respect to their member's use or nonuse of the drug?" The boundary of group consensus was the individual clique.

Maximum homogeneity occurred at eleven months when three-fourths of the doctors had begun to use the drug. Before and after this time period homogeneity was quite low. In this example contextual analysis enabled the investigators to relate individual attitudes with the perspectives of social groups; cliques were given an index score, based on the adoption patterns of individual members.

*Pair analysis* (Coleman, 1958, pp. 31–32) represents a third form of contextual analysis. With it the unit is a pair of individuals who are compared in terms of their attitudes toward some object. The first step in this analysis involves locating for each individual a relevant other person with whom comparisons can be made. This other may be discovered with the sociometric question "Who are your three best friends?" Or it may, as in our studies of mental patients, involve asking the patient, "Who are the five persons most important to you in your role of patient?" (Answers to this question enabled us to contact the persons designated most important and to compare their attitudes toward the same set of objects we had elicited from the patient. We were then able to develop discrepancy scores for each patient-other pair at different points in the career of patient and point to critical events that appeared to increase or decrease attitude similarity.)

## The Role of the Survey in the Study of Interaction

The deficiencies and flaws of the social survey have been extensively discussed and were found to revolve around internal and external validity, treatment of interaction, circumscribed time period, aggregate-individualistic bias, and failure to approximate the experimental model, thereby jeopardizing causal inferences. A final word on causal inference. Multivariant analysis, in conjunction with relational and contextual analysis, partially solves the causality problem, because comparative data are necessarily gathered. Multivariate analysis when used only in conjunction with statistical sampling models, however, is a poor second to the survey design that builds on theoretical sampling and the deliberate, ongoing selection of comparison groups. When comparison groups are constructed *after the fact*, as in the pure form of multivariate analysis, the investigator is manipulating data to create groups that should have been there initially. Systematically sampling comparison groups would be preferable.

The ideal survey would involve repeated observations, employ multiple comparison groups, combine theoretical with statistical sampling, and employ some form of relational analysis. I have said that the survey can contribute to symbolic interactionism. Despite the fact that survey designs necessarily involve commitment to a form of variable analysis just criticized, the survey can be employed as a method of determining the stable and routinized patterns of interaction that exist in social groups. Such patterns are often easily elicited, and there is reason to believe that they will be accurately reflected via the survey method. Lipset, Trow, and Coleman, for example, were able to elicit attitudes toward political activity in workshops and found them to be relatively stable within shops, and anthropologists have successfully employed a variant of the survey method in their kinship studies and have found, given agreement on the categories of analysis, that such structures can be reliably and relatively easily elicited. Public opinion polls of a national nature raise another issue, for—as Blumer (1948, pp. 542–54) has argued—the pollster too frequently fails to link the opinions he studies to their group context. There is reason to believe that opinion on such issues as a president's popularity or the desirability of entering a war cannot be accurately reflected in a social survey. Such opinions, tied as they are to small social networks, are often not clearly formed, perhaps not even existent. The forcing of a response into a *yes, no,* or *no opinion* continuum distorts the uncertain reality that opinion occupies in the symbolic world of the respondent.

Answers as to what attitudes and interactions are stabilized and what are in flux can only come from intensive field work and close observation. Going to the field with a precoded, rigidly structured interview schedule, but without prior knowledge about the issues at hand, is inappropriate. If early observations indicate there are clusters of routinized meanings and interactions, then the survey becomes an appropriate instrument to measure the nature of these forms.

Many survey analysts will never encounter these problems, particularly if they deal with data of a demographic or ecological variety: the information is relatively solidified and constant and is not open to multiple interpretations. When the investigator chooses to analyze such problems as face-work among strangers, however, or the labeling process among deviants and normals, or the process of self-other definition in encounters, or the emergent, and shifting reality of social groups, he will find that the survey is ill-equipped to handle his questions. Its very emphasis on structure and regularity makes it best suited for the study of processes and events of structure and regularity. To conduct a survey on the self-concept among a general population, or the process of labeling among the mentally ill, when such issues are theoretically defined as in flux, is to misapply the survey method.

Thus far I have treated the survey basically as a method of research and have not discussed it as a situation created by the investigator that is worthy of study. In Chapter 6 it was suggested that interviewing represents interaction among the unacquainted. Typically the survey involves the study of persons whom the investigator has not met before the interview and is unlikely to see afterward. A profitable line of inquiry for the interactionist would be the study of behavior as it occurs in encounters between the interviewer and the respondent. I suggest that rather than focusing on interviewer bias and respondent bias in the interview, that this interaction be systematically analyzed for what it tells and reveals about stranger encounters. Sociologists could then examine such processes as how embarrassment is controlled or courted in the interview, how selves are defined and negotiated, how involvement is maintained, how illegitimate side activities arise and detract from the interaction, how the encounter is opened, as well as ended, and so on. The survey, like the experiment, is both a method of research and a situation created by the sociologist. Its peculiarities are sufficiently different from those of the experimental laboratory to make its examination worthwhile.

## Notes

Relevant sources on survey design and analysis include Hyman (1955), Lazarsfeld and Rosenberg, (1955), and Hirschi and Selvin (1967). The reader should consult Campbell and Stanley (1963) for a more involved analysis of quasi-experimental designs.

Hyman's (1954) analysis of interviewing and the survey presents the first major set of findings on the reactive effects of interviewer-subject interaction. Stouffer's (1950, pp. 355–61) discussion of the one-shot case study should be examined for the general logic of comparison groups. Blumer's (1956, pp. 683–90) discussion of variable analysis and the survey provides a major criticism of the survey as a method and should be compared to Lazarsfeld's (1955) position. One of the earliest defenses of the survey and multivariate analysis is Durkheim's *The Rules of the Sociological Method* (1964 ed., Chap. 6). Written in 1895, this document provides a defense for the comparative method and anticipates many of the refinements presented by Lazarsfeld.

# 9    *Participant Observation: Varieties and Strategies of the Field Method*

The concept of participant observation . . . signifies the relation which the human observer of human beings cannot escape—having to participate in some fashion in the experience and action of those he observes.

*Herbert Blumer, 1966, p. vi.*

Participant observation is a commitment to adopt the perspective of those studied by sharing in their day-to-day experiences. The participation may be known to those observed, such that it is clear they are being studied, or the investigator may conceal his scientific role and attempt to become a "normal" member of the community, cult, organization, tribe, or club being studied. In both cases, the intent is to record the ongoing experiences of those observed, through their symbolic world, and such a strategy implies a commitment—either conscious or unconscious—by the observer to basic principles of symbolic interactionism. To comprehend scientifically the world of social man, sociologists must adopt the perspective of those studied—thereby avoiding the fallacy of objectivism; to adopt the perspective of those studied, means that the evolution and unfolding of social action through time and across situations must be followed as completely as possible, and this forces the investigator to analyze events that occurred before his presence in the field and to record all the relevant events that occur after his presence. Obviously events that occurred in the past can be only reconstructed by people who witnessed their occurrence. There is then a curious blending of methodological techniques in participant observation: People will be interviewed, documents from the past will be analyzed, census data will be collected, informants will be employed, and direct observation of ongoing events will be taken. For present purposes *participant observation* shall be defined as a field strategy that simultaneously combines document analysis, respondent and informant interviewing, direct participation and observation, and introspection.

In participant observation, interviews are typically open-ended, as opposed to closed-ended; census data, when analyzed, are usually not a central portion of the research process, but are used only to describe the characteristics of the population under study; and observation of ongoing events is typically less concerned with recording the frequency and distribution of events than it is with linking interaction patterns with the symbols and meanings believed to underlie that behavior. It is the thesis of the present chapter that participant observation may be most profitably treated as a method of qualitative analysis that requires observer submersion in the data and the use of analytic induction and theoretical sampling as the main strategies of analysis and discovery. As such, the method, when appropriately employed, entails a continuous movement between emerging conceptualizations of reality and empirical observations. Theory and method combine to allow the simultaneous generation and verification of theory. Participant observation is one of the few methods currently available to the sociologist that is well-suited to an analysis of complex forms of symbolic interaction. In contrast to the survey, which may be best suited to the analysis of stable forms of interaction, participant observation can better handle forms of interaction that are in change. As is the case with all methods, however, the method must be considered in terms of its ability to answer only certain kinds of problems—it is not a method that should be adopted every time a sociologist goes into the field.

## The Essential Features of Participant Observation

Participant observation is deliberately unstructured in its research design so as to maximize the discovery and verification of theoretical propositions. The attempt is to continually revise and test emergent hypotheses as the research is conducted. While this point will be discussed in detail when I turn to analytic induction, the following excerpt from Geer (1964, p. 337) points to the manner in which the hypothesis is treated with this method:

My use of hypotheses falls roughly into three sequential types. The first operation consisted of testing a crude yes-or-no proposition. By asking informants or thinking back over volunteered information in the data ("nearly all students today" or "no student"), I stated a working hypothesis in the comments and began the second operation in the sequence: looking for negative cases or setting out deliberately to accumulate positive ones. At the second stage, working with negatively expressed hypotheses gave me a specific goal. One instance that contradicts what I say is enough to force modification of the hypothesis. It is a process of elimination in which I try to build understanding of *what is* by pinning down *what is not*.

The third stage of operating with hypotheses in the field involves two-step formulations and eventually rough models. Hypotheses take the form of predictions about future events which may take place under specific conditions. . . . Needless to say, particularly in the first days in the field, the worker is never at the same stage with all his data; he may be operating at the yes-or-no level in one area and advancing to the model stage with another at any given time.

The hypothesis, then, in its final stage of development, frequently is not of the strict "A causes B" type. Instead propositional sets of an all-inclusive nature are developed so that the total arena of behavior under analysis may be incorporated in an explanatory network. Geer also suggests that the evidence presented for any given proposition will be of a variety of types (e.g., interviews, self-recollection, use of informants). Further, she points to the ongoing and developmental nature of participant observation.

*Assumptions of the Method*

A central assumption of participant observation is that the investigator shares as intimately as possible in the life and activities of those he is studying. This may involve, as in the case of the ethnologist, moving in with a tribe of Indians and living with them for an extended period of time, or it may consist of joining in the daily rounds of activity of medical students as they attend classes, make diagnoses of patients, conduct laboratory experiments, attend social functions at fraternities, and drink at local bars. In the latter case the investigator may not actually "live in" with his subjects, but he does partake in as many of their activities as possible. The experimenter or survey analyst, on the other hand, either brings his subject into his laboratory, or establishes only a fleeting relationship through a structured interview.

Direct participation on the part of the observer in the symbolic world of those he studies is also involved. This will often entail learning their language, their rules of etiquette, their eating habits, and their work patterns. Direct participation in their symbolic world is not easy. Learning a new language takes time and acquiring a knowledge of what nonverbal gestures mean is often difficult; Wax describes her difficulty in learning the meaning of Japanese conversational patterns:

When I began to make modest progress in the Japanese language, informants drilled me in simple phrases and were delighted when I remembered their instructions. While my exuberant and energetic personality prohibited any attempt to conform to the ideal standards of Japanese female behavior, my forceful remarks were not resented if they were conveyed with a veneer of self-deprecation. It was good manners to apologize for anything which conceivably merited an apology.

   . . . One of the most valuable pieces of advice given by informants was the repeated statement, "Japanese seldom lie: but they tell you anything to your face." More sophisticated informants . . . added that if the hearer has the intelligence to understand this suggestion, well and good, if not it is his misfortune. I took this advice to heart but was not able to apply it capably until I had learned far more about the center attitudes, simply because I often could not recognize the hints when they were given to me [1960, p. 170].

Learning and sharing the meanings inherent in another person's symbolic world poses problems for the participant observer, for he may cease to think entirely as a sociologist (or anthropologist) and, instead, begin to adopt the perspective of those he is studying. This "going native" can inhibit the development of hypotheses, for the observer finds himself defending the values of those studied, rather than actually studying them. Geer, for example, in the early days of her observation on college youth approached the field with a highly cynical attitude regarding the childish nature of the undergraduate college experience. As she began to make field contacts, however, her attitudes shifted and soon she found herself defending the very values she had earlier defined as immature. To guard against this shift in perspective, the field worker keeps day to day field notes on his own reactions and attempts to record shifts in his own perceptions.

A third assumption of participant observation is that there will be a continual attempt by the field worker to carve out a role for himself in the ongoing interactions he is observing. Cultures do not provide within their social structures a role called participant observer, and unlike the experimenter, who has convinced at least one culture of the veracity of his role, the participant observer must convince those he is studying to accept him and to allow him to question and observe them. Carving out of a role can be difficult, and may evolve through several phases (see Janes, 1961, pp. 446–50; Olesen and Whittaker 1967, pp. 273–81). Wax indicates that initially she approached her study of Japanese relocation camps with a high degree of insecurity regarding her role as observer. As she began to define her own role, she found that the Japanese began to define her as an observer and thereby validated the very role she was initially unsure of—but the role of observer did not exist until she began to act as one (see also Berreman, 1962).

Frequently the role eventually settled on represents a mix between the broad intents of the investigation and the personality and background of the observer. Wax, for example, was partially able to play the role of a Japanese female, but altered this role to fit her own personality. The general principle may be summarized by the dictum that the observer should not try to present himself as something he is not and he should use to advantage all the personal characteristics he possesses to enhance his observational role. Depending on the investigation, this may include drawing on such diverse past experiences as law violations, experiences as a mental patient, associations with drug users, and so on.

*Types of Observer Roles*

Four participant observer roles have been analyzed (see Gold, 1958, pp. 217–23). The first is the *complete participant.* The observer is wholly concealed, his scientific intents are not made known, and he attempts to become a full-fledged member of the group under investigation. A classic example is the study by Festinger, Riecken, and Schachter (1956) of a small group of persons who predicted the destruction of the world. The nature of the group led the authors to believe that if they presented themselves as sociologists, entry would be denied, so they posed as persons genuinely interested in the unusual predictions of the group and soon were able to penetrate its boundaries and become full-fledged members. They describe their strategy (1956, p. 234) as follows:

Our investigation was conducted without either the knowledge or the consent of the group members. . . .

Our first contact with the central figures of the group, their secrecy and general attitude toward non-believers made it clear that a study could not be conducted openly. Our basic problems were then obtaining entree for a sufficient number of observers to provide the needed coverage of members' activities, and keeping at an absolute minimum any influence which these observers might have on the beliefs and actions of members of the group. We tried to be nondirective, sympathetic listeners, passive participants who were inquisitive and eager to learn whatever others might want to tell us.

To gain entree, the observers posed as traveling businessmen who had learned of the group's activities and were interested in learning more. This gained them initial interviews, but soon raised a problem because one of the observers had fabricated a biography involving previous occult and supernatural activities in Mexico. The members of the group had begun to believe their predictions about the destruction of the earth, and the joining of a person with similar experiences reinforced this belief. The problem of altering the patterns of behavior of a group through disguised entry soon became apparent, and the authors were never sufficiently able to counteract this influence. The problem was further magnified when one of the observers was asked to lead a group meeting—an action for which he was ill-equipped and which he handled rather awkwardly.

A second problem confronting the observers was recording their observations. Obviously they could not make notes when in the presence of the group, so they resorted to the use of hidden tape recorders, recording notes in restrooms, and rushing back to their hotel late at night to tape their day's observations. As a result, doubt arose concerning the validity of certain of their field notes because of memory distortion, confusion of issues and speakers, and general field fatigue. (The problem of recording observations while in the disguised observer role is only a first difficulty, for once the investigation is complete the investigator finds himself with "mountains" of data, much of which have yet to be analyzed—a problem not peculiar to complete participation as a field method.)

Complete participation raises another problem, the issue of ethics in field research (given more complete treatment in Chapter 13). The Festinger, Riecken, and Schachter investigation was one of the first in a series of field studies that employed complete participation as the observer role and as such it caused a number of critics to comment on the unethical aspects of sociological research that does not give the subject an opportunity to refuse to be studied. The unintended harm that might arise from such observations, not to mention the publicity and the uncertain quality of the field observations themselves, has led some sociologists to reject all field observations that do not make the role of the investigator and the intent of his study known beforehand (see Erikson, 1967, pp. 366–73). While the ethical overtones of this problem have not been consensually defined by sociologists, it is my general position that any investigation that does not deliberately damage the reputation of those studied is ethically justifiable.

As a complete participant, the sociologist finds himself confronted with contradictory role demands—playing the disguised role and playing the role of sociologist. Role-pretense, as Gold terms it, is the basic theme of his activities; he knows he is pretending (Festinger, Riecken, and Schachter did not believe they were religious converts in the sect they studied). In effect, the complete participant finds himself simultaneously responding to demands of his hidden self, his pretended self, and his self as observer (Gold, 1958, p. 219). If his disguise is successfully carried off, he will achieve a sense of heightened self-awareness—an introspective attitude toward his own activities—because he must continually indicate to himself that the experiences he is sensing are due to his pretended role, not to his real self.

The *participant as observer* is the second type of role that may be assumed. Unlike the complete participant, the participant as observer makes his presence as an investigator known and attempts to form a series of relationships with his subjects such that they serve both as respondents and informants. This role is frequently employed in community studies, where an observer develops relationships with informants through time. Janes's description of his field research in a small midwestern community fits this activity:

Field work was begun by visiting town, county and school officials, and the newspaper editor to explain the purpose of the study and to ask their cooperation. Courthouse and school records and newspaper files were checked and interviews begun with officials and leading citizens. In time social interaction was initiated by attending church, joining a veteran's organization, returning visits of neighbors, and later spending social evenings with the families of several of the younger business men of the community [1961, p. 447].

While the observer is relieved of the tension that arises from role pretense, problems of establishing relationships, not going native, finding informants, and maintaining the observer-observed relationship must still be contended with. During early stages of his field work the investigator may encounter hostility. This may arise simply from misunderstandings concerning his presence, or it may represent a resistance to divulging information to a complete stranger. Previous investigations employing this role indicate that several phases are passed through as the investigator conducts his observations (see, for example, Olesen and Whittaker, 1967, pp. 273–81). In the first stage the investigator simply presents himself as a sociologist or anthropologist who is interested in making observations. He will be treated as a stranger and newcomer, and initial encounters are likely to be superficial. Subjects will try to place him in a recognizable social role and he will attempt to present himself in such a way that his role will be acceptable to them. Few of his subjects will be able to apprehend fully the meaning of his role; Oleson and Whittaker (1967, pp. 273–81) have noted, for example, that on several occasions during the early phases of their study of nursing students they were categorized as students, registered nurses, or faculty members—only infrequently as sociological observers. Because so few subjects will be familiar with the observer role, investigators find in this phase a greater reliance on roles that lie outside the boundaries of scientist or sociologist. For example, Oleson and Whittaker drew on their more global role experiences as previous students, as females, as music enthusiasts, and so on.

Once the parameters of the observer-observed relationship have been established, the investigator moves into a phase where he is accorded the status of provisional member. Respondents will begin to recognize him as a sociologist and may ask why they were selected for study. In this stage, as Wax has noted, there will be a deliberate attempt on the part of the observer to teach his respondents how to act toward him. This will include convincing them of the confidentiality of their conversations, as well as teaching them to accept the presence of an observer during their daily rounds of activity. As this process unfolds respondents will be teaching the observer how he may behave toward them. Backstage regions of behavior will be pointed out and acceptable topics for conversation will be conveyed. In the Olesen and Whittaker nursing study, the following observation was recorded:

As I opened the door I caught sight of Mary Jones at the bedside of her patient, facing the direction in which I was looking. Mary caught sight of me and remarked so that I could hear, "We're having our bath now." I said that I was sorry to have disturbed them and would be back a while later [1967, p. 275].

In the third stage the observer will be accepted as a "categorical member" of the community. By this time rapport will have been established, areas of observation will be agreed upon, and observer-observed roles will be consensually defined. Certain modifications in these roles will occur, particularly as the observer attempts to penetrate regions of observation initially defined as closed. His respondents and informants will now be bringing and giving information to him, and he must take care to insure that they do not define the boundaries of his observation too narrowly. In a recently completed study of interactions on a surgical ward in a large university hospital, I encountered difficulties of this sort in the ninth month of observation. Rapport and role relationships had been established, and I had observational rights in nearly every setting of the ward. A critical turning point occurred, however, when one of the departments involved on the ward began to institute a series of innovations regarding drug dispensing procedures. Members of the observational team felt it was imperative that we be present in the first days of this new operation, but the director of the unit, while sensitive to our observational needs, initially refused to allow us on the ward during this time, arguing that too many persons would be there and that nothing significant would be occurring. It was not until after a hurried meeting with the director had been called and our research needs respecified that we were permitted to be present during this period. What had occurred is clear—our informants and respondents had taken control out of our hands concerning what were and were not proper and necessary areas of observation.

The investigator will eventually find himself confronted with the problem of removing himself from the field, a process of role-disengagement. Field relationships will be terminated, and though friendships established will linger, continuous interactions with those observed will cease. Janes (1961, pp. 446–50) has called this the phase of "imminent migrant" and notes that in it respondents and informants take on a sense of urgency concerning how they are going to be described by the investigator in his written reports, and may try to exert pressure regarding the total investigation. For example, if the investigator has promised to maintain anonymity and later fails to do so he can be charged with violating an ethical contract. Further, if he has not made it clear that he is going to write a report as "he sees it," he may be flooded with a last round of data that are deliberately staged to make one last favorable impression on him. Janes describes his experiences in this phase as follows:

The final phase, imminent migrant, was initiated by an allusion to an expected date of departure from Riverville. Very quickly, literally overnight, townspeople began a new line of interaction. References to questions about the research findings were made. These remarks occasionally contained a tone of anxiety about what kind of impression the author held about the town. . . . Several parties and dinners in honor of the couple were held, but there was not a strong valedictory emphasis to these occasions. Rather, their conduct and tone were apparently intended to encourage the author to think well of his hosts [1961, pp. 446–50].

The difficulties surrounding role-disengagement will be contingent on the types of relationships established during the previous three phases. If those observed have come to regard themselves as friends of the observer and not merely informants, then their interpersonal demands on him will be greater than if a less intimate type of relationship has been established. If the field worker has come to regard his subjects as friends and not informants, he may find himself drawn into a network of role demands and expectations that influence his ability to evaluate the exact content of data gathered and relationships established. It is possible the field worker will overadopt the perspective of his respondents. Paradoxically, the persons observed may "go native" and overadopt the role of investigator to the extent that they cease to provide the kind of data that are needed. Whyte has provided an interesting instance of an informant going native in his description of Doc:

Doc found this experience of working with me interesting, and yet the relationship had its drawbacks. He once commented: "You've slowed me up plenty since you've been down here. Now, when I do something, I have to think what Bill Whyte would want to know about it and how I can explain it. Before, I used to do things by instinct" [1955, p. 301].

The *observer as participant* role is one in which investigations typically include only one visit—or interview—with the respondent. The nature of the contact is brief, highly formalized through the use of questionnaires, and there is no attempt to establish any sense of an enduring relationship with the respondent—the epitome of the stranger encounter. This represents the fundamental thesis underlying the social survey and, as such, has been treated in Chapter 8. The *complete observer* role removes the field worker entirely from interaction and is best seen in experiments where observations are recorded mechanically or conducted through one-way mirrors in the laboratory. I have treated this role extensively in Chapter 7. This brief discussion of observers-as-participants and complete observers is not intended to suggest that the participant-as-observer and the complete participant do not also employ these roles. For example, in our studies of interactions in a small psychiatric hospital, observations were frequently made through one-way mirrors of psychiatrists and patients during diagnostic sessions; in several instances neither party knew of the observation. This was the case despite the fact that we largely performed in the role of participants-as-observers. Similarly, we often interviewed patients only once, never again seeing them. Generally speaking, however, the type of experiences and problems I analyze in this chapter will be confined to the complete participant and the participant-as-observer. I will treat most extensively the latter of these two roles because what passes as participant observation in contemporary sociology is largely of this variety, and the problems of this field strategy may also be generalized to the less frequently used method of complete participation.

### Participant Observation's Solution to the Causal Inference Problem: The Case of Analytic Induction

At the heart of a causal proposition lies the demonstration of time order, covariance, and the exclusion of other causal factors. In the experiment this problem is explicitly treated by constructing two comparison groups—one exposed to the assumed causal variable and the other not exposed. The survey, I have noted, approximates the experimental model through multivariate analysis. In participant observation the experimental model is again approximated through the use of analytic induction, which is a strategy of analysis that directs the investigator to formulate generalizations that apply to all instances of the problem with which he is concerned. This differentiates analytic induction from multivariate analysis, for in the latter, concern is directed not to generalizations that apply to all instances of the phenomenon at hand, but rather to most or some of them.

Strategically analytic induction represents an approximation of the experimental model to the extent that explicit comparisons are made with groups not exposed to the causal factors under analysis. Conceptually this represents the classic before-after experimental design, and when employed in participant observation it calls for the investigator to search for empirical instances that negate his causal hypothesis. This general strategy, which combines the method of agreement and the method of difference previously discussed in the context of the experiment, is described by Lindesmith as follows:

The principle which governs the selection of cases to test a theory is that the chances of discovering a decisive negative case should be maximized. The investigator who has a working hypothesis concerning his data becomes aware of certain areas of critical importance. If his theory is false or inadequate, he knows that its weaknesses will be more clearly and quickly exposed if he proceeds to the investigation of those critical areas. This involves going out of one's way to look for negating evidence [1952, p. 492].

Described abstractly, analytic induction involves the following steps:

(1)  A rough definition of the phenomenon to be explained is formulated.
(2)  A hypothetical explanation of that phenomenon is formulated.
(3)  One case is studied in light of the hypothesis, with the object of determining whether or not the hypothesis fits the facts in that case.
(4)  If the hypothesis does not fit the facts, either the hypothesis is reformulated or the phenomenon to be explained is redefined so that the case is excluded.
(5)  Practical certainty may be attained after a small number of cases has been examined, but the discovery of negative cases disproves the explanation and requires a reformulation.
(6)  This procedure of examining cases, redefining the phenomenon, and reformulating the hypotheses is continued until a universal relationship is established, each negative case calling for a redefinition, or a reformulation (see Robinson, 1951, p. 813).

Lindesmith's (1947, 1968) research on opiate addiction provides an illustration of this method. The focus of his investigation was the development of a sociological theory of opiate addiction. He began with the tentatively formulated hypothesis that individuals who did not know what drug they were receiving would not become addicted. Conversely, it was predicted that individuals would become addicted when they knew what they were taking, and had taken it long enough to experience withdrawal distress when they stopped. This hypothesis was destroyed when one of the first addicts interviewed, a doctor, stated that he had once received morphine for several weeks, was fully aware of the fact, but had not become addicted at that time. This negative case, forced Lindesmith to reformulate his initial hypothesis to state:

Persons become addicts when they recognize or perceive the significance of withdrawal distress which they are experiencing, and that if they do not recognize withdrawal distress they do not become addicts regardless of any other considerations [1947, p. 8].

This formulation proved to be much more powerful, but again negating evidence forced its revision. In this case persons were observed who had withdrawal experiences and understood withdrawal distress, but not in the most severe form; these persons did not use the drug to alleviate the distress and never became addicts. Lindesmith's final causal hypothesis involved a shift on his part from

the recognition of withdrawal distress, to the use of the drug after this insight had occurred for the purposes of alleviating the distress [1947, p. 8].

This final hypothesis had the advantage of attributing the cause of addiction to no single event, but to a complex chain of events. The final hypothesis, which in reality represented a chain of propositions, involved the following:

1. Addiction rests fundamentally upon the effects which follow when the drug is removed, rather on the positive effects which its presence in the body produces.
2. Addiction occurs only when opiates are used to alleviate withdrawal distress, after this distress has been properly understood or interpreted. That is, after it has been represented to the individual in terms of linguistic symbols and cultural patterns which have grown up around the opiate habit.
3. If the individual fails to conceive of his distress as withdrawal distress brought about by the absence of opiates, he cannot become addicted, but if he does, addiction is quickly and permanently established through further use of the drug [1947, p. 165].

All of the evidence unequivocally supported the above theory, and Lindesmith concluded:

This theory furnishes a simple but effective explanation, not only of the manner in which addiction becomes established, but also of the essential features of addiction behavior, those features which are found in addiction in all parts of the world, and which are common to all cases [1947, p. 165].

Before reaching the conclusion that his theory explained all cases of opiate addiction, Lindesmith explicitly searched for negative cases that would force revision or rejection of the theory. He describes this process as follows:

Each succeeding tentative formulation was not constructed *de novo,* but was based upon that which had preceded it. The eventual hypothesis altered the preceding formulations sufficiently to include the cases which earlier had appeared as exceptions to the theory postulated.

It may be asked whether the search for negative cases was properly conducted and if the observer has not neglected evidence of a contradictory character. To this, of course, there is no final answer. It is probable that somewhere in the course of any study unconscious distortion takes place. Concerning the central hypothesis and the direct lines of evidence, however, certain procedures were followed which may be said to exclude bias. For example, when the theory had been stated in an approximation of its final form it occurred to the writer that it could be tested in cases where an individual had had two separate experiences with morphine or opiates, each of which was sufficiently prolonged to produce withdrawal distress but with addiction following only the second episode. Case 3 in Chapter Four is an example. It was concluded that if the theory was valid, the person would report that he had failed to realize the nature of withdrawal in that experience from which he had escaped without becoming addicted. Thereupon a thorough search was made for cases in which an individual had undergone such an experience with the drug prior to becoming an addict. All cases of this kind which could be found, or of which any record could be located, were taken into account. Any of these cases might have contradicted the final hypothesis, but none did so. The inference or prediction which had been drawn on the basis of the theory was fully borne out. This procedure was followed throughout the study wherever possible . . . [1947, pp. 9–10].

### The Intent of Analytic Induction

As Lindesmith's study reveals, a basic assumption underlying analytic induction is the search for propositions that apply to all cases of the problem under analysis. In other words, it is assumed that genuinely scientific causal propositions must be stated as universals. This belief forces the sociologist to formulate and state his theories in such a way as to indicate crucial tests of the theory and to permit the explicit search for negative cases. It is assumed

that the exceptional instance is the growing point of science and that cumulative growth and progressive development of theory is obtained by formulating generalizations in such a way that negative cases force us to either reject the generalization or to revise it [Lindesmith, 1947, p. 37].

This strategy not only forces the careful consideration of all available evidence, both quantitative and qualitative, but it makes necessary the intensive analysis of individual cases and the comparisons of certain crucial cases. Thus, Lindesmith did not confine his study only to analysis of individual addicts, but he also examined statistical reports on opiate addiction. In addition, he explicitly studied nonaddicts who had regularly received drugs in hospitals in order to isolate the causal conditions present in addiction and absent among nonaddicted hospital patients. This of course represents the use of the method of difference that forms the logic for the construction of control groups in the experimental design.

Another central feature of analytic induction is its reliance on theoretical rather than strict statistical sampling models. While Lindesmith made use of prior statistical studies of opiate addicts, his main strategy was to sample theoretically in a continual effort to find crucial cases that would invalidate his theory. In one sense the use of theoretical saturation as a criterion for concluding observations on a concept has its analogue in analytic induction's dictum that a theory is complete only to the extent that negative cases that invalidate it are not identified.

The use of the concept in participant observation and analytic induction represents somewhat of a departure from experimental and survey modes of research. Instead of an emphasis on strict variable analysis, concepts are used in a sensitizing fashion, as in Lindesmith's study, where opiate addiction was defined in terms of each crucial case. Such a strategy permits the investigator to work back and forth from his theory to his observations, altering when necessary both his theory and the definitions of his central concepts.

### Advantages of Analytic Induction

Analytic induction makes it possible to disprove theories while testing one theory against another. (Lindesmith was able to develop and test his theory of opiate addiction by testing it against psychological and physiological theories.) Analytic induction also provides a method by which old theories can be revised and incorporated into new theories as negative evidence is taken into account. (Lindesmith's initial theory was progressively refined in the light of each new piece of evidence.) Third, this method, with its extreme emphasis on the importance of the negative case, forces a close articulation between fact, observation, concept, proposition, and theory. Fourth, analytic induction provides one direct means by which theoretical and statistical sampling models can be brought together; that is, the investigator will find himself extending his propositions to representative cases not yet examined. One method of selecting cases will be the statistical sampling assumptions of randomization and representativeness. Theory will be of little use until it can be shown that the propositions apply to all cases of the phenomenon under analysis, and statistical sampling provides one method of doing this.

Fifth, analytic induction allows the sociologist to move from substantive, or middle-range theories to formal theories. Lindesmith, for example, hypothesized that the propositions in his theory would also apply to other forms of deviance such as alcoholism. While this is not completely representative of a formal theory as I have treated it in Chapter 3, it does indicate an attempt to work with a small number of generic concepts in a variety of different empirical settings to assess the utility range of those concepts and the underlying theory.

Sixth, analytic induction leads to developmental or processual theories, and these are superior to static formulations that assume variables either operate in an intervening or antecedent fashion on the processes under study. If the assumption that social events occur in a temporal-longitudinal sequence is correct, then it is incumbent on the sociologist to develop theories that take this element into account. Sociologists need theories and models of proof and inference that interpret social process.

### Deficiencies of Analytic Induction

As Turner (1953, pp. 604–11) has suggested, too frequently analytic induction is employed in a definitional rather than a causal fashion. That is, predictions concerning who would take a drug and who would not, or under what conditions withdrawal symptoms would be severe or not severe, were not contained in Lindesmith's theory. Instead it is a predictive system that explains the behavior of persons who have taken opiates. Furthermore, the emphasis on qualitative propositions of a universal nature creates problems when the processes studied are continuous variables that exhibit themselves in degree only. Lindesmith found that withdrawal symptoms had to be of a sufficient degree to cause the opiate user to become an addict. The precise amount of severity was never specified, hence it becomes difficult to test this critical assumption in the theory.

When the theorist identifies processes that do not present themselves in degree he avoids this difficulty, but continuous variables occur frequently. The only reasonable solution to the dilemma, of course, is to measure these events quantitatively along a continuum of degree, but this solution has seldom been employed. In effect then, if the theorist does not observe proc- esses that have universal occurrence he is forced to exclude them from consideration. Such events are the province of enumerative or statistical induction, with them the statistical method must be combined with the analytic induction. To fail to make this link is to forego the analysis of central pieces of information that would lead to greater specificity of the final theory.

A third disadvantage of analytic induction is an economical-temporal consideration. While relatively few cases will be analyzed, the time spent in the analysis typically will be much greater than that required in the ordinary experiment or survey. Lindesmith, for instance, intensively studied no more than seventy addicts, but spent several years in the collection, analysis, and presentation of his evidence. As the sophisticated participant observer em- ploys this method, he will utilize multivariate analysis to alternatively test different propositions and to identify the causal sequence of variables. The comparative method is central to the strategy because comparisons are made in situations where the causal propositions under development should not be present, and in these senses, it can be said that analytic induction should represent an attempted synthesis of all the methods of inference treated thus far.

## Participant Observation and the Problems of Validity

Just as the experiment and the survey are subject to the problems of internal and external validity, so too is participant observation. Can the observa- tions of the participant observer be generalized to other populations (ex- ternal validity)? Do the observations represent real differences, or are they artifacts of the observational process (internal validity)?

### External Validity and the Participant Observer

Ideally the use of analytic induction frees the participant observer from the question of external validity. In practice this issue has been one of the most frequent criticisms of the method. The criticism has taken the form that analysis of one case, or a series of cases, is not sufficient for scientific generalization because of the bias inherent in the cases chosen. The argument typically proceeds to state that at the essence of the scientific generalization lies a statistically representative sample of a large number of units from the population to which inferences are to be made.

Webb and associates (1966) have shown that the issue of generalizability to other populations involves three dimensions; these consist of population restrictions arising from any of the following: unique respondent characteristics, population instabilities over time, and population instabilities arising from spatial or geographical differences.

It is incumbent on the participant observer to demonstrate that the case(s) he studies are representative of the class of units to which generalizations are made. The sensitive participant observer is attendant to this demand, as the following statement from Burgess demonstrates:

This one autobiography of a delinquent career is a concrete and dramatic exemplification of what a case-study may reveal about the causes and treatment of delinquency that can never be arrived at by more formal techniques like statistics, which must depend very largely upon external data.

The case of Stanley appears also to be typical in a more real sense than can be verified by any statistical calculation. It is typical (i.e., belonging to the type) in the same way that every case is representative of its kind or species. This case is a member of the *criminal* species, and so of necessity must bear the impress of the characteristics and experiences of the criminal. It may not be the best specimen, perhaps only a good specimen or even a poor specimen. There can be no doubt that any case, good, bad, or indifferent, is a specimen of the species to which it belongs. . . . Hence, the study of the experiences of one person at the same time reveals the life-activities of his group [1966, pp. 185–86].

While Burgess's statement is formulated to defend the life-history method, it can be generalized to participant observation, which also involves intensive analysis of one case (an organization, primitive tribe, social club): a position that when coupled with the strategy of searching for negative cases provides data that bear on the three factors of population instabilities.

The participant observer will, however, have to know intimately the social and personal characteristics of his subjects, and be sensitive to any biasing features they possess. His investigations will also typically reveal characteristics of the cases studied that are not universally shared. For example, some opiate addicts may have college educations, while others may not have completed high school. The sample will not be homogeneous, and the resulting theory will have to be reformulated to handle heterogeneity. It remains for the participant observer and the user of analytic induction to demonstrate that he has answered the problem of external validity.

### Internal Validity and the Participant Observer

Internal validity sensitizes the observer to the biasing and distorting effects of the following intrinsic factors: historical factors, subject maturation, subject bias, subject mortality, reactive effects of the observer, changes in the observer, and peculiar aspects of the situations in which the observations were conducted. Each of these factors is present in any participant observation investigation. The earlier definition of participant observation stressed that it combines document analysis, respondent and informant interviewing, direct participation, observation, and self-introspection. Each of these methods may be viewed as a source of data that reflect on the seven dimensions of internal validity.

*History* refers to those events that either occurred before observations were made or to events that intervene between the first and last observation. If one was conducting a study of socialization in medical schools, potential historical factors might involve recent federal legislation that impinges on the medical profession, intrusions of other social systems such as economic depressions, war, and discussions in the press or even events that transpire within the study itself. In a broad sense historical factors involve subject maturation and observer changes. For present purposes, however, I will treat these as distinct dimensions. Specifically it is proposed that the participant observer, just as the survey researcher, make intensive use of the interview and existing documents to uncover the operation of historical factors that might jeopardize the internal validity of his study. The interview provides one means by which events that occurred prior to observations can be noted and analyzed, as does the document.

In a study currently underway on the life history of a mental health center, the author, in conjunction with Bernard Farber, George J. McCall, Bruce Johnson, Ralph Blankenship, and Robert Kapture is employing documents from various state and federal agencies to detail the specific events that transpired prior to the beginning of our study. In the course of the study documents are also utilized to measure shifts in opinion and varying external pressures on the organization. Interviews, in the early phase of the field work, were explicitly conducted to validate the document accounts and to fill in gaps in our knowledge. Obviously the use of interviews and documents supplies more than just data bearing on factors of internal validity; it also gives information regarding the historical dynamics of the organization under study. This establishes a point that bears repeating: Attention to factors of internal and external validity serves to answer theoretical interests of the investigation.

*Subject maturation* reflects a dimension that is particularly important in participant observation, because the investigator will be establishing relationships that will lead to changes in the subjects themselves. (The earlier quotation from Whyte's *Street Corner Society* regarding changes in Doc's perceptions bears directly on this maturational dimension, and most field workers note this factor.) It is typically the case that the subjects studied by the participant observer will be of one of two varieties—either respondents or informants. Depending on which category the subject falls into, the issue of maturation will be different. By informant I refer to those persons who ideally trust the investigator; freely give information about their problems and fears and frankly attempt to explain their own motivations; demonstrate that they will not jeopardize the study; accept information given them by the investigator; provide information and aid that could jeopardize their own careers. (Dalton, 1964, pp. 65–66; Naroll, 1968, pp. 265–67). These are ideal characteristics, and distinguish the informant from the respondent, who functions primarily as the person filling out or giving answers to a questionnaire in a social survey. The respondent will typically not bring special information to the investigator; not demonstrate special trust, nor give privileges of a special order; answer only questions he is asked and no more. In short, the respondent performs as a stranger, while the informant performs and relates as an intimate, a confidant, and a friend (Dalton, 1964, pp. 65–66).

The primary functions of the informant are to act as a *de facto* observer for the investigator; provide a unique inside perspective on events that the investigator is still "outside" of; serve as a "sounding board" for insights, propositions, and hypotheses developed by the investigator; open otherwise closed doors and avenues to situations and persons; and act as a respondent. Informants serve multiple purposes for the investigator, acting simultaneously as expert witnesses and as transmitters of information, and finally as informal sociologists in the field. In these various capacities the informant must be skilled at collecting, retaining and transmitting information (Back, 1960, pp. 179–87). This implies that they must be motivated to cooperate with the investigator. Furthermore, they will be knowledgeable in that they are exposed to the situations and topics central to the study. Whyte describes his key informant, Doc, as follows:

My relationship with Doc changed rapidly. . . . At first he was simply a key informant—and also my sponsor. As we spent more time together, I ceased to treat him as a passive informant. I discussed with him quite frankly what I was trying to do, what problems were puzzling me, and so on. Much of our time was spent in this discussion of ideas and observations, so that Doc became, in a very real sense, a collaborator in the research [1955, p. 301].

The motivations underlying an informant's cooperation often range from curiosity to a belief that extrinsic rewards are forthcoming, to a commitment to science as an enterprise, or to the sheer fact that conversing with an investigator provides a release of pent up aggression and hostility. Informants at any point in an investigation may be outsiders, frustrated rebels, marginal men, old hands, subordinates such as secretaries, or even leaders of bureaucracies. The investigator must be sensitive to these dual components of his informants (e.g., their social position in the setting and their motivations for cooperating), because during the trajectory of his study motives will change, positions will alter, and the quality and nature of information given will be changing.

Base-line interviews with respondents provide a standard for measuring the amount of change in them; day to day observations and their record in field notes measure the change in informants. The following excerpt from my field notes details one means of measuring this dimension:

In my first interviews and conversations with X I felt we were interacting on a purely surface-professional basis. In the last few months our conversations have dwelled more and more on his personal problems and on my career as a sociologist. X appears to be concerned that I not make the same mistakes he has—that I not overcommit myself to administrative duties. I feel that I have moved to a level of personal friendship with him and that this is primarily attributable to his recent illness.

In this excerpt several months of interaction are summarized and an explanation for the changes I have observed in the subject's relationship with me is developed.

*Subject bias* represents a major factor the participant observer must consider, particularly if he is developing propositions that apply to all persons under analysis. I have previously noted that nonhomogeneous characteristics of subjects will often be uncovered. Base-line interviews and the day to day field notes provide the main measure for this bias. Standard biographical questions concerning educational background, occupational history, religious preference, and so on, can be asked to attain a measure of the degree of subject bias present in the sample. Field observations supplement the interview, for here the observer will record interactional bias that emerges in his subjects.

*Subject mortality* is easily measured; the observer details those people who die, retire, move away, or in any other manner leave the research setting. Field notes supply data concerning the nature and motivation behind the departure, while interviewing and documents provide more standard means of measuring turnover rates, death statistics, and so on. In our study of a mental health center, monthly checkups are made on the organizational pay roll—a convenient data source for the mortality dimension.

*Reactive effects of observation* are the most perplexing feature of participant observation, since the presence of an observer in any setting is often a "foreign object." The creation of the role of participant observer inevitably introduces some degree of reactivity into the field setting. The excerpt from the Festinger, Riecken, and Schachter study of a small religious cult pointed this out: the presence of observers who had fabricated a social identity solidified the belief of the group that their prophecy was correct.

It is axiomatic that the observer must record what he perceives to be his reactive effect. He may treat this reactivity as bad and attempt to avoid it (which is impossible), or he may accept the fact that he will have a reactive effect and attempt to use it to advantage, in a quasi-experimental fashion. For example, Festinger and his colleagues could conceivably have introduced members who disparaged the belief system of the religious cult. Had they done so, they could have created experimentally a situation to test the response of the group to hostile outsiders.

The reactive effect will be measured by daily field notes, perhaps by interviews in which the problem is pointedly inquired about, and also in daily observations. In our mental health center study, we have made it a regular strategy to inquire about our reactive effects with certain key informants. This allows us to identify where our greatest reactive impact is felt and to discuss alternative means of observation.

*Observer changes* were noted earlier when it was suggested that many participant observers go "native" if they are in the field a long period. It is central to the method of participant observation that changes will occur in the observer, but the important point of course is to record these changes. Field notes, introspection, and conversations with informants and colleagues provide the major means of measuring this dimension. If the observer fails to record such changes, he risks losing the very objectivity gained by sharing in the events of those under study. The participant observer may just as easily commit the fallacy of objectivism as the survey analyst, for to be insensitive to shifts in one's own attitudes opens the way for placing naïve interpretations on the complex set of events under analysis.

The last category of internal validity relevant to the participant observer, are the *situations* in which observations are gathered. That all of human interaction is situated in social settings is fundamental to the analysis of observational data. The dynamics of these settings, the rules of etiquette that apply to them, the categories of participants who interact in them, and the varieties of action that transpire within them must be recorded and analyzed. All of the methods of participant observation should be brought to bear on this problem: formal documents to detail the nature of these settings and possibly even note who can and cannot enter them; behavioral observations to record their use and disuse; interviews to elicit the standard meanings persons hold toward them.

Becker and Geer (1960, pp. 267–89) have suggested that an important dimension of the behavior setting as a unit of analysis is the nature and number of participants present. They suggest that observations be recorded in terms of whether the investigator was alone with the subject or whether there was a group of respondents, since verbalized respondent attitudes will be shaped by group influence. If subjects are alone, they may say things that run counter to group opinion, but in the presence of the group express group consensus.

The situation, then, is a ubiquitous feature of all interaction, and recent evidence suggests that it, in combination with the definitions attached to it, significantly determines the behavior observed. The participant observer should devote a major portion of his early field observations to the nature of his investigation's situations; to ignore this dimension reduces the generality of his theoretical propositions.

**Steps in Participant Observation:
An Analysis of *Boys in White***

The basic forms of participant observation were shown to share the attempt on the part of the observer to carve out a role, learn the culture of the group and gain and maintain membership in the setting under study; the use of multiple methodologies such as documents, census data, open- and closed-ended interviews, statistical and theoretical sampling, and behavioral observations; and the development of complex causal propositions. The problems of role pretense, role disengagement, gaining entree, public recording of data, and "going native" are more difficult to control in the disguised participant role than in the participant-as-observer role, but both methods —in the domain of data analysis—approximate the experimental model through the use of analytic induction. Neither method is free from errors of validity; the detailed treatment of internal and external validity was meant to establish the relevance of these dimensions for the observational method generally.

I will illustrate the actual steps in an observation study by analyzing *Boys in White* (1961), a research monograph dealing with socialization in medical school conducted at the University of Kansas Medical School. First, however, the following steps may be noted. While these steps may not occur exactly in the order indicated, they are inherent in any investigation employing the observational method.

*Step 1:* Before actual field contacts and observations begin a general definition of the problem will be formulated. A theoretical perspective will be adopted, the relevant research literature will be reviewed, and an initial statement of research and theoretical objectives will be written.

*Step 2:* Next, a field setting will be selected, largely determined by the formulation of the problem as stated in Step 1. Flexibility in design will be present such that multiple settings can be considered for latter observations (e.g., as dictated by analytic induction and theoretical sampling).

*Step 3:* Upon selection of the research setting, initial field contacts will be made. Entree will be established, the purpose of the study will be made public to certain persons, and initial observations will be started.

*Step 4:* In this phase the initial implementations of Step 1 will occur. Working definitions of key concepts will be developed and multiple research methods will be employed. Statistical data on the setting and participants will be gathered, documents will be analyzed, and the historical context of the setting will be documented.

*Step 5:* Field research will be progressing by this phase. Informants will have been selected, approached, instructed, and the solicitation of interviews will occur. Early theoretical formulations will now be tested, reformulated, and tested again. Negative cases will be sought as the general method of analytic induction is followed.

*Step 6:* General categories for data analysis will be developed as hypotheses are formulated and tested. Indicators of key concepts are now being developed and refined as a coding and analysis scheme takes shape.

*Step 7:* Complex sets of propositions will be developed and validated with multiple methods and varieties of data. Comparison groups will be selected to further specify the causal propositions as a sequential, explanatory network is developed.

*Step 8:* This is the conclusion of the study, although additional observations may be made as necessary. Role disengagement will occur as the field workers begin to withdraw from continuous day-to-day observations. The actual writing of the research report now begins, and all earlier notes and observations are incorporated into a final picture of the events and processes studied. This phase is kept deliberately open-ended, since the observers may be drawn back for supplemental data.

### Boys in White

*Step 1. Formulation of Problem and Theory:* The basic theory employed was symbolic interactionism. While this framework delimited to a degree the types of processes that would be observed, it did not dictate explicit propositions, or problems to be examined. The authors describe their use of the theory as follows:

In explaining our further theoretical specification of the problem, we are tempted to make our decisions seem more purposeful and conscious than in fact they were . . . we went into the field and found ourselves concentrating on certain kinds of phenomena; as we proceeded, we began to make explicit to ourselves the rationale for this concentration of our interest. The areas we found ourselves concentrating on were consistent with our general theoretical assumptions but did not flow logically and inevitably from them. We studied those matters which seemed to be of importance to the people we studied, those matters about which they themselves seemed interested or concerned. Second, we studied those matters which seemed to be the occasion of conflict or tension between the students and the other social categories of persons with whom they came into contact in the school [1961, p. 20].

This statement illustrates the fluid-interactive relationship between theory and field observations that optimally exists in the participant observation study. A generic set of concepts is selected for study. The empirical indicators and meaning of the concepts are determined only after observations are begun. Subsequent to this rather vague statement of theory and research problem, the authors developed a working set of propositions that led them to examine the medical school as a complex network of social systems held together by competing group perspectives and definitions. This formulation further dictated their methodological strategy, as they note:

If we were going to look on the medical school as a social system, it seemed to us that a particular style of analysis was required. We would not be interested in establishing relationships between particular pairs or clusters of variables. Rather, we would be interested in discovering the systematic relationships between many kinds of phenomena and events considered simultaneously. . . . We did not propose hypotheses and confirm or disprove them so much as we made provisional generalizations about aspects of the school and the students' experience in it and then revised these generalizations as "negative cases"—particular instances in which things were not as we had provisionally stated them to be—showed us further differentiations and elaborations required in our model. . . .
Our theoretical commitment led us to adopt as our major method of investigation *participant observation* [1961, pp. 21–22].

*Step 2. Selection of Setting:* The setting for *Boys in White* was selected before the actual statement of problem and theory. The theoretical framework, however, demanded observations in multiple settings within the medical school. As a consequence, medical students and faculty were studied in such diverse situations as laboratories, fraternity houses, classrooms, wards of the hospital, offices, bars, and so on, enabling the authors to examine the specific impact of situations on the expressed attitudes of medical students toward the educational process generally, and toward faculty and other students specifically.

*Step 3. Establishing Entree and Initial Observations:* In this phase actual contact is made in the field, the purpose of the study is made public, and informal interviews are conducted to obtain an early picture of the field setting. Earlier excerpts in this chapter from Geer and Wax illustrate the problems in this phase.

*Step 4. Implementation of Working Hypotheses and Presentation of Doc-*

*ument and Historical Background Evidence:* The authors of *Boys in White* devote one entire chapter to the description of the research setting (1961, Chap. 2). The similarity of the University of Kansas Medical School to other North American medical schools is presented, as are statistical data on the background characteristics of students and faculty. Data from formal interviews with students are given to document their educational and occupational background. These data provided information on the personal characteristics of the students and as such yielded the evidence necessary to describe the special nature of the setting and participants under analysis.

*Step 5. Use of Informants, Testing of Propositions, and Analysis of Negative Cases:* Students generally functioned as respondents and informants in this study. Care was taken to simultaneously assess the validity of informant statements and activities by examining whether statements were volunteered or solicited; whether statements were made in a group context or made to the observer alone; whether activities were individual actions or whether they were indicative of a group context (see Table 9.1).

**Table 9.1:  Analytic Scheme Employed in *Boys in White***

|            |                                          | Volunteered N |        | Directed N |        | Total N |          |
|------------|------------------------------------------|---------------|--------|------------|--------|---------|----------|
|            | To observer alone                        | 23            | (17%)  | 17         | (13%)  | 40      |          |
| Statements | To others in everyday conversation       | 41            | (31%)  | 5          | (4%)   | 46      |          |
| Activities | Individual: Not seen by other students   | 1             | (1%)   | ....       | ....   | 1       |          |
|            | Group: Others present                    | 45            | (34%)  | ....       | ....   | 45      |          |
|            | Total                                    | 110           | (83%)  | 22         | (17%)  | 132     | (100%)   |

* Adapted from Table 10 in *Boys in White* (1961, p. 101) there titled, "Statements and Activities Expressing the Initial Perspective Classified by Those Present and Whether Volunteered or Directed" (September 10–October 3, 1956).

The relevance of this classification system is that it permits the observer to determine whether an expression of opinion by a student is a function of the observer's techniques—that is, a response to a direct question. If the answer to a question or a statement of opinion is accepted by the informant or respondent, the observer does not know if the informant is merely agreeing, or if it is an opinion he would ordinarily express even if not asked. Since the intent of any investigation is to determine what respondents actually feel, all statements should be analyzed in terms of this volunteered-directed dimension, and this classification system permits such an analysis. Becker and Geer recommend that the proportion of volunteered statements should always exceed the directed statements. The specific data presented in Table 9.1 under this dimension meets this criterion: the total volunteered statements were 48 per cent, while directed statements totaled only 17 per cent of the total set of observations analyzed.

The second advantage of this system is that it provides a means of determining whether statements or actions expressed are collective to "the degree that statements or actions occur in public." The authors state:

In the course of participant observation there will be many occasions when one of the persons observed will be alone with the observer and talk at some length about his problems and aspirations. Material of this kind can be considered evidence that the individual involved in the conversation held this view (and was willing to express it, at least in private) but does not give much clue as to whether the ideas expressed are held commonly or regarded as legitimate by all members of the group involved. It may, after all, be the case that many members of the group hold these opinions but hold them privately and neither express them nor act on them in the presence of their fellows [Becker and Geer, 1960, p. 286].

To check this point it was their strategy to classify all items according to whether they occurred in the presence of the observer alone, or when other members of the group were also present. They suggest (1960, p. 287) that there should not be an "overwhelming" proportion of items that are made or observed by the observer alone. (As shown in Table 9.1, on the expression of initial perspectives regarding medical school, 53 per cent of the statements and 98 per cent of the observed activities were made when others were present.) The authors conclude:

We note in Table [9.1] that nearly all observed activities and more than half (64%) the volunteered statements occur with more than one student present. As students do not challenge the statements or remark on the activities an unusual, we conclude they accept these expressions of the perspective as proper, legitimate behavior for students [1961, pp. 101–2].

The third advantage of this scheme is that it allows the field worker to determine what proportion of his observations are of activities and what proportion are statements. An overbalance of statements would be equivalent to observing "all talk" and no action. Observations of behavior with no accompanying statements would leave the investigator with a morass of behavioral observations with no links established to the attitudes and symbols underlying the activity. Becker, and Geer (1960, p. 287) recommend that there should be "a reasonable proportion of activities as well as statements . . . somewhere in the neighborhood of 20 to 25 per cent." Table 9.1 shows that 35 per cent of their items were activities, 65 per cent were statements.

Without further elaborating this analytic scheme it can be seen that it presents data on the nature of informant responses while providing a scheme that handles all behavioral and attitudinal observations made during the course of study.

Naroll (1968, p. 265) has presented a set of categories that usefully supplements the Becker-Geer scheme for analyzing informant-respondent activities and statements. He suggests that an informant may deliberately mislead the investigator because of a desire to please, or a belief that some benefit will come or injury be avoided by misrepresenting (e.g., escaping embarrassment). Further, an informant's statement may be incorrect because he generalizes from his experiences in one group context to the entire culture or organization under analysis. In short, "informants may err by describing ideal patterns as actual ones or by following a cultural or group stereotype [Naroll, 1968, p. 265]." In this respect it is the obligation of the observer to demonstrate the validity of his informant statements and activities by presenting the motives underlying the action (to the degree this is possible), and by indicating the degree of consensus of their actions or statements. While it is axiomatic that any individual's descriptions of a set of events represents his group perspective, it is problematic to assume that all other persons would agree with that statement.

The data reported in Table 9.1 were analyzed according to the *proportion* of students who expressed the initial perspective that students are obliged to learn everything presented in their classes. This form of analysis has been termed quasi-statistical and represents a main form of analysis that is

based on a body of observations which are not formally tabulated and analyzed statistically. . . . They include "quasi-distributions," "quasi-correlations," and even "quasi-experimental data" [Barton and Lazarsfeld, 1955, p. 346].

Suppose that the observer concludes that medical students

share the perspective that their school should provide them with the clinical experience and the practice techniques necessary for a general practitioner. His confidence in the conclusion would vary according to the nature of the evidence, which might take any of the following forms: (1) Every member of the group said, *in response to a direct question* that this was the way he looked at the matter. (2) Every member of the group *volunteered* to an observer that this is how he viewed the matter. (3) *Some given* proportion of the group's members either answered a direct question or volunteered the information [Becker and Geer, 1960, pp. 275–76].

This procedure makes quantitative use of qualitative data by converting observations into frequencies, proportions, correlations, and distributions. As such it permits the observer to determine which of his initial propositions are worthy of pursuit, for if his quasi-statistical formulations do not reveal support, he must search elsewhere. Second, this method provides a means of checking the frequency and distribution of the phenomenon under study, while at the same time pinpointing negative or nonsupportive cases for further study. Third, it permits the investigator to move from individual aggregate observations to conclusions that apply to the collective-group level. Table 9.2 (Becker and Geer, 1961, p. 125) indicates how quasi-statistical analysis can uncover negative cases for future analysis. These data portray the impact of students' initial perspective on study habits. They suggest that many more students express the provisional perspective in their statements or actions, than do not. The authors state:

Ninety-one per cent of the total (the sum of the positive columns) believe that there is more work to be done than they can do in the time available and solve this problem by taking short cuts to effective learning and studying only those things they consider important [1961, p. 126].

While 91 per cent of the students expressed this conclusion, Table 9.2 shows that five (9 per cent) did not agree. Interviews with these five students revealed that while they were not being selective in what they studied, they did believe that they could not learn everything presented. The following excerpt from the authors' field notes indicates how the quasi-statistical analysis revealed the negative cases that contradicted the major conclusion in Table 9.2:

Vic Morse, after telling me (in answer to my question) about his study schedule, went on. . . ," I think I have figured out their philosophy. They give us more than we can possibly do, but they want us to work up to our own capacity." (October 1, 1956. Single fraternity mn.) [1961, p. 126].

**Table 9.2. Frequency of Work Activities and Statements about Work With ( + ) and Without ( − ) Provisional Perspective (September 24–October 12, 1956)***

| Week of School | Statements + | − | Activities + | − | Total Observations |
|---|---|---|---|---|---|
| September 24– October 3 | 17 | 2 | 0 | 0 | 19 |
| October 8– October 12 | 31 | 3 | 6 | 0 | 40 |
| TOTAL | 48(81%) | 5(9%) | 6(10%) | 0 | 59(100%) |

* Adapted from Table 12 in *Boys in White* (1961, p. 125) there titled, "Frequency of Observed Work Activities and Statements About Work with ( + ) and without ( − ) Provisional Perspective" (September 24–October 12, 1956).

To summarize this step in the observational study, in it checks will be made on the frequency and distribution of phenomena, and negative cases—cases that contradict the initial propositions—will be examined; indices of major propositions will be developed; and informant and respondent statements will be assessed against the classification scheme offered earlier.

*Step 6. Refinement of Coding Scheme:* The same processes are going on in Step 6 as in Step 5. By this point, however, refined coding and analytic schemes will have been developed as more abstract propositions are examined. The observer will find himself confronted with a mass of seemingly unrelated data. The records of his field notes will have been typed in some continuous fashion, and it is quite likely that thousands of pages of notes will have been accumulated. Becker, *et al.*, describe their analysis of these notes as follows:

The records of our field notes and interviews occupy approximately 5,000 single-spaced typed pages. . . . A technical problem arises in considering how one can be sure that all pieces of evidence have been considered; it would clearly be impractical to search through 5,000 pages of notes every time one wished to check a proposition. To avoid this we indexed our field notes and labeled each entry with code numbers referring to major topics under which the given item might be considered. These entries were then reassembled by code number so that we had in one place all the facts bearing on a given topic, thus making possible a relatively quick check of our data on any given point [1961, pp. 30, 32].

The major topics included student commitment to initial perspective and student work patterns in preparation for examinations; other topics were the nature of student work in each year, patterns of cynicism and idealism throughout the student career, expressions of student perspective, and cultural patterns throughout the educational process. While the authors do not present a complete statement of their coding scheme, it can be assumed that all of these items were major categories of analysis under which any given observation could be multiply classified.

Becker and Geer (1960, pp. 281–82) suggest that the coding scheme should be inclusive to the extent that items are coded under as many categories as necessary. Many incidents will be coded under several categories. They provide the following excerpt from their field notes that was coded under "student-faculty relations" and "student cooperation on school activities":

Mann says that now that he and the other students have found out what Dr. Prince, the staff physician, is like, they learn the things they know he's going to try to catch them on and keep him stumped that way [1960, p. 281].

Ideally the coding scheme will treat incidents that are either expressions of attitudes or actions by individuals or groups. The coded incident should be reported in full. The following further illustrates observations coded under student-faculty relations.

The incident being coded should be summarized in all its relevant detail: the ideas expressed, the actions taken, the people present, the date, and the setting [Becker and Geer, 1960, p. 281].

Here are two samples of their summarized incidents that were coded as relevant to the student's perspective on student-faculty relations:

*5/25/6*
Jones talks about Smith not having done well on the OB oral—says Smith is really smart but of course they can get you on any oral, picking on something you don't know about.
*10/22/6*
Brown says he failed to get the lab work on a patient and got caught by Dr. Hackett. He copied the figures from the main lab, but drew some blood too in case Hackett checked up on him [Becker and Geer, 1960, p. 282].

In the community of mental health study referred to earlier, we have experimented with a variation on the Becker, *et al.*, coding scheme. This involves compiling a major data source book in which all units of observation are classified by date of observation, the setting where the observation occurred, the participants present, and the method of data collection (document analysis, structured interview, conversation, or behavioral observation). This master data file contains all of our major units of analysis, such topics as elements of formal structure in the organization; aspects of informal structure; career patterns in the organization; impact of external social systems on the organization; patterns of socialization and recruitment; development of common ideological perspectives, and so on. Each major category is broken down into as many subcategories as are deemed relevant. In the case of "career pattern" (a major category), we have some twenty subcategories designating key persons in the organization on whom we have career data.

Each topic in the master file is assigned a code number designating its location in the secondary data file where the actual unit of observation is located. Our code category for career patterns is "3," and each entry in that category is numbered consecutively from 01 to 20. This system allows us to classify any item into as many categories as are relevant. As a standard practice, we reproduce at least ten copies of each observational item, permitting us to maintain one file in which all observations are merely entered consecutively, and to break that unit of observation up into as many pieces as necessary. Thus if we have an interview with a key informant, we can take every piece of information of that interview that bears on a major category and file that portion of the interview under the appropriate major category. By keeping a continuous and consecutively entered file, we also have a regular means of assessing the nature and amount of our field work.

We have also employed the strategy of analyzing every unit of observation in terms of whether it is a behavioral observation or an interview, thus attempting to maintain the balance between these two dimensions suggested by Becker, *et al.* In addition we analyze each item by its reference to an individual statement of opinion; an observation of interaction between two or more persons and whether it refers to a collective statement or action. Thus we have a means of quickly determining where the bulk of our observations are falling. Since our study focuses primarily on day-to-day interactions, we attempt to gather more interactional than collective or individual observations.

*Step 7. Developing Complex Sets of Propositions and Use of Comparison Groups:* This step was illustrated in the earlier quotations from Lindesmith as he developed his final propositional system to explain opiate addiction. Here chains of propositions will be formulated, each of which builds on the preceding in a deductive manner. Becker, *et al.*, suggest that their general strategy in the medical student study was to develop a propositional network that would describe the entire medical school as a social organization.

The final stage of analysis in the field consists of incorporating individual findings into a generalized model of the social system or organization under study. . . . The kind of participant observation discussed here is related directly to this concept, explaining particular social facts by explicit reference to their involvement in a complex of interconnected variables that the observer constructs as theoretical model of the organization. In this final stage, the observer designs a descriptive model which best explains the data he has assembled [1960, pp. 276–77].

The form of these propositions may be a statement that predicts that medical students develop consensus about the amount of work they have to do because they are faced with a large amount of work, engage in joint activities, and face immediate dangers in the form of examinations. This statement includes reference to the necessary and sufficient conditions underlying the phenomenon and is based on a processual model that links each event to the next in a causal manner. As he formulates these propositions, the observer will employ the method of negative case analysis, which is one form of searching for comparison groups that verify or disqualify causal statements. In *Boys in White*, one final step in the analysis was a consideration of those cases that ran counter to their proposition that students shared a particular perspective. Their description of how the negative case was analyzed reflects the processual nature of analytic induction as a method of formulating propositions:

Because the statement of the perspective is refashioned many times in the course of the field work and later analysis with the idea of revising it to take into account as many of the negative cases as possible, this number will usually be quite small. Each one should be considered early, and whatever revisions it suggests should be incorporated in the analysis [1960, pp. 287–88].

They located two generic types of negative instances. In the one case there were students who did not make use of the perspective because they never learned it; in the other case were those students who made use of a perspective other than that postulated as the common one. Their explanation of these two types of students revealed that students who did not know the perspective were later taught it by fellow students. The students who shared another perspective led them to conclude that there exists "confirmed deviance in the student body, or that there may be marginal areas in which the perspective is not necessarily applied [1960, p. 288]." In this sense analytic induction also produces conditional propositions.

*Step 8. Role Disengagement and Final Writeup:* The writing of any research monograph based on participant observation will not really wait until this final phase: It will be written at every step along the way. (The fluid nature of the field method approach in one sense denies a logical order of steps as I have outlined them. *Boys in White*, for instance, was written every day the observers were in the field. Thus the eight steps I have outlined indicate a series of phases that will be covered in any study of this variety, although they may not occur in the order indicated.) The problem of role-disengagement was treated earlier in this chapter in the discussion of Janes' community study and will not be repeated here. I mention it to stress the fact that this will be one of the final issues in the field research.

## Boys in White *in Summary: Its Resolution of Recurrent Issues*

In many respects this study is a classic in the area of participant observation. Systematic attempts were made to treat qualitative observations in a quasi-statistical, quasi-quantitative fashion. Analytic induction was employed in its fullest sense, as represented by explicit efforts to formulate propositions based on negative case analysis. Internal and external validity were examined in a refined fashion, as illustrated by the scheme for analyzing informant and respondent statements. Theoretical and statistical sampling models were employed continuously when the authors moved from random samples of students to intensive treatments of diverse comparison groups.

Many critics of participant observation have argued that the data are too often impressionistic and hence can not be reproduced by future investigators. This was not the case in *Boys in White*. The presentation of data in tables is but one instance of how they moved above impressionistic data to a more rigorous level.

Others have suggested that too often participant observation studies become so circumscribed and case-bound that no generalizations are forthcoming. This was resolved in *Boys in White* by deliberately comparing its setting to other medical schools and establishing that it was quite similar to any other medical school setting that might have been selected (i.e., the resolution of external validity). Such standard problems as "going native," failing to present negative cases, failing to recognize bias in field data, and failing to present reliable and reproducible definitions of critical concepts and their empirical indicators were also resolved in this study.

Zelditch (1962, pp. 566–76) has argued that when appropriately used, participant observation studies employ not one, but three methods—participant observation, informant interviewing, and enumeration or sampling. To this I have added document analysis and introspection on the part of the observer. When correctly used, participant observation becomes triangulated with other methodologies.

### Participant Observations Compared with Other Methods

To highlight the unique features of participant observation, I now compare it with the survey and the interview. The following advantages may be noted. First, the participant observer is not bound in his field work by prejudgments about the nature of his problem, by rigid data-gathering devices, or by hypotheses, as he may be in the survey. The nature of the survey, when it relies on the logic of preplanned inclusion, is to formulate comparison groups, interview schedules, and hypotheses to be tested— before, not during, the research process. The fluid, interactive nature of participant observation allows the observer then to combine the best of the survey method with the best of his more unstructured approach.

Second, the observer can avoid the use of meaningless and irrelevant questions. Third, he is better able to make use of his impressions and reactions during the research process than is the survey analyst. Fourth, the observer is in a position to move behind the public selves of his respondents and penetrate the back regions of interaction—regions of behavior seldom open to the interviewer in the survey because of his fleeting relationship with the respondent. Fifth, the observer is well-equipped to link statements and actions of his respondents because he is present in the situations where they interact. When the survey analyst restricts his observations to one occasion, he must rely much more on indirect inferences about behavior and statements than does the observer. Sixth, the observer method is one in which the best-equipped person is closest to the data as they are collected. In the survey, the most adept person is typically the survey director and he is not the person who conducts the interviews in the field; this is too frequently left to the housewife, the part-time student, or the graduate assistant—there are a number of levels between the field director and the data—and this should not be the case with participant observation.

Seventh, in participant observation greater use is made of informant data and impressionistic reactions than in the survey. This places the field worker in a better position to impute motives from his observations, to pace his observations at a rate that leads to low levels of refusal, and to incorporate what may have first appeared to be irrelevant data into subsequent analysis. Too often the survey analyst is unable to do such pacing and ongoing analysis—although this need not be so, as *Union Democracy* demonstrated.

## Conclusions

I began this chapter with the claim that participant observation broadly defined is a method well-suited to the analysis of complex forms of interaction. This is but one way to conceptually distinguish this method from the survey, which I view as more appropriate for the study of stable, routine forms of behavior. Unfortunately this theoretical advantage has many empirical flaws, for whenever a method proposes to study change and process, factors jeopardizing internal validity must be carefully treated. In one sense, then, earlier criticism of participant observation as being narrow, and impressionistic become irrelevant, at least until the investigator answers the problems of internal validity.

I have attempted to show how the observational method is conducted, what its major forms are, how it can utilize analytic induction, and how, in one illustrative case, the issues of internal and external validity were resolved. It seems appropriate here to reconsider Trow's (1957, pp. 33–35) dictum that sociologists must carefully analyze each of their methodologies in terms of the kinds of questions they can best answer. To proclaim participant observation as *the* method of sociology is equivalent to stating that the experiment is the method of psychology. Obviously every discipline can and must employ more than one method, just as any theoretical perspective can and must employ more than one as it moves from vague hypotheses to observations and empirical tests. I have then broadly defined participant observation as a method that combines several other methodologies in the hope that sociologists will take the best from it as they work from their theories to the level of empirical reality.

## Notes

Useful reviews of participant observation include Bruyn (1967), Adams and Preiss (1960), and McCall and Simmons (1969). Zelditch's (1962) analysis of the various methods involved in participant observation should also be examined. For excellent discussions of the problems of field relations, Berreman (1962), Olesen and Whittaker (1967), and Schwartz and Schwartz (1955) should be read.

Howard S. Becker's (1958) review of the analytic principles involved in participant observation should be examined in conjunction with Glaser and Strauss' (1967) treatment of grounded theory. An early argument for analytic induction is contained in Znaniecki (1934, pp. 213–48), but an earlier and more interactionally based position is given in Mead (1917, pp. 176–227). In addition to Becker's discussion, Robinson's (1951, pp. 812–18) treatment of the method must be read. Turner's (1953, pp. 604–11) response to Robinson provides the major criticisms of analytic induction. Lest this chapter be interpreted as being lenient, I encourage the examination of Turner's position. My basic position is that analytic induction can be no better than its users—just as the survey and experiment can be no better than theirs. And because of participation observation's more unstructured nature, users of it must be even more critical of their own behavior. My long discussion of validity problems and participant observation was intended to provide a checklist for more rigorous use of the method.

A very good review of how the participant observer analyzes his field notes is given in Wolff's (1960, pp. 240–54) "The Collection and Organization of Field Materials: A Research Report." Anselm Strauss, *et al.* (1964), should also be examined in this respect.

# 10

# *The Life History Method*

Criteria drawn from the experimental model and used to evaluate single studies in isolation, however useful they may be in a variety of contexts, have had one bad by-product. They have led people to ignore the other functions of research and, particularly, to ignore the contribution made by one study to an overall research enterprise even when the study considered in isolation, produced no definitive results of its own. . . . We can perhaps hope that a fuller understanding of the complexity of the scientific enterprise will restore sociologist's sense of the versatility and worth of the life history.

*Howard S. Becker, 1966, p. xviii.*

In the 1930's and 1940's, under the influence of Robert E. Park and Ernest Burgess, sociologists trained at the University of Chicago, extensively employed the life history (or case study) method (see Becker, 1966; Park, 1952, pp. 202–9). With the rise of quantification and rigorous empirical measurement, however, sociologists in the last twenty years have turned away from the life history approach. My intent will be to present the major forms of the life history, detail the steps by which data are collected, discuss the method's analytic forms, and present what I feel are its unique advantages for contemporary sociology. The problems of the method will be treated, but my main thrust will show that—like participant observation—the life history method closely approximates the fit between theory and method advocated in earlier chapters.

**The Method Defined**

The life history presents the experiences and definitions held by one person, one group, or one organization as this person, group, or organization interprets those experiences. Becker (1966, pp. v–vi) describes it as

not conventional social science "data," although it has some of the features of that kind of fact, being an attempt to gather material useful in the formulation of general sociological theory. Nor is it a conventional autobiography . . . it is certainly not fiction. As opposed to these more imaginative and humanistic forms, the life history is more down to earth . . . less concerned with artistic values than with a faithful rendering of the subject's experience and interpretation of the world he lives in.

Life history materials include any record or document, including the case histories of social agencies, that throws light on the subjective behavior of individuals or groups. These may range from letters to autobiographies, from newspaper accounts to court records. A careful transcription of an interview, provided it does not intermix the interviewer's own interpretations, is as much a form of life history data as is a personal diary.

Every man, symbolic interactionism suggests, defines his world differently. If sociologists are to accurately explain these definitions and relate them to action, they must penetrate this subjective world of definitions, experiences, and reactions. Park, perhaps more than any other sociologist was sensitive to this methodological principle. He states:

In the case of human beings, it is the wide range of subjective life of mental and imaginative behavior which intervenes between stimulus and response, which makes human behavior fundamentally different from that of lower animals. It is this, too, which makes human behavior, particularly in the case of certain persons, so problematic and so difficult to understand. It is the purpose of the life history to get a record of this inner life [1927, p. 167].

*Assumptions of the Method*

Central assumptions of the life history are that human conduct is to be studied and understood from the perspective of the persons involved. All data that reflect upon this perspective will be employed. Clearly this is a case for taking the role of the acting other and actively sharing in his experiences and perspectives, and these notions of course lie at the heart of participant observation, which is one life history many times expanded, and are traceable to symbolic interactionism. Not to take the role of the other is to potentially supply the researcher's interpretations for the interpretations of those studied—and thereby slip into the fallacy of objectivism.

The sensitive observer employing the life history will be concerned with relating the perspectives elicited to definitions and meanings that are lodged in social relationships and social groups. Additionally, the variable nature of these definitions across situations will be examined. Concern will also be directed to recording the unfolding history of one person's, one group's, or one organization's experiences. This feature becomes a hallmark of the life history—the capturing of events over time. The sociologist employing the method becomes a historian of social life, be it the life of one person or of many persons similarly situated.

Finally it should be noted that because the life history presents the person's experiences as he defines them, the objectivity of the person's interpretations provides central data for the final report. The investigator must first, however, determine the subject's "own story." In fact, the subject's definition of the situation takes precedence over the objective situation because, as Thomas has argued:

There may be, and is, doubt as to the objectivity and veracity of the record, but even the highly subjective record has a value for behavior study. . . . Very often it is the wide discrepancy between the situation as it seems to others and the situation as it seems to the individual that brings about the overt behavior difficulty. . . . If men define situations as real, they are real in their consequences [1928, pp. 571–72].

In obtaining a life history, definitions of the situation will first be gathered and then the perspective of others who bear directly upon those definitions will be studied. This triangulation permits the analysis of varying definitions as they relate to the same behavioral unit. To understand definitions of the situation, the sociologist will first place his subject within the total range of units his single case represents. If the life history is of a juvenile delinquent, for instance, then a demographic and ecological analysis of the population of delinquents from which the single case is drawn must be presented. This permits generalizations to the broader population by studying a subunit from it—a basic principle of statistical sampling theory.

*Types of Life Histories*

Three basic forms of the life history can be distinguished: the complete, the topical, and the edited (see Allport, 1942, Chap. 6). *The complete life history* attempts to cover the entire sweep of the subject's life experiences. It will necessarily be long, many-sided, and complex. Shaw's life history of a juvenile delinquent, for example, initially ran some 200 pages, and was followed by a sociological interpretation. All of the forms, however, contain three central features: the person's "own story of his life," the social and cultural situation to which he and others see him responding, and the sequence of past experiences and situations in his life. Taking Shaw's life history as a case in point, the reader finds the subject describing his early childhood experiences, his educational history, his early contacts with the underworld, his initial reactions to being defined as a deviant, his association with other deviants, and finally his experiences in detention homes.

Juxtaposed against this first person description are data concerning the demographic and ecological features of the subject's neighborhood, information from psychiatrists and prison officials, and the subject's criminal record. The reader finds himself swept along by Stanley's report, feeling at various points the excitement that comes from reading a novel and sensing an identification with the author. This excerpt from the beginning of Stanley's story conveys this spirit.

To start out in life, everyone has his chances—some good and some very bad. Some are born with fortunes, beautiful homes, good and educated parents; while others are born in ignorance, poverty and crime. In other words, Fate begins to guide our lives even before we are born and continues to do so throughout life. My start was handicapped by a no-good, ignorant and selfish stepmother, who thought only of herself and her own children.

As far back as I can remember, my life was filled with sorrow and misery. The cause was my stepmother, who nagged me, beat me and insulted me, and drove me out of my own home. My mother died when I was four years old, so I never knew a real mother's affection. My father remarried when I was five years old [1966, p. 47].

The truthfulness of Stanley's statements was established by comparing them to interviews obtained from his stepmother, letters written by his sister, and formal records on his performance in the various detention homes to which he was sent. Presented with Stanley's definitions and those of his significant others, the reader is able to acquire a picture of Stanley's life up to the time the life history was prepared. This then is the central feature of the complete life history: a careful and studied representation of one person's, one organization's, or one group's entire life experiences.

*The topical life history* shares all of the features of the complete form except that only one phase of the subject's life is presented. Sutherland (1937), for example, in a presentation of the life of a professional thief, was only concerned with the experiences of one thief as they related to the social organization of professional crime. He describes his purpose as follows:

The principal part of this book is a description of the profession of theft by a person who had been engaged almost continuously for more than twenty years in that profession. This description was secured in two ways: first, the thief wrote approximately two-thirds of it on topics and questions prepared by me; second, he and I discussed for about seven hours a week for twelve weeks what he had written, and immediately after each conference I wrote in verbatim form, as nearly as I could remember, all that he had said in the discussion. I have organized this body of materials, written short connecting passages, and eliminated duplications as much as possible. In this organization I have attempted to preserve the ideas, attitudes and phraseology of the professional thief. The thief read the manuscript as organized and suggested corrections, which in all cases have been made [1937, p. iii].

There was little attempt by Sutherland to "objectify" the statement of his subject by reference to other sources or documents. What the reader finds is simply one man's conception of his profession with interpretations and annotations offered by Sutherland to clarify unusual terms and phrases. This is not to imply that the topical life history will never employ additional sources. In a study currently under way, I am obtaining a topical life history on the criminal experiences of a former professional con man who had been imprisoned for nearly twenty years. My main interest is in his activities as a professional thief and I am gathering data and materials from each prison he was in, from parole officers, from former employers, and from relatives. These statements are then placed against his interpretation of his life. I am retaining the form of Sutherland and Shaw by making the main body of the report a first person accounting.

The edited life history may be either topical or complete. Its key feature is the continual interspersing of comments, explanations, and questions by someone other than the focal subject. Sutherland, for example, approached an edited life history by his adding of annotations and interstitial passages. For purposes of theory construction and hypothesis testing, some degree of editing and interspersion of observer comments must be present. Without such intrusions, the life history must stand as its own sociological document.

## The Data of Life Histories

I began this chapter by noting that life history materials consist of any document that bears a relationship to a person's ongoing definitions and experiences. Two basic forms of these data may be noted: public archival records and private archival records (see Webb, et al., 1966, Chap. 3). The former are to be distinguished by the fact that they are prepared for the express purpose of examination by some set of others, often legally defined, as in the case of court records. The latter typically are not prepared for an audience. With the exception of a published autobiography, they seldom reach the hands of more than a few readers.

It is possible to introduce a classification of these two types of records, noting those that are primary in nature because of their direct reference to the subject and those that are secondary in nature. Secondary records represent reports that do not directly pertain to a specific subject, but instead to the class he represents. In addition, they may be sources written on the subject by a third person; it is possible to speak of letters written on a person, records of his family but not of him, and so on. The statements prepared by the subject are the personal documents of the life history. A complete life history will combine as many primary and secondary sources as possible, while focusing the report around the subject's own personal document.

## Public Archival Records

Generally speaking, the public archive is secondary in nature, although there will be occasions when court testimony, prison records, or newspaper accounts will directly refer to the focal subject. In these cases they become primary data sources. Four basic varieties of the public record may be noted (see Webb, *et al.*, 1966, Chap. 3). First are actuarial records concerning the personal and demographic elements of the population served by the record-keeping agency; these will range from birth and death statistics to records of marriages and divorces. Second are political and judicial records concerning court decisions, public votes, budget decisions, and so on. Third are other governmental or state documents such as weather reports, crime statistics, records of social welfare programs, and hospitalization records of the mentally and physically ill. Last are productions of the mass media pertaining to such issues as shifting political or social problems and instances of collective behavior. Mass media data may in addition involve the study of letters to editors, advertisements as business documents, comics and caricatures as works of fiction, and editorials and syndicated columns as expressions of opinion.

Landesco's (1964, pp. 559–76) study of organized crime in Chicago during the 1920's provides an illustrative case suggesting the ways in which these four types of public archival records may be combined to yield one life history of a social organization. The study was undertaken to arrive at a sociological accounting of the origin and growth of organized crime in Chicago and to trace the processes by which the underworld organization gained its control over the municipal governmental machinery of that city. His sources of data were several, involving participant observation, personal interviews with gangland leaders, political officials, and members of the police and the court system. Most important was his analysis of the following: County Board of Commissioners records; daily police bulletins; Chicago's major newspapers; records of the Crime Commission of Chicago; and reports from the Illinois Association for Criminal Justice.

In consulting these sources Landesco's intent was to arrive at a "Who's Who of Organized Crime in Chicago." By analyzing every name in the criminal news of the Chicago newspapers for a period of one year, a list of people involved was developed. He also categorized names appearing in the daily police bulletins. From these reports names of gang leaders were noted, as were the histories of the gangs for a 25-year period. This analysis yielded the names of gang members, gang leaders, and the names and activities of conflicting gangs and their leaders.

Life histories of the leaders in their gang settings were compiled and geographical locations of the gangs were determined. For a period of three and a half years, Landesco established personal contacts with gang members and leaders and prepared life histories on them. From official records of the Chicago Crime Commission and the Illinois Association for Criminal Justice, the probation and criminal records of the gang members were also determined. Out of these data, 7,000 records were secured and 400 names were selected for the "Who's Who in Organized Crime in Chicago." In constructing his final list, Landesco considered the following: a name had to appear in the news for a considerable period over the 25 years studied; a man had to occupy an important role in criminal news and criminal history; a man's place in organized crime had to be recorded; and the final list had to be cleared through the Bureau of Identification of the Police Department. A major discovery of his study was that most of the important gang leaders had only minor—some no—police records. Without further elaboration, it can be seen that public archival records should be combined with private and personal data if a comprehensive life history of a social organization is to be written. Histories that employ data only from the focal person(s) will usually be incomplete; as many different sources of data as possible should be gathered. If Landesco had relied only on police records, he would have uncovered very little data on the activities of gangland leaders.

*Private Archival Records*

The most important data for the life history are private records or documents. In these materials the subject's definitions of the situation emerge and it is precisely these definitions that the sociologist wants to juxtapose against the public document. Private documents include autobiographies; questionnaires, interviews, and verbatim reports; diaries, and letters; and artistic and projective materials. While no one of these sources is likely to provide a complete picture of the subject's life experiences, a combination of them will approach it closely.

## The Autobiography

The most common form of the personal document is the autobiography (see Allport, 1942, Chap. 6). It is often written on the basis of questions provided by the investigator and, of course, represents the subject's own interpretation of his life experiences. Two types of the autobiography may be distinguished: one that has been previously published, and one written at the request of the sociologist. With the previously published autobiography, the analyst must be aware of publication restrictions arising from canons of good taste and literary merit, and perhaps the goal of profit. On the other hand, the published form autobiography has the advantage of prior editorial criticism, which usually makes it easier to read. If it is the life of a distinguished and articulate person, it may also possess artistic and social significance. The unpublished autobiography will more strongly bear the imprint of the sociologist requesting it and will reflect the life of persons not ordinarily accorded social recognition or prestige.

Allport (1942, Chap. 6) has distinguished three types of the autobiography that correspond to the three types of the life history, the first a comprehensive autobiography, which covers the subject's life from the earliest point he can remember to the time of writing. It will deal with a relatively large number of lines of experience, giving, Allport suggests, a picture of variety, roundness, and interrelatedness of life.

The topical autobiography—for example, Sutherland's treatment of a professional thief—is an excision from the life of the subject. As such it invites comparison with other kinds of lives. Sociologists, for instance, might profitably compare the life of the professional thief with the professional experiences of the burglar, the con artist, or the embezzler on the basis of similarly constructed topical life histories.

Edited autobiographies, the third type of autobiography, have as their virtue the elimination of the length and repetitiousness of the comprehensive and topical autobiographies: The sociologist deliberately monitors the statements of his subject, selects certain materials for amplification, deletes others, and so places his stamp on the final product. (In a sense, all autobiographies bear this imprint because the subject probably would not have written his life history without prodding from the sociologist.)

But what portions of the material should be edited, and what should stand as stated by the subject? Allport (1942, p. 78) proposes the general guideline that unique styles of expressions (argot and colloquial phrasing) remain unedited; editing for the sake of clarity, or to remove repetitious material would seem justified.

When confronted with an articulate subject, the sociologist is able to test and refine his hypotheses through successive questions and probing. A single case or a series of such cases can then be employed to develop a grounded theory. This was the strategy of Lindesmith (1947) as he refined his theory of opiate addiction. Each statement of the subject and each phase of his life represents a universe of experiences that potentially confirms or negates hypotheses. As noted earlier, Sutherland monitored and edited and each modification and interpretation was subsequently presented to his subject who then responded to it.

The great merit of the autobiography, as Allport (1942, p. 77) states, is that it provides an "inside picture" of the subject's life, a side that is neither fully apparent nor fully public. It happens, however, that the author of the autobiography may not always be fully aware of what has occurred in his life. Furthermore, he may dress up, beautify, or hide what he is aware of. It is the job of the sociologist to probe and uncover such topics. What our subject's acts have been and what his habits are, we can know, as Park tells us. It is more important to learn:

What is it that habitually engages his attention? What are the subjects of his dreams and reveries? . . . In addition to these facts of his history, it is important to know however, his incompleted acts: what he hopes; what he dreams; what his vagrant impulses, "temptations," are [Park, 1952, p. 204].

In the autobiography the sociologist must keep the record of experiences separate from the interpretation given them. Here the triangulation of perspective becomes relevant. The sociologist hopes to discover the differences in definition and meaning attached to those events that form the core of his subject's experiences. This was the line taken by Shaw, in the case of Stanley. He states:

An important initial step in the study of the delinquent child is to procure a rather complete and accurate description of his delinquencies and other behavior difficulties. Among other things this description should show the specific offenses in the order of their occurrence, the chronological age of the child at the time of each offense, the immediate circumstances in which each offense occurred, and the number of persons involved. . . . In the present chapter materials are presented to give an objective picture of Stanley's difficulties. . . . The subjective and personal aspects of these problems (without which the picture is necessarily incomplete) are revealed in the boys "own story" which follows in subsequent chapters [1966, p. 32].

The final life history will not be a conventional autobiography. Life histories and the autobiographies they rest on

have rather the character of confessions, intimate personal documents intended to record not so much external events as to reveal sentiments and attitudes [Park, 1952, p. 204].

The sociologist who incorporates autobiographies into his life history should take steps to minimize the slighting of any relevant event. He must also insure that the subject's interpretations are accurately reported. These are two features often not present in the published autobiography because the subject may deliberately distort his life history to bring it into line with his present behavior. Further, the sociologist tries to keep his subject

oriented to the questions sociology is interested in, asks him about events that require amplification, tries to make the story jibe with matters of official record and with material furnished by others familiar with the person, event, or place being described [Becker, 1966, p. vi].

## The Diary

While few sociologists have employed the diary as a source of life history data, Allport has suggested that the spontaneous, intimate diary is the personal document par excellence because in it

the author sets down only such events, thoughts, and feelings as have importance to him; he is not so constrained by the task-attitudes that frequently control the production in letters, interviews, or autobiography [1942, p. 95].

In the diary the author may express self-feelings he otherwise would never make public, and in its ideal form the diary is unsurpassed as a continuous record of the subjective side of a man's life. Ideas are set down, disappear with age, are replaced with new thoughts, new feelings, new experiences. Turning points and reactions to personal tragedies may be recorded, and in the long-term diary sociologists may find a record surpassing the autobiography.

In contrast to the autobiography, the diary represents the immediate recording of experiences, unimpaired by reconstructions and distortions of memory. Because of the reconstructed nature of the autobiography, it may suffer from the *fallacy of motive attribution*; the diary is less susceptible to this. Observers frequently find the author of an autobiography constructing motives to explain his past behavior which, while realistic at the moment, may not be correct. In William Wordworth's poetic autobiography *The Prelude*, there is a deliberate attempt to reinterpret childhood experiences with nature from the literary and philosophical positions of Romanticism and pantheism. The interpretations are forced and inconsistent. Had Wordsworth kept a diary, critics would have another criterion by which to assess the credibility and authenticity of his autobiography.

Diaries may take several forms. Allport (1942, Chap. 7) proposes the following classification: the intimate journal, the memoir, and the log.

The intimate journal is perhaps the most useful of the three types for it contains "uncensored outpourings"—the entries being written discontinuously, either daily or at longer intervals of time. The biography of Dylan Thomas (Read, 1964) contains portions from his personal diary, notes kept by Thomas on poems he was writing, reflections on his financial status, and comments on his acceptance in the artistic world. For the sociologist interested in the private life of a public figure, the intimate journal provides data not elsewhere available.

At times the intimate journal approaches the status of a confessional diary in which the subject sets down his emotions and responses to particularly critical events. The recent work of Douglas (1967) on the social meanings of suicide has made extensive use of the confessional diary. At one point (pp. 291–310) he draws heavily from the diary of a suicide victim who over a four-year period kept a continuous confessional diary. In this instance, material not contained in the diary indicated that the subject (Marion) was a high school graduate living with her mother and sister in a middle-class Chicago residential neighborhood. She had met a young clerical worker, Thomas Whitford, at a high school dance and five months later married him. They moved out of her mother's home into a transient residential area near to Chicago's South Side. The first entry in her diary was made about two months after her marriage and indicates her concern with love, money, and the quarrels she was having with her husband. In the early part of 1913 she had an abortion, and she entered in her diary:

I asked Tom what he wished to do, if we could go on, and he suggested that we separate. . . . All of a sudden I seemed really to know what that would mean for me and I thought I would go mad. I certainly am an unhappy woman with him now sometimes; how should I feel without him? [Douglas, 1967, p. 291]

On her twenty-first birthday in February of 1915 she wrote "I hope that next year I won't be here to write." Early in January of 1916 she entered a period dominated by death wishes and after learning that Tom had spent a night with another woman wrote:

For the first time in my life I had the desire to kill, to plunge a dagger in her [the other woman's] heart. She's innocent. She didn't know he was married, and even so, she is not to blame. He is all wrong. . . . Oh, God, tell me. Let someone explain. . . . Is there any answer but the one? . . . All this is killing me, but thank God, I want to go. I want and beg to go home, to drop off this earth where there is no place for me—where I don't want a place. . . . I wish to God I could drop off the earth and just end my life, but it is not so [Douglas, 1967, p. 291].

A little more than a year later, she and Tom parted, and she began living with another man, Bert. Her despondency continued, and the next-to-last entry in the diary reads:

He lay on the lounge, and I sat and looked at him. He told me it was none of my business what he does. Oh, God, I'm miserable. This is the last straw, to have him untrue, and to lie about it. . . . I told Bert he was playing with fire, but he will not take seriously anything I say [Douglas, 1967, pp. 293–96].

On the next day Bert phoned her and they met for lunch. She writes

I'm glad I didn't phone first. I am all broken up about Bert. My sense of honor (Oh God, how ridiculous that sounds, for me) tells me to leave my Bert, who belongs to another. Someday I will have the strength [p. 296].

This was the last entry in her diary. What happened between Marion and Bert when they met is not known, but Bert stayed with her the night of May 6, and sometime while he slept Marion shot and killed him and then killed herself.

From these data Douglas extracts a number of salient themes, noting the recurrent statements by Marion of "dying in order to go home to rest at peace with God." In addition he notes her attempt to "blame others" for suicidal wishes. But a point that also emerges is Marion's wish to take along with her the "other" who caused her pain and dishonor. Douglas concludes by classifying Marion's suicide as a form of substantial self-escape from this world that also represents a transformation of suicide into a reunion with a loved one. Douglas' interpretation and Cavan's (1928, from which Douglas drew the diary materials) would have been substantially improved had they possessed more complete life history material, however. Nowhere does the reader find data from the men involved in Marion's life, for example. Hence, the observer is left with only Marion's "story"—it is not possible to juxtapose this story against the interpretations of her significant others—and an elaborate explanation of Marion's suicidal motives on the basis of just her story is tenuous. As a general rule, then, diaries should always be combined with other life history materials.

The memoir is the second form of the diary. It is basically impersonal in nature and may be written in a few sittings. In this respect it may resemble the autobiography, although it typically contains much less about the subject and his personal life. It becomes more of an objective "accounting" of his affairs. Records kept by foreign correspondents represent the memoir, as does William Shirer's *Berlin Diary*, for example. Faris' (1967) recent accounting of one phase in the University of Chicago Department of Sociology's history takes on the flavor of a memoir, although it draws on the perspectives of more than one person. Still, its data are mainly career biographies, records of publications, courses taught in the department, and so on. The impersonality of the memoir substantially reduces its sociological significance for many interactional purposes.

The log is an "account book," a record of events, of happenings, a list of meetings, of visits, of trips and so on. It may also contain time-budget accounts, but its typical form is depersonalized. This is not to degrade its importance as a personal document. When placed against a topical autobiography, the log may fill gaps concerning the subject's day-to-day patterns of interaction that would not otherwise appear. Recent work by Barker and Wright (1954) has made excellent use of the log in depicting the ordinary patterns of interaction of members in one small community. Time budgets on a large number of like-situated persons—in an organization, for example —can provide a vibrant picture of the daily rhythm of conduct in the setting. Again, however, logs taken alone are too depersonalized to suffice as complete life history data.

## Letters

In contrast to diaries and autobiographies, which are directed (initially at least) to only one person (the author), the letter has a dual audience—the writer and the recipient. This fact introduces an element that must be considered in letter analysis, for the document may reveal more about the relationship between the author and the recipient than about either alone. The analyst of letters (Allport, 1942, pp. 108–10) must consider who the recipient is, what the relationship is between the writer and the recipient, and who the author is. The topic of the letters and the nature of the relationship represented by the letter must also be considered. In many senses letters may be said to reveal as much about the letter writer as they do about the person receiving them. The style of address, the mode of presentation, the topics covered and the frequency of writing all reveal elements about one person's perception of another. In the letter the author raises his own experiences up for examination and presents them to another in a fashion that he feels will be acceptable and interpretable. Allport comments:

If they are defective in revealing many sides of one personality, they are undoubtedly successful in revealing the tie between two personalities. Dyadic relationships, tapped by letters, constitute a neglected chapter in social psychology [1942, pp. 108–9].

This seems almost too restrictive, for the letter may reveal a good deal about the personality of the author, particularly if observers have access to a cross-section of letters that go to more than one person. The recently published letters of Dostoevsky (Magne, 1964), for example, reveal his conception of his friends and family while presenting the emergent personality of the author over a period of fifty years. In Dostoevsky's letters the reader finds the purest form of his autobiographical memoirs. Put with the sometimes thinly veiled autobiography of his novels and stories, his letters provide a major source for reconstructing his private life, for in the letters the reader finds the progressions Dostoevsky underwent from a moody adolescent to a budding author, to his life as a convict, to his years as a successful author.

Sociologists have been prone to ignore the value of the letter as a source of data, but historians and literary critics have made extensive use of such data as they attempt to reconstruct the life of important literary and historical figures (see Gottschalk, 1945: Chap. 2). With few exceptions, sociological uses of the letter have dealt with the products of the deviant, the immigrant, and the social outcast. Thomas and Znaniecki (1927) for example made extensive use of letters of the Polish peasant to uncover the transitional problems involved in moving from one social setting to another.

Two recent uses of this form of the personal document have been the suicide studies of Garfinkel (1967) and his associates and the study of a religious cult (1966) by Lofland. In Lofland's study of a small California religious cult that predicted the coming of a "Christ-Messiah" in the year 1967, letters were analyzed to reveal the conversionary and proselytizing efforts of the group. In the course of his study Lofland discovered that after the period of acceptance into the cult, the new member developed a rhetoric to neutralize his emotional conflicts. The following open letter to his family by a young soldier conveys the "powerful (and classic) content of this facilitating and justifying rhetoric":

I wrote my family a very long, detailed, but yet very plain letter about our movement and exactly what I received in spiritual ways, plus the fact that Jesus had come to me himself. The weeks passed and I heard nothing, but I waited with deep trust in God.

This morning I received a letter from my mother. She . . . surmised that I was working with a group other than those with the "stamp of approval by man." She . . . called me a fanatic, and went on to say: "My fervent constant prayer is that time will show you the fruitlessness of the way you have chosen before it consumes you entirely. A real true religion is deep in the heart and shines through your countenance for all to see. One need not shout to the house tops either."

At first it was the deepest hurt I had ever experienced. But I remember what others in our [Divine Precepts] family have given up and how they too have experienced a similar rejection. But so truly, I can now have a little rejection that our beloved Master experienced [Lofland, 1966, p. 55–56].

The letter goes on to praise others who have shared the same rejections. The letter reveals an important element of the author's personality. He is willing to experience rejection from a significant other for a higher good. The letter also reveals his interpretation of the personality of his mother. She simply does not understand the goal he is striving for. Lofland's study surpasses the usual investigation that relies on only one source of life history data. He meticulously weaves a complete life history of all his central subjects around the intents of the cult movement. Their family histories are recorded, as are their educational and occupational histories. In addition, personal interviews are woven around letter and diary analysis, and last, he complements these data with direct observations of the subjects. Thus a behavioral component of the life history is combined with the personal document.

Jacobs' (1967, pp. 60–72) analysis of 112 suicide notes is use of yet another type of letter: messages written by a person to which no reply is intended. The suicide note represents a truncated form of communication, but more than the ordinary letter that assumes a reply, it reveals the termination of a relationship. Jacobs analyzed the notes into six categories. *First form notes* represented the largest single category of the notes (1967, p. 67) and were characterized by the author's begging for "forgiveness or request for indulgence," as the following excerpt illustrates:

It is hard to say why you don't want to live. I have only one reason. The three people I have in the world don't want me.
Tom, I love you so dearly but you have told me you don't want me and don't love me [Jacobs, 1967, p. 67].

The author of the note makes similar statements to her father and mother, and concludes:

I love you all dearly and am sorry this is the way I have to say goodbye.
Please forgive me and be happy.
Your wife and your daughter [1967, p. 68].

Jacobs extracts from this note the hypothesis that the author is involved in a complex of long–standing problems. Unable to solve them, she has no other alternative than to take her own life. To justify this extreme act, she begs indulgence and forgiveness on the part of the survivors.

The problem of analyzing the suicide note, or any note when it is taken out of relational context, becomes apparent. Lacking direct data from the suicide victim, Jacobs is forced to construct *his* definition of the meaning contained in the note. While it may be that one motive for committing suicide is the confrontation of insurmountable problems, this must be taken as only a hypothesis and not a conclusion. To substantiate such a hypothesis the sociologist would need other data from and on the victim: interviews with the relatives mentioned in the note, previous notes or letters written by the suicide, and certainly standard life history data involving previous problems.

While notes, suicidal or otherwise, represent a peculiar form of the letter, they should not be taken at face value, nor should they be used singly; their meaning must be challenged, and triangulated beyond the sociologist's interpretation.

## Questionnaires, Interviews and Verbatim Reports

Earlier I pointed out that for a life history to have a broad sociological significance, it necessarily must be oriented to "the questions sociology is interested in." Obviously these questions will vary according to the theoretical and research orientations of each sociologist, but the point stands: Extensive use must be made of the questionnaire, the interview, and the verbatim report. The reason for such inclusions is to keep the subject mindful that many of his life experiences are of sociological importance even though they may appear unimportant to him. The questionnaire, or life history guide as it more properly becomes, serves as a guide to the subject as he orders his thoughts and conveys them to the sociologist. It also insures topics will not be forgotten or overlooked. In addition, it will become the major source of operationalization for the concepts contained in the theoretical framework under analysis.

In this context, it is justifiable to admit as life history data any questionnaire or interview schedule that permits the subject to express his opinions. Allport (1942) would *exclude* as sources of data structured and scaled questionnaires, or self-administered questionnaires that force the subject into a predetermined format. Tape recordings of interview sessions and short essays written on open-ended questions will become the major forms taken by this element of the life history.

There will be dimensions of the interview guide that may become quite structured, however—such sociopersonal dimensions as age, sex, years of education, occupational history, mobility patterns, religious and political preferences, perceived social status, and so on. But if a structured format is employed, even if only on a few items, the investigator must continually enable the subject to "personalize" the questions and bring them within his frame of reference. The subject, thus can be told to use the questions as guides and props and instructed to

disregard questions having no vital application to his life; he can be encouraged to rearrange his exposition so that the order of topics suits his convenience and style. In short, the suggestive influence of the guide can to some extent be counteracted so that only its value as a prod to memory remains [Allport, 1942, p. 89].

### Guidelines for the Questionnaire and Interview

If life histories are to be compared, some guidelines must be established for purposes of comparability, but there seems little consensus in the psychological and sociological literature concerning the form these guidelines should take. Each spokesman seems to speak only for his own theoretical perspective. My position holds that some set of uniform standards must be established, but that they should be broad enough to permit each investigator to adopt them to his specific case.

Such standards must not sacrifice "the spontaneity of self-written accounts produced by the subject in his own way, in solitude, and at his own convenience [Allport, 1942, p. 94]." In this context it is useful to review several proposals for ordering the life history guide. Dollard, a cultural-psychoanalyst, proposes a Freudian model for the life history. He stresses (1935) the following dimensions: The subject must be viewed as a specimen in a cultural series; the organic motors of action ascribed must be socially relevant; the peculiar role of the family group in transmitting the culture must be recognized; the specific method of elaboration of organic materials into social behavior must be shown; the social situation must be continuously specified as a factor; the continuous related character of experience from childhood to adulthood must be stressed; the life history material must be organized and conceptualized.

Dollard's formulation directs attention to early family influences on the subject, while pointing to the impact of cultural settings in the developmental process. Noticeably absent in his formulation is the consideration of the interaction factor in personality development (K. Young, 1952, pp. 305-6). If the self arises out of interaction, then those crucially developmental interactions that shape the self must be recorded. Dollard also fails to mention the importance of standard demographic and sociopersonal data. If, as I have previously argued, the subject of any life history represents a set of similarly situated units, then the objective features of this set must be identified. Certainly researchers must have such data as educational history, age, and occupational experiences. A further difficulty with Dollard's formulation is its individualistic bias. Life histories may be gathered on groups, organizations, and even communities. His outline presents few guidelines for movement above the individual to larger collectivities.

Kimball Young (1952, pp. 303-11, 320-22, 687-93) has presented perhaps the most elaborate guideline for the life history. He divides his proposal into the following areas: data on the family (including the subject, his father and his mother); developmental history of the individual, including experiences confronted in childhood, pre-adolescence, adolescence, and adult life; the nature and meaning of the inner (subjective) life, including such topics as emotional stabilities, sense of the self, power devices, recreational and avocational activities, basic satisfactions, and work as a value. This proposal completely covers the life-cycle. It has the advantage of being so complete that it could be used with a group, or members of an organization. It also contains recommendations concerning data on demographic and sociopersonal aspects. Thus Young suggests that the age, sex and names of all family members be collected. Residential patterns, ethnic variations, health histories, major occupations, educational levels, religious and political affiliations, and perceived social status are other dimensions he suggests examining. These factors lend themselves to a structured format, although they are stated so that each person can attach his own meaning to them.

Lemert (1951, pp. 445–46) has proposed a more focused format for the organization of the life history. His is a guide for the study of the deviant and entails:

1. *The nature of the deviation*, including information on the ways the deviant is different from normals in terms of his patterns of interaction and so on. Data also should be collected on the subcultural nature of the deviance, its relationship to a social organization and the deviant's role in that organization.

2. *The societal reaction to the deviant*, including the general reaction to the deviation (e.g., acceptance, rejection, or inconsistent). Also record the degree of social distance between the deviant and his community, and make note of the social definitions attached to him and his deviance. Last, has society's reaction to deviant made him more dependent or independent of that society?

3. *The natural history of the deviant*, including a description of childhood and adult development. Are there crisis points in the history at which the self-conception changed? How did the family react and was the deviance learned in the family? What sort of self-conception does the deviant presently have and does this correspond with the social definitions attached to him?

4. *Social participation*, in which data will reflect deviant's occupational status and income and the impact of his deviance upon these dimensions. Additional data should be collected on the impact of the deviance on his sex, family participation, political, religious, educational, and recreational activities.

In many aspects Lemert's proposal mirrors Young's, except that it is explicitly focused on the deviant. Although Young's is much longer, it can be adopted to any category or subject.

## The Natural History Approach to Life Histories

The strength of Young's and Lemert's proposals lies in the emphasis on the natural history of events over time. The best can be taken from Young and Lemert, keeping in mind that any set of standards should be flexibly viewed. I would begin with standard personal-social data of the subject and his significant others. The natural history flavor of Lemert's approach can then be adopted to any category of participants or social collectivities. Next, the nature of the interaction to be studied would be recorded. This might be deviance, proclivities for social organization, or the orderly development of a normal personality. Third, the natural history of this interaction pattern would be examined. Critical points of reference, early societal reactions, and points of stabilities would be studied in this section.

When the investigator employs the life history guide, his first step will be to list the objective career points in the subject's life. If the study is of a deviant, it would focus first on the deviant's behavior problems, his arrests, court appearances, and commitments. These experiences are then arranged in the order of their occurrence and presented to the subject as a guide in writing his "own story" (see Shaw, 1966, p. 22). These experiences become reference points that the subject speaks to. His instructions will be to give a complete and detailed account of each experience, the situation in which it occurred, and the impression it made on him.

The sociologist may find that the subject's initial attempt at reconstructing his life history is meager and incomplete. If so, the analyst will take specific instances from the subject's life and have him more fully elaborate them. This process of obtaining a complete ordering of the subject's life will necessitate a long series of interview sessions—which typically follow after the subject has prepared some statement. Through continual interaction, the life history begins to take shape. Previous omissions are filled and elaborated, and refinements are brought out.

If the natural history outline approach is employed, the subject becomes the main source of data on the outline. The sociologist functions to draw out the critical experiences and sociologically relevant aspects of the life as it transpired.

## The Data of the Life History in Summary

I have presented forms of data utilized in the life history. Unfortunately few users of the method have concerned themselves with combining as many data sources as possible. Thus some use only interviews, while others analyze notes and letters, and still others use only the extended autobiography. In practice, "we still find various techniques intermingled, with personal documents playing only an incidental role [Allport, 1942, p. 121]." I have argued repeatedly that triangulation is the best strategy. The life history can also be conceived of as a triangulated research technique. Letters, diaries, notes, interviews, and personal compositions by the focal subject must be simultaneously combined to yield the final product. The best focus for the life history becomes, then, the "prolonged interview" in which subject and sociologist continuously interact and reflect upon the subject's statements. This prolonged interview becomes the strategy for combining observations, introspective reports, testing, and questionnaires. The findings of one method reinforce and validate the findings of another. Indeed, as Allport states:

The internal consistency, or self-confrontation, of evidence obtained by such polydimensional approaches is almost the only test we have for the validity of our researches. So by all means let personal documents fall into a larger battery of methods [1942, p. 121].

An additional point: The life history must contain reports from persons other than the subject. Not only must users of life histories triangulate methodologies, but they must also triangulate perspectives. The analysis of diaries and suicide notes indicated the problems that arise when only the subject's report is employed. Unless the perspectives of others are brought to bear upon the subject's statements, observers have no way of assessing the idiosyncrasies of those interpretations.

## Analytic Strategies and Dimensions of the Life History

Thus far I have discussed the major forms of the life history and the various data it rests upon. Remaining to be treated are the forms of data analysis employed in the method, and categories of internal and external validity as they relate to life history analysis.

### The Causality Problem

In solving the causality problem, I recommend that the sociologist employ analytic induction in his analysis of life history materials. The thrust of analytic induction, as noted in Chapter 9, is to formulate, through progressive revisions of the research hypothesis, a series of propositions that have universal application. The life history method becomes the paradigmatic form of this analysis, for the investigator *assumes* that the case, or cases, he has intensively analyzed portray the universe from which they were selected.

Analytically (Allport, 1942, Chap. 4) the sociologist may choose to formulate either idiographic or nomothetic propositions and explanations. If he chooses the latter, his attempt will be to generalize the cases analyzed to the total population; if the former, his analysis will relate only to the case under study. Idiographic analysis is the intensive study of one case with the attempt being to formulate lawful statements that pertain only to that case. The rationale for it rests in the assumption that because no two lives are the same, causal propositions will never be identical from case to case. Therefore the laws of science must rest fundamentally on the idiographic mode of analysis.

Nomothetic analysts, on the other hand, claim that the only scientific laws are statistically derived from the analysis of a large number of cases; they disparage the case study method. Lundberg, for example, makes the case document "a helpless tail to the statistical kite":

It is the thesis of this paper that the assumed opposition or incompatibility between these two methods is illusory for three principle reasons: (1) The case method is not in itself a scientific method at all, but merely the first step in the scientific method; (2) individual cases become of scientific significance only when classified and summarized in such form as to reveal uniformities, types, patterns of behavior; (3) the statistical method is the best, if not only, scientific method of classifying and summarizing large numbers of cases. The two methods are not, therefore, under any circumstances opposed to each other, nor is the one a substitute for the other. . . . Thus, the only possible question as to the relative value of the case method and the statistical method resolves itself into a question as to whether classification of, and generalizations from, the data should be carried out by the random, qualitative, and subjective method of common observation or through the systematic, quantitative and objective procedures of the statistical method [1926, p. 61].

Lundberg's statement is quite clear—the life history, case method is unscientific, impressionistic, and of use only in the exploratory phases of research. Allport replies to this interpretation by offering the rationale of the idiographic method.

*What for the nomothetist is hard to contemplate is the very real possibility that no two lives are alike in their motivational processes.* To assume that causation is identical from case to case is to overlook the point that Lewin has emphasized, namely that *lawful determinism* need not be based upon the frequency of occurrence in multitudes of cases, but may apply to onetime happenings (to the single life). If each personality harbors laws peculiar to itself; if the course of causation is personal instead of universal, then only the intensive idiographic study of a case will discover such laws [1942, p. 57].

Unfortunately this dialogue has ignored the fact that it is possible to discover propositions that pertain to a total population by the use of a single or small set of life histories. This is the solution offered by analytic induction. Each case studied, and each event within each case, becomes a critical source of data that either validates or disconfirms a previous hypothesis.

Lundberg errs by charging that the life history lacks a scientific base. There certainly is no better way to establish covariance and time order between a set of variables than with a method that explicitly focuses on events over time. Because analytic induction, when employed in conjunction with the triangulated methodology, rests on several distinct sources of data, the observer is aided in the discovery of contradictions as well as confirmations of emergent research hypotheses.

An example is in order. In the previous chapter I extensively quoted from Lindesmith's study of the opiate addict to show how universal propositions may be uncovered with the life history method. Lindesmith's study provides a base against which all life histories should be judged. Analytic induction was his model of proof and inference and each case was viewed as potentially negative in the sense that it could invalidate a previous hypothesis.

Lemert's (1958, pp. 141–48) study of the systematic check forger extends Lindesmith's approach. His purpose was to test Sutherland's theory that all professional thieves are involved in a behavior system that validates and supports their illegal behavior. Through the intensive analysis of 72 check forgers Lemert challenges the applicability of Sutherland's formulations by showing that with this category of thief, no systematic behavior system is present. He shows (1967, p. 116) that the class characteristics and backgrounds of systematic forgers incline them to avoid intimate association with other criminals. His use of the life history method leads him to invalidate a previous theory, and he then proceeds in a series of other papers to present a theory that does account for their conduct [see Lemert, 1967].

## Sampling Models and the Life History

If analytic induction provides the model of inference for the life history method, then it is apparent that the sampling model becomes a variant of theoretical sampling theory. However, a statistical sample model may be employed in the early state of the research when the cases for analysis are selected. Thus if observers are collecting life histories on imprisoned criminals, they might randomly select a handful of such persons. Random selection removes any initial bias that might otherwise be present. If we are interested in unique cases not widely distributed, however, nonrandom sampling models are in order. Once the case has been selected, theoretical sampling becomes the main method of selecting topics for analysis; theoretical saturation becomes centrally relevant. If the life history is topical, then every event during the period covered must be thoroughly saturated before other events can be analyzed. Burgess (1966, pp. 188–97) suggests that all life histories begin with the objective career points in the subject's life. This would entail the subject's report, as well as statements by all other persons involved in his experiences. Also, as many different types of data would be brought to bear upon each phase as are available and empirically possible.

Employing theoretical sampling in conjunction with analytic induction, the sociologist searches for contradicting data and takes his observations to all areas of his subject's life that have relevance for the topic at hand.

Theoretical saturation occurs when all available and relevant sources of data have been exhausted. It must be remembered that theoretical saturation may not correspond to what the subject regards as a complete statement. When such situations occur it is better to permit the subject's statements to run their course, than to prematurely cut him off—but the sociologist must consider the sociological explanation. There can be no hard and fast rule in this respect—saturation may occur at any point in the study and the only criterion the investigator can employ is the compatibility of each statement with all that preceded it. If contradictions are located, then saturation has not been achieved. If no contradictions appear and if no more data are available or relevant, then saturation has occurred. It is important to record all sources of data systematically in terms of their compatibility and internal consistency. The sociologist must continually monitor the data as they are collected. A life history is written at every point in the collection process, and thus it becomes quite difficult to conceive of the life history going through the phases of conceptualization, hypothesis formulation, hypothesis testing, analysis, and writeup. Analytic induction and theoretical sampling, as interrelated strategies, prohibit such a classification.

*Problems of Internal and External Validity*

In the discussion of participant observation, the factors of internal and external validity were intensively treated. In many respects it is unnecessary to repeat that discussion, for nearly every statement concerning that method has direct relevance to the life history. For example, external validity demands that the sociologist demonstrate that his case selected for study is representative of the population to which he wishes to generalize. He must also show that the restrictions arising from time and spatial location have been considered and adequately treated. These latter two dimensions of external validity most frequently account for noncomparability between life history investigations. Thus Lemert's findings that the systematic check forger is not a member of a behavior system contradicts Sutherland's earlier findings in this regard. As one causal proposition, Lemert (1967, pp. 109–18) suggests that historical factors intervening between his study and Sutherland's account for his difference: The check forger in the 1950's is responding to a different set of cultural and historical conditions than the forger in the early 1920's. If continuity between life history investigations is to occur, each investigator must carefully document the historical conditions operative on his subject at the time of data collection.

Internal validity raises a peculiar class of problems with the life history, for when dealing with one case researchers must be aware of their reactive effects and of changes that are going on as the subject reconstructs his life. Because the life history variously rests on public and private archival data, this problem is confounded by the fact that certain pieces of information may never be validated in a triangulated sense. A lost letter, a discarded diary, and a newspaper account by a deceased reporter are a few instances of data that must be accepted on face value.

The dimensions of internal validity refer to events that occur *both before and after the study has begun.* They are intrinsic to the research act. Thus, when the subject is reconstructing his life he certainly responds to his perception of maturational influences present in the various phases of his life. But also, once the study has begun, both he and the sociologist will be undergoing changes, maturationally and symbolically, that may influence the validity of all subsequent observation. Consideration must be given both aspects of internal validity, first with interactions that occur after the life history is begun. *Historical factors may not* have relevance in production of the life history, but if the time lapse is great, extending over several years, they certainly must be considered. If the time span is relatively short (e.g., less than a year) then distortion would be decreased, though it cannot be ignored. Again, the perspective of the subject must be brought forth, and if he defines certain situations as important and as intrusive, they must be recorded.

*Maturational variables* should be treated just as historical factors, although the investigator must be sensitive to an interaction between the two. For example in Shaw's *The Jack-Roller,* the first interview with Stanley was conducted when he was sixteen years and eight months old. In that interview a list of his behavior difficulties, delinquencies, and commitments up to that time was secured and he prepared a brief document based on those experiences. One month later he was arrested and charged with burglary and "jack-rolling" and was committed to the Chicago House of Correction for one year. The life history was not resumed until one year later, at which time Stanley was informed that his first story was "an excellent summary of his life, but lacked detailed descriptive material [Shaw, 1966, p. 23]." In response to a request for elaboration, he prepared a document of approximately 250 typewritten pages. Neither Shaw, nor Burgess who summarized this life history, made note of the potential changes Stanley had undergone as a result of his one-year experience in a correction home, nor did they make reference to historical changes that might have transpired during that time period that would have led Stanley to alter the definitions and interpretations contained in the earlier and much shorter personal document. As a general rule it is recommended that all life histories extending over a significant length of time, or which are interrupted by movements in the subject's life during the time of preparation, carefully consider any reactive changes that might arise because of this time delay or interruption. At the very least the investigator should have the subject reconsider all earlier statements in light of the changes undergone. Modifications should be made and noted, linking them, if possible, to the maturational and historical variables.

The problem of *subject bias* should be of little relevance in the life history, since biasing features should have been treated in the early selection and sampling phase. *Subject mortality* could conceivably leave the investigator with an incomplete life history, and because only a few subjects are being considered at any one time, the mortality factor looms as a major threat to this research strategy.

*Reactive effects of the observer* should be seriously considered, because it is the observer's presence that is likely to lead the subject to write a life history, and intrusions of the observer's personality must carefully be recorded and guarded against. This is a subtle factor to control, because until the observer develops a "relationship of substance" with the subject, he will be unable to assess any reactive effects. After the relationship is established, several strategies are available. The observer may have the subject go back over their earlier conversations and productions and reevaluate them in terms of his present feelings. The observer may keep a notebook on what he feels his impact has been. Such an ongoing record permits a detailed analysis that may later be added to the life history. By all means, the subject's aversions to certain topics of his life, and his preservation of others, should be noted. In the course of a life history now under collection, I have become aware of this reactive effect. Initially I began by having the subject (an ex-criminal) record his formal experiences with crime and then give me detailed statements on each. I became aware that he was deliberately avoiding a series of crimes committed in a specific period of his life. Some months later he confessed that he had deliberately withheld this information until he felt he could trust me. He then prepared a long statement on those episodes. Precisely what had transpired over that time and what I had done to convey my "trustworthiness" was unclear to me, but I kept a running log on our relationship and have noted this turning point.

Reactive effects of the observer are closely related to *changes in the observer* over the course of the study. He may begin the study with certain aversions concerning his subject's life and subsequently modify these definitions. Certainly he will become more knowledgeable concerning the subject, forming a social relationship with him. In fact it is quite probable that the subject and the observer will become friends before the study is over. Just what impact this may have on the final product is again unpredictable. It may lead the observer to delete undesirable materials and to overemphasize others. This is difficult to quantify and the burden fundamentally rests on the sociologist to determine, assess, and record such changes. It is suggested that the observer maintain a logbook over the entire period of the study; the publication of such logs would go far toward objectifying these dimensions. If they were presented alongside the subject's personal document, their analysis would permit other sociologists to assess the final objectivity and validity of the published life history (see Kluckhohn, 1945, pp. 150–55). They would also permit others to learn from one's own mistakes and to employ to advantage those strategies that seemed to work best.

The relevance of such logs is seen in Thrasher's *The Gang* (see 1963 ed.), which is based on life history material gathered from 1,113 gangs in

Chicago. Nowhere in Thrasher's monograph is the reader told how the materials were gathered, what their sources were, or what the author's relationship was to those who gave him the materials (see Short, 1963, pp. xvii–xxiv). Consequently, the internal validity of Thrasher's report becomes suspect. And it is virtually impossible to replicate this portion of his study.

I have suggested that *the situations of observation* have important influences in participant observation, experiments, and surveys. They seem to be of less importance in the life history. Generally, the core interviews will be gathered in one setting, frequently the office of the sociologist, or in some other mutually agreeable location. Sutherland states, for example, that the interviews with Chic Conwell were conducted in his office over a twelve-week period. Becker (1961) has reported that the interviews constituting his and the Hughes' life history on a female drug addict were largely conducted in his home. Obviously this situation will vary by the subject, the topic at hand, and the relationship between the observer and the subject. Unless behavioral observations occupy an important role in the final document, it seems accurate to state that situational variations will be of little import in the life history. The observer should, however, inform his readers where his observations were gathered and in what situations his subject prepared the personal documents contained in the study.

## The Subject and Internal Validity

Researchers must be sensitive to the fact that each of the above dimensions also has direct reference to the subject and the reports he prepares. In a sense, the subject becomes a sociologist during the course of the study, and it is reasonable to assume that his own self-attitudes, definitions, and feelings will be drastically altered during the course of this activity. Focusing, as he must, upon his own life, he is likely to adopt a peculiar self-stance—a stance that begins to challenge the past autobiographies he has constructed.

All persons, located as they are at various points in their own moral careers, construct a personally convenient and socially acceptable picture of their life up to and including the future. Goffman has suggested:

Given the stage any person has reached in a career, one typically finds that he constructs an image of his' life course—past, present, and future—which selects, abstracts, and distorts in such a way as to provide him with a view of himself that he can usefully expound in current situations. Quite generally, the person's line concerning self, defensively brings him into appropriate alignment with the basic values of his society, and so may be called an apologia. If a person can manage to present a view of his current situation which shows the operation of favorable personal qualities in the past and a favorable destiny awaiting him, it may be called a success story. If the facts of a person's past and present are extremely dismal, then about the best he can do is to show that he is not responsible for what has become of him, and the term sad tale is appropriate [1961, pp. 150–51].

The sociologist must be aware that his subject is likely to present some variation on the success story in his life history. Under unusual conditions a subject may focus on a sad tale, but it is likely to cover only certain areas of his life. Quite obviously an accurate life history will lie somewhere between these two extremes. It is the function of the sociologist to bring his subject around to this middle ground—around to a picture of his life that includes more than the good or only the bad.

During this process the subject will adopt the peculiar self-stance of the sociologist, while maintaining a portion of his former self. He will call forth unpleasant experiences and attempt to cover them up. On occasion the unpleasant will become socially acceptable topics to him. At such times the relationship established with the sociologist becomes centrally important. The observer's integrity and trustworthiness may be challenged, just as the character of the subject may now be challenged by virtue of the statements being made.

To the extent that the above processes operate during the collection of the life history, the observer must record the subjective changes (maturational and otherwise) his subject is undergoing. If such changes are not noted, the life history may suffer because of shifts in perspective that occur over the period of collection. Matters are further complicated when it is realized that events occurring years ago may be called forth by the subject. The actual occurrence of such events, the role of the subject in them, the situation in which they occurred, and the outcome of interaction within them must all be called forth and contemplated by the subject. His memory may have faded, leading him to present any of the above factors incorrectly. He may also have incorrectly interpreted them at their time of occurrence. Given such possibilities, what may the sociologist do?

There are several alternatives. First, it must be remembered that the objectivity of a recalled event is of less value than is its subjective impact on the person recalling it. It is appropriate to repeat Thomas' statement, "If men define situations as real, they are real in their consequences." The subjective remembrances and interpretations must be taken at face value— but in addition to these, as many different perspectives as possible must be brought to bear upon that specific event and situation. Herein lies the tremendous importance of letters, diaries, and the personal reflections of others. Under certain conditions it may be possible to consult the records of public agencies to triangulate the interpretation of the subject. Court records could, for example, be placed against a juvenile delinquuent's report of what went on at his hearing. Records of prison officials can be compared to a convict's statement that he was a "loner." The possibilities seem infinite in this regard and as many as possible should be employed.

During the subject's life, historical events may have transpired that he feels have had important influences upon him. Being sent to prison, drafted during war time, being married and divorced, and having been forced out of a job during an economic depression are events that could have drastically altered his life and life chances. Any such event that is assigned importance by the subject must be noted.

*Further Problems in the Analysis of Life History Data: Some*
*Comments on the Historical Method*

The sociologist compiling a life history is confronted with many of the same problems historians resolve through the use of what is termed the historical method (see Gottschalk, 1945). Examples of such problems include imputing a motive to the deceased author of a crucial document (e.g., the suicide note); analyzing a document that appears inauthentic; establishing the fact that the author of a document is in fact the author; discovering the meaning of a document after its authenticity has been established. These are issues that lie at the heart of any form of document analysis. The sociologist is aided by the fact that his subject is typically "before" him, and hence some of these problems can be overcome. But on many occasions the author will not be present, or the sources of other critical documents may not be.

Any method that attempts to collect, record and analyze documents from the past and to weave these documents into a meaningful set of explanations is historical. The reconstruction of the past from such data is termed *historiography* (Gottschalk, 1945, pp. 8–9). Clearly the sociologist compiling a life history engages in some form of historiography. The sources of data employed by the historian parallel those of the sociologist (contemporary records, confidential reports, public reports, questionnaires, government documents, expressions of opinion in editorials, essays, fiction, song, poetry, and folklore). The historian classifies these data as primary sources (those involving the "testimony of an eyewitness") and secondary sources (those involving the testimony, or report of a person not present at the time of the events recorded) (see Gottschalk, 1945, pp. 10–14).

The historian's classification of the primary source refers to a document directly related to the subject (e.g., a letter written by him); the historian's secondary sources are those that refer not directly to the subject but to the class of persons he represents (e.g., court records on juvenile delinquents). Accordingly, I term the historian's primary sources first-hand reports, his secondary sources as second-hand reports. This permits me to classify primary sources by whether they are prepared by the subject or by some other person. It is necessary to consider the delay between the occurrence of an event and the time at which it was reported. The majority of life history data will of course be primary in nature, and of the first-hand variety. However, when the reports of others are brought in, then their second-hand nature must be considered. Thus, while a document by a focal subject may be contradicted by another's statement, observers would be led to suspect that statement if it was second-hand in nature, based, perhaps on hearsay. The problem is further confounded when we consider what literary critics and historians term *the reality distance problem.* That is, the analyst often finds himself several times removed from the problem he is studying. This may be stated in the following form: *reality* (subjectively perceived) leads to *subject's* interpretation, which is *translated* into a document (poem, letter, etc.) *perceived, interpretated and analyzed by the investigator* (art critic, historian, sociologist). A chain of interpretations can thus be envisioned. Each person who reads the document brings to it his general bias and feelings which may further distort its meaning. Analysts are thus brought back to the difficulty of communicating consensual meaning. It is impossible to escape the Thomas dictum regarding definitions of the situation—each person's statement initially has as much validity as any other persons. Furthermore, it must be recognized that no statement is ever interpreted exactly as it was intended by the speaker or author. All symbolic statements, Camus tells us: "always transcend the one who makes use of it [the author] and makes him say in reality more than he is aware of expressing [1960, p. 92]." Camus suggests "In this regard, the surest means of getting hold of it [the work] is not to provoke it, to begin the work without a preconceived attitude and not to look for its hidden currents [1960, p. 92]." However, even this cautioning principle is difficult to abide by. All observers approach their "realities" with preconceptions. The point, however, stands—when analyzing ambiguous documents, analysts must try to permit them to speak for themselves.

Still, there must be some general rules for judging the reliability and validity of a document. Following Gottschalk's (1945) discussion I state the following. First, the closer a subject is to the event he reports, the greater the validity and reliability. Second, because

Documents differ in *purpose* (some being intended purely as records or aids to one's own memory, some as reports to other persons, some as apologia, some as propaganda, and so on), the more serious the author's intention to make a mere record, the more dependable the source [Gottschalk, 1945, p. 16].

This rule presupposes the fact that analysts can infer the reason behind a document's preparation—a point that will be considered shortly. The third principle is based on the number of persons the document is intended for. Because, as Gottschalk notes, the tendency to embellish and dramatize a document may increase as the number of persons it is intended for increases, the greater the confidential nature of the report, the greater its probable validity. The fourth rule states that because the testimony of schooled or experienced observers is generally "superior to that of the untrained and casual reporter" researchers must give greater validity to those reports prepared by the more expert observer. Essentially this rule suggests that analysts give greater favor to those reports prepared by persons either closest to the event under study or who are trained at observation. Sociologists then suspect the naïve reports of a person who learns of an event at a distance. Similarly, the greater the familiarity of the author with the event, the greater the validity of his statements.

### External Criticism

Thus far I have assumed that the documents that come under analysis are authentic (i.e., are what their author and their content claim them to be). It may often be the case that the authenticity of a document is doubtful, however. For example, observers may come upon forged or garbled documents, and be forced to accept the subject's claim for their meaning and authenticity. Establishing the fact that a document represents what it is claimed to represent is the goal of *external criticism* (Gottschalk, 1945, p. 29).

To distinguish a hoax or a misrepresentation from a genuine document the sociologist (or historian) first establishes the date of the document (as nearly as possible) and then examines the materials to see whether or not they are anachronistic (which may show themselves in the material on which the document is written, if it was typewritten or in ink, or if it should, say, describe a labor strike that had not occurred at the time the letter was supposedly written).

Then, making his best guess as to the author of a document, the sociologist tries to identify the handwriting. If observers have handwritten documents from their subjects, they can place these specimens against other letters or materials. Third, the style of presentation will be examined. Peculiar phrases, spelling patterns, the use of proper names, and most importantly signatures can be analyzed and compared to authenticated documents. Fourth, having authenticated a text as well as possible, the sociologist is then "faced with the task of determining its meaning [Gottschalk, 1945, p. 33]." This problem was acutely recognized by Douglas in analyzing the suicide's diary discussed earlier.

Before I note what seems to me to be the most important aspects of this case study, it might be well to note a few important rules for analyzing such reports. First, given the complex, quickly changing nature of human communications, it seems unwise to place too much importance on any single statement. We must look primarily for basic, recurring patterns. And, in close relation to this, we must not emphasize particular words or phrases *unless* the communicator himself uses them in such a way as to indicate by a consistent pattern that they have a particular meaning and importance to the communicator. The words must also be seen in their context, above all in the context in which the communicator purposefully places them. We must also be wary of assuming that a word or phrase used by the communicator means the same for him that it means for us [1967, pp. 296–97].

To achieve all this, a sense of "historical-mindedness," or the ability to accurately take the role of acting others and view the world from their perspective, is necessary (Gottschalk, 1945, p. 33). It is inappropriate to analyze documents out of context, or to analyze only portions of them— they must be situated and analyzed in their completeness (see Garfinkel, 1967). Failure to do so may lead to a misinterpretation of a document's meaning or intent. Thus Douglas was cautious in interpreting what Marion meant when she said "go the limit" with her lover. Did this have the sexual connotation persons now ascribe to the phrase? Or did it mean she should either kill herself or kill Tom—that is, was killing Tom equivalent to going to the limit? When phrases such as this are in question, the general rule is to not give them special meaning unless they are given such meaning by the author; if a phrase is repeated over and over, researchers are justified in giving it a special place in the analysis.

The meaning of a document will never be completely established because symbols are never exactly interpretated as they were communicated. Observers can only infer meaning, but the closer they are to the subject, the easier this becomes.

*Internal Criticism*

Having established an authentic text and discovered as completely as possible what the author intended, the sociologist, or historian has "established what the witness' testimony is [Gottschalk, 1945, p. 34]."He has yet to determine whether that testimony is credible and, if so, in what parts—the job of internal criticism. In asking, "Is this document credible?" the sociologist is less concerned with whether or not what it describes is what actually happened. Rather, he asks:

*Is this as close to what actually happened as we can learn from a critical examination of the best available sources.* The historian thus establishes *credibility or verisimilitude* . . . rather than truth [Gottschalk, 1945, p. 35].

Sociologists recognize, then, that a completely accurate rendering of the event under analysis will seldom be achieved; instead, they strive for approximation and valid inference.

In approaching a document the analyst begins with a series of questions that may be noncommittal, such as, Did this subject really intend suicide? or What were the details of her life prior to the suicide attempt? Or he may have full-fledged hypotheses, "though only implicit and in interrogative form" [Gottschalk, 1945, p. 35]:" Did Marion commit suicide because of her lover's infidelity? or "Why did she commit suicide at the time she did?" Putting the prediction in the interrogative form facilitates the researcher progressively to modify and reformulate his hypotheses as he becomes more familiar with the data.

*General Rules for the Interrogative Hypotheses:* To admit any piece of evidence as pertinent to the interrogative hypothesis, the historian demands that it pass the following four tests:

1. Was the ultimate source of detail (the primary witness) *able* to tell the truth?
2. Was the primary witness willing to tell the truth?
3. Is the primary witness *accurately reported* with regard to the detail under examination?
4. Is there any *external corroboration* of the detail under examination? [Gottschalk, 1945, p. 38].

Any detail that passes these tests is good historical and sociological evidence.

*Ability to Tell the Truth:* As a general rule I have noted that the ability to tell the truth rests upon nearness to the event. The reliability of a witness' account will vary directly by his own remoteness from the event in time and space, and the remoteness of his record from the event in time and space. This rule rests on the fact that all sociological statements pass through at least three steps: observation, recollection, and recording (not to mention the sociologists' own perception of the witness' report). Geographical and temporal closeness to the event affects all three steps.

Returning to Douglas' study of Marion, which was largely based on her personal diary, it is necessary to ask, How able was Marion to tell the truth in her diary? Lacking data to triangulate her report, the critic has no way of knowing how much of a time lag transpired between her various entries. This raises serious problems, for if she was unable to record accurately the events that led up to her suicide, then analysts are left with inaccurate data.

A similar problem is encountered when researchers analyze newspaper reports of an event, or study government documents. To establish that these data pass the tests of external and internal criticism requires that the author be located in time and space. The author's nearness to the event must be reported, as should the time lag between the occurrence and the reporting of the event.

Obviously all witnesses, even if equally close to the event, are not equally competent witnesses. Competence will vary by age, expertness, education, memory, narrative skill, degree of attention maintained at the time, and the amount of self-attachment to the event being reported (Gottschalk, 1945, p. 39). Noting these dimensions, the analyst could certainly say that

Marion (Douglas' suicide subject) had the greatest degree of self-attachment to the event she reported. She would then be the most competent person to record the events leading to her suicide. But, having proven competence, observers still must ask, Was the subject willing to tell the truth? In this regard Marion may well have been distorting certain factors to make her suicide more socially acceptable.

*Willingness to Tell the Truth:* A subject may be able to report an event accurately, but for any number of reasons fails to do so (Gottschalk, 1945, pp. 40–47). If he is an interested witness, he may have a self-stake in the record and deliberately attempt to please or displease the reader. This of course introduces an element of bias that must be uncovered. If observers have comparable documents reporting the same event, and one presents it in a favorable light and the other in an unfavorable light, they must inquire into the personalities of the two authors to discover who has the largest stake in the record. Often, too, literary style will lead to a distortion of the record. This bias is likely to be nondeliberate, as in autobiographies where the author assumes the role of "omniscient observer" and ceases to employ qualifying phrases such as *if,* or *but,* or *it is perhaps safe to say.* (Gottschalk, 1945, p. 41). Frequently this will occur when the subject is asked to take the role of the larger body of persons he represents. Suddenly he ceases to be precise in his statements and begins saying, "All ex-cons feel this way." The truth of such generalities must be doubted.

Occasionally there are laws and conventions that restrict a subject's ability to tell the truth (Gottschalk, 1945, p. 41). For instance, laws of libel and good taste restrict the exact reporting of certain events. Sociologists themselves abide by the "anonymity rule" and quite frequently find themselves not reporting certain features of their study because of the damage or harm it could bring to the subject.

Unwillingness to tell the truth, whether intentional or subconscious, leads to misstatement of fact more often than omission of fact. When the same witness is both unable and unwilling to tell the truth (almost always is this the case to some degree at least), the historian has before him a document that commits errors both of omission and commission. Yet he must continue to bear in mind that even the worst witness may occasionally tell the truth and that it is the historian's business to extract that iota of truth, if he can [Gottschalk, 1945, p. 42].

*Conditions Favorable to Credibility:* There are certain conditions favorable to accurate recording. When the truth of a statement is a matter of indifference to the subject, he is likely to be unbiased. Thus if observers ask a subject his age or ask him to describe some nonthreatening feature of his life, he is likely to be truthful in his response. Conversely, if a statement is prejudicial or intimidating to the subject, he is likely to be untruthful. If observers ask an ex-convict how many crimes he committed that were undetected by the legal authorities and that have occurred within the last seven years, it is very probable that he will either not report these crimes or he will give an incorrect report. Matters of common knowledge, however (a man's age, the time of parole violation, years of education, etc.), are less likely to be mistaken.

When the sociologist (or historian) is unable to obtain data from the primary witness, he must resort to hearsay and secondary evidence. In these situations he asks: On whose testimony is the witness' statement based? Did the secondary witness accurately report the primary witness? If not, what details did he accurately report? Answers to these questions may allow the analyst to reconstruct the primary witness' account and move on to other events and issues. Thus he asks of second-hand evidence the same questions he asks of first-hand reports. (This problem may be particularly acute when newspaper accounts are placed against a subject's statement. Landesco, for example, in his study of organized crime encountered problems of newspaper biasing.)

*Corroboration:* The historian will not accept a document, or a particular from a document, as reliable and valid unless it is corroborated by the independent testimony of two or more witnesses (Gottschalk, 1945, p. 45): the principle of triangulation. The importance of the independence of witnesses is obvious—although it may not be easy to establish. Where any two witnesses agree, it may well be that they agree because they are testifying or reporting independently to an observed fact. But it may be that they agree because they have decided on the same points beforehand, or one may have copied from the other or in some other way been influenced by the other. Finally, both sources may have been influenced by a third person. This problem cuts wider than the analysis of life history data. In survey interviews, for example, it may be that subjects unwittingly influence one another when filling out an interview schedule. The reporting of annual salary, for example, seems to be one topic on which husbands and wives seldom independently report. Further, it may be that during the interaction between subject and interviewer all independence of observation is lost— the interviewer begins to lead the subject into answers. *"Unless independence of observers is established, agreement may be confirmation of a lie, or of a mistake rather than corroboration of fact* [Gottschalk, 1945, p. 45]."

Gottschalk notes that observers are frequently unable to locate either independent documents or witnesses. In these situations they are forced to look for other kinds of corroboration. Thus in suicide studies it may be impossible to locate the other persons involved; or in the study of illicit and deviant activities, externally validating sources may be absent. In some situations, however, the absence of other reports may be taken as confirmation, or analysts may accept the reputation of the author and the absence of self-contradiction in his document as sufficient proof of its truthfulness. Thus the absence of contradiction in other sources helps to determine credibility.

Because the credibility of an entire document can be no greater than the credibility of its parts, observers must always be alert to internal contradiction in their documents. Corroboration by general credibility is weak, as is corroboration by silence, or conformity, or agreement. Hence a document for which there is no external and independent corroboration is always weaker than the document for which there is (Gottschalk, 1945, p. 46).

Many of the validity questions raised in document analysis will never be satisfactorily answered, for there may be only one reliable witness—the subject himself—and sociologists must again return to the central feature of the life history, which is the elicitation of one person's perceptions and definitions, remembering that many times they can only establish inferentially the veracity of his statements. His emotions, ideals, wishes, failures, images of self, private opinions, and motives are his alone, and only he can give good testimony on them, unless they are externally manifested to others who can report them validly.

Even when these inner experiences are known from the testimony of others to whom the subject may have told them, they rest ultimately upon his own powers of introspection. The biographer is in this regard no better off than the psychologist—and worse off in that his witness is dead and beyond interview. And all history, we have said, is biographical in part. The biographer does, however, have one advantage over the psychologist—he knows what his subject is going to do next. He therefore can reason from response to sensation, from act to motive, from effect to cause [Gottschalk, 1945, p. 47].

**Organization and Synthesis of Life History Materials**

The organizational and synthetic problems of preparing a life history report are briefly as follows:

*Step 1:* Select a series of research hypotheses and problems to be answered or explored in the life history. Formulate tentative operationalizations of key concepts.

*Step 2:* Select the subject(s) and determine the form the life history is to take.

*Step 3:* Record the objective events and experiences in the subject's life that pertain to your problem. These events should be triangulated by source and perspective so that contradictions, irregularities and discontinuities can be established.

*Step 4:* Obtain the subject's interpretations of these events as they occurred in their chronological, or natural order.

*Step 5:* Analyze all reports and statements collected thus far in terms of internal validity, internal criticism, external validity, and external criticism.

*Step 6:* Resolve the validity of the above sources, and establish the priority of sources for subsequent hypothesis tests.

*Step 7:* Begin testing hypotheses that have emerged to this point, search for negative evidence, and continue to modify, generate, and test these hypotheses.

*Step 8:* Organize an initial draft of the entire life history and submit this to the focal subject(s) for their reactions.

*Step 9:* Rework the report in its natural sequence in light of the above reactions. Present the hypotheses and propositions that have been supported. Conclude with its relevance for theory and subsequent research.

Rather than viewing these as inflexible steps, they should be seen as relevant criteria against which any life history may be assessed. There is a built-in bias here: theory is assumed to be the major guiding force in the organization of the materials. In this respect I disagree with those spokesmen who feel life histories cannot be employed to generate and validate theory.

### Current Status of the Life History Method

In 1945 Robert Angell reviewed some 22 sociological studies that made extensive use of the life history method between the period 1920–40. He observed that upon the appearance of Thomas and Znaniecki's *Polish Peasant*, sociologists had responded to this relatively new method in a disappointing fashion. Few systematic investigations employing the method appeared, and few modifications of it. He concluded his review with the following note:

Perhaps the most important factor in limiting the number of sociologists using personal documents has been the "climate of opinion" in the sociological field during the last twenty years. In reacting from the "armchair sociology," many have gone to the extreme of wishing to deal only with what they believe to be cold, hard facts. Conceptualization has been suspect; it has been thought that facts could speak for themselves. Particularly shunned have been approaches which give a large place to the "subjective" aspect of social life. Science, so runs the popular doctrine, requires that attention be given only to those phenomena that can be dealt with in terms of counting or of physical measurement. So strong has been this "objective" tendency that most younger sociologists have been carried along by it. To those who subscribe to this doctrine personal documents are altogether too unreliable for any but the most elementary scientific use. They may be considered of some value in locating new "objective" variables, or in suggesting new relationships, but it is felt that their service in these ways is distinctly preliminary and exploratory. The real research must be done in other ways. The point is that those who adopt this view minimize the importance of conceptualization. They do not believe that the prime importance of sociology is a better theory [Angell, 1945, pp. 231–32].

Angell reached this conclusion in 1945, despite the fact that his review revealed that the users of the life history method had shown the feasibility of gathering such materials, and indicated that life history materials had been employed to develop new hypotheses as well as to verify existing theory. Furthermore, a review of the 22 studies indicated that theory could emerge out of the materials, and that life history data were equally as valid as questionnaire data (see Cavan, Hauser and Stouffer, 1930, pp. 200–3). Angell suggested, in addition to the shift in scientific opinion regarding the method, that too few persons were willing to invest the time and effort in such a research strategy. His indictment is valid today. Howard S. Becker, in his preface to a revised edition of Shaw's *The Jack-Roller* states:

Given the variety of scientific uses to which the life history may be put, one must wonder at the relative neglect into which it has fallen. Sociologists, it is true, have never given it up altogether. But neither have they made it one of their standard research tools. They read the documents available and assign them for their students to read. But they do not ordinarily think of gathering life history documents themselves or of making the technique part of their research approach [1966, p. xvi].

The history of the life history method in sociology provides a useful documentary on current views toward theory and research. Becker states:

Sociologists became more concerned with the development of abstract theory and correspondingly less interested in full and detailed accounts of specific organizations and communities. They wanted data formulated in the abstract categories of their own theories rather than in the categories that seemed most relevant to the people they studied. The life history was suited to the latter task, but of little immediately apparent use in the former [1966, p. xvi].

Concomitant with the above is the current view that defines single studies (surveys or experiments) as more expedient and desirable than a long chain of life histories that cumulatively yield a grounded theory of some segment of social interaction. The life history, of course, demands a huge time commitment on the part of the investigator and is most applicable when conceived in terms of a series of such studies. Thus the life histories collected by Park's students together yield a viable picture of life in one community (Chicago) over a 20-year period.

The stance of Lundberg some 35 years ago still seems to be applied to the method. Conceiving the life history as an adjunct to the survey and statistical analysis leads most observers to regard it as of only exploratory usefulness. Few sociologists have considered the powerful utility of life histories in generating theory. Earlier references to Landesco, Thrasher, Lindesmith, and Lemert were meant to demonstrate its use in theory construction. It is a curious historical anomaly that Stouffer demonstrated in 1930 that life history data were at least as valid and reliable as structured questionnaire data. The view that such data are unreliable and of only exploratory value seems to still obtain, however, despite this early demonstration.

## Unique Relevance of the Life History for Sociology

Given the stereotypes commonly ascribed to the method, what are its most appropriate uses for the contemporary sociologist? Shibutani aptly states one:

Whatever else social psychologists must know, it appears obvious that the effective study of human behavior requires some familiarity with the intimate details of the lives of a variety of people. But many students have been so well protected that they know little of what goes on outside of middle-class communities. One economical way of overcoming this handicap is the extensive reading of first-person documents—autobiographies, letters, diaries and the clinical reports of psychiatrists [1961, p. v].

The method's relevance extends beyond sheer exposure to other points of view, however. If sociologists take Mead's social behaviorism seriously, they are obligated to formulate methodologies that begin with men's overt, observable interactions, and to interpret these acts in terms of the meanings and definitions attached to them. Mead states:

Social psychology is behavioristic in the sense of starting with an observable activity—the dynamic, ongoing social process, and the social acts which are its component elements—to be studied and analyzed scientifically. But it is not behavioristic in the sense of ignoring the inner experience of the individual—the inner phase of that process or activity. On the contrary, it is particularly concerned with the rise of such experience within the process as a whole. It simply works from the outside to the inside instead of from the inside to the outside, so to speak, in its endeavor to determine how such experience does arise within the process [1934, pp. 7–8].

This ability to interpret ongoing social acts from the perspective of the persons involved has been one criterion I have brought to bear against all methodologies. The life history becomes a method par excellence in this light because it rests on the assumption that records of man's subjective experiences form the core data of sociology. Sociologists should, then, view life histories as points against which interview, questionnaire, and observational data would be assessed. If analysts can obtain meaningful statements of the "subjective" life from an interview that cannot be excelled by a life history document, then they have a triangulated piece of data. But if they find that the interview is lacking in this regard, then they must turn to a form of the personal document as supplementary data.

Becker (1966, pp. x–xviii) has extended the functions of the method beyond this. He suggests it may serve as a "touchstone" by which other theories, hypotheses, and propositions may be evaluated. (When Lemert applied Sutherland's theory of professional crime to the systematic check forger, he uncovered a negative case that led to a revision of the original Sutherland formulations.) The life history can function, then, as a negative case against which existing theories may be assessed. Second, life histories can be useful in providing data on the subjective side of routine institutional experiences and processes. While criminologists have elaborate theories concerning the effects of prisons on convicts, they frequently lack data concerning the subjective side of such experiences. By explicitly focusing on the subjective, the life history can extend their theories further into this realm of organizational experience. Third, the method may open avenues of inquiry into areas that appear resolved. Thus while small-group research appears to have run its course in such areas as leadership and group process, a set of life histories on the actual experience of group leaders might well expand existing theories and raise problems that heretofore have appeared to be resolved.

Fourth, the method has the potential of providing the data observers are presently unable to obtain from the more behavioristic experiments and retrospective surveys. That is, if analysts assume that a full-blown naturalistic methodology must link overt interactions with subjective experience, then they can employ life histories to establish the links other methods are incapable of providing.

To the above functions I add the following. The life history may be the best available technique for studying such important social psychological processes as adult socialization, the emergence of group and organizational structure, the rise and decline of social relationships, and the situational response of the self to daily interactional contingencies. It is easy to conceive of life histories carried out on entire organizations, social groups, or even communities. Indeed, this is one strategy employed by the cultural and social anthropologist as he writes the history of a community. Key community leaders can be interviewed, their trajectories of public experience can be noted, and the objective career points in the community's history can be described by persons in varying social positions.

On a more methodological level, life histories represent a major approach to the "sensitizing concept" strategy of theory development and verification. Beginning with vague, yet generic concepts, sociologists can derive operationalizations from the subject's point of view—thus allowing him to attach his meanings to a conceptual framework. In addition, because the life history requires demographic reports, interview data, document analysis, and participant observation, it permits the merger of several discrete methodologies into a single strategy.

A theme running through this discussion has been the close relationship between the life history and symbolic interactionism. I have argued that a theory that stresses the "subjective" side of social experience demands a methodology that explicitly focuses on such data. Herein lies the tremendous value of the life history—it permits sociologists to balance the "objectivism" of the experiment, the survey, and participant observation with the internal, covert, and reflective elements of social behavior and experience.

### Notes

I have found the following sources to be the best statements on the life history method: P. Young (1966, Chap. 10), K. Young (1952), Thomas and Znaniecki (1927), Blumer (1939), Allport (1942), and Gottschalk, Kluckhohn, and Angell (1945). The Allport and the Gottschalk, Kluckhohn, and Angell sources present the most thorough presentations. I have drawn my remarks on the historical method primarily from Gottschalk; my classification of life histories drew heavily from Allport. Howard S. Becker's preface to the 1966 edition of Shaw's *The Jack-Roller* offers a concise review of the method's major assumptions. (*The Jack-Roller* is also a very good illustration of the best use of the method.)

Statements concerning the relevance of the life history for organizational analysis can be found in the 1924 edition of Park and Burgess' *Introduction to the Science of Sociology* (especially relevant are pp. 152–59 and 210–16). Blumer's (1939) critique of the *Polish Peasant* should be examined for its review of this classic document and for its critical review of the life history as a method.

A very recent quasi-life history is Eldridge Cleaver's (1967) *Soul on Ice*. This contains a number of letters and essays relevant to the construction of a life history on Cleaver.

I am indebted to Mark F. Denzin for the discussion of the reality-distance problem in document analysis. Albert Camus' essay on the works of Franz Kafka in *The Myth of Sisyphus and Other Essays* offers an excellent example of how a document might best be approached. Camus' position on the symbol and its interpretations is concisely stated by the interactionist J. E. Hulett, Jr., in his "Communication and Social Order: The Search for Theory": "We could say with some justification that the message received is never the same as the message that was sent [1964, p. 466]." This captures the essential problem of document analysis.

This chapter is longer than my treatment of other methods because I wish to restore the life history to greater prominence within the sociological enterprise. I have also offered a more extended discussion because materials on the method are not readily available.

# 11

# Unobtrusive Measures: The Quest for Triangulated and Nonreactive Methods of Observation

Today the dominant mass of social science research is based upon interviews and questionnaires. We lament this overdependence upon a single, fallible method. Interviews and questionnaires intrude as a foreign element into the social setting they would describe, they create as well as measure attitudes, they elicit typical roles and responses, they are limited to those who are accessible and will cooperate, and the responses obtained are produced in part by dimensions of individual differences irrelevant to the topic at hand.

*But the principle objection is that they are used alone.*

Eugene J. Webb, et al., 1966, p. 1.

An unobtrusive measure of observation is any method of observation that directly removes the observer from the set of interactions or events being studied. Public archival documents represent one major class of unobtrusive measures; the conditions that lead to their production are in no way influenced by an intruding sociological observer. Unobtrusive measures range from the public and private archive to simple behavior observations of persons at work or play, from contrived observations based on mechanical equipment (such as tape recorders and video cameras) to physical trace analysis.

## Assumptions of the Method

In many senses the use of unobtrusive measures represents an extreme behavioristic stance on the part of the sociologist. By removing himself from the flow of interaction, he is only permitted to make inferences concerning the interpretations and definitions that gave rise to the behavior studied and recorded. The chief utility of unobtrusive measures is realized when they are combined with methods of observation that probe the subjective factors of interaction.

Because contemporary social science has relied excessively upon interviews and questionnaires as its major research methodology, a tradition has developed that "allowed them to become the methodological sanctuary to which the myopia of operational definitionalism permitted a retreat [Webb, *et al.*, 1966, p. 172]." Unobtrusive measures propose new techniques of research that buttress findings from questionnaire and interview research. A fundamental strategy underlying their use is the triangulation of methodologies—a strategy I have repeatedly advocated. Not only may a variety of unobtrusive measures be combined (triangulated), but they may also be combined with the more traditional methodologies of the survey, experiment, observation, and life history.

The use of unobtrusive measures represents an awareness on the part of the sociologist that his presence as an observer is foreign, and therefore in some sense reactive, thus raising problems of internal validity. The presence of an observer is a potentially reactive factor, since he may produce changes in behavior that diminish the validity of comparisons. Arsenian, for example, has shown that an adult sitting near a door seemed to lend assurance to a group of nursery-school children [1943, pp. 225–49]. Further, the effect of an observer may erode over time and hence produce a selective contamination in observational data (Webb, *et al.*, 1966, p. 113). Schwartz and Schwartz make the following statement concerning their effect upon patterns of interaction on a small psychiatric ward:

The mere presence of the observer means that movements are made and orientations are developed toward him which would not otherwise have occurred. The "typicality" of these movements, their difference from or similarity to other activities undertaken by the observed before the observer role had been established may alter the course of events, even when the observer is temporarily absent. Conspicuous during the early stages of our research was the great amount of feeling aroused in both patients and staff by the investigator's presence. The patients were curious and, at times, hostile to the investigator; they watched him closely and sometimes attacked him verbally, insisting they did not want to be guinea pigs. . . . However, these feelings gradually diminished, and at the end of six months the observed no longer reacted to the observer with strong negative feelings, and responded to him as they would to a regular ward staff member [1955, p. 346].

Observer presence may also jeopardize external validity:

No matter how well integrated an observer becomes we feel he is still an element with potential to bias the production of the critical data substantially. The bias may be a selective one to jeopardize internal validity, or perhaps more plausibly, it may cripple the ability of the social scientist to generalize his findings very far beyond his sample [Webb, *et al.*, 1966, p. 113].

### Varieties of Unobtrusive Measures

*Physical Trace Analysis*

Physical traces and signs left behind by a population (see Webb, *et al.*, 1966, Chap. 2) are generated without the producer's knowledge of their future use by sociologists, and thus such data have none of the reactivity that arises when a subject knows he is being studied. *Erosion measures,* which are the natural remnants of some population's activity that has selectively worn certain objects, are one of two basic types of physical traces. (Webb, *et al.*, have noted such erosion measures as the wear on library books as an index of their popularity, and the study of replaced tiles in museums as a record of the popularity of certain exhibits.) Perhaps of more sociological relevance is the analysis of the erosion and depletion of critical resources and objects in locales through which particular populations pass —for example, Hayner's study of the "souvenir habit" in large urban hotels. This habit, as defined by a hotel detective, includes "everything from the taking of a carnation from the lobby bouquet to the theft of hundreds of dollars worth of silver and linen at a time [Hayner, 1964, p. 322]." Hayner's study of theft patterns in the urban hotel provided him with a central clue to the motivations and self-conceptions of hotel residents. He pointed to the impersonality that pervades hotel living and suggested that the "souvenir habit" was only one index of the feeling of estrangement and transitoriness that characterizes a large majority of hotel dwellers.

The study of deteriorated dwelling units provided Wallace (1965) with an index of the low level of subsistence characteristics of men living in skid row. A study of the destructive habits of inmates in various total institutions might point to the degree of boredom inherent in such settings. The number of miles accumulated by police patrolmen in their patrol cars measures their daily activity—as does the number of times their tires have to be replaced.

The second form of physical trace analysis is *the accretion measure,* or the recording of population deposits over time. In this, observers reverse the rationale for erosion analysis and examine those remnants that exist through time and attempt to make inferences about the people leaving such traces. Wallace's study of life in skid row revealed that one index hotel clerks employ to measure a man's relationship with legal authorities is the number of possessions he leaves behind. Wallace states:

When a resident gets picked up by the police, his spare clothing, all his possessions, and any rent paid in advance are endangered. The hotel clerk nearly always knows when one of his tenants is caught. . . .

In such cases the manager has several courses of action. He may quite legally wait until the tenant's rent runs out, and then enter the room and confiscate all property. The tenant loses everything. Or if he is so inclined, the manager may promptly remove all of the tenant's property, store it safely, and re-rent the room [1965, pp. 35–36].

Other accretion measures might include the study of deposits of love letters in waste containers as a measure of troubled interaction patterns. Gold (1964, pp. 1–49) included such data in his study of janitors and their relationships with tenants, and Siu's (1964, pp. 429–42) study of the Chinese laundryman included an analysis of how frequently calendars of nude female figures were hung in laundry shops. The differential distribution of these calendars revealed that such displays appeared more frequently in the shops of younger men who were labeled sexual deviants. But more important, these calendars referenced the fact that Chinese laundrymen viewed it as legitimate to associate with prostitutes; the display of nude calendars merely reinforced this belief pattern. These data are one form of the physical trace—the deposit of certain materials in human social-interactional quarters. Other forms of depository analysis can be imagined. Students of bureaucratic life, for instance, could focus on the wall-hangings and desk decorations in offices as an index of prestige in an organization. Similarly, the extent to which office dwellers attempt to personalize their quarters with pictures and displays reveals something about their personality and their perceived relationship to the organization. In this case the nature of the display, as well as the fact that a display is present, reveals something about the office's occupant.

Experimental intervention with respect to physical trace analysis may also be conducted (see Webb, *et al.*, 1966, pp. 43–50). Waiting for deposits or erosions that occur naturally may take time and the dross, or loss rate, may be high. For example, an investigator may begin a study of what men in skid row rooming houses leave behind and find after a period of observations that he has stationed himself in the wrong setting or that the data he collects are inappropriate. Clerks in rooming houses might then be asked to cooperate in the selection of a setting, or police could be consulted. The sociologist may also experimentally introduce objects in certain situations to observe differential erosion and depository reactions toward them. An investigator interested in the ritualism associated with seating patterns in bars, for example, might vary the quality and location of chairs and booths. Or if studying the differential readiness of certain persons to inscribe initials upon booths and walls, he might vary the quality or texture of booths.

*Problems with Physical Trace Analysis.* The time taken for collection, the dross rate, and the quality of the data are restrictive factors, but more important is the fact that too frequently the observer lacks sufficient data on the population making the physical traces to justify generalizations and valid comparisons to other situations. Also, certain undetected response sets may be operating to give a pattern to such traces. Siu found, for example, that only certain Chinese laundrymen displayed calendars and that these were displayed in particular areas of the shop. The reason for this differential location was not recorded—that is, the response set that might have explained this variation remained unstated.

Physical traces may also be selectively found at only various time intervals and in only certain social settings. For example, Chinese laundrymen may no longer display calendars with nude women, or they may only make such displays when their wives are not living with them. In this respect it would be inappropriate to draw conclusions about their relationship to a sexual ideology without data on the temporal and spatial dimensions.

While experimentation may be possible, with certain types of physical traces it is impossible; and in the absence of experimentation, generalizations should be made cautiously. Conditions that would prohibit experimentation include inaccessibility of the population that initially made the deposits because of spatial and temporal factors. (Certainly, for example, Chinese laundrymen today, to the extent that they still exist, are likely to be considerably different from their counterparts in the 1920's when Siu made his study.) Or the objects on which deposits or erosions once occurred may no longer be available or within the everyday pattern of interaction of the population being studied. Hence it would be impossible to reintroduce such objects and observe the behavior directed towards them.

In summary, physical trace analysis is most appropriately viewed as a strategy for recording the incidence, frequency, and distribution of social acts toward certain social objects through time and in various situations. The ideal physical trace analysis would compare different populations in different settings at different times in terms of their actions toward one uniform set of objects [also see Rowe, 1953: 895–940 on archeological techniques relevant in this context]. Such investigations would permit valid generalizations beyond the single sample. In addition, data would be gathered on the population characteristics and, if possible, on the motivations and definitions underlying their actions toward those objects, combining unobtrusive measures with interviews, questionnaires, and intensive observation.

*Archival Record Analysis*

The second major form of unobtrusive measures is the analysis of public and private archival records. These data—which include actuarial records, political and judicial records, records of government agencies, and data from the mass media—were taken up in the previous chapter, and that discussion will not be repeated here, but it should be noted that public and private archives have relevance beyond the life history and are properly viewed as forms of unobtrusive data. Prepared by a person in a given organizational position, they represent a peculiar stance toward the issues contained in the report under study, and observers must be sensitive to the selective bias introduced by the person preparing such reports. Further, analysts must realize that any public archival document represents the imprint of the organization that produced it, and thus bias arises simultaneously from both the author and from his organization. The problem is further compounded when changes over time are considered; shifts in language, in population characteristics, and in organizational personnel all lead to potential dissimilarities across time in any agency's report or in the reports from agencies of the same class.

Observers must realize that the reality of any archival producing agency is a reality representing that agency's interpretations of what has occurred, what is to be reported, and what is to be saved for future generations. The "agency perspective" becomes particularly acute when sociologists propose temporal analyses of such matters as crime rates, birth and death statistics, marriage and divorce rates, hospitalization statistics, and the like (see, for example, Kitsuse and Cicourel, 1963, pp. 131–39; Garfinkel, 1967).

If the problem of death is considered, the ambiguity of official, archival statistics becomes more clear. All persons understand what it means to die and what the word *dead* means, but Sudnow has shown that:

The actual occurrence of a death involves the operation of a rather specific set of mechanisms, none of which is currently understood in great detail. To "die," some say, the heart must cease beating, and that can occur as a direct result of one or more of a series of quite specific biochemical-physical occurrences, e.g., the heart can burst open in certain kinds of trauma, the nerve tissue which provides the heart with its electrical stimulation can be damaged, or weakened through a loss of blood supply, etc. Yet cessation of the heart is currently considered by some to be merely a "sign" of death, and not definitive of it. In certain medical circles there is considerable disagreement over the precise biological meaning of death; some argue that the cessation of cellular activity constitutes death, others insist upon a more specific attention to properties of cellular multiplication [1967, p. 65].

Medical experts cannot agree on when death has occurred, nor can they agree on what definition will be attached to that biological and social status termed death. The problem is further complicated when it is asked under what conditions a newborn infant is considered to have died? Citing observations from one hospital, Sudnow reports the following definitions that are used to describe *newborn infants.*

At County Hospital, there is a system of definitions and weights intended to describe the status of fetuses. According to its weight, length and period of gestation at the end of which it is delivered (or "expelled"), a fetus is either considered "human" or not. At County, the dividing line is 550 grams, 20 centimeters, and 20 weeks of gestation. Any creature having smaller dimensions or of less embryonic "age" is considered nonhuman . . . and if "born" without signs of life, is flushed down the toilet or otherwise simply disposed of, placed in a jar for pathological examination, or the like. . . .

The fetus that passes the definitional limit and is considered a "human," dead or alive, is, however, not always treated as the regulations require. . . .

While some flexibility is permissible in assigning these statuses, there is always care exercised in attempting to treat that which might be properly considered as a "human" by disposal [1967, pp. 109–11].

Not only do hospitals have different problems to confront when a human, as opposed to a "thing," is born, but they must also prepare official statistics to report such occurrences. If a fetus is not accorded "human" status, then a death statistic is not generated; however, the conditions that generate such data are ambiguously determined and subject to a great deal of modification and negotiation. Sudnow notes, for example that Catholic parents are more likely to have their fetuses defined as human (even if they immediately die) than are Protestants. These observations challenge the generalizability of archival data on birth and death rates from one hospital to another. More broadly, of course, they suggest that similar organizations processing the same set of events (e.g., police departments, mental hospitals, courts of law) may not generate comparable data on those events. Before observers can confidently make valid comparisons across organizations and through time, they must consider the potential bias that arises from differing "organizational perspectives" on those events. It is a plausible hypothesis (and one which must be answered before analysis proceeds) that variations in such matters as delinquency rates, or shifts in birth and death statistics, do not represent true differences in the occurrence of those events. They may represent only differences in organizational bookkeeping.

In a recent study of juvenile courts in two communities, this problem was sensitively treated by Cicourel (1968), who found that the social organization of juvenile agencies in the two communities accounted for variations in their recorded rates of delinquency. Political pressures, previous experiences with juvenile officers, the presence or absence of lawyers, and the social status of the potential delinquent's family all affected the decision of whether or not a given adolescent would be defined as delinquent. These findings supported the earlier study of Kitsuse and Cicourel (1963, pp. 131–39) on rates of delinquency in a wealthy Chicago suburb; they found that the chief of police normally and routinely released potential delinquents with a reprimand and a statement that "kids from good families don't get into trouble."

Cicourel suggests that a meaningful analysis of public archival data (at least data on delinquency rates) cannot proceed until the investigator has "taken the role" of the members in the organization that is producing the records under analysis. He states:

Attempts to estimate crimes now known to the police are exceedingly difficult, but it is also difficult to evaluate the cases that are uncleared in police files and for which there are no suspects. Add to this the crude and ambiguous classificatory and descriptive materials making up police and probation files, along with the practical circumstances governing the assembly of official statistics, and the reader can only wonder how the conventional literature can use official materials after only the usual perfunctory remarks about their drawbacks . . . such materials cannot be interpreted unless the observer is able to demonstrate the theoretical and empirical grounds for assigning sense to both the member's activities and his own coding operations that produced the "data" [1968, p. 330].

In the previous chapter I discussed the conventional problems surrounding official, archival data (e.g., internal and external validity of those records). Cicourel suggests that observers study the generation of organizational records as they would study the formation of rumor, gossip, and history in everyday activities (see Shibutani, 1966). In analyzing such records, sociologists are dealing with the transformation of conversations, haphazard observations, and negotiated interpretations into formalized and consensual statements concerning the occurrence of a particular set of events, the motivations underlying such occurrences, and the actions of the record keeper toward them.

These issues return the discussion to the problem of ever achieving a complete and accurate rendering of any set of events, a problem further complicated because the sociologist works with imperfectly constructed records as he elaborates his own interpretations and explanations. The meanings he brings to bear upon those records, the coding procedures he goes through, and his final explanations represent still more steps away from the actual events being analyzed. Cicourel states:

I earlier referred to rumors and collective behavior because I want to underscore the problematic features of the social organizations I have discussed throughout this book. The policeman's conception of "typical" juveniles, "punks," "good kids," his recognition of typical sociological arrangements, family organization, and the like, are integral to understanding how behavior comes to be labeled "delinquent" . . . the "delinquent" is an emergent product, transformed over time according to a sequence of encounters, oral and written reports, prospective reasonings, retrospective readings of "what happened," and the practical circumstances of "settling" matters in everyday agency business [1968, p. 333].

His study challenges the conventional view of sociologists that delinquents, mental patients, birth and death rates, marriages and divorces and the like are ". . . natural social types distributed in some ordered fashion and produced by a set of abstract 'pressures' from the social structures [Cicourel, 1968, pp. 335–36]." Observers must take as problematic the natural distribution of such events, but most important, they must take as problematic the archival documents and records that report the occurrence of such events. The central assumption of this alternative view is:

that members' categories, the things to which they refer, members' objectivication and verification procedures for deciding delinquency, and members' rules for expressing and deciding "what happened" become the source of data [Cicourel, 1968, p. 336].

The existence of delinquents, dead children, married women, and mental patients assumes that such "objects" have an objective social existence uniformly perceived by all qualified persons. The position I am advocating holds that the occurrence of such "objects" in a social reality is always a negotiated existence subject to alternative interpretations, definitions, and symbolic meanings. Therefore their reported existence in public and private archives must be treated as a "peculiar" interpretation that may or may not have been reported in the same fashion by another agency or another person at another time. Each archival report must be interpreted within its "situated" context. The failure to achieve this "situated interpretation" can only further challenge the internal validity and more greatly distort the authenticity and meaning of such analyses.

## Simple Observations

Simple observations are the third basic variety of unobtrusive measures. Here I refer to those situations

in which the observer has no control over the behavior or sign in question, and plays an unobserved, passive and unobtrusive role in the research situation [Webb, et al., 1966, p. 112].

The strategy underlying simple observations is to remove the reactivity that arises when a "known" observer is present. Simple observations bypass this reactivity by removing the known observer, but remain first-hand observations because the investigator is still present in the situation. Their simplicity derives only from the fact that "the investigator does not intervene in the production of the material [Webb, et al., 1966, p. 115]. In all other respects they take on the complexity of participant observation or any other observational method.

Simple measures are also distinctive because they rely nearly totally on visual cues perceived and recorded by the observer—yet they retain the behavioristic flavor of all unobtrusive measures. Unless follow-up interviews are conducted, the investigator is left with observations of behavior alone.

*There are five types of simple observations. The first are observations of exterior body and physical signs* that are indicative of some behavior pattern or some inferred pattern of definition. These signs are displayed in an exterior fashion, although some may take the form of signs and symbols. Each of these exterior signs represents categories of informational cues about the self, or the possessor and displayer of them. These signs or cues are often unconsciously displayed, although, as in the case of dress, their appearance may be deliberate. Their meaning for interaction lies in the consensual definitions attached to them by others in the course of day to day conduct.

Examples of such signs include the study of clothing and dress as indicators of the self and personal identity. Stone, one of the few sociologists who has focused on this unobtrusive measure, writes:

We can note how one's name is established by dress if we imagine Teddy Roosevelt without the pince-nez, F.D.R. without the cigarette holder, or Thomas Dewey without the moustache. One of our informants, a small-time real estate operator, was aware of the significance of clothing in his attempts to personalize his occupational identity. Asked, "What do your fellow workers say and think when you wear something new for the first time on the job?" he replied: "Well, I always have a new hat, and I suppose my clientele talks about it. But, you know, I always buy cheap ones and put my name in them. I leave them around in restaurants and places like that intentionally. It has advertising value." [1962, p. 95]

When this respondent was asked if he chose to wear a greater variety or small variety of clothes when at work he replied: "A smaller variety so you look the same everyday. So people will identify you. They look for the same old landmark [Stone, 1962, p. 95]." Stone's study goes beyond the method of simple observations and achieves a synthesis with another methodology—the interview. Beginning with the unobtrusive observation that clothing revealed categories of the self, Stone validated and explained the dimensions of this process by the interview.

Ehrlich's (1963, pp. 264–72) study of the swastika epidemic that swept the United States in 1959 and 1960 represents another ingenious use of the simple observation. Working with data furnished by the Anti-Defamation League, Ehrlich attempted to explain the wide occurrence of anti-Semitism in American communities. His data on the nature of this epidemic consisted, in part, of the following observations:

—a college building painted with swastikas
—the front sidewalk of a Hillel House painted with a swastika
—anti-Semitic message painted on the door of a Jewish doctor

—swastikas found painted on boards in a lumberyard
—over 100 window panes of a school building shattered and swastikas painted on the walls of four washrooms [1963, p. 265].

Within the period December 26, 1959, through March 1, 1960, approximately 637 separate incidents of an anti-Semitic nature were recorded. Ehrlich's study proceeds with these data and correlates size of community and other demographic variables with the appearance of these signs. The study demonstrates that exterior signs can be recorded and woven into meaningful sociological analyses. Parallel studies could be conducted on the fads and fashions of various other movements and ideologies. The recent display of signs reading "God is Dead" in college communities could be recorded as one index of the present generation's challenge to the values of their parents. Inscriptions on the walls of restrooms reflect private, but often consensual definitions of sexual fantasies.

Phillips reported a study employing multiple indicators to document the changes in Miami resulting from the influx of a hundred thousand Cubans. Two years following the Castro revolution, he observed

—Bilingual street signs (No Jaywalking; Cruce por la Zona)
—"A visitor hears as much Spanish as English"
—Latin-American foods on restaurant menus
—Supermarkets selling yucca, malanga, and platanos [1962, p. 85; also Webb, et al., 1966, p. 119].

This study resembles Ehrlich's to the degree that exterior signs in public places are observed as indices of social change and public ideologies.

Symbols, in addition to clothing, street signs, menus, and the like, could be studied with the simple observational method. Hair styles worn by members of different social classes or occupational positions demonstrate the impact of fads and fashions; the use of jewelry by women reveals self-imputed class position; the display of vicariously consumed prestige items, so prominent in Veblen's analysis of the American class structure, shows the shifting mosaic of prestige items in the American social structure. An endless list of these symbols could be presented. They are easily accessible for observation, and when their study is combined with follow-up measures, the sociologist can achieve the interactional explanations stressed in this book.

Simple observations are not without weakness, however. Despite the fact that the investigator is on the scene of observation, he may become fatigued, bored, or develop a response set. Multiple observers and the construction of indices of reliability lessen these problems. (When I discuss physical location analysis as another strategy of simple observations, a series of indices will be presented.)

Temporal and spatial population restrictions may jeopardize the external validity of exterior sign analysis. The observer is largely confined to observing public patterns of behavior in public settings and thus his conclusions are necessarily restricted to conduct and symbols displayed in those situations. A simple variation on Stone's study of dress could be designed that focused on "dress at home" as opposed to "public dress." As yet, however, no studies (to my knowledge) have been designed to examine the "privateness" of this symbolic order. As a consequence, Stone's data are restricted to public modes of dress and public presentations of the self.

The dross, or loss factor was considered as a potential flaw of physical trace analysis, and it also has relevance for the above measurements. The investigator may place himself in poor situations for study, or focus on the wrong populations and hence find that the data he is after either are not present or occur at too low a frequency to be useful. This problem can be overcome by judicious field work prior to observations.

*Expressive movement* analysis represents a second form of the simple observation. With it concern is directed to the various features of the body that are manipulated, often in unconscious ways, to convey definitions of self and interpretations of situation. The study of the eye, the face, the limbs and the body generally is termed "kinesics"—or the analysis of learned, patterned, body-motion behavior. Sociologists have been slow to analyze this form of conduct, although Simmel, as early as 1908 (pp. 646–51) pointed to the tremendous import of the face and visual interaction in routine encounters. Perhaps the strongest rationale for examining the expressive features of the body is to remember that face to face interaction can only occur when persons confront one another with their physical presence. Therefore the analysis of such encounters leads to the question of how it is that persons bring their expressive body movements in line with their verbal utterances and statements.

If observers focus on how the body is brought into line with what is spoken, two distinct conditions can be described. The first, called *embodied posturing,* arises when all the expressive movements of the body validate and support the spoken definitions of self and other. Thus, when a person at a party states that he is "getting high," that statement would be validated only if appropriate body movements corresponded with that utterance. (These might include relaxed limb gesturing, smiles, and open gazes and glances.) When the movements of the body fail to correspond with what is spoken, there is *disembodied posturing.* Students who claim full attention in the classroom may, for example, give themselves away by relaxed limb posturing or by long gazing out the window or around the room.

Webb, *et al.* (1966, p. 122), propose a study of the superstitious behavior of baseball players as one area of expressive conduct. They hypothesize that the extent to which superstitious behavior is engaged in may be directly related to whether or not the player is in a slump or in the middle of a hot streak. Murphy and Murphy (1962, pp. 253–76) have reported differences in facial expressions between young and old Russians, showing that the faces of old people seemed resigned, tired, and sad, while the faces of children seemed lively, friendly, and full of vitality.

Studies of facial and body gestures must first confront the question of what a particular gesture means. A smile may mean happiness, relief, a full stomach. A frown may indicate disagreement, involvement in thought, displeasure, or too full a stomach. The meanings must be determined for the persons expressing them and for their recipient. In addition, the situation in which the gesture is expressed must be analyzed. A smile at a funeral probably means something quite different than a smile at a wedding.

*Physical location analysis* represents the third form of the simple observation. The basic intent of this strategy is to record and analyze the ways that humans locate their bodies and interactional equipment through a social space. While ethnologists and primatologists have long studied the ecology of physical spacing among infrahuman organisms, social scientists have given little attention to this problem [e.g., proxemics]. The investigation of expressive movements and of physical location complement one another because each refers to forms of nonverbal conduct that reflect ongoing definitions in the interactional process.

Hall, who has made the study of physical spacing, or territoriality, a major component in his theoretical analysis of culture, compares the study of this dimension between man and animals as follows:

Territoriality is the technical term used by the ethnologist to describe the taking possession, use, and defense of a territory on the part of living organisms. Birds have recognizable territories in which they feed and nest; carnivorous animals have areas in which they hunt, bees have places in which they search for honey, and man uses space for the activities in which he engages. . . . Territoriality reaches into every nook and cranny of life. . . . The history of man's past is largely an account of his efforts to wrest space from others and to defend space from outsiders [1959, p. 51].

An analysis of physical spacing reveals subtle status patterns maintained by the distance between participants. It also reflects the nature of ongoing social relationships and perhaps tells more about what persons are thinking than do their verbal statements. Hall (1959, pp. 163–64) has made the following classification of the distances kept by Americans and suggests the corresponding relationship that may be inferred:

1. *Very close* (3 in. to 6 in.)          Soft whisper; top secret
2. *Close* (8 in. to 12 in.)              Audible whisper; very con-
                                          fidential
3. *Near* (12 in. to 20 in.)             Indoors, soft voice; out-
                                          doors, full voice; con-
                                          fidential
4. *Neutral* (20 in. to 36 in.)          Soft voice, low volume;
                                          personal subject matter

| 5. *Neutral* (4½ ft. to 5 ft.) | Full voice; information of nonpersonal matter |
| 6. *Public Distance* (5½ ft. to 8 ft.) | Full voice with slight overloudness; public information for others to hear |
| 7. *Across the room* (8 ft. to 20 ft.) | Loud voice; talking to a group |
| 8. *Stretching the limits of distance* | 20 ft. to 24 ft. indoors; up to 100 ft. outdoors; hailing distance, departures |

In Latin America the interaction distance is much less than it is in the United States, and Hall suggests that Latin Americans cannot talk comfortably unless they are within a distance that would evoke either sexual or hostile feelings for Americans. Consequently, when Americans and Latins interact a continual readjustment process is observed, with Latins moving closer and Americans moving away.

Hall's observations provide useful clues for laboratory and field experimentation. Studies could be designed in which the rules outlined by Hall are violated and the subsequent reactions carefully, and unobtrusively recorded (see, for example, Sommer, 1968). Different public and private behavior settings could also be examined to reveal potential violations of these spacing rules. Observers might compare the spacing rules employed by a professor in his office with students to the rules employed when in the company of his family, or with close friends or colleagues.

Sommer (1959, pp. 247–60; 1961, pp. 99–110; 1962, pp. 111–16; 1966, pp. 206–14; 1967, pp. 654–60; 1968) has conducted a series of experiments on the hypotheses suggested by Hall. He notes initially that it is important to distinguish between territoriality, and what he terms "personal space" (1959, p. 248). Territory is always stationary, not moving with the person. Personal space however, is carried around with, and is established every time persons engage in interaction. Thus, even a person walking along a sidewalk is contained within a personal space—a space encompassing his visual and physical movements. Personal space has the body as its locus or center, while the territory does not. Sommer has shown that Americans routinely locate themselves at distances up to three feet for normal conversation. When located around a table, persons are more likely to converse with others seated at the corners, as opposed to adjacent chairs. When persons situate themselves in pairs or dyads for conversation they are also more likely to choose corners than adjacent chairs. Persons diagnosed as schizophrenics are more likely to violate this norm, choosing instead to locate at greater distances from one another.

In a study of group leadership, Sommer found that leaders preferred end positions at tables, and when the leader did not occupy the end position, the other people sat opposite or across, rather than beside him. Leaderless groups also preferred to sit around one end of the table. When the normal distance for daily interaction was violated, Sommer and Felipe (1966, pp. 206–14) found that the person encroached upon moved from the encroacher within 30 minutes. Other, more subtle devices were observed being used to protect personal space; these included moving one's shoulders so that the other person's vision was blocked, or building minor walls around oneself with notebooks, purses and coats.

Cavan (1966, Chap. 5) has observed that in public bars the general rules formulated by Hall concerning physical location are translated into the number of bar stools between patrons. When patrons are located at adjacent stools, intimate conversation ensues. When three bar stools separate them, interactional overtures may be made, but "when the distance is four or more stools, they generally are not [1966, p. 90]." The nature of bar interaction is such, however, that declarative, or loud and general conversation may be engaged in over a four-stool distance. Tied to these rules of physical spacing and conversation are more subtle norms concerning the reciprocity of drink gift-giving that vary by the distance between persons. The sex of patrons also influences this spacing pattern. In cross-sex encounters, females typically begin the conversation and the male is under obligation to move closer, while same-sex encounters between males appear not to follow this pattern (Cavan, 1966, pp. 92–95).

Davis, Seibert, and Breed (1966, pp. 298–306) have reported an investigation that examined interracial seating patterns on New Orleans public buses. Beginning with an explicit commitment to unobtrusive measures, they employed a refined form of physical location analysis. During the months of April and May, 1964, they stationed three students on 11 of the 39 transit lines operating during morning and afternoon peak hours in New Orleans. Their purpose was to develop an index of the degree of interracial integration on these transit lines by examining the seating patterns of Negroes and whites at the time of entry on the bus. Three variables were coded: race (Negro or white), sex and age (16 years and under, or 17 to 45, 45 or over). Eighty-seven observations were charted on diagrams showing the exact placement of every seated passenger at the time of sampling, and recording age, sex, and race.

Computations based on these data provided their index of the degree of integration. Before a reliable index could be constructed, however, two problems had to be overcome. The first derived from the obvious fact that there were no physical barriers on the buses demarcating white and Negro compartments. Therefore, if a Negro sits in front of a white, the question must be raised, "Who has entered whose section?" The authors note that "an analyst who wishes conceptually to partition a bus must introduce his own cutting lines [1966, p. 300]. A second problem arose because even among adjacently seated persons degrees of integration may differ. Sitting side by side seems different from "sitting front to back, or diagonally tangent, or across the aisle from; and sitting side by side on transverse seats is probably different from the same relation on lengthwise seats [1966, p. 300]." The presence of vacant seats and spaces between seats also introduces problems of analyzing the degree of integration.

These difficulties led the authors to develop four different measures—each of which computes the "number of persons who violate the old pattern of white precedence over Negroes [1966, p. 300]." A perfectly integrated bus was defined as one on which "half the seated passengers are precedence violaters [1966, p. 300]." The first method was derived from the number of whites who sat behind Negroes. Beginning with the front of the bus, any white who was seated further back than the first seated Negro was defined as a precedence violator. The second method simply computed the number of Negroes sitting in the front half of the bus as opposed to whites sitting in the back half. Method three was based on the percentage of seated passengers who were white. "Any Negroes seated in that proportion of seats from the front and any whites in the remaining seats" were defined as precedence violators (1966, p. 300). Method four was based on the number of seated whites and the location of Negroes within that number. "Any Negroes seated among that number from the front and any whites beyond that number were precedence violators (1966, p. 300)."

Each of these methods has shortcomings. With method one, a single Negro on the front seat of the bus would make all whites seated behind him precedence violators. Method two is imperfect because it overestimates the amount of precedence violation on crowded buses where the racial balance departs from unity. For example, on a fully occupied bus in which three-fourths of the passengers were Negro, every fourth rider would be defined as a precedence violator. Method three would similarly overreport a lightly occupied bus in which Negroes sat behind whites: if all persons sat near the front, an imperfect index of integration would be derived. Method four results in a double counting of all whites and Negroes.

White males and Negro females were the most frequent precedence violators; older persons, of both races, violated less frequently. This study suggests that reliable data on behavior in public behavior settings can be collected through unobtrusive measures and put to relevant theoretical use. In a 1967 article Davis and Levine (pp. 84–91) point to the relative neglect by sociologists of the study of conduct in the settings our society has created for public transit. Ocean voyages, air flights, train trips, subway trips, and passage in elevators all represent settings in which a great deal of "aggregate time" is spent by persons in modern industrial society, but the norms governing conduct in these settings have not been identified. Lyman and Scott (1967, pp. 236–49) have extended the notions of territoriality and personal space developed by Hall and Sommer and have suggested the following typology: *Public territories* are those in which the person has a great deal of freedom of access—can come and go at relative will; public transit facilities and entertainment establishments (beaches, bars, theaters) are public territory. *Home territories* are areas controlled by the regular participants, and in them an intimacy and freedom of conduct is legitimate; Homes, certain classes of offices, certain bars, club houses, and hobo jungles are representative of the home territory. They are relatively closed behavior settings, with access limited to those persons included in the group that routinely inhabits it. *Interactional territories* "refer to any area where a social gathering may occur [1967, p. 240]." A party, a lecture, a concert —in short, any situation in which persons are engaged in focused and direct interaction—is an interactional territory. These territories have fragile boundaries which can be broken at a moment's notice. The entry of the wrong person, a misinterpreted phrase, lack of proper attention, or the absence of necessary equipment are only a few of the elements that can force the dissolution of the territory. *Body territories* resemble Sommer's notion of personal space and include the space "encompassed by the human body and its anatomical parts [Lyman and Scott, 1967, p. 241]." Body territories accompany interactants wherever they go and automatically become incorporated into any other territorial locale.

While Lyman and Scott discuss some of the strategies of control and manipulation in these various locales, still unexamined are the peculiar rules of body location that obtain in each. In addition, observers must not forget that each locale (with the exception of the body or personal) can become transformed into any of the other types, given the presence of proper definitions and persons. Cavan, for example, has noted that a given bar can at differing times of the day function as a public and home territory, while continuously representing an interactional locale.

Hall's rules on body distance could be tested in these types of locales. Experimental variations with "stooge" observers could be developed and subsequent reactions recorded. Sommer has skillfully developed experimental designs in libraries, cafeterias, and hospital wards. Similar studies could be formulated for bars, elevators, public transit facilities, and even private territories such as the home. The studies so far undertaken are only a beginning in the empirical study of physical location and body propriety as they relate to a comprehensive framework for the analysis of face to face interaction.

Instabilities of populations over time and situations may restrict the generality of such analyses, however. Davis, Seibert, and Breed examined instabilities over time by systematic samplings at different times of the day. This is one procedure that partially solves the problem of population instability, because variances in time should also reflect variances in persons inhabiting such settings. Observer reliability must also be considered. Fortunately most of the physical location measures discussed are simple in form and thus permit reliable observations. Davis, Seibert, and Breed report a high degree of reliability between their observers, although an exact ratio is not given. (Sommer has reported reliability ratios between his observers as high as .91.) Another factor that must be reckoned with is that of observer fatigue. If an investigator is stationed for a long period in one situation he may become bored, develop a response set, or in some other way become less reliable in his observations. This difficulty can be overcome by the use of multiple observers whose findings are correlated for reliability.

*Observations of language* behavior represent the fourth form of simple unobtrusive observations. The study of language ranges from complex linguistic analyses of verbal utterance, to the history of a group's linguistic categories, to the ways in which languages are transmitted. Unobtrusive language analysis focuses primarily on conversation sampling and the interrelationship of speech patterns to locale, categories of persons present, and to time of day. Excluded from this category of observation is much of modern linguistic analysis. As Webb, *et al.,* state:

Language is a hoary subject for observation, with everything from phonemes to profanity as legitimate game. Our interest here is more circumscribed and centers on language samples collected unobtrusively [1966, pp. 127–28].

Language analysis combines the study of physical locations with expressive movements; both of these categories represent languages given off in some consensual fashion to some audience. For purposes of convenience I will restrict language analysis to the study of verbal utterances—remembering, however, that this bears a close relationship to the other categories.

Cavan (1966) employed a form of unobtrusive language analysis in her study of bar interactions. She systematically recorded conversations between bar patrons to test the hypothesis that when in nonserious behavior settings persons were under no obligation to present accurate histories of themselves. The norms of conduct in bars are such that persons can routinely sever "themselves from their biographies in a number of ways [Cavan, 1966, p. 79]." Since the rules of bars require only a demonstration of legal drinking age, one need "only carry with him those identity papers that establish his date of birth [Cavan, 1966, p. 79]." The remaining components of his personal and social identity are established through his verbal and nonverbal communications. Cavan states:

Insofar as one can expect that exchanges therein will rarely if ever subject one to encounters outside the bar, the patron is also at liberty to prefabricate an entire life for himself with little likelihood that it will later be exposed as a sham [1966, p. 80].

The study of conversations in bars, followed up by personal interviews with patrons, would test more rigorously the hypothesis that biographies are constructed on the spot to foster a special definition of self.

Cavan's strategy could be extended to other behavior settings as well. Conversations in business offices could be compared to conversations by the same persons in lunch counters, cafeterias, or cocktail lounges. Family and home interaction could be compared to the topics of conversations engaged in while in the presence of "outsiders."

Psathas and Henslin (1967, pp. 424–43) have presented one of the most imaginative studies of language behavior. Their study blends formal linguistic analysis with the unobtrusive method. They examined the rules and definitions employed by cab drivers as they located points of delivery and pick-up on the basis of dispatcher messages. The dispatcher's messages were tape recorded by Henslin while he was employed as a cab driver, and were subjected to a complex analysis that included all information given in the message and the action taken by the driver. A coding procedure recorded the part of town referred to in the message, the street number and name, special features of the location (if given), information on how to find the passenger, his name (if given), and any other special features of the passenger. Each item of information was then assigned a special category that represented unique directions for the cab driver. Thus, if a driver was told to "Drive up and get out," he

must do more than merely drive up. His instructions involve getting out of the cab and actively looking for the passenger in a place where the passenger is presumed to be [Psathas and Henslin, 1967, p. 433].

Through their decoding process, Psathas and Henslin were able to arrive at an interesting depiction of the activities cab drivers routinely carry out when they fulfill the simple assignment of picking up and delivering a fare. Their investigation was couched in the tradition of ethnomethodology and was conceived as a test of that perspective. They note that their method requires one further step.

To determine whether this classification is psychologically real would require verification by means of systematic interrogation or further observations of the behavior of drivers. For example, one type of message could be presented to drivers who would then be asked to say all that they can about the particular place, what they think it looks like and how they would go about finding a passenger there [1967, p. 442].

Such a follow-up strategy would permit an analysis of what types of drivers use what elements from the messages. At the encoding end of the message, dispatchers could be interviewed to ascertain what types of information they routinely give drivers and why they give one kind of description and not another.

Telephone conversations could be monitored in a similar fashion, only in this case the observer might want explicit knowledge about the participants. Various locales could be studied to uncover the forms of expressive movements persons employed when speaking on the telephone. Do telephone booths lead to greater expressive movements than open phones? Do booths, as opposed to open phones lead to longer conversations? These examples suggest that the topic of conversation may be only one element of the unobtrusive analysis. The length of conversation, and the nature of expressive movements provide two other sources of observation.

Sidewalk conversation sampling could become a form of analysis to supplement other data on the uses of various public locales. In studying the behavior of college students, observers might locate themselves on their main thoroughfares at varying times of the day to learn the salient topics of conversation. This form of study could also be adopted to organizational studies (see Strauss, 1968, pp. 515–30).

On one occasion during the study of a large state mental hospital I happened into a large connecting tunnel between two treatment buildings and discovered virtually hundreds of messages scrawled on the walls. An analysis of these messages would reveal elements of the private thoughts and relationships of mental patients. Waiting rooms in hospitals, doctor's offices, employment agencies, and outside psychological laboratories could be studied for the nature of conversations that transpire within them. Language behavior, expressive analysis, exterior signs, and physical location all represent forms of data that complement one another. It is more appropriate to visualize these as mutually triangulated methodologies.

With *time sampling analysis* the investigator directs his attention to the social organization of time and some set of ongoing events in a specified population. This may take the form of analyzing the social meanings persons hold toward time and its passage, or it may simply involve recording the amount of time persons spend in various activities. The theoretical importance of time analysis derives from the fact that man does not live in a world strictly governed by calendar time (see Sorokin and Merton, 1937, pp. 615–29). The passage of calendar days and months is often collapsed into seasons, semesters, or significant activities. An entire four-year period in college may simply be described as "my undergraduate days." Even physical distance may be expressed in the amount of time it takes to move from one point to another. Thus persons will say "it is a ten minute drive," or "it takes three days." When dealing with time, its organization, and its relationship to ongoing interactions, analysts are chiefly referring to the social meanings attached to calendar time. The same interpretation holds for the analysis of physical space, and distance and location. It is appropriate to ask how it is that man defines and acts toward time and space in his daily activities such that those activities have a regularity and predictability for subsequent interactions.

The major unobtrusive strategy of time analysis is the simple, nonreactive observation of what persons do over a specified time period. The investigator follows his subject(s) around, recording all of the subject's activities toward the objects under study. Brookover and Back (1966, pp. 64–70) report a time sampling technique in which nurses were routinely observed as they passed through predetermined locales and their conduct in those settings was recorded.

Perhaps the earliest study of this nature was one by Booth (1903, pp. 47–56; see also 1967, pp. 305–12) that focused on the activities of London families on the weekends. Through a combination of diaries, interviews, and unobtrusive observations, Booth developed a series of hypotheses concerning the typical Sunday and holiday interaction patterns of the Londoner. In one observation he made the following report of a parishioner's activity on a Sunday (as viewed by a deacon):

They get up at nine or ten, and as he passes to his chapel he sees them sitting at breakfast half-dressed or lounging in the window reading *Lloyd's Weekly Newspaper*. After they are washed and dressed the men wait about until the public-houses open, and then stay within their doors till three o'clock when they go home to dinner, which meanwhile the women have been preparing. At half-past twelve, as he goes from chapel after the morning service, the minister often meets women laden with baskets of provisions from the street-market near by. . . . After dinner the men, if they have drunk too much, may go to bed, but the better sort take a stroll. In the evening the young people pair off for walking out, while the elders may perhaps go to a concert or Sunday League lecture [Booth, 1967 pp. 305–306].

Booth's study merges the social organization of time with the investigation of time spent in relationship to a class of objects. Two distinct approaches may be taken when engaging in either of these forms of analysis. The first is to saturate a given period of time by continuous observations; the second is to sample from a time period only certain hours, minutes, or months for study (Webb, *et al.*, 1966, p. 137). Thus Brookover and Back's study more properly becomes a time-sample investigation. The research of Barker and Wright (1954) represents a time-saturation approach. Their strategy is to follow a given class of subjects continuously over a specified period of time. For example, observations were made of one child's activity during an entire day; eight observers were used and it was felt that observer effects were negligible. Time saturation as a technique poses significant problems if a large class of subjects or a long period of time are to be studied. It is most practical for relatively short periods of time and for small numbers of persons. It is difficult to adopt this approach to groups or organizations, because the number of observers soon equals the number being observed.

A second technique of time analysis is the use of diaries or record books kept by the focal subjects in which they record their activities over a certain period of time. This approach has the danger of reactivity and of subject bias, for observers may lack external validations of statements. While not strictly an unobtrusive measure, the use of diaries with observers unobtrusively located provides a valuable triangulation of methods.

In Brookover and Back's (1966, pp. 64–70) time analysis of nursing students, an experimental design was developed to compare the relative validity of the diary and unobtrusive observational method. Sophomore nursing students in the School of Nursing at Duke University were placed in one of two experimental groups or a control group. Students in the first experimental group were instructed to keep a diary, or time budget, in which they answered the following questions concerning their behavior on specified days: if exposed to communication during the day, the number of persons present and their identity; the type of activity engaged in; the purpose of the activity; the type of exposure to the activity; who initiated the discussion or activity; who dissented in the discussion or activity; and whether the respondent agreed or disagreed with the major viewpoint expressed. Eight time intervals between 7:00 A.M. and 11:00 P.M. were chosen randomly and assigned to the subjects as focal periods to be recorded. At each time the subjects filled out the questionnaire, during four sets over a two- to three-day sequence.

The second experimental group was termed the "time-place group" and with it a presumably unobtrusive investigator was placed in a situation to observe their interactions. The locales for observation were determined by asking the subjects to note where they were at particular times of the day in the week preceding the experiment. These settings included hospital wards, the dormitory, libraries, classrooms, and the cafeteria.

A comparative analysis of the diary and time-place groups revealed substantial agreement between reported and actually occurring events. For example, both forms stated that interaction with men was greatest on Saturdays, and after 6:00 P.M. No association was reported, in either record, with nursing instructors after 6:00 P.M. daily or on Sunday. Although Brookover and Back do not state a preference for the two methods, it is recommended that when possible both approaches be employed. At the very least initial pretests should be conducted to establish their validity. If the time-place method is employed, some amount of prior questioning and diary or time-budget analysis would prove useful for subsequent allocation of observers to the setting under study.

Reiss (1959, pp. 182–95) describes a pilot study that tested the hypothesis that personal contacts of urban, rural nonfarm and rural farm residents differed in the direction of urban dwellers having fewer face to face and intimate contacts during an average day. Random samples of males over 20 years, white and full-time employed from Nashville, Tennessee, and two village communities located near Nashville were drawn and presented with a series of questions concerning what they had done on the previous day. The time-budget opened with the statement:

"Now, we would like to know how you spent your time yesterday. We want to know just how much time you spent doing different things during the day and whom you spent time with. Suppose we begin with the time you got up yesterday: what time did you get up?" [Reiss, 1959, pp. 183–84]

This question was followed by a "What did you do when you first got up?" Respondents were then asked, "Did you spend the time with anyone, or were you more or less alone?" If they were with someone, they were asked "Whom were you with, and how close are they to you?" Each new activity or block of time was similarly examined until the person said he went to sleep. Interviewers were instructed to obtain the information so that it could be coded into one of the following mutually exclusive categories:

1. *Intimate kinship,* such as nuclear family members.
2. *Close intimate friends* defined as "very close," "my best friend," etc.
3. *Close associate or client,* e.g., derived from work.
4. *Good friend,* a friend defined as "close."
5. *Distant associate or casual acquaintance,* either a fellow worker who is not defined as a friend or a person with whom one has a "speaking acquaintance."
6. *Cordial recognition* defined as person whom one recognizes in address, or "just someone to whom I say, hello."
7. *Pure client,* defined as person whom one doesn't know personally, but one with whom contact is made, or with whom interaction takes place in a client relationship [Reiss, 1959, p. 184].

For analytical purposes categories 1–4 were defined as "primary contacts," 5–7 as "secondary contacts," and 6–7 as "impersonal." [Reiss, 1959, p. 184].

Analysis of these data revealed that there were no significant differences in respondent social status and types of interpersonal contact. Urban males spent a greater average of time in primary contacts than rural nonfarm, or rural farm males, but "this was due largely to difference in primary contacts at work [1959, p. 182]." Urban and nonfarm males were likely to have a greater mean amount of *impersonal* contact (categories 6–7) than were rural farm males. These findings lend support to the Sorokin and Zimmerman (1929) statement that the study of rural sociology is fundamentally a study of an occupational group and that this fact leads to a series of other differences "between the rural and the urban communities [Reiss, 1959, p. 194]." Earlier statements by Simmel (see Wolff, 1950) had suggested differences in interpersonal contact derived basically from place of residence and not occupational position. Reiss' study supports the Sorokin and Zimmerman hypothesis and suggests that future investigations should examine other occupational groupings and the nature of their interpersonal relationships.

In a massive analysis of leisure-time activities in modern industrial societies that de Grazia (1962, pp. 422–23) performed on a national sample of 7,000 separate households, a secondary analysis asked respondents about the amount of time they spent between 6:00 A.M. and 11:00 P.M. for a two-day period during March–April of 1954. Each individual in the sample maintained a complete diary of his activities for specific quarter-hour intervals during the two-day period. Among the findings were the following: Males spend over three times as much time away from home at work as do females; on Sundays this reduces to 1.2 hours for males and .3 hours for females; on weekdays females spent approximately twice as much time at a friend's or relative's house as males; nearly all household chores are performed by females during the week, although on weekends males share this activity at a greater proportion.

In reference to the sample and the diary technique, de Grazia states:

By all tests, the sample appeared representative of the population of the country. The distribution of the respondents in the sample by geographic areas, by number and make of cars owned, by home ownership, by color, by income, and by telephone ownership—all the distributions were extremely close to independent estimates for the United States [1962, p. 423].

Of the diary technique he argues:

By limiting the period for which diaries had to be maintained to two consecutive days, some of the usual objections to the diary approach were met. In addition, following the personal visit during which the diaries were left with the respondent, a reminder telephone call was made the next day. Apparently the elaborate system of cross-checks that was possible not only enabled the editors and coders to achieve a high degree of accuracy but also revealed a high degree of accuracy in the original entries [1962, p. 423].

The Reiss and de Grazia investigations move beyond mere time-budget analyses and link the social organization of time with elements of the social structure. They indicate the tremendous importance of time analyses, and that this simple approach can be combined with the survey method. Diary analysis departs from pure unobtrusive methodology, but when large samples of persons are to be studied, some form of the diary appears necessary.

I began this discussion of time analysis with the statement that the meanings assigned to time, and its relationship to social organizations are of more theoretical value than simple time-budget accounts. In an incisive analysis of dying in the modern hospital, Glaser and Strauss (1964; 1968) stress this point, especially in their examination of post-mortem stories. They state:

Another important feature of the post-mortem story is its description of the temporal aspects of the patient's trajectory which we call "time-jamming" and "time-spreading." As personnel review the case they may jam months of lingering into a few moments of discussion and spread out a few strategic moments of the trajectory into a detailed 20-minute discussion of, say, what everyone was doing when the patient's tubes fell out without notice. Time-jamming and time-spreading indicate the relevant parts of the pre-death story that bothered the staff. Subsequently, the story is steered purposively, if unwittingly, in a clearly negative or positive manner so as to balance out sentimentally what happened [1968, p. 235].

The study of time and its passage in the hospital will reveal a great deal about the value assigned to a patient by the staff. Accidents, transmissions of incorrect information, and the inappropriate location of staff at critical dying periods can be partially explained by the definitions attached to time and the activities engaged in at that moment.

Similar organizational studies of time could be developed. The icons or symbols assigned to time and its passage could be examined (Strauss, 1968); in some institutions it is a bell that signals its occurrence, in others it is the clock, and in prisons it may be the time left until one is paroled. Organizations have their own timetables, with categories of persons assigned activities at certain moments. Janitors in the modern university appear after five, while secretaries begin early in the day. Night and day people in organizations have their own conceptions of time, and according to their time schedule all other segments of their life must be organized accordingly (see Lipset, Trow, and Coleman, 1962, pp. 153–59). The simple observational techniques are best viewed as complementary. A complete interactional study would employ all of them, as well as more structured and reactive techniques. Expressive movement analysis, for example, properly conceived, would require data on time, physical location, exterior signs and language. If precedence is given to any of these methods, physical location and time analysis should be favored, for they explicitly demand data on the two major sources of population instabilities—time and space.

### Sources of Invalidity with the Simple Measure

Errors that arise from population instabilities over time and locale can be partially overcome by sampling multiple locales at varying times. Even so, with the simple observation only relatively small populations can be studied and generalizations to cities, occupational groups, or entire organizations must be quite tentative when only the simple measure is employed. Error may also occur from infallibilities of the observer. Unless multiple observers are employed, response sets arising from fatigue, boredom, or theoretical preconceptions can emerge to challenge an investigation's internal validity. An additional problem with the simple observation is the restrictive nature of the behavior that can be observed. If the observer is to remain unnoticed, then the settings most amenable to this strategy will be public. Private settings such as the home, the executive's office, or an analyst's couch are unlikely to become open to such study. Finally, dross rates, or the gained-loss factor in theoretically useful data, may be quite high with this method. Unless prior investigations are conducted, observers may be staked out in settings where critical behavior does not occur at a high frequency. This of course is a good reason for the use of questionnaires, informants, and interviews as combined research strategies.

Perhaps the greatest strength of the simple observation is, as Hall has stated, that "what people do is frequently more important than what they say (1959, p. 15)." As I noted in opening this chapter, however, much of the data gathered by unobtrusive measures fail to offer the "why" and offer instead only an observed relationship (Webb, *et al.,* 1966, p. 127).

*Intervening Unobtrusive Analysis: The Use of Hidden Recording Devices*

Unobtrusive measures that rely chiefly on the nondetected observer suffer from all of the fallibilities of observers noted, as well as an inability to monitor and control the quality and quantity of incoming data. The last method to be discussed in this chapter overcomes these flaws to a certain extent because the observer is removed from the observational scene and replaced by hidden recording equipment (see Webb, *et al.,* 1966, pp. 142–70).

With such equipment, observational settings can be systematically varied without loss of observer time and a permanent record of observations can be obtained. In addition, such devices provide useful reliability checks on subsequent observations where human observers are employed. A further advantage is that the mechanical recorder can be placed in private behavior settings where human unobtrusive observers would not be permitted. Hidden recording devices include tape recorders, audiotapes, one-way mirrors, and still and moving photography. Additional techniques would include physiological measuring mechanisms that record body movements ranging from the eye's to the entire body's. The most extensive use of mechanical equipment in sociology thus far has been in small-group, laboratory investigations—where one-way mirrors, and hidden microphones are used. Unfortunately the laboratory strategy is seldom unobtrusive in design or execution. Subjects are aware that they are subjects and often realize that their behavior is being coded and analyzed by persons they can neither see nor hear. But the small-group strategy can conveniently be transported into the natural field situation. Tape recorders and microphones can be installed in offices, places of work, or even in private behavior settings. Telephones can be monitored, and video cameras can be installed to provide permanent records of actions and utterances. One of my colleagues experimented with hidden tape recorders during a field trip to Latin America. Forced to leave the major routes of transportation and travel into the mountains, he installed a transistorized tape recorder on the back of one of his pack horses. The recorder was automatically activated by a small voice microphone contained in his shirt pocket. He routinely taped field notes at the end of each day with this and often employed it when speaking with critical informants, a strategy that could be adapted to field work in urban settings as well; the main recording devices would be installed in the investigator's automobile and could be activated at distances up to a mile away by transistorized microphones. The hidden microphone permits more fluid field interactions than the notebook or the open recorder into which the respondent is encouraged to pour out his intimate thoughts, and the investigator can operate as his own experimental stimuli, varying his style and mode of presentation to test hypotheses with much of the rigor found back in the laboratory.

Photographic equipment can also be employed to take pictures of respondents, locales where observations occurred, or even as a behavior measure of expressive movements, physical location patterns, or exterior signs and traces. Anthropologists have long used the camera as a standard piece of field equipment, although often in a reactive fashion. Photos of natives, their dwelling units, their tools of agriculture and hunting and even styles of dress have frequently been taken to provide a permanent record for future investigators and to document field notes (see Lewis, 1953, pp. 452–75; Rowe, 1953, pp. 895–940).

Webb, *et al.* (1966, p. 146), suggest that a large untapped data domain as yet unused by sociologists is the archives of the radio and television networks; these contain visual and auditory records of significant historical events that could be put to meaningful analysis by the sociologist. The study of trends in fashion, shifts in public opinion, reactions to national crises, and the like could all be made from these data. It must be remembered, however, that such records necessarily have a reactive quality that derives from the initial selective recording of the events. Network policy combined with the realization by a respondent that his statements are being recorded for posterity challenge the internal validity of such documents. Their value has as yet gone unexplored, however, and problems of internal validity seem relatively insignificant in view of their advantages.

The mechanical recording of body movements—a logical extension of physical location analysis—can be achieved by attaching simple recording devices to pieces of furniture. Cox and Marley (1959, pp. 57–60) devised a movement measure in a study of the effects of drugs on restlessness among patients. Their device involved a series of pulleys and springs set under the springs of the bed that recorded the displacement of the mattress whenever the patient moved. Their technique could be elaborated to include polygraph chartings of such movements, thus making even more precise the final record. Other investigators have similarly wired baby cribs, office desks, and chairs.

*Experimental Variations*

Without explicit monitoring and control of the hidden recording device, this form of unobtrusive analysis can suffer from the flaws of a high dross rate and an inability to record the needed observations (see Webb, *et al.*, 1966, pp. 155–56). Therefore, experimental interventions in the field setting must often be designed. The television show "Candid Camera" resorted to various experimental designs because simple observations produced high dross rates in the desired data. Webb, *et al.*, report that in the early days of the show, its originator, Allen Funt, relied totally on film and audio recordings of gestures and conversations. With conversations

Funt found that a large amount of time was required to obtain a small amount of material, and he finally turned to introducing confederates who would behave in such a way to direct attention to the topic of study [1966, p. 156].

Confederates, or persons deliberately instructed to behave so as to elicit hypothesized reactions, remain nonreactive factors to the extent that they go unnoticed. In the "Candid Camera" sequences, the confederates were seldom detected and the sociological significance of the show was reflected in the natural reactions of persons confronted with unusual and unexpected stimuli in their taken-for-granted daily encounters. In one sequence, males in several different cultural settings were requested to carry the suitcase of a female confederate to a corner.

Filmed abroad, the episodes centered on a girl indicating she had carried the suitcase for a long time and would like a hand. The critical material is the facial expression and bodily gestures of the men as they attempted to lift the suitcase and sagged under the weight. It was filled with metal. The Frenchman shrugged; the Englishman kept at it [Webb, *et al.*, 1966, p. 156].

Studies of social interaction in public entertainment settings could be designed to vary the mode of entertainment normally expected by patrons. Rock and roll groups could be sent into a normally quiet night club and audience reactions to the performance taped with hidden recorders. Confederates could be located in bars to study the reactions of patrons when they received the wrong drink, or confederate bartenders and barmaids could be instructed to vary their reaction to a patron when he receives the wrong order. Variations in dress, style of speech, and expressive movements could also be manipulated to assess their effects on a patron's willingness to complain, or quietly accept.

Sechrest has reported experimental variations in the study of automobile traffic behavior. One study was concerned with the willingness of drivers to accept a challenge to "drag" at stop signals. The investigators challenged by pulling alongside

a car, gunning the engine of their car, and looking once at their "opponent." They used different stimulus cars and recorded several attributes of the responding cars. Results showed a strong decline in acceptance of the challenge with increasing age and with presence of passengers other than the driver in the respondent's car. As for the stimulus cars? Very few drivers wanted to drag with a Volkswagen [Webb, et al., 1966, p. 163].

Filmed accounts of such episodes could be made. Similar variations in other forms of traffic behavior are conceivable; for example, "bumping and stumbling" on sidewalks could be studied. What do normal participants on our streets and sidewalks do when another person cuts in front of them and bumps them or stumbles across their path? Experimental confederates varying in mode of dress (as an indicator of social class) might be introduced and the reactions filmed.

### An Assessment of Hidden Recording Devices

With the techniques just discussed the observer moves out of his passive, unobtrusive role and actively guides the data. The use of hidden recording equipment insures permanent data records, thus permitting later reliability and secondary analyses. Yet the hardware has its drawbacks. Some devices are static in nature and hence restrictive in their experimental value. Wired chairs, stationary microphones, and the like do not permit the kind of fluid locale-temporal sampling strategy necessary to overcome problems of population instabilities over time and space. Also, copying data from these records is costly. In one of the few analyses of the tape-recorded interview, Bucher, Fritz and Quarantelli (1956, pp. 359–64) state that for many research projects the time-cost factor automatically rules out the possibility of using tape recorders. Quality tape recorders cost from one hundred to more than a thousand dollars, and the cost of tape ranges from two to four dollars a reel, depending on the size of the reel and the quality of tape. Transcription costs from a single seven and one-half inch tape can run as high as twenty dollars, and this is before multiple reproductions of the transcription are produced. Bucher, Fritz and Quarantelli estimated that

approximately 700 tape recorded NORC interviews required a total of over 4,200 hours of transcription time and 1,800 hours of proofing and correction. Specifically for each hour of original recording, an additional 6.3 hours of skilled typing time and 2.8 hours of checking were required [1956, p. 363].

They state that a minimum of twenty-five dollars per hour of tape-recorded interview should be estimated, this over and above the initial cost of obtaining the interview. If movies or extensive series of photographs are produced, similar and even higher costs must be expected.

Another problem is the presentation of data gathered by a hidden recording device: Journals and monographs are ill-prepared to present long series of photographs. Further, repositories for data of this nature would need to be established so that future investigators could procure them to conduct independent analyses.

The problem of detection looms large when in the disguised role, and this is magnified when hidden recording devices are employed. Finally, the ethics of disguised observation are debatable. If an observer is discovered while using a hidden device, he can expect reactivity from his subjects and criticism from certain spokesmen in the discipline. (The ethical issues involved are treated in Chap. 13.)

## Some Additional Considerations

*Sampling Strategies and Unobtrusive Analysis*

Several types of sampling strategies may be employed in any investigation (e.g., interactive, noninteractive theoretical, or statistical), but a further classification of sampling strategies is in order involving a distinction between *situational and temporal sampling*. Unobtrusive analysis combines spatial and temporal sampling methods with theoretical sampling to a much greater degree than any of the methods thus far discussed.

Webb has spoken of what he calls "oddball sampling" as a logical extension of the unobtrusive methods presented in this chapter. As quoted in Chapter 4, he states:

Thus far, the emphasis has been on data sources and overlapping classes of data. We might also profitably explore the possibility of using multiple samples. Again, this is different from the usual definition of multiple samples. In addition to sampling a number of different classrooms, or groups of students or cities, one may ask are there different types of categories of samples available for the variable under study. Is there a group of natural outcroppings among occupations, already formed social and interest groups, or people who have common experiences? Can we economically exploit for research purposes the broad spectrum of already formed groups which may be organized along some principle of direct substantive applicability to the investigation [1966, p. 37]?

Criticizing the normal strategy of statistical sampling theory, Webb goes on to argue:

Because one sometimes doesn't know the universe for a study and because of cost restraints, subjects are most often selected because of proximity. Our subjects are typically drawn from the subject pool of the introductory class, from friends, friends of friends, or those unlucky enough to be members of the institution of the investigator, be it the school, the hospital or the prison [1966, pp. 37–38].

Oddball sampling, or the use of natural outcroppings of data, as Webb calls them, complements theoretical sampling. Webb proposes as natural groups the following: airport travelers, firemen, men aboard ship, grand prix automobile drivers, self-help groups of a deviant nature (e.g., Alcoholics Anonymous, Gamblers Anonymous, etc.). In studies of isolation and its effects on the self, Webb suggests "interstate truck drivers, pilots flying missions alone at night, orthopedic patients in iron lungs, and anecdotal reports of prisoners in solitary confinement, shipwrecked sailors and explorers [1966, p. 39]." These natural groups are situated by locale, not time. Similar groups, persons, and occupational types could be sampled by time as well; day and night people in organizations would be an example.

When observers begin to sample by locale, time and subject statistical models take on their greatest relevance. Analysts can randomly sample different times of the day, different locales, or different persons who pass through certain locales by time of day, situational location and so on. The student employing unobtrusive methods should search for naturally occurring groups and locations for his studies, and abandon the college student and housewife as the main classes of subjects.

*Problems of Causality and Unobtrusive Analysis*

A viable causal hypothesis will demonstrate covariance between the variables examined while establishing that the independent variable preceded the dependent variable in time. Further, such hypotheses will be tested against rival explanations. The two generic classes of rival hypotheses repeatedly treated in this book have been factors deriving from internal and external validity. To summarize Webb's discussion, errors in validity may arise from the following sources:

1. *Reactive Measurement Effect*
   1. Awareness of being tested
   2. Role playing
   3. Measurement as change
   4. Response sets
2. *Error from Investigation*
   5. Interviewer-observer effects
   6. Change in observer-fatigue, boredom, etc.
3. *Varieties of Sampling Error*
   7. Population restriction (idiosyncrasies, etc.)
   8. Population stability over time
   9. Population stability over areas

4. *Access to Content*
   10. Restrictions to content
   11. Stability of content over time
   12. Stability of content over areas
5. *Operating Ease and Validity Checks*
   13. Dross or loss rate
   14. Access to descriptive cues
   15. Ability to replicate [Webb, 1966, p. 36].

These five categories of invalidity are some of the major sources of error treated in earlier discussions of internal and external validity. I have now adopted these dimensions to unobtrusive measures and the discussion thus far has variously indicated the relevance of each for unobtrusive measures. Returning to the causality problem, it is clear that unobtrusive measures effectively handle reactive measurement effects—this is their explicit intent. Errors from the investigator are mitigated by the use of hidden recording equipment. Varieties of sampling error can be solved by systematic samplings over time and across situations. Access to content can be similarly handled, and hidden equipment permits access to otherwise denied areas of observation. Problems of operating ease and validity checks are not serious with the unobtrusive approach. When multiple observers are employed, reliability checks can be made and with permanent audio and visual records this problem becomes negligible.

Unobtrusive methods adequately solve problems of internal and external validity, then, but what of the other two elements in a causal hypothesis? On these counts unobtrusive analysis is exceedingly weak, because when taken alone such strategies leave out the "why" in the causal hypothesis. They offer only a correlation or establish the existence of a relationship. Webb, *et al.*, verify this point:

Barch, Trumbo and Nangle (1957) used the behavior of automobiles in their observational study of conformity to legal requirements. We are not sure if this is more properly coded under "expressive movement," but the "physical location" category seems more appropriate. They were interested in the degree to which turn-signaling was related to the turn-signaling behavior of a preceding car. For four weeks, they recorded this information:

1. Presence or absence of a turn signal
2. Direction of turn
3. Presence of another motor vehicle 100 feet or less behind the turning motor vehicle when it begins to turn
4. Sex of drivers.

Observers stood near the side of the road and were not easily visible to the motorists. There was the interesting finding that conforming behavior, as defined by signaling or not, varied with the direction of the turn. Moreover, a sex difference was noted. There was a strong positive correlation if left turns were signaled. But on right turns, the correlation was low and positive. Why there is a high correlation for left turns and a low one for right turns is equivocal. The data, like so many simple observational data, don't offer the "why," but simply establish a relationship [1966, p. 127].

If unobtrusively gathered data suffer from an inability to forge meaningful causal hypotheses, what is their proper role for the sociologist interested in causal analysis? To answer this question, it is necessary first to consider why such measures do not immediately lend themselves to causal analysis. My position is that the extreme behavioristic bias of the unobtrusive approach leads to the failure. Unless observers have means of systematically probing the subjective dimensions of social conduct, inferences will always be causally weak and superficial. Symbolic interactionism suggests that the meaningful elements of social forces, of symbols, of time and space, occur only after these forces have been transformed and translated into ongoing lines of action. This translation process may of course not always be conscious and deliberate. Custom, habit, and tradition often lead persons to do things they give little or no thought to—but the fact is that custom, habit, and tradition reflect this process of translating social forces into lines of action. I am necessarily led to the position that a complete methodology of the social sciences is one that combines the behavioristic and symbolic elements of human conduct. Accordingly, unobtrusive methods of observation, like all other strategies, realize their fullest potential when they are combined with methods that probe the subjective side of human conduct.

**Notes**

My major source in this chapter has been the groundbreaking work by Webb, *et al., Unobtrusive Measures: Nonreactive Research in the Social Sciences* (1966). This must be read for a more complete understanding of the method.

It is relevant to note, I believe, that Erving Goffman's studies of face to face interaction (see, for example, 1967) offer a theoretical perspective on the unobtrusive method. At one point he states:

The acts or events, that is, the sign-vehicles or tokens which carry ceremonial messages are remarkably various in character. They may be linguistic, as when an individual makes a statement of praise . . . and does so in a particular language and intonation; gestural, as when the physical bearing of an individual conveys insolence or obsequiousness; spatial, as when an individual precedes another through the door . . . ; task-embedded, as when an individual accepts a task graciously . . . ; part of the communication structure, as when an individual speaks more frequently than the others, or receives more attentiveness than they do [1967, p. 55].

These elements of the ceremonial message (linguistic, gestural, spatial, task-embedded, and communication) reflect a theoretical concern with many of the components of unobtrusive analysis. My treatment of simple measures of observation reflects a concern with these dimensions of the ceremonial-interactional process.

Two excellent sources on the use of hidden and technical hardware are Lewis (1953, pp. 452–75) and Rowe (1953, pp. 895–940). Lewis' discussion is limited to the camera and photographic equipment; Rowe's deals with motion pictures, infrared photography, ultraviolet light techniques, aerial photography, and sound recording. Rowe also discusses some of the techniques employed by archeologists relevant to physical location analysis.

Part IV
# Strategies of Triangulation and the Art of Doing Sociology

# Strategies of
# Multiple Triangulation

Every cobbler thinks leather is the only thing. Most social scientists, including the present writer, have their favorite methods with which they are familiar and have some skill in using. And I suspect we mostly choose to investigate problems that seem vulnerable to attack through these methods. But we should at least try to be less parochial than cobblers. Let us be done with the arguments of "participant observation" *versus* interviewing—as we have largely dispensed with the arguments for psychology *versus* sociology —and get on with the business of attacking our problems with the widest array of conceptual and methodological tools that we possess and they demand. This does not preclude discussion and debate regarding the relative usefulness of different methods for the study of specific problems or types of problems. But that is very different from the assertion of the general and inherent superiority of one method over another on the basis of some intrinsic qualities it presumably possesses.

*Martin Trow,* 1957, p. 35.

Advocating triangulation, or the combination of methodologies in the study of the same phenomena, has been a basic theme of this book. I have repeatedly suggested that the sociologist should examine his problem from as many different methodological perspectives as possible. My definition of each method has implied a triangulated perspective. Participant observation was seen as combining survey interviewing, document analysis, direct observation, and observer participation. Similarly, unobtrusive measures were defined as involving multiple data approaches, as were the life history, the experiment, and the survey. Remaining to be treated are the strategies by which the sociologist may meaningfully combine these methods so that fully grounded and verified theories can be generated.

### Research Methods as Lines of Action

Research methods represent lines of action taken toward the empirical world. Many sociologists assume that their research methods are neutral "atheoretical tools" suitable for valid scientific use by any knowledgeable user; I have attempted to indicate that on the contrary, research methods represent different means of acting on the environment of the scientist. Surveys, for example, dictate a stance toward the invariant and stable features of this reality, while participant observation assumes a reality continually in change and flux. Hence, when a sociologist adopts any one of these methods, he is necessarily led to lines of action different from those he would have pursued had he employed another method. Each research method reveals peculiar elements of symbolic reality. When a sociologist adopts a method, his definitions of that method serve to make his final observations in some way different from those of any other user—past, present, or future. Thus, not only do methods imply different lines of action, but their sociological users lend unique interpretations to them. Add to these factors that the reality to which sociologists apply their methods is continually in a state of change, and we find, as Shibutani has argued

that what is called "reality" is a social process; it is an orientation that is continuously supported by others. . . . Societies, no matter how stable they may appear, are ongoing things. The world is in a state of continuous flux, and as life conditions change, knowledge must keep pace. In this sense all knowledge is social [1966, pp. 170–171; 182].

*Sociology's Negotiated Reality*

When I speak of triangulated research strategies oriented toward common units of observation, I mean that these units of observation are social objects in the environment of the scientist. These objects represent the reality of the scientist, and their meaning arises out of his experiences. It is to be hoped that the definitions attached to these objects will be public and consensual. Indeed, scientists demand a certain degree of consensuality, but that consensuality will never be complete, since each method implies a different line of action toward that reality—hence each will reveal different aspects of it, much as a kaleidoscope, depending on the angle at which it is held, will reveal different colors and configurations of objects to the viewer. Methods are like the kaleidoscope—depending on how they are approached, held, and acted toward, different observations will be revealed. This is not to imply that reality has the shifting qualities of the colored prism, but that it too is an object that moves and that will not permit one interpretation to be stamped upon it.

A second source of variance arises from the users of methods. Each sociologist brings to these lines of action his own interpretations of them, and to an extent these will be unique. When two investigators employ participant observation as a strategy for uncovering the stratification system in a local community, different results can be expected simply because each has defined the method in a different fashion. One may have taken pains to insure a rigorous statistical sample, while the other may choose a theoretical sampling strategy. Or one may conduct long training sessions for his observers, while the other merely hands out information sheets. An endless variety of subtle differences in interpretation may be present in the two studies—which ideally are comparable. The subtle differences may make them quite dissimilar, however.

A third reason consensuality can never be complete arises from the definitions brought to bear upon the units observed. Each user approaches these units from a unique perspective that reflects his past experiences, personal idiosyncrasies, and current mood. If, for example, one were examining the stratification system in a local community, past experiences would condition the persons observed, the questions asked, and ultimately the results. Vidich and Shapiro (1955, pp. 28–33) have shown that in one community study the participant observer systematically overobserved middle-class, professional males; females and persons from the labor force were underrepresented in the final analysis. While Vidich and Shapiro suggest that the observer's role in the community dictated this sampling strategy, it seems fair to conclude also that his own preferences and abilities to interact with persons most like him may also have contributed to his choice.

The fourth factor that leads to distortions is that the world of observations is in a state of continuous change. This necessarily makes observations at one point in time different from any other set of observations. What Campbell and Stanley have termed population instabilities arising from time and space refer to this factor of change. Student revolts are an example; student activity in 1969 was fundamentally different from similar actions by students at any other time. The meanings attached to universities, the political role of students, their self-conceptions, their ideologies and values have all changed; hence, comparisons between historical periods demands a sensitivity to the meanings attached to the units observed by those generating the meanings. Student protest today may appear similar to actions in the 1930's, but it would be unreasonable to conclude that the same processes are operating.

The activities of the sociologist are in many ways no different from those of the persons he studies. All humans are involved in the process of making sense out of this social object called reality and they do so by agreeing on the definitions attached to it. Until sociologists recognize the fundamental elements of symbolic interaction embedded in their own conduct, sociology will not move closer to the status of a mature, self-aware science that understands its own activities and subject matter.

But while the scientist shares a good deal with his subjects, he takes a peculiar stance toward his own activities. What is meant by the sociological method represents this commitment to a set of rules and values that set sociologists apart from others. Observations must be made public and they must be assessed against agreed-upon rules of inference and proof. The stress in this book upon rules of inference, internal and external validity, and interrelationship of observations to theory represents my view of these rules.

It is important, however, not to overlook the human-personalistic element in the scientific process. I have suggested that this element intrudes into every step of the scientific process; from the selection of research methods to research problems flowing from a favored theory, personal values and preferences shape decisions. Despite the existence of public rules governing the enterprise called science, the values, definitions and ideologies of each scientist significantly determine the translation of rules of method into the scientific process. These aspects of what might be called "doing science" will be treated in the next chapter. I note their relevance here to present both sides of the scientific coin before returning to the topic of triangulation.

*A Recapitulation*

Sociology's empirical reality is a reality of competing definitions, attitudes, and personal values. As such, it is a social object in the symbolic environment of the scientist. Any attempt to approximate knowledge of this object must acknowledge this fact. The act of doing research is an act of symbolic interaction. Each sociological method and, in fact, each sociologist generates different lines of action toward this object. Thus, complete agreement between methods and their users can never be expected. But there are rules of method that govern the sociologist's conduct. His actions—from the use of methods, to the personal values that shape the sociological act—must be made public.

Triangulation, or the use of multiple methods, is a plan of action that will raise sociologists above the personalistic biases that stem from single methodologies. By combining methods and investigators in the same study, observers can partially overcome the deficiencies that flow from one investigator and/or one method. Sociology as a science is based on the observations generated from its theories, but until sociologists treat the act of generating observations as an act of symbolic interaction, the links between observations and theories will remain incomplete. In this respect triangulation of method, investigator, theory, and data remains the soundest strategy of theory construction.

## Types of Triangulation

It is conventionally assumed that triangulation is the use of multiple methods in the study of the same object (see Campbell and Fiske, 1959; Webb, *et al.*, 1966). Indeed, this is the generic definition I have offered, but it is only one form of the strategy. It is convenient to conceive of triangulation as involving varieties of data, investigators, and theories, as well as methodologies. The four basic types of triangulation are *data*, with these types; (1) time, (2) space, (3) person, and these levels (1) aggregate (person), (2) interactive (person), (3) collectivity (person); *investigator* (multiple vs. single observers of same object); *theory* (multiple vs. single perspectives in relation to the same set of objects); and *methodological* (within-method triangulation and between-method triangulation).

*Data Triangulation*

Not only may observers triangulate by methodology, but also by data sources. In a very loose sense, theoretical sampling is an example of the latter process; that is, researchers explicitly search for as many different data sources as possible which bear upon the events under analysis. Data sources, in this sense, are to be distinguished from methods of generating data. The latter refer to research methods per se, and not sources of data as such. By triangulating data sources, analysts can efficiently employ the same methods to maximum theoretical advantage. Thus, if studying the social meanings of death in the modern hospital, it would be possible to employ a standard method (e.g., participant observation) but deliberately take this method to as many different areas as possible. Researchers might examine different role groups within the hospital and then turn to family members of dying persons. Death rituals in other settings might also be examined by the same process. Primitive societies could be studied. Highway deaths, deaths at home, at work and even at play are other examples. Each of these represent significantly different data areas within which the same generic event (death) occurs. Basically this would be the use of dissimilar comparison groups as a sampling strategy, but it more properly reflects a strategy of triangulation. By selecting dissimilar settings in a systematic fashion, investigators can discover what their concepts (as designators of units in reality) have in common across settings. Similarly, the unique features of these concepts will be discovered in their situated context.

All sociological observations relate to activities of socially situated persons—whether they are in groups, or organizations, or aggregately distributed over some social area. A focus on time and space as observational units recognizes their relationship to the observations of persons. A major focus in time observations will be its relationship to ongoing interactions; observers can sample activities by time of day, week, month, or year. Similarly, they also can sample space and treat it as a unit of analysis (e.g., ecological analysis), or as a component of external validity. Personal data point, of course, to the most common unit of analysis—the social organization of persons through time and space. These three units—time, space, and person—are interrelated. A study of one demands a study of the others. Returning to the instance of dying, an investigation could be designed that triangulated data by these three dimensions. Death in the early morning in the emergency room of the hospital could be compared to midday deaths in the presence of nonhospital personnel, for example.

Three distinct levels of person analysis can be treated. The first is what is commonly found in the social survey; individuals are selected for study, not groups, relationships, or organizations. I term this aggregate analysis because of the failure to establish social links between those observed. Random samples of housewives, college students, and blue-collar workers are instances of aggregate-person analysis. The second level I term interactive. Here the unit becomes interacting persons in either laboratory or natural field settings. Small groups, families, and work crews are examples. What sociologists commonly associate with participant observation, small-group experiments, and unobtrusive measures represents this form of analysis. The unit is interaction and not the person or the group. Goffman's (1961) studies of face to face encounters in hospital surgery rooms are excellent examples. Surgeons, nurses, and the hospital social structure were studied only as they interacted in generating a series of interactive episodes.

The third level, the one commonly associated with structural-functional analysis, is the collectivity. Here the observational unit is an organization, a group, a community, or even an entire society. Persons and their interactions are treated only as they reflect pressures and demands of the total collectivity.

The three levels of analysis can be illustrated by returning to the example of dying in the hospital. An aggregately oriented investigation might simply sample the various attitudes held by hospital personnel toward the dying process. An interactional study would examine how these attitudes are generated out of the encounters between personnel. Last, the collectivity-oriented investigator might examine how the structural features of the hospital (e.g., its organizational chart, role positions), dictate certain attitudes and practices on the part of its members. Any one investigation can combine all three levels and types of data; in fact those studies commonly regarded as classic make these combinations: time, space, and persons are alternatively analyzed from the aggregate, interactive, and collective levels.

*Boys in White* represents such a synthesis. Medical students were randomly sampled and interviewed, groups of interacting students were observed, and the role demands of hospital staff, as they related to these interactions, were analyzed. Situation and time sampling were also used. Student study patterns during critical examination periods were compared to patterns during nonexamination periods. Study habits in laboratories, fraternities, and the class room were also compared.

Investigator triangulation simply means that multiple as opposed to single observers are employed. Most investigations in fact do employ multiple observers, although all of them may not occupy equally prominent roles in the actual observational process. What Roth (1966, pp. 190–96) has termed hired-hand research represents an inappropriate use of multiple observers: the act of making observations is delegated to persons who lack the skill and knowledge of the primary investigator. The use of undergraduates as coders, graduate students and housewives as interviewers, and computer specialists as data analysts represents a delegation of responsibility that places the least well-prepared persons in crucial role positions. When multiple observers are used, the most skilled observers should be placed closest to the data. Triangulating observers removes the potential bias that comes from a single person, and insures a greater reliability in observations, a rationale well illustrated by Strauss, *et al.*, in their observational study of interactions in mental hospitals:

There were three fieldworkers subjected for the most part to the same raw data. Search for pinpointing and negative evidence was abetted by the collective nature of our inquiry. If the colleague reported the same kind of observation as another without prior consultation, confidence grew. If after hearing the report of an observation, a colleague was himself able unquestionably to duplicate it, it indicated that our observational techniques had some degree of reliability. If no colleague did corroborate an observation—which did happen—if it seemed important then, or later, further inquiry was initiated. Something like a built-in reliability check was thus obtained because several fieldworkers were exposed directly to similar or identical data [1964, p. 36].

Theoretical triangulation is an element that few investigations achieve. Typically a small set of hypotheses guide any study and data are gathered that bear on only those dimensions, but there would seem to be value in approaching data with multiple perspectives and hypotheses in mind. Data that would refute central hypotheses could be collected, and various theoretical points of view could be placed side by side to assess their utility and power (see Westie, 1957, pp. 149–54). Such strategies would permit sociologists to move away from polemical criticisms of various theoretical perspectives, since pitting alternative theories against the same body of data is a more efficient means of criticism—and it more comfortably conforms with the scientific method.

The necessity of considering theoretical triangulation as an integral feature of the research process is shown in those areas characterized by a high degree of theoretical incoherence—contemporary theory in the area of small-group analysis, for example. Some sociologists argue that exchange theory explains interaction in groups, while others stress a functionalist perspective; at the same time, interpersonal attraction and balance theorists debate the efficacy of their approach, while symbolic interactionists propose their own framework. Empirical data go unorganized, and each theorist searches for data appropriate to his hypotheses. As a consequence, no solidly grounded theory has emerged in this area. Each new investigator has typically taken one of the following lines of action. Some resort, as Westie has shown in the field of race relations, to

a rigid empiricism in which the "facts" (meaning the empirical findings) are seen to speak for themselves. The utility of such research is often bound to the particular moment, place and project [1957, p. 149].

A second strategy is to select from among the

many contradictory propositions already held in the field, a particular proposition or set of propositions, which are relevant to the problem at hand and which appear to make sense in terms of what the investigator already knows about the aspect of society under investigation [Westie, 1957, p. 149].

The obvious difficulty with this approach is that what one "already knows" is very limited in scope and range and hence hardly reliable enough to provide a solid basis for selecting propositions and hypotheses.

The third line of action leads the investigator to develop his own propositions and theory. These represent additional formulations to those currently existing in the area and hence detract from any ongoing synthesis of theory and research. These small theories come close to what Merton has termed middle-range theory; more properly they must be viewed as small ad hoc theories that only pertain to the data under analysis. Glaser and Strauss (1967) have recently called for grounded, substantive sociological theories, a position more in line with my criticisms. Their theory of dying in the hospital is one example of what they call for.

The recommended procedure is to utilize all of the propositions that currently exist in a given area as one designs his research. As Westie has described this process, it involves the following steps:

1. A comprehensive list of all existing propositions in a given area is constructed.
2. For each of these propositions a list of possible interpretations is made.
3. The actual research is conducted to determine which of the presupposed empirical relationships actually exist.
4. Those presupposed relationships that fail to survive the empirical test are thrown out, as are the interpretations attached to them.

5. The best interpretations, from the many contradictory propositions initially formulated, are selected through subsequent empirical investigations.
6. Conclude with a list of those propositions that passed and failed the empirical test and reassess the theories from which they were derived.
7. State, now, a reformulated theoretical system—basing it at all points on the empirical tests just conducted [1957, pp. 150, 153].

The process can be illustrated by a hypothetical investigation in the area of small-group, face to face behavior. Erving Goffman, George Homans, and Herbert Blumer form the basis of comparison. Each of these theorists presupposes a series of propositions that would explain variations in face to face encounters as they occur in small groups or any intimate social setting. Homans sets forth a series of propositions that assumes an exchange principle operating in human transactions. To paraphrase one of his propositions: *The more costly* (in terms of punishments) *a particular activity is to the person, the less frequently that act will be emitted.* Thus, in a small-group setting if a person is criticized for his mode of dress, Homans' propositions predict that the person will modify his dress. Goffman, on the other hand, presupposes a "threat and deceit motivation" underlying face to face interactions. When persons present themselves for interaction they have special goals in mind and will do all they can to achieve those goals. This may involve dressing in a special fashion, making particular statements, or employing any of a number of dramaturgical devices. Thus, Goffman's proposition might read: *The more important a goal is to the person, the more deceptive he will become as he moves toward that goal.* Blumer, working from a Meadian-interactional perspective, assumes that persons interact as they define situations, and that any encounter has an emergent character to it such that novel lines of behavior have the potential of emerging. In this system what might initially begin as a goal, a value, or a threat in the encounter could suddenly be transformed as the interaction emerges. Blumer's proposition might read: *Lines of action in an encounter vary as the situation, self, and other participants are variously defined during the trajectory of interaction.* These definitions would be seen as emerging in the conversations each person carries on with himself during the encounter. Stable lines of action would flow from those definitions the person is most strongly committed to.

The three theorists offer quite different explanations; each assumes a different principle of motivation; each directs attention to a different set of empirical processes; each would admit different data as tests of their propositions. If the unit of observation is the number of interactions directed toward a focal object, the incompatibility of the three perspectives can be seen. Homans would direct attention to the cost-reward structure of the encounter; Goffman would stress the interactional strategies and goal structures of the respective participants; Blumer would direct attention to the definitions that emerge out of the interaction and the relationship of these definitions to the overt behavior.

Homans' proposition would focus on overt behavior as it displays a cost and reward structure; Goffman would stress this behavioristic element as well, but would lay emphasis on the initial definitions held by the interactants; Blumer would combine the analysis of overt physical actions with the covert conversations of each participant. To summarize, each perspective directs analysis to different data areas, suggests different research methods, and contradicts the explanations of the other two.

Theoretical triangulation would permit a tentative resolution of these issues. Beginning with the three propositions, a common unit of observation would be selected. Propositions specific to that unit, yet deducible from the perspectives, would be made. Operational measures of each critical concept and its relationship to propositions would then be formulated. Empirical observations would next be collected and, finally, each proposition would be assessed against these data. In such a study, a face to face encounter in a small-groups laboratory could become the empirical unit. The strategy of data triangulation could be employed because each perspective demands different data. Hence, an investigator might collect verbal recordings, photographs, interview data, and other unobtrusive measures of physical activity. Investigator triangulation could also be employed to avoid explicit theoretical bias that might otherwise be introduced. By triangulating theory, data, investigators, and methods, a reliable and valid set of data could be generated. Armed with these data, the analyst would be in an excellent position to assess the relevance, utility, and strength of each perspective.

The advantages of this theoretically triangulated strategy are several. As Westie notes, it

minimizes the likelihood that the investigator will present to himself and the world a prematurely coherent set of propositions in which contradictory propositions, however plausible, are ignored [1957, p. 154].

The procedure demands that all relevant propositions be considered and made explicit before the investigation begins, a stricture that should lead researchers away from particularistic explanations of their data.

A second advantage is that triangulation permits the widest possible theoretical use of any set of observations. Sociologists can move beyond theory-specific investigations to generalized-theoretical studies. The strategy makes the investigator more broadly aware of the "total significance of his empirical findings [Westie, 1957, p. 154]." Westie states:

Where, as in the usual procedure, the investigator is concerned with upholding or refuting a particular theory, he may be completely unaware of the fact that his empirical findings actually add confirmation, or doubt, as the case may be, to numerous other theoretical propositions extant in the area or in related areas [1957, p. 154].

A last advantage of triangulation is that it encourages systematic continuity in theory and research. At the moment it is rare that one sociological investigation unambiguously supports or refutes a set of propositions. Similarly, when there is little in the way of theory to guide interpretation,

subsequent empirical investigations of alternative interpretations are often necessary. Where alternative interpretations are made explicit from the beginning of the project they are more likely to survive as alternatives after the fact of investigation: the present procedure encourages research programs rather than isolated projects [Westie, 1957, p. 154].

Rather than searching only for support of their propositions, investigators should deliberately seek negative evidence, a parallel to the strategy from analytic induction that directs the observer to view each data unit as a potential negative case that must be explained before further observations are gathered.

Sociologists should also think in terms of a theoretical synthesis. It may well be that each proposition contains a kernel of truth. A final propositional network might combine features from hypotheses that were initially contradictory. Taking the example of Homans, Goffman, and Blumer once again, it might be found that under certain conditions exchange, threat, and emergent motivational principles *all* operate. If so, the final theory should reflect the discriminatory power of each perspective.

*Methodological Triangulation*

This is the last generic form of triangulation, and the one stressed in earlier chapters. Two forms can be noted, the first being within-method triangulation, which is most frequently employed when the observational units are viewed as multidimensional. The investigator takes one method (the survey) and employs multiple strategies within that method to examine his data. A survey questionnaire might be constructed that contains many different scales measuring the same empirical unit. Taking the famous case of alienation scales, many recent investigations have employed five distinct indices. The obvious difficulty is that only one method is employed. Observers delude themselves into believing that five different variations of the same method generate five distinct varieties of triangulated data. But the flaws that arise from using one method remain, no matter how many internal variations are devised. As Webb states:

Every data-gathering class—interviews, questionnaires, observation, performance records, physical evidence—is potentially biased and has specific to it certain validity threats. Ideally, we should like to converge data from several different data classes, as well as converge with multiple variants from within a single class [1966, p. 35].

A much more satisfactory form of method triangulation combines dissimilar methods to measure the same unit, what I call between or across-method triangulation. The rationale for this strategy is that the flaws of one method are often the strengths of another, and by combining methods, observers can achieve the best of each, while overcoming their unique deficiencies. This balance-checklist approach to method evaluation is well expressed by Webb, *et al.* I repeat the quotation offered in Chapter 1:

So long as one has only a single class of data collection, and that class is the questionnaire or interview, one has inadequate knowledge of the rival hypotheses grouped under the term "reactive measurement effects. . . ." It is too much to ask any single class that it eliminate all the rival hypotheses subsumed under the population-, content-, and reactive-effects groupings. As long as the research strategy is based on a single measurement class, some flanks will be exposed, and even if fewer are exposed with the choice of the questionnaire method, there is still insufficient justification for its use as the only approach. No single measurement class is perfect, neither is any scientifically useless [1966, pp. 173–74].

By employing multiple methods researchers may more confidently assume that:

When a hypothesis can survive the confrontation of a series of complementary methods of testing it contains a degree of validity unattainable by one tested within the more constricted framework of a single method [Webb, *et al.*, 1966, p. 174].

Methodological triangulation can take many forms, but its basic feature will be the combination of two or more different research strategies in the study of the same empirical units. With five distinct research methods that overlap in design, a variety of combinations can be constructed; a completely triangulated investigation would combine all five. Thus, if the basic strategy was participant observation, researchers would employ survey interviewing with field experiments, unobtrusive methods, and life histories. Most sociological investigations can be seen as stressing one dominant method (any of the five), with combinations of the other four as additional dimensions.

*Principles of Methodological Triangulation*

The nature of the research problem and its relevance to a particular method should be assessed. If data from large numbers of persons located over a wide geographical area are needed, then the survey will probably become the primary method. More localized methods such as participant observation could be adopted to certain locales or particular problems within the total investigation. Often it will be found that each method demands a degree of modification to fit the problem at hand. In organizational studies, for example, it is extremely difficult to launch large-scale participant observation studies when the participants are widely distributed by time and place. In such situations participant observation may be adapted only to certain categories of persons, certain events, certain places, or certain times. The interview method can then be employed to study those events that do not directly come under the eyes of the participant observer. Archival analysis will record events that occurred prior to the study and may be additionally used to validate respondent reports during the interviewing period. As methods are adapted to the special problems at hand, their relative strengths and weaknesses must again be assessed. It may be, for example, that the reactivity of a known observer is substantially reduced in some field settings where prior knowledge exists, and thus an important threat to internal invalidity is removed.

It must also be remembered that each method has unique strengths and weaknesses. All methods that involve direct observation and interviewing have the problems of reactivity which arise from the investigator's presence. On the other hand, such methods permit the direct study of behavior and allow the investigator to combine subject perceptions with his interpretations. In designing triangulated investigations, the methods that are combined should reduce as much as possible all threats to internal and external invalidity.

A third principle stresses that methods must be selected with an eye to their theoretical relevance. I have suggested that surveys are well suited to studying stable patterns of interaction, while participant observation best reveals interactions in their most complex forms. Obviously if a researcher sets out to test a series of propositions concerning emergent identities in a small-group setting, the survey would be inappropriate as a major method. To maximize the theoretical value of their studies, investigators must select their strongest methods. There may, however, be value in combining methods that initially seem inappropriate, much as contradictory theoretical propositions are brought to bear upon the same data. By employing this strategy, analysts may reveal aspects of the problem that their strongest method would overlook.

Vidich and Shapiro's (1955, pp. 28–33) investigation of the stratification system in a small community illustrates this point. They combined participant observation and survey interviewing. As noted earlier, the survey revealed that the participant observer had oversampled persons most like himself. The unsampled group involved a disproportionate number of persons with low prestige. Commenting on this fact, Vidich and Shapiro state:

Thus, even though the observer made deliberate efforts to establish contact with lower prestige groups, his knowledge of community members was biased in favor of individuals with higher prestige. . . . Yet, despite all efforts to counteract the tendency, definite selectivity is indicated, and it would be surprising if the selective association of the observer with the community did not somehow influence his understanding of the local culture. Without the survey data, the observer could only make reasonable guesses about his areas of ignorance in the effort to reduce bias. The survey data gave him more exact information regarding the degree and line of selectivity operating, and thereby allowed him to make better compensatory allowances in planning his observational activities [1955, p. 31].

Researchers must be flexible in the evaluation of their methods. Every action in the field provides new definitions, suggests new strategies, and leads to continuous modifications of initial research designs. Like other forms of interaction, sociological research reflects the emergent, novel, and unpredictable features of ongoing activity; this is the fourth principle: No investigation should be viewed in a static fashion. Researchers must be ready to alter lines of action, change methods, reconceptualize problems, and even start over if necessary. They must continually evaluate their methods, assess the quality of the incoming data, and note the relevance of the data to theory.

To summarize, methodological triangulation involves a complex process of playing each method off against the other so as to maximize the validity of field efforts. Assessment cannot be solely derived from principles given in research manuals—it is an emergent process, contingent on the investigator, his research setting, and his theoretical perspective.

## Strategies of Multiple Triangulation

Multiple triangulation exists when researchers combine in one investigation multiple observers, theoretical perspectives, sources of data, and methodologies. Thus sociology moves beyond studies that triangulate only by data source, method, theory or observer—all are simultaneously combined in the analysis of the same set of events. I set forth this strategy as the most refined goal any investigation can achieve. With it, all of the advantages that derive from triangulating single forms are combined into a research perspective that surpasses any single-method approach. To illustrate, I take the problem of generating a grounded theory of interaction in face-to-face settings. The basic unit of data will be the interaction that flows between two or more persons when they come together in an encounter. I will triangulate data sources by examining encounters in a variety of different situations—marital interactions, encounters at work, and behavior in nonserious settings will be the major data sources. More specifically, I will examine the nature of face-to-face interaction as it occurs in office settings, in private homes, and in public cocktail lounges and bars.

My methodologies will include interviews, participant observation, unobtrusive analysis, life histories of the persons interviewed, and natural field experiments. Theoretically I will adopt the perspectives of Goffman, Homans, and Blumer. Specific propositions from each theorist will be derived and tested in terms of the above strategies.

My use of data triangulation will include all three types—space, time, and personal. Interactions in the three settings will be sampled by time of day, number of persons present, and their location at the time of observation. The use of survey methods will permit the gathering of aggregate data, for I can draw a random sample of persons and ascertain their attitudes toward behavior and activity in the three settings.

Participant observation will be the major strategy for uncovering patterns of interaction, but this will be used in conjunction with the life history and unobtrusive measures. Once I have captured the flavor of interaction in these three situations, confederate observers will be used to introduce natural field experimentations.

In this study the collectivity level of data will be examined only as it impinges on interaction in these settings. Thus, through the use of survey interviews, contextual analysis, and participant observation, the constraining structural features of the settings will be analyzed.

The major goal of this investigation will be the test of these three perspectives and the propositions derived from them. To avoid the bias that might arise from a single observer partial to any of the theories, multiple observers will be employed. Observer triangulation will also serve to increase the reliability of the unobtrusive observations.

*Problems in Designing Multiple Triangulated Investigations*

Several difficulties arise when as many different approaches as I am proposing are combined in a single study. The first and most obvious problem is locating a common unit of observation against which various theories can be applied. If each theory proposes a different set of propositions, then it follows that each also designates a different set of relevant data. How then, may observers be assured so that any test of these perspectives is valid and comparable? The only solution is to select one common data base and simply force the theories to be applied to those data. Thus an analyst can take a given interactional episode—an incident of social change, a revolution, a hospitalization, a death, a deviant act—in short, any common data unit and apply the theories to that base. It may be advantageous to apply the theories to data that commonly are not accepted within their domain. This maximizes the appearance of negative cases and hence uncovers the weakest elements in the theories.

When researchers select a common data base the use of multiple methodologies becomes crucially important. Unless they approach those data from several empirical perspectives, elements of method-bias will appear and there is the danger of presenting only certain features of those data. This rationale also holds for employing multiple observers (that is, the removal of observer bias).

A second problem may be that restrictions of time and money make it impossible to employ multiple observers, multiple methods, and multiple data sources. In this situation all that can be hoped is the best possible use of what is available. It may not be feasible to employ multiple observers, but multiple data sources may be available. A hierarchy of alternatives can be imagined in which the most valid and reliable investigation is developed given only limited resources. In this hierarchy of alternatives, the scarcest resource would probably be multiple observers. This lack is significantly mitigated when multiples of the other triangulated elements are employed. It seems likely that any investigation, no matter how limited in scope, can be designed so that multiple data areas and multiple methods are employed —nor would a lack of theoretical perspectives seem to be a problem, though a problem may arise in certain situations when the available methods and theories appear inappropriate or irrelevant. If such is the case, the investigator must simply adopt what is available to his needs; the principle of multiple triangulation would still be relevant.

Serious consideration of a problem will often reveal that what appears unique is in reality a special case of a problem previously treated by standard theories and methods. Donald Ball (1968, pp. 59–75) recently resolved a problem such as this in his analysis of telephone interactions. In his review of the sociological literature, few investigations were found that had taken this problem as a focus. Many sociologists would have either formulated their own theory or simply engaged in raw empiricism. Ball, however, adopted the strategy I am advocating; working with the interactional perspectives of Simmel, Mead, and Goffman, a theoretical framework was developed that treated telephone conversations in terms of the contingencies rising from voice to voice, as opposed to face to face, interaction.

A final problem involves the inaccessibility of critical data areas, types, or levels. A theory may demand observations of private behavior settings such as the home, the confession booth, or the psychiatrist's office. These are settings normally not made available to sociological observation. While certain unobtrusive measures might permit entry into these settings, this will not always be possible. In such situations a hierarchy of desired empirical areas can be constructed and if one area is closed, observers simply move to the next most desirable. Thus, if psychiatrists' offices are closed, study could focus on interactions in other types of offices (those of bankers, clergymen, faculty) where similar interactional processes were assumed to exist.

*A Recapitulation*

I began this chapter with a statement on the inherent difficulties of generating valid sociological data. The shifting nature of the empirical world and the unique bias that arises from theories, methods, and observers make doing sociology a task fundamentally different from that of the other sciences. I have suggested that the resolutions to this difficulty are two-fold. First, sociologists must realize that their growth as a science is contingent on the recognition of these elements. Second, multiple strategies of triangulation are proposed as the preferred line of action. By combining multiple observers, theories, methods, and data sources, sociologists can hope to overcome the intrinsic bias that comes from single-method, single-observer, single-theory studies.

**Notes**

My use of the concept of triangulation draws heavily from Campbell (1963, pp. 94–176), Campbell and Fiske (1959, pp. 81–105), Webb, *et al.* (1966), and Webb (1966). My view of the scientific process has been influenced by Mead's "Scientific Method and Individual Thinker," (1917, pp. 75–85) where the problem of individual perspectives and scientific conduct is discussed.

An interesting line of research is implied by the hypothesis that different methods and different sociologists provide incomparable data regarding the same empirical units. My hypothesis suggests that any argument for comparability must first demonstrate that factors intrinsic to the research act are neglible test factors. If this cannot be demonstrated, claims for comparability are considerably weakened. gible test factors. If this cannot be demonstrated, claims for comparability are considerably weakened.

My notion of data levels parallels the traditional discussion of nominalism, realism, and interactionism as distinct sociological strategies; see, for example, Park and Burgess (1924).

My use of theoretical triangulation must in no way be construed as a defense of eclecticism. Indeed, sociologists committed to a given perspective will probably not employ theoretical triangulation. The great value of this strategy, as I see it, however, is its assurance that no study will be conducted in the absence of some theoretical perspective. In this sense it is most appropriate for the theoretically uncommitted, as well as for the analysis of areas characterized by high theoretical incoherence.

# 13 On Ethics and the Politics of Doing Sociology

As every researcher knows, there is more to doing research than is dreamt of in philosophies of science, and texts in methodology offer answers to only a fraction of the problems one encounters. The best laid research plans run up against unforeseen contingencies in the collection and analysis of data; the data one collects may prove to have little to do with the hypothesis one sets out to test; unexpected findings inspire new ideas. No matter how carefully one plans in advance, research is designed in the course of its execution. The finished monograph is the result of hundreds of decisions, large and small, made while the research is under way and our standard texts do not give us procedures and techniques for making these decisions. . . . I must take issue with one point . . . that social research being what it is, we can never escape the necessity to improvise, the surprise of the unexpected, our dependence on inspiration. . . . It is possible, after all, to reflect on one's difficulties and inspirations and see how they could be handled more rationally the next time around. In short, one can be methodical about matters that earlier had been left to chance and improvisation and thus cut down the area of guesswork.

*Howard S. Becker,* 1965, pp. 602-603.

A single theme has guided my discussion in this book: I set out to show that sociological methods represent different lines of symbolic interaction the sociologist carries on with his empirical reality, and I suggested quite early that research methods can no longer be viewed as "atheoretical tools" suitable for use by any knowledgeable sociologist. Each method implies a different data reality for the sociological theory; these realities and their attendant lines of action were indicated in each of the methodology chapters. I fear, however, that this discussion may have suffered from the flaw Becker and others have suggested is present in all methodology texts—that I have presented too idealized a view of the process of doing theory and research. In this chapter I hope to remedy this.

*Methodological Misconceptions*

The sociological enterprise of theory and research has been presented as an idealized process, immaculately conceived in design and elegantly executed in practice. My discussions of theory, measurement, instrumentation, sampling strategies, resolutions of validity issues, and the generation of valid causal propositions by various methods proceeded on the assumption that once the proper rules were learned, adequate theory would be forthcoming. Unfortunately, of course, this is seldom the case. Each theorist or methodologist takes rules of method and inference and molds them to fit his particular problem—and personality. Concepts do not automatically generate operational definitions, and theories do not fall into place once all the data are in. Rather, theoretical formulations arise from strange sources— often out of personal experiences, haphazard conversations with friends and colleagues. And many times these formulations bear only a distant relationship to data.

If I have made too public and rational the process of theory construction, then, a further deficiency has been the implication that the researcher carries on a dyadic relationship with his subjects and data, that each sociologist learns a method and then goes out and designs a study to which that method is applied. This is not the way research gets done. What typically occurs is a complex form of interaction between the demands subjects place upon observers and the actual research carried out. Some subjects are randomly selected, as the idealized view of research assumes, but more frequently they are not. Some are clients who finance research efforts and thus expect a payoff for their cooperation; others are subjects in the traditional meaning of the term, but they also expect something in return. Some subjects are friends, colleagues, students, and with them the reciprocity of demands becomes even more complex. Their cooperation demands a certain stance. Paying students to volunteer in an experiment overlooks the deeper obligation observers have toward them. Their cooperation permits research to be done. Sociologists are obligated to demonstrate the outcome of their studies to them. In addition, subjects should be made as much a part of the scientific process as possible; they are not objects to be manipulated for personal or scientific ends.

Few studies are conducted in entire isolation. The sociologist is involved in a complex web of social relationships that formally and informally influence his actions. The following may be noted (see Sjoberg, 1967, pp. xi– xvii). If a project is funded from government or university sources, there is an obligation to produce results, this may imply that only certain problems will be studied (often those currently in vogue). Further, it implies that only certain findings will be reported. Negative results seldom go into final grant reports—researchers tend to show positive findings. To produce negative findings suggests a faulty sociological self—good sociologists do not design studies that fail (see Record, 1967, pp. 25–49).

Obligations also fall upon the sociologist from his formal role position in an organizational hierarchy. The sociologist employed by the university is expected to do research and regularly to publish his findings. He is also expected to demonstrate his ability to do research. Also, many sociologists at a university are evaluated by the amount of money they bring in to do research; these funds are then used to hire graduate assistants and secretaries—to build research organizations. Unfortunately, when research organizations are created, the problems of bureaucracy arise (Roth, 1964, pp. 190–96). Divisions of labor are made to delegate responsibility and authority for different tasks, and varying interpretations of the goals of the organization appear. Some persons commit themselves deeply to the organization's projects; others become alienated and begin to substitute means for goals (getting a job done may become more important than attaining valid field results, for example). People of different training, skill, and commitment will be hired, and the possibility always exists that the least able are placed in the most important positions (graduate students with no field experience become field directors; secretaries who have never coded questionnaires become coding directors; untrained undergraduates become field interviewers). These possibilities can challenge the validity of the research that is generated. (Untrained persons *can* perform adequately in an organizational setting for research—but their presence increases the likelihood that invalid results will be produced.)

Location in an organizational setting also creates problems for the principal investigator and his associates. When the allocation of data rights (who can publish what) arises, there may be arguments because initially no agreements were made. If investigators of equal status are directing a project, personalities may come into conflict—each feeling he has responsibilities and skills not possessed by his associate.

Then there is the question of ethics (see Shils, 1959, pp. 114–57). To whom does the sociologist owe the greatest moral obligation? Can he study persons with hidden recorders? Must he elicit permission from subjects before his study begins? Must he maintain anonymity in his final reports? Does he owe society at large a responsibility not to pry into private behavior settings? These questions represent ethical issues of the highest order and they must be answered at some point in every investigation.

A further problem is the sociologist's involvement in value decisions. Can sociologists legitimately view their research as free of value implications, and can they avoid making value commitments as they do research? Some persons argue that values have no role in the scientific process, while others say value commitments are made every step of the way (see Becker, 1967, pp. 239–48).

The problems of ethics, organized research, subject responsibility, value positions, informal demands on the investigator, and a misconception of the subject represent issues that lie at the heart of doing sociology and science in general, yet they are not adequately treated in most methodology texts. In the remainder of this chapter these problems will be examined. I have held a discussion of them to the last because to begin with them gives a distorted view of the sociological enterprise.

## Toward a Rationalization of Unplanned Contingencies in the Research Process

The following section treats a series of contingencies that may arise during the research process. Solutions to some of them do not exist. It is hoped, however, that a systematic presentation of some of them will lead others to build upon this discussion and make more rational and predictable what up to now have been untreated elements in the research process.

### Theory Construction, Resistant Data, and Emergent Conceptualizations

A pervasive problem in nearly any investigation is the relationship between the theory one begins with and the data gathered to test, validate, or extend that theory. Ideally, researchers assume that appropriate data are always gathered to test their theories; this seldom happens, however. The following contingencies make this link between theory and research quite elusive and at times unpredictable: first, theories may initially be so vague as to deny precise data designations, and the analyst may resort to raw empiricism, feeling that worthwhile theory will not come from his observations. It is possible to refine elusive theory through research, however. In this case observers speak of a grounded theory arising out of empirical observations. Ideally, the investigator should steer a path between these two extremes. Theory and data, no matter how imprecise, should work hand in hand. An excellent example of this strategy is reported by Reisman and Watson (1964, pp. 235–321). Theirs was a long-term research project aimed at developing a theory of sociable interaction in modern American middle-class society. Little theory was forthcoming, however, and the authors offer the following reasons:

Our task was to study the nature and significance of sociable interaction in modern middle-class society. In order to do this, we felt we could not begin with conventional methods of data management and that we had to expose ourselves in a rather more open and intuitive manner to the complexities of our subject. Our emphasis was on exploration rather than the collection of systematic information for the testing of specific hypotheses. We sought to find new ways of thinking about sociability, new ways of interpreting it, new ways of understanding what may be gained and lost in the course of sociable interaction [Reisman and Watson, 1964, p. 236].

They go on to state the nature of their problem more directly:

There was no line of inquiry which we wished to pursue, no established tradition of research upon which to build. Georg Simmel's scintillating essay on sociability, for example, was a stimulus to reflection and speculation but scarcely a program for research. Indeed, our project was an effort to be systematic and even quantitative in areas that on the whole, had been dealt with previously in diffuse and theoretical fashion. Under these conditions, the project was shaped by the intellectual preoccupations and curiosities of the principal investigators [1964, p. 239].

The investigation was guided, then, by little theory, and took shape as interactions grew around the investigators. The authors state:

In immersing ourselves in the study of sociability, we found that unconscious or irrational elements of the personality were brought to bear on the research, as well as conscious and rational ones. . . . The wide differences which existed among us initially with respect to training and experience in research, our different and often opposed commitments regarding the processes and preferred outcomes of research, were sometimes aggravated, often assuaged, and always blurred by the urgent need, which we each felt, to discover in our associates congenial partners in research. The emergent ethos of the project with its emphasis on pluralism in style and method, diffusion of initiative and responsibility, and compulsive attention to the processing of data, seems to flow from many sources; the vagueness and difficulty of the research task, the quality of sociability as a projective, expressive form of interaction rather than an instrumental one; the existence of wide differences in personal and professional style among the individuals who were committed to work together as a research team; and an eventual consensus of temperament favoring permissive and receptive methodologies for both internal and external operations of the research staff [1964, pp. 236–37].

Their project's development thus demonstrates many of the contingencies that may arise in any long-term research project. In the absence of well-defined theory and methodology, the individual personalities of the participating investigators take precedence, and the final product reflects more of those personalities than it does of the theory and data.

Given the absence of coherent theory, what may an investigator do? One line of action is to take whatever existing theory one can find and formulate it to fit the specific problem at hand. Diverse perspectives may be relevant, and in this case I recommend theoretical triangulation. There seems little excuse for going into an investigation with *no* theory; vague frameworks can at least be reworked to fit current needs.

A second problem is that research tools may be inappropriate to the theory and research problem, and unless compromise designs are formulated, the needed data may not be available. This problem emerged in the sociability project; Watson, trained in the rigors of experimental and quantitative design, felt that sociable interaction could and should be studied quantitatively, while Reisman was inclined toward a more qualitative, "soft" approach to data collection. No firm decision was ever reached on this methodological issue, and consequently the data that were collected never adequately fitted their conceptualizations of sociability.

James A. Davis (1964, pp. 212–34) describes another research project that initially began with a vaguely defined theory and because of the limitations of time, budget, and client demands was forced to develop a compromise survey-sampling design. His project reflects the problems that arise when a study is funded and guided by clients who have little interest in sociological theory. The client was The Fund for Adult Education, which wanted an evaluation of the effectiveness of its Great Books adult study program. The Fund wanted to know the impact of reading classic books upon their reader's attitudes. Davis states:

It was this program which was to be evaluated, to the end of discovering whether the effects on the participants were such as to justify the continuation or expansion of Fund for Adult Education support. . . . The design of such research falls naturally into two parts, which can be thought of as sampling . . . and questionnaire construction. . . . Of the two, sampling presented the fewest problems. It so happened that this is one social-science situation for which there is a clear-cut textbook sample design. According to the course I teach in research methods, one should collect a large number of people, arrange for a random subgroup to participate in Great Books, prevent the remainder from participating in the program, and measure both groups on the dependent variables, before and after the experiment. . . . It also happened that, as usual, the textbook design was out of the question. Such an experimental study would be "possible," although there would be an enormous number of difficulties—making sure that the controls do not get Great Books or equivalent experience, establishing community programs which mask the mechanics of the sample design, and so forth. The major obstacle turned out to be time. We began active work on the study in the late summer of 1957 and had to deliver a report by fall 1958. It would have been plainly impractical (as well as quite expensive to get a field experiment organized in two months before the 1957–1958 Great Books year got under way, and results of a spring 1958 follow-up assessed by fall 1958. In addition, we all agreed, that if the program's effects were as expected, some of them might not show up until several years of exposure to the program [1964, pp. 218–19].

The combined effects of limited resources, a time deadline, and the belief that effects of the program would be long-term, led Davis to formulate a compromise sampling design that selected persons in various years of the Great Books program. A second problem was that the Great Books Foundation felt their program had no specific purposes. How then was he to devise a research strategy that would evaluate it? Failing in an attempt to have the program state its goals, Davis still felt compelled to devise an adequate study. "I was perfectly willing to let the facts speak, but I was not going out of my way to disappoint somebody who had given me $40,000 to do research [1964, p. 222]." Thus an attempt was made to gather data that adequately reflected the true nature of the program, but Davis also wanted to extract a "worthwhile" sociological product from the investigation, and he devised subsequent sampling strategies that in no way reflected the needs of his client. As a result, an important variation on contextual analysis as a survey strategy was developed.

In other words, unplanned contingencies shaped the research process. Client demands, limitations of time and money, and the investigator's sociological and personal motives combined to make the final Great Books project quite different from what its initial plans implied. Davis' study represents one solution to the problem of inappropriate research plans; a thorough knowledge of existing sociological methods and an awareness of new methodological developments permitted him to salvage a valuable study from what otherwise would have been just another research report to a client. As a general rule, the best weapon for dealing with methodological limitations is a thorough knowledge of what has preceded one theoretically and methodologically. Without such knowledge, there is the danger of conducting an amorphous study such as the sociability project.

Another, and related strategy is to employ what I have earlier termed methodological triangulation. Rather than limiting studies to one method (which increases the risk of that method being inappropriate), sociologists can judiciously utilize multiple methods, thereby escaping the inherent limitations of a single field strategy. While Davis, for example, overcame the problem of one method by a compromise design, he could have handled the same problem by using a variety of research methods. Small-scale case studies could have been conducted on a handful of Great Books study groups, and these data would have usefully complemented the survey data.

A third difficulty arises when theory and methods are perfectly blended but the collected data fail to yield the kind of observations needed. This, in one sense, was the difficulty confronted by Davis. He wanted a longitudinal field experiment, but the data and field demands would not permit it. His solution was to modify the research design. A better illustration of this difficulty is offered in the sociability project. Since it lacked a clear theoretical and methodological focus, this investigation combines all of the difficulties so far discussed, and illustrates the type of compounding influences that may arise when theory, method, and data sources are never precisely formulated. In their chronicle of their project, Reisman and Watson repeatedly stress their difficulty in locating one data source that would meet their needs. They alternatively employed interviewers, informants, direct observation at parties, and at one point even joined an adult recreational camp to gain access to another observational setting. Summarizing these difficulties, they state:

Eventually we decided that the only solution was to draw on our own sociable contacts, extending the range of our sociable activity, soliciting and accepting invitations from persons whom we knew only slightly, using brokers to introduce us to parties where we might not otherwise be asked, and in general using whatever resources were available to us as individuals for maximizing the range of our sociable experiences [1964, p. 259].

This strategy made the investigators observers of their own interactions and later gave rise to severe ethical problems.

Still, the investigation ran its course with no suitable data source ever having been selected. Had they made a list of all the potential data sources they could have employed, with their attendant methodologies and theoretical values—had they triangulated data sources—a full-fledged investigation might have been designed to overcome the inherent weaknesses of any single data body.

A classic investigation of this kind is Blau's (see 1963; 1964, pp. 16–49) *The Dynamics of Bureaucracy*. Faced with problems similar to those of Reisman and Watson, Blau employed what I would term a multiple triangulated field strategy. Impressed with the Mertonian revisions of functional theory, and utilizing a Weberian model of bureaucracy, Blau conducted a comparative case study of two governmental agencies. He describes his strategy as follows:

In the weeks before I started observation in the first government agency, I designed a detailed schedule for the research procedures. This was completed after I had entered the organization and become acquainted with the actual setup. I had earlier decided to use three basic methods—direct observation, interviewing, and analysis of official records—and to employ various quantitative as well as qualitative research techniques under each. Thus, I planned not only to observe whatever I could notice about the relations among colleagues in the office but also to obtain a systematic record of all their social interaction for a specified period; not only to interview selected members of the organization on specific issues but also to administer a semistructured interview to all members of the work groups intensively studied; not only to read the procedure manual but also to abstract some quantitative information from it. I put each research problem I had outlined on 5 x 8 slips . . . which were cross-classified by the various research procedures. . . . The resulting file indicated the different substantive problems that might be studied with any given research procedure [1964, p. 21].

While he entered the intensive phase of observations with a field guide to observations, Blau purposely kept this guide flexible. It underwent continuous revisions as new data appeared, as field problems arose, and as his theoretical image of research settings took shape.

The research critic can compare Blau's investigation with the Watson-Reisman sociability project and perhaps find solace in the fact that even when some of the hypotheses one begins with undergo revision or are abandoned during the course of study, valuable theoretical insights can be forthcoming. Still, whether one begins his study with a clear perspective, or starts with many vague notions and no precise hypotheses, the idea that this process can be

classified neatly into hypothesis-testing and insight-supplying is grossly misleading, since these are polar types that appear in actual investigations in various admixtures. The double aim is always to develop and refine theoretical insights which explain reality . . . and to discriminate between the correct and the false explanatory principles [Blau, 1964, p. 20].

Some observers of this process have claimed that ultimately all of science is intuitional and art-like in execution. They suggest that scientists cannot rationalize the scientific process. Polanyi, a former physical chemist states, for example:

The scientist's procedure is of course methodical. But his methods are but the maxims of an art which he applies in his own original way to the problem of his choice [1958, p. 311; also see Dalton, 1964, p. 52].

Bridgeman, the Nobel Prize physicist similarly argues that:

There is no scientific method as such. . . . The most vital feature of the scientist's procedure has been merely to do his utmost with his mind, *no holds barred*. . . . The so-called scientific method is merely a special case of the method of intelligence, and any apparent characteristics are to be explained by the nature of the subject matter rather than ascribed to the nature of the method itself [1947, pp. 144–45; also see Dalton, 1964, p. 51].

While I fundamentally subscribe to the position that doing sociology represents more than learning the rituals of the scientific method, it is too easy to take an extreme position and say all of science is a form of art. I prefer, instead, Davis' description of survey analysis.

Thus, if survey analysis is an art, it is not an art like sculpture or painting, in which one can make almost anything out of the raw materials. Rather it is an art very much like architecture, in which it is possible to show disciplined activity by producing elegant structures while working with raw materials characterized by limited engineering properties and for clients with definite goals and finite budgets. Balance between discipline and creativity is very difficult in social science. By and large, the fashionable people in sociology are "action painters" who dribble their thoughts on the canvas of the journals, unrestrained by systematic evidence, while at the opposite pole there are hordes of "engineers" who grind out academic development housing according to the mechanical formulas of elementary texts. It is not easy to steer between these courses, and I am not claiming that I did so in this study, but my opinion is that the fun lies in trying to do so [1964, p. 233].

Some of the many problems that emerge before and during an ongoing investigation to create an undesirable distance between one's theory and data have been illustrated from the chronicles kept by persons who attempted in some way to resolve them. I have suggested that a dedicated commitment to a triangulated perspective during the research process can greatly reduce the magnitude of these problems. Certainly doing sociology requires a keen mind and an ability to see relationships others have ignored, but sociologists can systematize this process by explicitly imposing a rigor and discipline to their activities, and one element in this activity should be the use of triangulated perspectives, methods, data sources, and observers.

## The Research Relationship: Subjects Talk Back

A second major contingency that may arise during the research process is a failure to consider the social context within which subjects are located. Closely related to the contextual location of the subject is the type of relationship observers establish with them. (This latter point raises the broader question of values and ethics and will be discussed shortly). A continuum of effects subjects may have upon research activities can be constructed. Persons randomly selected in a social survey seldom influence total research efforts, of course, but at the other extreme recalcitrant informants, persons who refuse interviews, or even entire communities and nations, can tremendously influence individual studies and indirectly affect the total discipline.

To analyze subject effects first demands an analysis of the types of subjects sociologists conduct research *on, toward* and *for*. Some subjects remain strangers to us and to them our research is of little importance. Shils has described the typical small-group experiment as one in which little feedback occurs because of the nature of this relationship.

In the first place, the groups on which experiments are carried out are small. The situations are very often no more than quasi-real at best. They are contrived by the experimenter; they are seldom recurrent, and they are usually of brief duration, falling mainly between a half-hour and two hours. The stimuli or the variables in the situation are rarely of great significance to the experimental subjects and as far as is known—it has never been followed up—leave no lasting impression on the personality or outlook of the subject. Since, furthermore, the groups which are the objects of the experiment usually have had no anterior life of their own, they disappear from memory with the end of the experiment [Shils, 1959, p. 141].

In these circumstances few alterations in the research design would be expected, but there are subjects with whom observers establish an in-depth relationship. They may be students who become subjects, friends who formerly were subjects, or they may be colleagues from whom data are gathered, and analysts can expect demands from such subjects. They may, for example, ask that certain features of their behavior not be reported, or some may quarrel with the researcher's interpretations, others attempt to ingratiate themselves. If prior agreements have not been made concerning the research relationship, severe repercussions can occur.

Janes reported the attempts by one community to ingratiate themselves with him as his study neared completion (1961, p. 449; see Chap. 9 of this book, p. 192–3). A community that did far more than attempt to ingratiate the observer is reported by Vidich and Bensman (1964, pp. 313–49). Their study represents perhaps the most severe form of reaction that can be generated when no clear agreements are made with the people giving their consent for observation. Beginning as another community study that focused on stratification, prestige, and political patterns of interaction, the study soon became an investigation that commanded the attention of the American Anthropological and Sociological Associations. From the start, the townspeople wanted to know what the research was about and how the town would be affected by it. In answering these questions, Vidich and Bensman implicitly made future promises to the town. Here is the formal statement made to the community.

We are not interested in the negative features of the town because too much fruitless work on that has been done already. A positive approach is needed. We are interested in constructive activities because from this we feel we can help other people in other communities to live better lives. Springdale is a laboratory which may help us find important solutions. We are especially interested in the Community Club because it is a democratic organization that brings *all people* together and there are no restrictions on membership and no entrance fees. We have to get back to the older values of the individual, neighboring and the neighborhood, and Springdale seems to provide an opportune setting for this. We enlist your cooperation in helping us to solve this scientific problem [1964, pp. 327–28].

This statement was made to enlist the town's support and cooperation—yet in the early stages of the study, the researchers did not know what the project would be studying. And by giving "nonexistent" answers to community inquiries when the project's methods and results are indefinite, the project, unfortunately, becomes committed to those answers [Vidich and Bensman, 1964, p. 328].

The greatest concern of the subjects was how they were going to be portrayed in the final research report. In some instances the concern "bordered on anxiety and in other instances an exhibitionism with a desire to only appear in a desirable light [1964, p. 328]." In their concern to maintain community rapport and cooperation, the researchers promised that no one would be identified in the book. Key members of the community developed the impression that the entire report would be statistical, and this feeling spread to members of the project as well. While this was not an explicit policy of the project, it became an implicit promise to the community. The final report (1958), however—which appeared as the book *Small Town in Mass Society*—failed to maintain complete subject anonymity. Code names were used, but the analysis of certain community problems immediately made it clear to the community participants who were being portrayed. Hence, the authors had implicitly violated their promise to the town and soon they found themselves denounced not only by the community, but also by their university and their research project.

Vidich and Bensman quote this review given their book by a newspaper in a community near Springdale:

## THE SMALL TOWN IN MASS SOCIETY— [SPRINGDALE] SAYS IT ISN'T SO

*Small Town in Mass Society,* by Arthur J. Vidich and Joseph Bensman (Princeton University Press, $6.00).

An accurate review of this book should be from the viewpoint of a professional sociologist since it is intended as a text book for the social sciences.

Lacking that point of view, our interest in the book stems from the fact that it is written by a former resident of [Springdale] and concerns itself with "class, power and religion" in [Springdale], called Springdale in the book.

Mr. Vidich is currently about as popular in [Springdale] as the author of *Peyton Place* is in her small town and for the same reason—both authors violate what Vidich calls the etiquette of gossip [1964, p. 339].

The review goes on to state that the statistical survey of the community was "fairly accurate" but that Vidich's report was completely in error.

The lesson should be clear—when an investigator makes promises to his subject, no matter how implicit, he will be held to them. Such promises can take a number of forms, depending on who the subject is, what the investigator-subject relationship is, and what the investigator's intents and purposes are. It is nearly axiomatic that all subjects expect something in return for their cooperation. In the Springdale case it was a favorable picture of their community; in a small-group experiment it may be money. Except for small amounts of money, the sociologist has very little he can offer in return. He can show subjects his final report (knowing they may not understand it), and occasionally he may be able (and willing) to make policy recommendations concerning a social problem, but that is about all. He must, however, always be aware that subjects do indeed talk back, and the nature of this dialogue can significantly shape his final results.

### The Political Context of Research: Sociology's Pressure Groups

A third, and highly variable, contingency in the research process is the political and social context in which the sociologist finds himself, a complex, political world of competing, conflicting, and only infrequently complementary values, perspectives, and ideologies. In short, a world of settings defined differently by each of many competing reference and pressure groups. The existence of such perspectives means that sociological activity in some way reflects the interpretation given them. When a researcher attempts to meet the needs of a client while satisfying the goals of his profession (as did Davis), he finds himself compromising the demands of each when he attempts to bring his own goals into the process.

The following groups may impinge on the sociologist's actions: clients, subjects, respondents, informants, research organizations, granting agencies, academic communities, students, colleagues, scientific and professional societies, and even local, national, and international political communities (see Sjoberg, 1967, p. xiii). To the extent that these groups and their perspectives are differently recognized and brought into the sociologist's lines of action, it is possible to speak of differing social relationships and interpretations emerging between them and the sociologist. A researcher may be simultaneously responding to the demands of a client, a network of colleagues, and his respective university as he engages in a single act of research. What is the effect of these variously recognized pressure groups upon their activities as sociologists?

The literature abounds with instances in which one pressure group was ignored to please another. In such cases, the sociologist runs the risk of endangering the project, if not indeed his career. Vidich and Bensman jeopardized the perspective of Springdale for a commitment to the perspective of sociology, and challenged the perspective of their university and research organization. In Davis' Great Books' study, a relatively amiable compromise was struck between his client's needs and his own professional perspective. He phrases the potential conflict that exists between a client and a study director as follows:

This brings us to the subject of money. I think it may be stated as a matter of indisputable fact that there is no money available in the contemporary

United States for unrestricted support of large-scale social research. . . .
Thus is born "the client," typically a large foundation or a government
agency with a particular research question which it feels is worth the exor-
bitant costs and personal frustrations involved in commissioning research.
And with the birth of the client comes the eternal triangle of client, organization and study director. It is the operation of this triangle which is the key
to the poignant histories of surveys. . . . The root of the problem, I think,
lies in the difference between generality and specificity. Clients commission
research because they are interested in something specific: who has health
insurance, whether enough people are training for careers in biochemistry.
. . . Sociology is, however, the enemy of the specific. Even though the
facts of social life in modern America are less well documented than the
facts of marine life at the bottom of the ocean, the academic sociologist
(the ultimate judge, employer, or journal editor whom our young Ph.D.
wants to impress) has a phobia against research that "merely" describes.
This is "nose-counting," "dust-bowl empiricism," "trivia," and so forth and
is not part of the grand scheme for building the science of sociology. . . .
Therefore, the academically oriented study director is faced with a dilemma. If he completes his research in such a fashion as to satisfy the
sponsors, it will lack academic glamour. If, on the other hand, he completes
a piece suitable for academic publication, it will probably tell the sponsor
nothing about the questions which led to the research [Davis, 1964, pp.
212–15].

Unless the sociologist is of such eminence that the client will feel fortunate
to receive his services, he finds himself compromising these competing perspectives, and too often the compromise shifts in the direction of the client
or granting agency, with sociology taking second-best. This would not be so
unfortunate if it were not for the fact that client money is typically tied to
the analysis of social problems. The sociological analysis of social problems
is appropriate, of course—but what is a social problem one year may not be
so the next, and in such cases sociologists find their research being directed
by another's perspective. It would seem that a more reasonable strategy for
building a science of sociology would be long-term programmatic research
projects that permitted the sociologist to pursue his problems in an atmosphere free from a client's demands and needs.

Not only may granting agencies and clients exert demands on the investigator, but so too may the public at large. Reisman and Watson report the
"negative press" they received from a national news magazine when it was
learned that they were studying cocktail parties and other sociable gatherings. They describe this reaction as follows:

In the winter of 1959–1960, *Newsweek* telephoned Reisman to ask about
the Sociability Project, and it was clear from the dialogue that they meant
to ridicule the project as a waste of taxpayer's money, as well as presenting
the amusing picture of a "name" social scientist attending cocktail parties
in pursuit of his dreary specialty [1964, p. 317].

While he attempted to remove all degree of responsibility from the granting agency (the National Institute of Mental Health), shortly after the conversation

*Newsweek* appeared with a "National Affairs" story and cartoon of a cocktail party with sloshing glasses and sleuthing social scientists. [Reisman and Watson, 1964, p. 317].

There then ensued phone calls from newspapermen, broadcasters, and indignant and inquiring letters from taxpayers, congressmen, and senators. Fortunately, for the investigators, the granting agency stood behind them. But while the impact of such publicity upon subsequent observations and the public reputation of sociology can only be guessed at, it is probable that little good came from it.

Moving to the international level, I make note of the now infamous Project Camelot (see Sjoberg, 1967, pp. 141–61; Horowitz, 1965, pp. 3–7, 44–67; 1966, pp. 445–54). This was a short-lived investigation financed by the Defense Department that was envisioned as having a budget close to $6,000,000. While its focus was never clear, it purportedly was brought into existence to permit large-scale gathering of data on the nature and causes of revolutions in underdeveloped countries. It was also aimed at finding ways of eliminating the causes of revolution. For a variety of reasons that are as yet unclear, several eminent American social scientists were brought into the project. Conceived in late 1963, the project was dead by 1965. It is instructive to briefly review the involvement of social scientists in it. Horowitz has listed the following points on which the social scientists directing the project seemed to agree. First, they were men who felt the need for a large-scale project in social science, and they wanted to create a sociology relevant to contemporary, world-wide social problems. They viewed Camelot as an opportunity to do fundamental research with relatively unlimited funds at their disposal. Horowitz states:

(No social science project ever before had up to $6,000,000 available.) Under such optimal conditions, these scholars tended not to look a gift horse in the mouth. As one of them put it, there was no desire to inquire too deeply as to the source of funds or the ultimate purpose of the project [1966, p. 448].

Second, most social scientists involved with the project felt there was a greater freedom associated with militarily sponsored research than was currently possible at universities or colleges. They were also convinced that their findings would significantly influence the military. Third, none of them felt they were spying for the government in their research roles. Fourth, these men were highly committed to the project itself, and felt they owed a moral and ethical obligation to carry on in a highly undefined situation.

Given these beliefs, Horowitz asks, "Was Project Camelot workable?" To answer this question, it is necessary first to inquire into the circumstances that led to its demise. Ultimately the decision to terminate the project came from President Johnson. The events leading to his decision revolved around a professor of anthropology who was a former citizen of Chile. This individual had requested an appointment with Camelot in its early stages and was refused. He subsequently planned a trip to Chile and again requested authorization from the Camelot staff. It was understood that he was going to Chile on his own, and not as a representative of the project, but, soon after his arrival in Santiago, he had a conference with the Vice-Chancellor of the University of Chile to discuss Project Camelot. Their second meeting was attended by a Chilean sociologist who asked the visiting anthropologist to state the exact nature of the study. Before he could reply, the Chilean sociologist read a copy of a statement prepared by John Galtung, denouncing the project. This document was simultaneously released to the Chilean Senate and the left wing Chilean press.

Almost immediately political pressure from concerned State Department officials and reactions from members of Congress halted the Project. In a memo to Secretary Rusk, President Johnson stipulated that "no government sponsorship of foreign area research should be undertaken which in the judgment of the Secretary of State would adversely affect United States foreign relations [Horowitz, 1966, pp. 447–48]."

Given these rapid, and rather brutal reactions by our highest government officials, what can be said about the feasibility of the Camelot Project? . Horowitz states that from the beginning the research design was plagued by ambiguities.

It was never quite settled whether the purpose was to study counterinsurgency possibilities, or the revolutionary process. Similarly, it was difficult to determine whether it was to be a study of comparative social structures, a set of case studies of single nations "in depth," or a study of social structure with particular emphasis on the military. In addition, there was a lack of treatment of what indicators were to be used, and whether a given social system in Nation A could be as stable in Nation B [1966, p. 452].

In addition, there was a peculiar value bias running through the early documents. The question was never raised concerning the efficacy and utility of revolutions per se. Rather, it was asked, "How can we prevent revolutions?" Perhaps a more telling flaw was the failure of those involved to consider the role of social science in a federally sponsored project. They apparently did not feel that the autonomy of the social sciences was being challenged, despite the fact that the State Department had the final say of approval or disapproval.

This last issue raises the general problem of ethics and social research. In Camelot, professional scientists let the client assume nearly all control. As Horowitz states:

What is central is not the political motives of the sponsor. For social scientists were not being enlisted in an intelligence system for "spying" purposes. But given their professional standing, their great sense of intellectual honor and pride, they could not be "employed" without proper deference for their stature. Professional authority should have prevailed from beginning to end with complete command of the right to thrash out the moral and political dilemmas as researchers saw them. The Army, however respectful and protective of free expression, was "hiring help" and not openly and honestly submitting a problem to the higher professional and scientific authority of science [1966, pp. 453–54].

The right of the Army to define, delimit, and give support to the project was never questioned. This, as Horowitz states, "is a tragic precedent; it reflects the arrogance of a consumer of intellectual merchandise [1966, p. 454]." Had the government maintained its respect for the scholars and disciplines involved, this issue might not have been raised. The question of who sponsors our research is of less importance than is their stance toward sociology and the use they make of our findings.

Sponsorship is good or bad only insofar as the intended outcomes can be predetermined and the parameters of those intended outcomes tailored to the sponsor's expectations [Horowitz, 1966, p. 454].

In the case of Camelot, the sponsoring agency clearly determined the outcome, and thereby removed all sense of intellectual integrity that could have been found in the project.

Sociologists must ask, "Who was at fault?" Was the government wrong in expecting a study that met their needs? In one sense they were not—but their stance toward the social scientist was certainly indefensible. Few other clients remove complete control from the hands of those they support and sponsor.

On the other hand, the involved social scientists cannot be absolved of responsibility. Social science research in the 1960's is not so new that one entering it can be completely unaware of the consequences of accepting federal money—especially if as in Camelot the granting agency is the Department of Defense and the problem under analysis is revolution in politically troublesome countries. Both parties were at fault and the lessons to be learned from the incident should be taken seriously. As Horowitz states:

Project Camelot was intellectually, and from my own perspective, ideologically unsound. However, and more significantly, Camelot was not cancelled because of faulty intellectual approaches. Instead, its cancellation came as an act of Government censorship, and an expression of the contempt for social science so prevalent among those who need it most. Thus it was political expedience, rather than lack of scientific merit, that led to the demise of Camelot, because it threatened to rock State Department relations with Latin America [1966, p. 454].

A second major consequence of the project was President Johnson's directive concerning complete censorship rights over all federally sponsored foreign research; all other government granting agencies are now under this censorship rule. Thus the National Institute of Mental Health, the National Science Foundation, the Office of Education, and other agencies are under the veto power of the State Department when foreign research projects are under consideration. It is appropriate to conclude this summary of Camelot with Horowitz's statement:

We must be careful not to allow social science projects with which we may vociferously disagree on political and ideological grounds to be decimated or dismantled by Government fiat. Across the ideological divide is a common social science understanding that the contemporary expression of reason in politics is applied social science, and that the cancellation of Camelot, however pleasing it may be on political grounds to advocates of a civilian solution to Latin American affairs, represents a decisive setback for social science research [1966, p. 454].

## On Ethics: The Value-Laden Context of Sociological Research

I have thus far argued that all sociological activity occurs within a context of shifting political pressures. It follows that a fourth major contingency shaping sociological activity is the values and ethical stances sociologists either voluntarily or involuntarily assume. While most sociologists now agree that it is impossible to conduct research in the absence of personal and political values, few are agreed on the exact nature of these values and the precise role they should occupy in their activities.

My previous comments on social relationships suggest that sociologists may have as many value and ethical stances as they have relationships. Thus, clients may expect certain findings, while colleagues expect another. In this respect, I must make clear what is meant by the term *ethics*. There seems to be general agreement that ethics (and values as well) refer to an "ought" world. When researchers make a decision to study prisoners and not prison officials, they are making a value decision. When they say the relationship between X and Y is negative, they are making a scientific statement. Science, is "an *is world,* a set of facts growing out of consensus among a small group [Dalton, 1964, p. 60]."

When I say that all sociologists *should* honor their relationships with subjects, I am making an ethical statement. When some sociologists do not honor these relationships they are branded as unethical. It must be remembered that ethics and values, like scientific findings, are not statements that come from an invariant source. They do not reside in a world of abstract ideals. Rather, ethics (as all plans of action) are symbolic meanings subject to the most complex political arguments. Hence, when I speak of values and ethics in the scientific process, I refer to meanings that are subject to negotiation and redefinition. What is ethical in one period, one university, one profession, or one group may be unethical in another.

It is impossible not to take ethical and value stances in the process of research. When analysts choose to enter one social setting, and not another, they have made an implicit value decision that one is better than the other for their purposes. When I state that sociology should be scientific, I make a value statement. Values and ethics are with sociologists at all times. According to such spokesmen as Lundberg and Parsons, values have no role in the scientific process; they say that science studies the world of facts, and that scientists do not make value decisions. To the contrary, I would agree with Becker, who suggests:

To have values or not to have values: the question is always with us. When sociologists undertake to study problems that have relevance to the world we live in, they find themselves caught in a crossfire. Some urge them to not take sides, to be neutral and do research that is technically correct and value free. Others tell them their work is shallow and useless if it does not express a deep commitment to a value position. This dilemma, which seems so painful to so many, actually does not exist, for one of its horns is imaginary. For it to exist, one would have to assume, as some presumably do, that it is indeed possible to do research that is uncontaminated by personal and political sympathies. I propose to argue that is not possible and, therefore, that the question is not whether we should take sides, since we inevitably will, but rather whose side are we on [1967, p. 239].

A consideration of values and ethics in sociology must answer first this question: to whom are sociologists accountable when they make observations? My position is that they are responsible to many differing pressure groups. A good deal of the debate today over the uses of sociology represents an inability to agree on which pressure groups should take precedence. I would reject Shils' treatment of ethics; he states:

Ultimately, the ethical quality of social science research—i.e., the ethical quality of the relationship of the investigator to the person he interviews or observes—is derived from the social scientist's relations, as a person and as a citizen, with his society and with his fellow man [1959, p. 147].

This denies the important and significant role played by the variety of pressure groups earlier considered. Sociologists find themselves in a complexly variegated world of changing values, ethics, and political perspectives. No one ethic, value, or ideology uniformly applies to their activities.

A second major question concerns differing ethical consequences of sociological activities. For example, do certain methodologies raise different moral and ethical questions than others? Is it reasonable to state that participant observation in a disguised role is more unethical than a public survey (Erikson, 1968, pp. 505–6)? Closely related to the methodological issue is the question of what stance the sociologist should take toward the implications of his findings. Are sociologists obligated to move into the outside world and actively promote social change? Or is their role more restricted, primarily involving the pursuit of knowledge? In my discussion of these questions, the main interest will be in demonstrating that unless sociologists recognize the role played by values and ethics in their daily affairs, closer ties between theory, method and data will not be forthcoming.

Two incompatible solutions to the question of how the sociologist resolves his obligations to those observed may be distinguished. On the one hand, there are what may be termed *ethical absolutists* who argue that one set of ethics uniformly applies to all sociological activity. On the other hand, there are the *ethical relativists* who suggest that the only reasonable standard is the one "dictated by the individual's conscience [Becker, 1964, p. 280; Dalton, 1964, pp. 50–95]."

The ethical absolutist's position was best summarized by Shils (1959, pp. 114–47) and repeated by Erikson (1967, pp. 366–73). Before presenting this position, a word on my own position is in order. Briefly, I disagree with those who suggest that the sociologist has no right to observe those who have not given their consent. I suggest that the sociologist has the right to make observations on anyone in any setting to the extent that he does so for scientific purposes. The goal of any science is not harm to subjects, but the advancement of knowledge. Any method that moves us toward that goal without unnecessary harm to subjects, is justifiable. The method employed cannot in any deliberate fashion damage the credibility or reputation of the subject, and the sociologist must take pains to maintain the integrity and anonymity of those studied—unless directed otherwise. This may require the withholding of certain findings from publication entirely, or until those observed have moved into positions where they can be done no harm. My position holds that no areas of observation should *a priori* be closed to the sociologist, nor should any research methods be *a priori* defined as unethical, a position clearly at odds with that of the ethical absolutists.

Ethical absolutism begins with the assumption that one can ascribe to modern Western society a value structure that stresses individual autonomy. The dominant moral theme of this social order is the fundamental right of privacy and autonomy for each individual. From this basic assumption a number of ethical principles can be derived for the social scientist (Shils, 1959, pp. 114–47), the first of which is that, he has no right to invade the personal privacy of any individual. Thus, disguised research techniques such as participant observation or unobtrusive methods are defined as unethical when they invade this private order and hence potentially challenge the right of individual autonomy. Second, sociologists as scientists are morally obligated to contribute to their society's self-understanding. In this respect they can only manipulate their subjects and intrude into their private quarters when their activities have therapeutic and/or genuinely scientific purposes, such as the cumulative value of knowledge.

Third, because intrusions into private quarters, and the deliberate disguising of research intents potentially causes harm to subjects, sociologists can only legitimately practice their science in public spheres with openly defined methods (e.g., public surveys).

This ethical system does contain a number of qualifications. Shils, for example, suggests that under certain circumstances it is permissible to invade private spheres of conduct. That is, he suggests that sociologists can legitimately study public institutions such as the law and polity when they do not unduly challenge the moral order and sacredness of those institutions. He states:

I myself see no good reason, therefore, other than expediency, why these "sacred" secular subjects should not be studied by social scientists or why they should not be studied by legitimate techniques. I can see no harm that can come from such inquiries, carried on with judicious detachment and presented with discretion. I can see no moral issue here, such as I can see in the case of manipulation by interviewers and observers or in the case of intrusions of privacy [1959, pp. 138–39].

Despite this, Shils argues that excessive publicity given to sacred-secular institutions

not only breaks the confidentiality which enhances the imaginativeness and reflectiveness necessary for the effective working of institutions but also destroys the respect in which they should, at least, tentatively, be held by the citizenry [1959, p. 137].

That this position contradicts his other ethical mandates seems not to bother him, however, for he goes on to state:

The former consideration is purely empirical and has a reasonable probability of being right. It stands in contradiction to the liberal-democratic and particularly to the populistic-democratic principles of "the eyes of the public constituting the 'virtue of the statesman.' " It restricts the freedom of social scientists. The second consideration is genuinely conservative, as it implies that authority must have some aura of the ineffable about it to be effective. It contradicts a postulate of liberalism and of the social science which is a part of liberalism and which has on the whole proceeded on the postulate of unlimited publicity and an easy-going irreverence toward authority [1959, pp. 137–38].

To summarize, Shils—as an ethical absolutist—argues that there are only two conditions under which the sociologist can legitimately engage in his science: when the results contain some potential therapeutic value (the alleviation of a social problem), or when they contribute to the total body of scientific knowledge. It is clear, however, that the value of science for science's sake takes a position subordinate to science for purposes of therapy. Shils seems to see the function of all human activity as being one of upholding the morality of the attendant social order. This deliberately conservative bias contradicts what I regard as the necessary stance of modern social science.

Commenting on those sociologists who feel that there is little, if any, conflict between the goals of the scientist and those he studies, Becker notes:

The impossibility of achieving consensus, and hence the necessity of conflict, stems in part from the difference between the characteristic approach of the social scientist and that of the layman to the analysis of social life. Everett Hughes has often pointed out that the sociological view of the world —abstract, relativistic, generalizing—necessarily deflates people's view of themselves and their organizations. Sociological analysis has this effect whether it consists of a detailed description of informal behavior or an abstract discussion of theoretical categories. The members of a church, for instance, may be no happier to learn that their behavior exhibits the influence of "pattern variables" than to read a description of their everyday behavior which shows that it differs radically from what they profess on Sunday morning in church. In either case something precious to them is treated as merely an instance of a class [1964, p. 273].

Becker states that sociologists inevitably take someone's side to the potential injustice of another, and hence inevitably present things as some people do not wish to see them; to this, Shils would reply that sociologists should simply avoid circumstances where such consequences could arise. This of course represents an irreducible conflict. If sociologists true to their calling represent the seamier sides of life, then how can it be proposed that they examine settings where no injustice to any perspective would occur?

It seems to me that the ethical absolutists share many of the biases of their counterparts in philosophical idealism, who presume that it is possible to have a complete knowledge of his society's values. The idealists claim to have an image of good and bad, and hence one set of ethical mandates can be constructed. What they ignore is that ethics, like values and other lines of action humans direct toward social objects, are symbolic meanings that emerge out of a political context. Morality, ethics, and values emerge out of interaction. The absolutist has ignored this fundamental feature of human interaction.

It is totally indefensible to state that sociologists ought not to challenge the sacred order of their secular institutions, just as it is indefensible to define beforehand what methods, goals, and strategies sociologists ought to employ. While this position is clearly value-laden, I feel it is justified by the interactionist perspective. Further, it seems to be supported by the activities sociologists routinely engage in. Sociology is abstract and sociological observations necessarily reveal elements of social behavior that persons in everyday life would prefer not to have revealed.

What then is the solution? I have suggested that each sociologist necessarily determines his own ethics. If no one set of standards will apply to sociological activities, then in each situation encountered a slightly different ethical stance will be required. To take this position of course presumes a view of the sociological process that assumes that each sociologist is committed to "telling it as it is," and that he is relatively free to make such statements. That is, I assume that despite the existence of multiple competing pressure groups, the sociologist can manage to maintain his scientific integrity. I further assume that his social location in this political world is such that he is free to make value and ethical decisions. In short free to choose, the value he chooses is that of science for science's sake, and this becomes his only ethical mandate.

Several conditions will affect the translation of this ethical standard into daily sociological conduct. In the simplest cases, as Becker notes, the sociologist may "be taken in" by those he studies and cannot tell it "as it is." To take research in organizational settings as instances of this situation, it is possible to note cases where observers are permitted access to certain behavior settings, but those giving this permission may structure the situation so that researchers see only what they want them to see. To counteract organizational management of the situation, a thorough knowledge of the field situation and an awareness that things are often not what they are presented to be are required. The researcher may also be taken over by the values of those he is studying and lose his sociological objectivity. To guard against this, I have earlier recommended periodic absences from the field by the observer so that a renewed perspective may be established.

The sociologist may be forced into an undesirable ethical stance because of promises he has made to his subjects, the problem confronted by Vidich and Bensman; to secure observation rights, they had to make promises that were later violated. Commenting on these promises, Becker suggests:

> Because of the far-reaching consequences such an agreement could have, most social scientists take care to specify, when reaching an agreement with an organization they want to study, that they have the final say as to what will be published, though they often grant representatives of the organization the right to review the manuscript and suggest changes [1964, p. 278].

Ostensibly the solution to this problem appears to lie in the kinds of agreements observers make with those studied. Upon analysis, however, this can be seen as sidestepping the issue. Ultimately the kinds of bargains sociologists should strive for are those that give complete freedom to study what is deemed necessary. Few subjects will agree to this, feeling always that they know more than sociologists about their problems, a conviction that conveniently permits them to limit researcher access to settings that might be viewed as crucial. In situations where subjects do accept an open-data rights bargain, it is likely that they will not understand the full implications of such an agreement.

The people who agree to have a social scientist study them have not had the experience before and do not know what to expect, nor are they aware of the experiences of others social scientists have studied. Even if the social scientist has pointed out the possible consequences of a report, the person whose organization or community is to be studied is unlikely to think it will happen to him; he cannot believe this fine fellow, the social scientist with whom he now sees eye to eye, would actually do something to harm him. He thinks the social scientist, being a fine fellow, will abide by the ethics of the group under study, not realizing the force and scope of the scientist's impersonal ethic and, particularly, of the scientific obligation to report findings fully and frankly. He may feel easy, having been assured that no specific item of behavior will be attributed to any particular person, but will he think of the "tone" of the report, said to be offensive to the inhabitants of Springdale [Becker, 1964, p. 280]?

Making a proper research agreement, as a solution to the problem of publication and one's obligations to those studied, is insufficient, because each scientist must ultimately decide for himself what he will do or not do, publish or not publish. These decisions must rest with his conscience, for he more than any other person has the intimate knowledge of the consequences of his actions. Abstract ethical rules cannot solve the issues that daily arise in sociological research. For example, certain officials in an organization may have access to study manuscripts and daily observations, while low-level line workers are not even aware of the investigators' presence. To those officials made aware of such studies, are observers ethically obligated to reveal how line workers avoid certain forms of work? Must observers tell all persons they study that they are sociologists? Can they tell line workers that their managers care little about the quality of their products? These are only a few of the problems that arise in any investigation. Their resolution must come from the persons involved—the individual scientist and his subjects.

One mandate thus governs sociological activity—the absolute freedom to pursue one's activities as one sees fit. This rule will be variously translated into individual projects; it is contingent ultimately on the researcher's conscience and on what those in the field situation permit him to do and see. When making an agreement, an additional line of action may be of value: researchers can warn those studied of the effect of publication and help to prepare them for possible consequences. As Becker (1964, pp. 270–83) suggests, a carefully thought out educational program may help those studied to come to better terms with what the sociologist reports. Such programs might take the form of seminars, small-group discussions, and even the circulation of the final report before it is published. In presenting his results to the group studied, the investigator can make clear the kinds of consequences that may be forthcoming. As Becker notes, he can point out the effect of his study on other groups with which those studied are in interaction (the press, national organizations, clients, citizens, and the like) and show them that his findings may endanger their standing with respect to these groups. But in so doing he can make clear that their problems are not unique—that they are shared by many other organizations and communities. Given this perspective, they can better defend their own difficulties and perhaps move in directions for needed social change.

Second, the sociologist can make clear the kinds of interpretations his report may generate. He can make his value judgments clear and indicate what his biases were. With this information, the subjects can better defend their own setting by making reference to the scientific document generated on and about them. Third, the investigator may open new avenues of action and perception among those studied. Organizational leaders may be ignorant of the dysfunctional aspects of certain programs, and an exposure to the sociologist's findings may correct their misconceptions.

Dangers to the sociologist's integrity may arise during this process of education. Hostile factions he was previously unaware of may come forth and challenge the credibility of his study. Faced with this pressure, he may be inclined to alter certain elements of his study. While it may appear that deletions from his report would appease certain parties, under no circumstances should such deletions be sanctioned. As Becker states:

> Although he may be sensitive to the damage his report might do, he should not simply take complaints and make revisions so that the complaints will cease. Even with his best efforts, the complaints may remain because an integral part of his analysis has touched on some chronic sore point in the organization; if this is the case, he must publish his report without changing the offending portions [1964, p. 282].

It may appear, however, that there are features of his report that can be deleted without changing its significance. Embellishments on a point previously well established can be removed if their presence would unduly jeopardize some person. If, however, their presence is necessary to establish the credibility of a point, they should remain. In this situation, if it appears to the investigator that his findings will bring harm or loss of respect to some subject, he may withhold publication until the subject has moved into a situation where such harm would not occur, or at least would be minimized. The sociologist must know his field situations thoroughly before he can adequately and confidently resolve these ethical issues. His theory and data must be well in hand so that when the problem of deciding what to publish arises he can, with full confidence, defend his deletions and inclusions.

Closely related to the above issues is the question of whether or not various research methods have differing ethical implications. Basically, the ethical absolutist argues for the exclusion of all research strategies that hide or disguise the true nature of sociological activities. To him, disguised observer roles and many unobtrusive methods are unethical because permission for their use has not been obtained from those studied. The most recent proponent of this absolutist position is Erikson (1967, pp. 366–73). In presenting his argument, the counter-perspective of the ethical relativist will also be discussed (see Denzin, 1968, pp. 502–4; Polsky, 1967, pp. 117–49; Ball, 1967). Erikson's first argument against disguised observation is that it represents an invasion of privacy. Such an interpretation of course assumes that the sociologist can define beforehand what is a private and what is a public behavior setting. Cavan's (1966) findings suggest that any given behavior setting may, depending on the time of day and categories of participants present, be defined as either public or private. The implication is that the "privateness" of a behavior setting becomes an empirical question. To categorically define settings as public or private potentially ignores the perspective of those studied and supplants the sociologist's definitions for those of the subjects. Erikson continues his argument by suggesting that when sociologists gain entry into private settings via disguised roles, they potentially cause discomfort to those observed; and because the sociologist lacks the means to assess this induced discomfort, he has no right to disguise his intent or role in the research process.

If the research of Goffman is taken seriously, the statement that wearing masks, or disguising one's intents raises ethical questions and causes discomfort during the research process may be challenged, for the proper question becomes, not whether wearing a mask is unethical (since no mask is any more real than any other), but rather, "Which mask should be worn?" There is no straightforward answer, for sociologists assume a variety of masks, or selves, depending on where they find themselves (the classroom, the office, the field). Who is to say which of these are disguised and which are real? My position is that any mask intelligently assumed and not deliberately donned to injure the subject is acceptable. To assert that an assumed role during the research process is *necessarily* unethical and harmful is meaningless.

Second, Erikson argues that the sociologist who assumes a disguised role jeopardizes the broader professional community, because in the event of exposure he could simultaneously close doors to future research and taint the image of his profession. My position is that any research method poses potential threats to fellow colleagues. The community surveyed twice annually for the past ten years can just as easily develop an unfavorable image of sociology and refuse to be studied as can a local Alcoholics Anonymous club studied by a disguised sociologist. Every time the sociologist ventures into the outside world for purposes of research, he places the reputation of the profession on the line. To argue that disguised observations threaten this reputation more than the survey or the experiment ignores the potential impact these methods can and often do have.

Third, Erikson argues that sociologists owe it to their students not to place them in situations where they might have to assume a disguised research role. The assumption of such roles, Erikson suggests, poses moral and ethical problems for the investigator, and students should not have this burden placed on them. My position, based on my own experiences and experiences related by other colleagues, is that this feeling of uncertainty and ethical ambiguity can just as easily arise from the circumstances surrounding the first interview with an irate housewife in a social survey. Certain persons feel more comfortable in the role of disguised observer than in the roles of survey interviewer, known participant observer, or laboratory observer. The belief that encounters with subjects when in the role of disguised observer cause more investigator discomfort than other kinds of investigation may be questioned. I suggest there is nothing inherent in the role that produces ethical or personal problems for the investigator.

Erikson's fourth argument is that data gathered via the disguised method are faulty because sociologists lack the means to assess their disruptive effects on the setting and those observed. I propose that sociologists sensitive to this problem of disruption employ the method of post-observational inquiry recently adopted by psychologists; the investigator asks the subject what he thought the experiment entailed. After completing observations in the disguised role, the researcher's presence could be made public and those observed could then be questioned concerning the effect on them. Such a procedure would provide empirical data on these perceived disruptive effects, thus allowing their assessment, and it would permit sociologists to measure empirically the amount of discomfort or harm their disguised presence created. Further, the investigator might make greater use of his day to day field notes to measure his own perceived impact. Every time the sociologist asks a subject a question, he potentially alters behavior and jeopardizes the quality of subsequent data. It seems unreasonable to assume that more public research methods (e.g., surveys) do not also disrupt the stream of events under analysis. To argue that disguised roles cause the most disruption seems open to question.

Erikson concludes by noting that sociologists never reveal everything when they enter the field. I suggest that not only do they never reveal everything, but frequently it is not possible for them to reveal everything; they themselves are not fully aware of their actual intentions and purposes (e.g., in long-term field studies).

Summarizing his position Erikson, offers two ethical dictates: it is unethical for researchers to deliberately misrepresent their identity to gain entry into private domains otherwise denied them, and it is unethical to deliberately misrepresent the character of research. My reactions are perhaps in the minority among contemporary sociologists, but they indicate what I feel is a necessary uneasiness concerning the argument that sociologists are unethical when they investigate under disguise or without permission. To accept this position has the potential of making sociology a profession that only studies volunteer subjects. I suggest that this misrepresents the very nature of the research process; sociologists have seldom stood above subjects and decided whom they had the right to study and whom they were obligated not to study. Instead, they have always established their domain during the process of research, largely on the basis of their own personal, moral, and ethical standards. (In retrospect this can be seen to be so, given the fact that such categories of persons as housewives, homosexuals, mental patients, and prostitutes are now viewed as acceptable and legitimate persons for observation.)

To summarize, I suggest that in addition to these ethical questions, sociologists might also concern themselves with the fact that at this point in the history of their science they lack the automatic moral-legal license and mandate to gain entry into any research setting; nor do they have the power to withhold information from civil-legal authorities after their data have been obtained. As Project Camelot demonstrated, sociology as a profession has little stature in the eyes of the public and broader civil-legal order. To put ourselves in a position that only sanctions research on what persons give us permission to study continues and makes more manifest an uncomfortable public status. Certainly this need not be the case, as the current status of psychiatry, medicine, the clergy, and the law indicates.

I have placed the burden of ethical decision on the personal-scientific conscience of the individual investigator. My value position should be clear: I feel sociologists who have assumed those research roles and strategies Erikson calls unethical have contributed more substantive knowledge to such diverse areas as small-group research, deviant behavior, medical and organizational sociology than have those who have assumed more open roles. But again this is a matter of individual, as well as collective, scientific conscience and standards. The entry into any scientific enterprise potentially threatens someone's values—be they other sociologists or members of some society. As Becker said, sociologists must always ask themselves, "Whose side are we on (1967, p. 239)?" I feel that Erikson's position takes away from the sociologist the right to make this decision. Perhaps rather than engaging in polemics and debate, the best course of action would be for sociologists as a profession to open these matters to public discussion and empirical inquiry.

*Sources of Variance and the Art of Sociology*

Ultimately the sociological analyst must return to the fact that his science represents a human studying fellow humans. This condition dictates sociology's fate as a discipline—an imperfectly perceiving object is examining objects that react. No matter how technically perfect methods become, variance in observations will always arise, because the sociological observer is a social animal subject to the same whims and fancies, the same pressures and ideologies as those he studies.

Given this, it is perhaps appropriate to ask once again the hoary question of whose side is the sociologist on when he acts as a sociologist? Whose values are influencing him? What ideologies does he hold? What are his personal preferences for one type of method as opposed to another?

If, as I have suggested, sociologists will always be criticized because they disclose a perspective or point of view that someone wished concealed, then they must recognize this as a potential contingency shaping their activities. If sociologists remain true to their discipline, this will always be the case, for above all the sociologist is dedicated to the pursuit of knowledge. Some will say that the wrong group was studied, others that someone's methods were unethical, and some may dislike the researcher's theory. Some critics may even say that sociologists are not involved enough in the "real world" —that they do not adequately concern themselves with the social consequences of their research findings. To these persons, the researcher can only answer that

We take sides as our personal and political commitments dictate, use our theoretical and technical resources to avoid the distortions they might introduce into our work, limit our conclusions carefully, recognize the hierarchy of credibility for what it is, and field as best we can the accusations and doubts that will surely be our fate [Becker, 1967, p. 247].

This book represents only one position among many on the current issues surrounding theory and method in sociology. The programmatic theme dominating my discussion has been deliberate. I believe that the sociologist can no longer treat theory and method as separate subdivisions within his discipline. Each represents intertwined, yet significantly different ways of acting on the symbolic environment. The two must be brought together in an integrated fashion, and my efforts represent a tentative and provisional attempt in this direction. It is my hope that the issues discussed in this book will be debated by others—such is the nature of interaction in any context.

## Notes

There are several excellent sources relevant to the social aspects of doing sociology. These include Bensman and Stein (1964), Hammond (1964), and Sjoberg (1967). A text that appeared after the major portions of this book were completed is Sjoberg and Nett's *A Methodology for Social Research* (1968). It offers a sociology of knowledge approach to social research and must be examined for its position, which in many ways parallels my own.

A problem I have not explicitly treated in this chapter involves the ethical issues surrounding experimentation on human subjects. Sources that may be examined in this context include Wolfle (1968), Hilmer (1968, pp. 324–30), Beecher (1966, pp. 45–46), Lear (1968, pp. 61–70), and the Spring, 1969, issue of *Daedalus*. The ethical position I have offered assumes a humanitarian commitment on the part of the researcher, a commitment that combines a belief in the values of science with a concern for significant aspects of the human condition. I assume that no researcher will engage in studies that would sacrifice the sanctity of human life or self-respect. Ultimately, however, I believe that ethical decisions must be resolved by the individual researcher. I obviously assume a great deal in this respect: I assume a dedication to the scientific study of the human condition.

Some readers of this chapter have suggested that I have not adequately treated the kinds of contingencies and ethical decisions that confront the beginning student of sociology. They proposed a treatment of such problems as tailoring research reports and papers to the demands of a major professor. I do not deny the existence of such pressures, but I assume that the beginning student can best learn how to handle these problems by examining how practicing sociologists have confronted the problems that arise during the actual research process. The ethical and political issues are fundamentally the same. A clear and self-conscious commitment to one's perspective and to the enterprise of sociology is appropriate for the resolution of such issues at whatever level.

I have also not treated the problems surrounding the plea for a more applied sociology. Many sociologists now call for a more active involvement in the world of social problems. Such a stance, I contend, demands a reconception of the sociologist's role—a reconception that I reject. It demands a more active involvement in the political as opposed to the scientific aspects of doing sociology. It calls for a professional as opposed to a scientific conception of sociology as an enterprise. In my judgment the efforts of applied sociologists to treat social problems have been relatively fruitless. Neither a betterment of social conditions nor the improvement of sociological perspectives has been forthcoming.

The proper perspective—and this of course is a value commitment on my part—is a dedication to sociology for its own sake. This at least insures the theoretical direction of applied activities. It has the additional potential of making applied activities one variation on the act of empirical research.

# References

Adams, Richard N., and Jack D. Preiss, eds. 1960. *Human Organization Research: Field Relations and Techniques*. Homewood, Illinois: Dorsey.

Allport, Gordon W. 1942. *The Use of Personal Documents in Psychological Research*. New York: Social Science Research Council.

Anastasi, Ann. 1961. *Psychological Testing*. New York: Macmillan.

Back, Kurt W. 1960. "The Well-Informed Informant." In *Human Organization Research: Field Relations and Techniques*, Richard N. Adams and Jack D. Preiss, eds., pp. 179–87. Homewood, Ill.: Dorsey.

Ball, Donald W. 1967. "Conventional Data and Unconventional Conduct: Toward a Methodological Reorientation." Paper presented to the Pacific Sociological Association, March, 1967, at Long Beach, California.

——. 1968. "Toward a Sociology of Telephones and Telephoners." In *Sociology and Everyday Life*, Marcello Truzzi, ed., pp. 59–75. Englewood Cliffs, N.J.: Prentice-Hall.

Barker, Roger G. and Wright, Herbert F. 1954. *Midwest and Its Children: The Psychological Ecology of an American Town*. Evanston, Ill.: Row, Peterson.

Barton, Allen H. and Lazarsfeld, Paul F. 1955. "Some Functions of Qualitative Analysis in Social Research." *Frankfurter Boiträge Zur Soziologie* 1: 321–61.

Becker, Howard S. 1953. "Becoming a Marihuana User." *American Journal of Sociology* 59 (November): 235–42.

——. 1954. "Field Methods and Techniques: A Note on Interviewing Tactics." *Human Organization* 12 (Winter): 31–32.

——. 1955. "Marihuana Use and Social Control." *Social Problems* 3 (July): 35–44. Reprinted in *Human Behavior and Social Processes*, Arnold M. Rose, ed., pp. 589–607. Boston: Houghton Mifflin.

——. 1956. "Interviewing Medical Students." *American Journal of Sociology* 62 (September): 199–201.

——. 1958. "Problems of Inference and Proof in Participant Observation." *American Sociological Review* 23 (December): 652–59.

——. 1961. Postscript to *The Fantastic Lodge: The Autobiography of a Girl Drug Addict*, Helen MacGill Hughes, ed., pp. 203–6. Boston: Houghton Mifflin.

Becker, Howard S. 1963. *Outsiders: Studies in the Sociology of Deviance*. New York: Free Press.

————. 1964. "Problems in the Publication of Field Studies." In *Reflections on Community Studies*, Arthur J. Vidich, Joseph Bensman, and Maurice R. Stein, eds., pp. 267–84. New York: John Wiley.

————. 1965. Review of *Sociologists at Work*, Philip E. Hammond. ed. *American Sociological Review*, 30 (August) : 602–03.

————. 1966. Introduction to Clifford Shaw, *The Jack-Roller*. pp. v–xviii. Chicago: University of Chicago Press.

————. 1967. "Whose Side Are We On?" *Social Problems* 14 (Winter) : 239–48.

Becker, Howard S. and Geer, Blanche. 1957. "Participant Observation and Interviewing: A Comparison." *Human Organization* 16 (Spring) : 28–32.

————. 1960. "Participant Observation: The Analysis of Qualitative Field Data." In *Human Organization Research: Field Relations and Techniques*, Richard N. Adams and Jack D. Preiss, eds., pp. 267–89. Homewood, Ill.: Dorsey.

Becker, Howard S., Geer, Blanche, Hughes, Everett C., and Strauss, Anselm L. 1961. *Boys in White*. Chicago: University of Chicago Press.

Beecher, Henry E. 1966. "Documenting the Abuses." *Saturday Review* (July), pp. 45–6.

Benney, Mark, and Hughes, Everett C. 1956. "Of Sociology and the Interview: Editorial Preface." *American Journal of Sociology* 62 (September) : 137–42.

Berger, Joseph, Zelditch, Jr., Morris, and Anderson, Bo. 1966. *Sociological Theories in Progress*. Boston: Houghton Mifflin.

Berreman, Gerald D. 1962. *Behind Many Masks*. Cornell University, Ithaca, N.Y.: Society for Applied Anthropology.

Bierstedt, Robert. 1959. "Nominal and Real Definitions in Sociological Theory." In *Symposium on Sociological Theory*, Llewellyn Gross, ed., pp. 121–44. New York: Harper and Row.

————. 1960. "Sociology and Humane Learning." *American Sociological Review* 25 (February) : 3–9.

Blalock, Hubert M. 1960. *Social Statistics*. New York: McGraw-Hill.

————. 1967. "Causal Inferences in Natural Experiments: Some Complications in Matching Designs." *Sociometry* 30 (September) : 300–15.

Blalock, Hubert M. and Ann B. Blalock, eds. 1968. *Methodology in Social Research*. New York: McGraw-Hill.

Blau, Peter M. 1963. *The Dynamics of Bureaucracy*. Chicago: University of Chicago Press.

————. 1964. "The Research Process in *The Dynamics of Bureaucracy*." In *Sociologists at Work*, Phillip E. Hammond, ed., pp. 16–49. New York: Basic Books.

Blumer, Herbert. 1931. "Science Without Concepts." *American Journal of Sociology* 36 (January) : 515–33.

————. 1939. *Critique of Research in the Social Sciences I: An Appraisal of Thomas And Znaniecki's Polish Peasant*. New York: Social Science Research Council.

————. 1940. "The Problem of the Concept in Social Psychology." *American*

*Journal of Sociology* 45 (May): 707–19.

Blumer, Herbert. 1948. "Public Opinion and Public Opinion Polling." *American Sociological Review* 13 (October): 542–54.

———. 1954. "What is Wrong With Social Theory?" *American Sociological Review* 19 (February): 3–10.

———. 1955. "Attitudes and the Social Act." *Social Problems* 3 (Summer): 59–65.

———. 1956. "Sociological Analysis and the 'Variable'." *American Sociological Review* 21 (December): 683–90.

———. 1962. "Society as Symbolic Interaction." In *Human Behavior and Social Processes*, Arnold M. Rose, ed., pp. 179–92. Boston: Houghton Mifflin.

———.1964 "Comment." *Berkeley Journal of Sociology* 9: 118–22.

———. 1966. "Sociological Implications of the Thought of George Herbert Mead." *American Journal of Sociology* 71 (March): 535–44.

———. 1966. Foreword to Severyn T. Bruyn, *The Human Perspective in Sociology: The Methodology of Participant Observation*, pp. iii–vii. Englewood Cliffs, N.J.: Prentice-Hall.

———. 1969. "The Methodological Position of Symbolic Interactionism." In *Symbolic Interactionism*, Herbert Blumer, pp. 1–60. Englewood Cliffs, N.J.: Prentice-Hall.

———. 1969. *Symbolic Interactionism.* Englewood Cliffs, N.J.: Prentice-Hall.

Bonjean, Charles M., Hill, Richard J., and McLemore, S. Dale. 1967. *Sociological Measurement: An Inventory of Scales and Indices.* San Francisco: Chandler.

Booth, Charles. 1967. *On the City: Physical Pattern and Social Structure*, Harold W. Pfautz, ed. Chicago: University of Chicago Press.

Boyle, Richard P. 1969. "Algebraic Systems for Normal and Hierarchical Sociograms." *Sociometry* 32 (March): 99–119.

Bradley, J. V. 1968. *Distribution-Free Statistical Tests.* Englewood Cliffs, N.J.: Prentice-Hall.

Brookover, Linda and Back, Kurt W. 1966. "Time Sampling as a Field Technique." *Human Organization* 25 (Spring): 64–70

Bruyn, Severyn. 1966. *The Human Perspective in Sociology: The Methodology of Participant Observation.* Englewood Cliffs, N.J.: Prentice-Hall.

Bucher, Rue, Fritz, Charles E., and Quarantelli, E. L. 1956. "Tape Recorded Interviews in Social Research." *American Sociological Review* 21 (June): 359–64.

Burgess, Ernest. 1966. "Discussion." In *The Jack-Roller*, Clifford Shaw, pp. 185–97. Chicago: University of Chicago Press.

Burke, Kenneth. 1965. *Permanence and Change.* Indianapolis, Indiana: Bobbs-Merrill.

Camilleri, Santo F. 1962. "Theory, Probability, and Induction in Social Research." *American Sociological Review* 27 (February): 170–78.

Campbell, Donald T. 1957. "Factors Relevant to the Validity of Experiments in Social Settings." *Psychological Bulletin* 54 (July): 297–312.

———. 1963a. "From Description to Experimentation: Interpreting Trends as Quasi-Experiments." In *Problems in Measuring Change*, Chester W. Harris, ed., pp. 212–42. Madison, Wis.: University of Chicago Press.

Campbell, Donald T. 1963b. "Social Attitudes and Other Acquired Behavioral Dispositions." In *Psychology: A Study of a Science*, 6, *Investigations of Man as Socius,* S. Koch, ed., pp. 94–176. New York: McGraw-Hill.

Campbell, Donald T. and Fiske, Donald W. 1959. "Convergent and Discriminant Validation by the Multitrait-Multimethod Matrix." *Psychological Bulletin* 56: 81–105.

Campbell, Donald T. and Stanley, Julian C. 1963. *Experimental and Quasi-Experimental Designs for Research.* Chicago: Rand McNally.

Camus, Albert. 1960. *The Myth of Sisyphus and Other Essays.* New York: Vintage Books.

Cavan, Ruth. 1928. *Suicide.* Chicago: University of Chicago Press.

Cavan, Ruth, Hauser, Phillip M. and Stouffer, Samuel A. 1930. "Note on the Statistical Treatment of Life History Material." *Social Forces* 9 (December): 200–3.

Cavan, Sheri. 1966. *Liquor License.* Chicago: Aldine Publishing Company.

Cicourel, Aaron V. 1964. *Method and Measurement in Sociology.* New York: Free Press.

———. 1967. "Fertility, Family Planning and the Social Organization of Family Life: Some Methodological Issues." *The Journal of Social Issues* 20 (October): 57–81.

———. 1968. *The Social Organization of Juvenile Justice.* New York: John Wiley.

Cleaver, Eldridge. 1968. *Soul on Ice.* New York: McGraw-Hill.

Coleman, James. 1958. "Relational Analysis: The Study of Social Organization with Survey Methods." *Human Organization* 17 (Spring): 28–36.

Conwell, Chic, and Sutherland, Edwin H. 1937. *The Professional Thief.* Chicago: University of Chicago Press.

Cooley, Charles Horton. 1922. *Human Nature and the Social Order.* New York: Charles Scribner.

———. 1926. "The Roots of Social Knowledge." *American Journal of Sociology* 32 (July): 59–79.

Coser, Lewis. 1963. *The Sociology of Literature.* New York: Macmillan.

———. 1965. (Ed.) *Georg Simmel.* Englewood Cliffs, N.J.: Prentice-Hall.

Costner, Herbert L. and Leik, Robert K. 1964. "Deductions from 'Axiomatic Theory'." *American Sociological Review* 20 (December): 819–35.

Cox, G. H., and Marley, E. 1959. "The Estimation of Motility During Rest or Sleep." *Journal of Neurology, Neurosurgery and Psychiatry* 22: 57–60.

Cronbach, Lee J. 1957. "Proposals Leading to Analytic Treatment of Social Perception Scores." In *Person Perception and Interpersonal Behavior,* Renato Tagiuri and Luigi Petrullo, eds., pp. 353–79. Stanford, California: Stanford University Press.

———. 1960. *Essentials of Psychological Testing.* 2nd ed. New York: Harper and Row.

Daedalus. 1969. "Ethical Aspects of Experimentation with Human Subjects." Spring, entire issue.

Dalton, Melville. 1964. "Preconceptions and Methods in *Men Who Manage.*" In *Sociologists at Work,* Phillip E. Hammond, ed., pp. 50–95. New York: Basic Books.

Davis, James. 1964. "Great Books and Small Groups; an Informal History of a National Survey." In *Sociologists at Work*, Phillip Hammond, ed., pp. 212–34. New York: Basic Books.

Davis, Morris and Levine, Sol. 1967. "Toward a Sociology of Public Transit." *Social Problems* 15 (Summer): 84–91.

Davis, Morris, Seibert, Robert, and Breed, Warren. 1966. "Interracial Seating Patterns on New Orleans Public Transit." *Social Problems* 13 (Winter): 298–306.

de Grazia, Sebastian. 1962. *Of Time, Work and Leisure*. Garden City, N.Y.: Doubleday.

Denzin, Norman K. 1966. "The Significant Others of a College Population." *Sociological Quarterly* 7 (Summer): 298–310.

———. 1968. "On the Ethics of Disguised Observation." *Social Problems* 15 (Spring): 502–4.

Deutscher, Irwin. 1969. "Looking Backward: Case Studies on the Progress of Methodology in Sociological Research." *American Sociologist* 4 (February): 35–41.

Dollard, John. 1935. *Criteria for the Life History*. New Haven: Yale University Press.

Douglas, Jack D. 1967. *The Social Meanings of Suicide*. Princeton, N.J.: Princeton University Press.

Drabek, Thomas E. and Haas, J. Eugene. 1967. "Realism in Laboratory Simulation: Myth or Method?" *Social Forces* 45 (March): 337–46.

Edwards, Allen L. 1957a. *The Social Desirability Variable in Personality Assessment and Research*. New York: Dryden Press.

———. 1957b. *Techniques of Attitude Scale Construction*. New York: Appleton-Century-Crofts.

Ehrlich, Howard J. 1963. "The Swastika Epidemic of 1959–1960: Anti-Semitism and Community Characteristics." *Social Problems* 9 (Winter): 264–72.

Erikson, Kai T. 1967. "A Comment on Disguised Observation in Sociology." *Social Problems* 14 (Spring): 366–73.

———. 1968. "A Reply to Denzin." *Social Problems* 15 (Spring): 505–6.

Erskine, Hazel G. 1967. "The Polls: More on Morality and Sex." *Public Opinion Quarterly* 31 (Spring): 116–28.

Faris, Robert E. L. 1967. *Chicago Sociology: 1920–1932*. San Francisco: Chandler.

Festinger, Leon. 1953. "Laboratory Experiments." In *Research Methods in the Behavioral Sciences*, Leon Festinger and Daniel Katz, eds., pp. 136–72. New York: Holt, Rinehart and Winston.

Festinger, Leon, Riecken, Henry, and Schachter, Stanley. 1956. *When Prophecy Fails*. New York: Harper and Row.

Fiedler, Fred E. 1967. *Theory of Leadership Effectiveness*. New York: McGraw-Hill.

Freedman, Ronald. 1950. "Incomplete Matching in Ex Post Facto Studies." *American Journal of Socioolgy* 55 (March): 485–87.

French, John R. P., Jr. 1953. "Experiments in Field Settings." In *Research Methods in the Behavioral Sciences*, Leon Festinger and Daniel Katz, eds., pp. 98–135. New York: Holt, Rinehart and Winston.

Friedman, Neil J. 1967. *The Social Nature of Psychological Research*. New York: Basic Books.

Furfey, Paul H. 1959. "Sociological Science and the Problem of Values." In *Symposium on Sociological Theory*, Llewellyn Gross, ed., pp. 509–30. New York: Harper and Row.

Garfinkel, Harold. 1967. *Studies in Ethnomethodology*. Englewood Cliffs, N.J.: Prentice-Hall.

Geer, Blanche. 1964. "First Days in the Field." In *Sociologists at Work*, Phillip E. Hammond, ed., pp. 322–44. New York: Basic Books.

Glaser, Barney G. and Strauss, Anselm. 1964. *Awareness of Dying*. Chicago: Aldine Publishing Company.

———. 1967. *The Discovery of Grounded Theory*. Chicago: Aldine Publishing Company.

———. 1968. *Time for Dying*. Chicago: Aldine Publishing Company.

Glock, Charles Y. 1955. "Some Applications of the Panel Method to the Study of Change." In *The Language of Social Research*, Paul F. Lazarsfeld and Morris Rosenberg, eds., pp. 242–50. Glencoe, Illinois: Free Press.

Goffman, Erving. 1959. *The Presentation of Self in Everyday Life*. Garden City, N.Y.: Doubleday.

———. 1961. *Asylums*. Garden City, N.Y.: Doubleday.

———. 1961. *Encounters*. Indianapolis, Indiana: Bobbs-Merrill.

———. 1963. *Stigma*. Englewood Cliffs, N.J.: Prentice-Hall.

———. 1963. *Behavior in Public Places*. New York: Free Press of Glencoe.

———. 1967. *Interaction Ritual*. Chicago: Aldine Publishing Company.

Gold, Raymond L. 1958. "Roles in Sociological Field Observations." *Social Forces* 36 (March): 217–23.

———. 1964. "In the Basement—The Apartment Building Janitor." In *The Human Shape of Work: Studies in the Sociology of Work*, Peter L. Berger, ed., pp. 1–49. New York: Macmillan.

Goode, William J. 1965. *Women in Divorce*. New York: Free Press of Glencoe.

Goode, William J. and Hatt, Paul K. 1952. *Methods in Social Research*. New York: McGraw-Hill.

Gorden, Raymond L. 1969. *Interviewing: Strategy, Techniques and Tactics*. Homewood, Ill.: Dorsey Press.

Gordon, Chad. 1968. "Self-Conceptions: Configurations of Content." In *The Self in Interaction*, Vol. I, Chad Gordon and Kenneth J. Gergen, eds., pp. 115–36. New York: John Wiley.

Gottschalk, Louis, Kluckhohn, Clyde, and Angell, Robert. 1945. *The Use of Personal Documents in History, Anthropology, and Sociology*. New York: Social Science Research Council.

Gouldner, Alvin. 1962. "Anti-Minotaur: The Myth of a Value-Free Sociology." *Social Problems* 9 (Winter): 199–213.

———. 1968. "The Sociologist as Partisan: Sociology and the Welfare State." *American Sociologist* 3 (May): 103–16.

Green, Bert F. 1954. "Attitude Measurement." In *Handbook of Social Psychology*, Vol. I, Gardner Lindzey, ed., pp. 335–69.

Greenwood, Ernest. 1945. *Experimental Sociology*. Morningside, N.Y.: King's Crown Press.

Gross, Edward and Stone, Gregory P. 1963. "Embarassment and the Analysis of Role Requirements." *American Journal of Sociology* 70 (July): 1–15.

Guttman, L. 1944. "A Basis for Scaling Qualitative Data." *American Sociological Review* 9 (February): 139–50.

————. 1947. "The Cornell Technique of Scale and Intensity Analysis." *Education and Psychological Measurement* 7: 247–79.

————. 1950a. "The Problem of Attitude and Opinion Measurement." In *Measurement and Prediction*, S. A. Stouffer, and others, pp. 46–59. Princeton, N.J.: Princeton University Press.

————. 1950b. "The Basis for Scalogram Analysis." In *Measurement and Prediction*, S. A. Stouffer, and others, pp. 60–90. Princeton, N.J.: Princeton University Press.

Hall, Edward T. 1959. *The Silent Language*. New York: Doubleday.

Hammond, Phillip E. 1964. (Ed.) *Sociologists at Work*. New York: Basic Books.

Hayner, Norman S. 1964. "Hotel Life: Proximity and Social Distance." In *Contributions to Urban Sociology*, Ernest S. Burgess and Donald J. Bogue, eds., pp. 314–23. Chicago: University of Chicago Press.

Hickman, C. Addison and Kuhn, Manford H. 1956. *Individuals, Groups and Economic Behavior*. New York: Dryden Press.

Hill, Richard J. 1953. "A Note on Inconsistency in Paired Comparison Techniques." *American Sociological Review* 18 (October): 564–66.

————. 1969. "On The Revelence of Methodology." *et al.* 2 (May): 2, 26–9.

Hilmer, Norman A. 1968. "Anonymity, Confidentiality, and Invasions of Privacy: Responsibility of the Researcher." *American Journal of Public Health* 58 (February): 324–30.

Hirschi, Travis and Selvin, Hanan C. 1967. *Delinquency Research: An Appraisal of Analytic Methods*. New York: Free Press.

Homans, George Caspar. 1950. *The Human Group*. New York: Harcourt, Brace and World.

————. 1964. "Contemporary Theory in Sociology." In *Handbook of Modern Sociology*, R. E. L. Faris, ed., pp. 951–77. Chicago: Rand McNally.

Horowitz, Irving Louis. 1965. "The Life and Death of Project Camelot." *Transaction* 3 (November-December): 3–7, 44–47. Also reprinted in *American Psychologist* 21 (May, 1966): 445–54.

Hovland, Carl, and Sherif, Muzafer. 1952. "Judgmental Phenomena and Scales of Attitude Measurement." *Journal of Abnormal and Social Psychology* 47 (October): 822–32.

Hughes, Everett C. 1956. *Men and Their Work*. Glencoe, Ill.: Free Press.

Hughes, Everett C., and Hughes, Helen McGill. 1952. *Where Peoples Meet*. Glencoe, Ill.: Free Press.

Hulett, J. E., Jr. 1964. "Communication and Social Order: The Search for a Theory." *Audio-Visual Communication Review* 12 (Winter): 458–68.

Hyman, Herbert. 1954. "The General Problem of Questionnaire Design." In *Public Opinion and Propaganda*, Daniel Katz, and others, eds., pp. 665–74.

Hyman, Herbert. 1954. *Interviewing in Social Research.* Chicago: University of Chicago Press.
————. 1955. *Survey Design and Analysis: Principles, Cases and Principles.* Glencoe, Ill.: Free Press.

Jacobs, Jerry. 1967. "A Phenonological Study of Suicide Notes." *Social Problems* 15 (Summer): 60–72.
Janes, Robert W. 1961. "A Note on the Phases of the Community Role of the Participant Observer. *American Sociological Review* 26 (June): 446–50.
Johnson, Harry. 1960. *Introduction to Sociology.* New York: Harcourt, Brace.

Kahn, Robert L., and Cannell, Charles F. 1962. *The Dynamics of Interviewing: Theory, Technique, and Cases.* New York: John Wiley.
Katz, Elihu and Lazarsfeld, Paul F. 1955. *Personal Influence.* Glencoe, Ill.: Free Press.
Kendall, Patricia L., and Wolf, Katherine M. 1955. "The Two Purposes of Deviant Case Analysis." In *The Language of Social Research,* Paul F. Lazarsfeld and Morris Rosenberg, eds., pp. 167–70. Glencoe, Ill.: Free Press.
Kinch, John W. 1963. "A Formalized Theory of the Self-Concept." *American Journal of Sociology* 68 (January): 481–86.
Kish, Leslie. 1953. "Selection of the Sample." In *Research Methods in the Behavioral Sciences,* Leon Festinger and Daniel Katz, eds., pp. 175–239. New York: Holt, Rinehart and Winston.
————. 1965. *Survey Sampling.* New York: John Wiley.
Kitsuse, John I., and Cicourel, Aaron V. 1963. "A Note on the Uses of Official Statistics." *Social Problems* 11 (Fall): 131–39.
Kuhn, Manford H. 1962. "The Interview and the Professional Relationship." In *Human Behavior and Social Processes,* Arnold M. Rose, ed., pp. 193–206. Boston: Houghton Mifflin.
————. 1964. "The Reference Group Reconsidered." *Sociological Quarterly* 5 (Winter): 5–21.
————. 1964. "Major Trends in Symbolic Interaction Theory in the Past Twenty-five Years." *Sociological Quarterly* 5 (Winter): 61–84.
Kuhn, Manford H., and McPartland, Thomas S. 1954. "An Empirical Investigation of Self-Attitudes." *American Sociological Review* 19 (February): 68–76.

Landesco, John. 1964. "Organized Crime in Chicago." In *Contributions to Urban Sociology,* Ernest W. Burgess and Donald J. Bogue, eds., pp. 559–76. Chicago: University of Chicago Press.
La Piere, Richard T. 1934. "Attitudes vs. Actions." *Social Forces* 13 (March): 230–37.
————. 1969. "Comment on Irwin Deutscher's 'Looking Backward'." *American Sociologist* 4 (February): 41–42.
Lazarsfeld, Paul F. 1954. "The Art of Asking Why: Three Principles Underlying the Formulation of Questionnaires." In *Public Opinion and Propaganda,* Daniel Katz, and others, eds., pp. 675–86. New York: Holt, Rinehart and Winston.

Lazarsfeld, Paul F. 1955. Foreword to Herbert Hyman, *Survey Design and Analysis*, pp. ix-xvii. Glencoe, Ill.: Free Press.

———. 1955. "Intrepretation of Statistical Relations as a Research Operation." In *The Language of Social Research*, Paul F. Lazarsfeld and Morris Rosenberg, eds., pp. 115–25. Glencoe, Ill.: Free Press.

———. 1958. "Evidence and Inference in Social Research." *Daedalus* 87: 99–130.

Lazarsfeld, Paul F., and Menzel, Herbert. 1961. "On the Relation Between Individual and Collective Properties." In *Complex Organization: A Sociological Reader*, Amitai Etzioni, ed., pp. 422–40. New York: Holt, Rinehart and Winston.

Lazarsfeld, Paul F., and Rosenberg, Morris. 1955. (Eds.) *The Language of Social Research*. Glencoe, Ill.: Free Press.

Lazarsfeld, Paul F., Berelson, Bernard, and Gaudet, Hazel. 1955. "The Process of Opinion and Attitude Formation." In *The Language of Social Research*, Paul F. Lazarsfeld and Morris Rosenberg, eds., 231–42. Glencoe, Ill.: Free Press.

Lazerwitz, Bernard. 1968. "Sampling Theory and Procedures." In *Methodology in Social Research*, Hubert A. Blalock, Jr., and Ann B. Blalock, eds., pp. 278–328. New York: McGraw-Hill.

Lear, John. 1968. "Do We Need Rules for Experiments on People?" *Saturday Review* (February, 5): 61–70.

Leik, Robert K. 1965. " 'Irrelevant' Aspects of Stooge Behavior: Implication for Leadership Studies and Experimental Methodology." *Sociometry* 28 (September): 259–71.

Lemert, Edwin A. 1951. *Social Pathology*. New York: McGraw-Hill.

———. 1958. "The Behavior of the Systematic Check Forger." *Social Problems* 6 (Fall): 141–48.

———. 1967. *Human Deviance, Social Problems and Social Control*. Englewood Cliffs, N.J.: Prentice-Hall.

Lewis, Oscar. 1953. "Controls and Experiments in Field Work." In *Anthropology Today*, A. L. Kroeber, ed., pp. 452–75. Chicago: University of Chicago Press.

Liebow, Elliot. 1967. *Tally's Corner*. Boston: Little, Brown.

Lindesmith, Alfred R. 1947. *Opiate Addiction*. Bloomington, Ind.: Principia Press.

———. 1952. "Comment on W. S. Robinson's 'The Logical Structure of Analytic Induction'," *American Sociological Review* 17 (August): 492–93.

———. 1968. *Addiction and Opiates*. Chicago: Aldine Publishing Company.

Lipset, Seymour Martin. 1964. "The Biography of a Research Project: *Union Democracy*." In *Sociologists at Work*, Phillip Hammond, ed., pp. 96–120. New York: Basic Books.

Lipset, Seymour Martin, Trow, Martin, and Coleman, James. 1962. *Union Democracy*. Garden City, N.Y.: Anchor Books, Doubleday.

Lofland, John. 1966. *Doomsday Cult*. Englewood Cliffs, N.J.: Prentice-Hall.

Lundberg, George A. 1926. "Case Work and the Statistical Method." *Social Forces* 5: 60–63.

———. 1955. "The Natural Science Trend in Sociology." *American Journal of Sociology* 61 (November): 191–202.

Lundberg, George A. 1956. "Quantitative Methods in Sociology." *Social Forces* 39 (October): 19–24.

Lyman, Stanford M., and Scott, Marvin B. 1967. "Territoriality: A Neglected Sociological Dimension." *Social Problems* 15 (Fall): 236–49.

Maccoby, Eleanor E., and Maccoby, Nathan. 1954. "The Interview: A Tool of Social Science." In *Handbook of Social Psychology*, Vol. I, Gardner Lindzey, ed., pp. 449–87. Reading, Mass.: Addison-Wesley.

MacIver, R. M. 1931. "Is Sociology a Natural Science?" *American Journal of Sociology* 25 (May): 25–35.

Manning, Peter K. 1967. "Problems in Interpreting Interview Data." *Sociology and Social Research* 15 (April): 302–16.

Mayne, Ethel Colburn. 1964. (Trans.) *Letters of Fyodor Michailovitch Dostoevsky*. New York: McGraw-Hill.

McCall, George J., and Simmons, J. L. 1969. (Eds.) *Issues in Participant Observation: A Text and Reader*. Reading, Mass.: Addison-Wesley.

McGrath, Joseph E., and Altman, Irwin. 1966. *Small Group Research: A Synthesis and Critique of the Field*. New York: Holt, Rinehart and Winston.

Mead, George Herbert. 1917. "Scientific Method and Individual Thinker." In *Creative Intelligence: Essays in the Pragmatic Attitude*, John Dewey, ed., pp. 176–227. New York: Holt, Rinehart & Winston.

———. 1927. "The Objective Reality of Perspectives." In *Proceedings of the Sixth International Conference of Philosophy*, Edgar Sheffield Brightman, ed., pp. 75–85. New York: Longmans, Green.

———. 1934. *Mind, Self, and Society*. Chicago: University of Chicago Press.

Merton, Robert K. 1946. *Mass Persuasion*. New York: Harper and Brothers.

———. 1967. *On Theoretical Sociology*. New York: The Free Press.

Merton, Robert K. and Kendall, Patricia L. 1946. "The Focused Interview." *American Journal of Sociology* 51 (May): 541–57.

Miller, Delbert C. 1964. *Handbook of Research Design and Social Measurement*. New York: David McKay.

Mills, C. Wright. 1959. *The Sociological Imagination*. New York: Oxford University Press.

Mueller, John H., and Schuessler, Karl F. 1961. *Statistical Reasoning in Sociology*. Boston: Houghton Mifflin.

Murphy, G. and Murphy, L. 1962. "Soviet Life and Soviet Psychology." In *Some Views on Soviet Psychology*, R. A. Bauer, ed., pp. 253–76. Washington, D.C.: American Psychological Association.

———. 1950. *Social Psychology*. New York: Dryden Press.

Naroll, Raoul. 1968. "Some Thoughts on Comparative Method in Cultural Anthropology." *Methodology in Social Research*, Hubert M. Blalock, Jr., and Ann B. Blalock, ed., pp. 236–77. New York: McGraw-Hill.

Olesen, Virginia L., and Whittaker, Elvi Waik. 1967. "Role Making in Participant Observation: Processes in the Research-Actor Relationship." *Human Organization* 26 (Winter): 273–81.

Orne, Martin T. 1962. "On the Social Psychology of the Psychological Experiment: With Special Reference to Demand Characteristics and Their Implications." *American Psychologist* 17 (October): 776–83.

Osgood, C. E., Suci, G. J., and Tannenbaum, P. H. 1957. *The Measurement of Meaning*. Urbana, Ill.: University of Illinois Press.

Park, Robert E. 1931. "The Sociological Methods of William Graham Summer, and William I. Thomas and Florian Znaniecki." In *Methods of Social Science: A Case Book*, Stewart A. Rice, ed., pp. 154–75. Chicago: University of Chicago Press.

————. 1952. Human Communities: *The City and Human Ecology*. Everett C. Hughes, and others, eds., Glencoe, Ill.: Free Press.

Park, Robert E. and Burgess, Ernest W. 1924. *Introduction to the Science of Sociology*. 2nd ed. Chicago: University of Chicago Press.

Parsons, Talcott. 1950. "The Prospects of Sociological Theory." *American Sociological Review* 15 (February): 3–16.

Parsons, Talcott and Shils, Edward A. 1959. *Toward a General Theory of Action*. Cambridge, Mass.: Harvard University Press.

Paul, Benjamin D. 1953. "Interview Techniques and Field Work." In *Anthropology Today*, A. L. Kroeber, ed., pp. 430–51. Chicago: University of Chicago Press.

Phillips, R. H. 1962. "Miami goes Latin under Cuban Tide." *New York Times*, 111 (March, 18): 85.

Polanyi, Michael. 1958. *Personal Knowledge*. Chicago: University of Chicago Press.

Polsky, Ned. 1967. *Hustlers, Beats, and Others*. Chicago: Aldine Publishing Company.

Psathas, George and Henslin, James J. 1967. "Dispatched Orders and the Cab Driver: A Study of Locating Activities." *Social Problems* 14 (Spring): 424–43.

Read, Bill. 1964. *The Days of Dylan Thomas*. New York: McGraw-Hill.

Record, Jane Cassels. 1967. "The Research Institute and the Pressure Group." In *Ethics, Politics, and Social Research*, Gideon Sjoberg, ed., pp. 25–49. Cambridge, Mass.: Schenkman Publishing Company.

Redfield, Robert. 1948. "The Art of Social Science." *American Journal of Sociology* 55 (November): 181–90.

Reisman, David and Watson, Jeanne. 1964. "The Sociability Project: A Chronicle of Frustration and Achievement." In *Sociologists at Work*, Phillip E. Hammond, ed., pp. 235–321. New York: Basic Books.

Reiss, Albert J., Jr. 1959. "Rural-Urban Differences in Interpersonal Contracts." *American Journal of Sociology* 65 (September): 182–95.

————. 1968. "Stuff and Nonsense about Social Surveys and Observation." In *Institutions and the Person: Papers Presented to Everett C. Hughes*, Howard S. Becker, and others, eds., pp. 351–67. Chicago: Aldine Publishing Company.

Richardson, Stephan A., Dohrenwend, Barbara Snell, and Klein, David. 1965. *Interviewing: Its Forms and Functions*. New York: Basic Books.

Robinson, W. S. 1951. "The Logical Structure of Analytic Induction." *American Sociological Review* 16 (December): 812–18.

Rose, Edward. 1960. "The English Record of a Natural Sociology." *American Sociological Review* 25 (April): 193–208.

Rosenthal, Robert. 1966. *Experimental Effects in Behavioral Research*. New York: Appleton-Century-Crofts.

Ross, John A., and Smith, Perry. 1965. "Experimental Designs of the Single-Stimulus, All-or-Nothing Type." *American Sociological Review* 30 (February): 68–80.

Roth, Julius A. 1966. "Hired Hand Research." *American Sociologist* 1 (August): 190–96.

Rowe, John Howland. 1953. "Technical Aids in Anthropology: A Historical Survey." In *Anthropology Today*, A. L. Kroeber, ed., pp. 895–940. Chicago: University of Chicago Press.

Roy, Donald. 1952. "Quota Restriction and Goldbricking in a Machine Shop." *American Journal of Sociology* 57 (March): 427–42.

Sarbin, Theodore R. 1967. "On the Futility of the Proposition that some People Are Labeled Mentally Ill." *Journal of Consulting Psychology* 31 (October): 447–53.

Scheff, Thomas J. 1966. *Being Mentally Ill*. Chicago: Aldine Publishing Company.

Schrag, Clarence. 1967. "Philosophical Issues in the Science of Sociology." *Sociology and Social Research* 51 (April): 361–72.

Schwartz, Morris, and Schwartz, Charlotte Green. 1955. "Problems in Participant Observation." *American Journal of Sociology* 60 (January): 343–53.

Seeman, Melvin. 1967. "Powerlessness and Knowledge: A Comparative Study of Alienation and Learning." *Sociometry* 30 (June): 105–23.

Selltiz, Claire, Jahoda, Marie, Deutsch, Morton, and Cook, Stuart W. 1965. *Research Methods in Social Relations*, rev. one-vol. ed. New York: Holt, Rinehart and Winston.

Shaw, Clifford R. 1966. *The Jack-Roller*, Phoenix ed. Chicago: University of Chicago Press.

Sherman, Susan Roth. 1967. "Demand Characteristics in an Experiment on Attitude Change." *Sociometry* 30 (September): 246–61.

Shibutani, Tamotsu. 1961. *Society and Personality*. Englewood Cliffs, N.J.: Prentice-Hall.

———. 1966. *Improvised News: A Sociological Study of Rumor*. Indianapolis: Bobbs-Merrill, Inc.

Shils, Edward A. 1959. "Social Inquiry and the Autonomy of the Individual." In *The Human Meaning of the Social Sciences*, Daniel Lerner, ed., pp. 114–57. Cleveland: Meridian.

Short, James F., Jr. 1963. "Introduction to the Abridged Edition" of Frederic M. Thrasher, *The Gang*, pp. xv–liii. Chicago: University of Chicago Press.

Siegel, Sidney. 1956. *Nonparametric Statistics for the Behavioral Sciences*. New York: McGraw-Hill.

Simmel, Georg. 1908. "Sociology of the Senses: Visual Interaction." In Georg Simmel, *Soziologie*, pp. 646–51. Leipsig: Duncker and Humbolt. Also translated and adapted by Robert E. Park and Ernest W. Burgess in *Introduction to the Science of Sociology*, 2nd ed., pp. 356–61. Chicago: University of Chicago Press.

———. 1950. *The Sociology of Georg Simmel*, Kurt Wolff, tran. New York:

Siu, Paul C. P. 1964. "The Isolation of Chinese Laundryman." In *Contributions to Urban Sociology*, Ernest W. Burgess and Donald J. Bogue, ed., pp. 429–42. Chicago: University of Chicago Press.

Sjoberg, Gideon. 1967. (Ed.) *Ethics, Politics, and Social Research*. Cambridge, Mass.: Schenkman Publishing Company.

Sjoberg, Gideon, and Nett, Roger. 1968. *A Methodology for Social Research*. New York: Harper and Row.

Smelser, Neil J. 1968. *Essays in Sociological Explanation*. Englewood Cliffs, N.J.: Prentice-Hall.

Sommer, Robert. 1959. "Studies in Personal Space." *Sociometry* 22 (September): 247–60.

———. 1961. "Leadership and Group Geography." *Sociometry* 24 (June): 99–110.

———. 1962. "The Distance for Comfortable Conversation: A Further Study." *Sociometry* 25 (June): 111–16.

———. 1967. "Sociofugal Space." *American Journal of Sociology* 72 (May): 654–60.

———. 1968. *Personal Space*. Englewood Cliffs, N.J.: Prentice-Hall.

Sommer, Robert, and Felipe, Nancy Jo. 1966. "Invasions of Personal Space." *Social Problems* 14 (May): 206–14.

Sorokin, Pitirim A., and Berger, Clarence Q. 1938. *Time-Budgets of Human Behavior*. Cambridge, Mass.: Harvard University Press.

Sorokin, Pitirim A., and Merton, Robert K. 1937. "Social Time: A Methodological and Functional Analysis." *American Journal of Sociology* 42 (March): 615–29.

Sorokin, Pitirim A., and Zimmerman, C. C. 1929. *Principles of Rural-Urban Sociology*. New York: Henry Holt.

Spitzer, Stephan P., and Denzin, Norman K. Forthcoming. *The Career of the Mental Patient*.

Spitzer, Stephan P., Stratton, John R., Fitzgerald, Jack D., and Mach, Brigitte K. 1966. "The Self Concept: Test Equivalence and Perceived Validity." *Sociological Quarterly* 7 (Summer): pp. 265–80.

Spykman, Nicholas J. 1966. *The Social Theory of Georg Simmel*. New York: Atherton Press.

Stevens, S. S. 1951. "Mathematics, Measurement, and Psychophysics." In *Handbook of Experimental Psychology*, S. S. Stevens, ed., pp. 1–49. New York: John Wiley.

Stinchcombe, Arthur. 1968. *Constructing Social Theories*. New York: Harcourt, Brace and World.

Stone, Gregory P. 1954. "City Shoppers and Urban Identification: Observations of the Social Psychology of City Life." *American Journal of Sociology* 60 (July): 36–45.

———. 1962. "Appearance and the Self." In *Human Behavior and Social Processes*, Arnold M. Rose, ed., pp. 86–118.

Stone, Gregory P. and Farberman, Harvey A. 1967. "On the Edge of Rapprochement: Was Durkheim Moving Toward the Perspective of Symbolic Interaction?" *Sociological Quarterly* 8 (Spring): 149–64.

———. 1970. (Eds.) *Social Psychology from the Standpoint of Symbolic Interaction*. Boston, Mass.: Blaisdale.

Stouffer, Samuel A. 1930. *Experimental Comparison of Statistical and Case History Methods in Attitude Research*. Unpublished Doctoral Dissertation, Department of Sociology, University of Chicago.

————. 1950. "Some Observations on Study Design." *American Journal of Sociology* 55 (January): 355–61.

Strauss, Anselm L. 1959. *Mirrors and Masks*. Glencoe, Ill.: Free Press.

————. 1968. "Strategies for Discovering Urban Theory." In *The American City: A Sourcebook for Urban Imagery*, Anselm L. Strauss, ed., pp. 515–30. Chicago: Aldine Publishing Company.

Strauss, Anselm L., and Schatzman, Leonard. 1955. "Cross-Class Interviewing: An Analysis of Interaction and Communicative Styles." *Human Organization* 14 (Summer): 28–31.

Strauss, Anselm L., Schatzman, Leonard, Bucher, Rue, Ehrlich, Danuta, and Sabshin, Melvin. 1964. *Psychiatric Ideologies and Institutions*. New York: Free Press.

Sudnow, David. 1967. *Passing On: The Social Organization of Dying*. Englewood Cliffs, N.J.: Prentice-Hall.

Svalastoga, Kaare. 1964. "Social Differentiation." In *Handbook of Modern Sociology*, R. E. L. Faris, ed., pp. 530–75. Chicago: Rand McNally.

Thomas, W. I., and Thomas, Dorothy Swaine. 1928. *The Child in America*. New York: Alfred A. Knopf.

Thomas, W. I., and Znaniecki, Florian. 1927. *The Polish Peasant*. New York: Alfred A. Knopf.

Thrasher, Frederick M. 1963. *The Gang*, abridged ed. Chicago: University of Chicago Press.

Thurstone, L. L. 1927. "Psychophysical Analysis." *American Journal of Psychology* 38: 368–89.

Thurstone, L. L., and Chave, E. J. 1929. *The Measurement of Attitude*. Chicago: University of Chicago Press.

*Time*. 1967. "Editorial Preface." July 7, p. 11.

Torgerson, W. S. 1958. *Theory and Methods of Scaling*. New York: John Wiley.

Trow, Martin. 1957. "Comment on Participant Observation and Interviewing: A Comparison." *Human Organization* 16: 33–35.

Turner, Ralph H. 1953. "The Quest for Universals in Sociological Research." *American Sociological Review* 18 (December): 604–11.

Upshaw, Harry S. 1968. "Attitude Measurement." In *Methodology in Social Research*, Hubert M. Blalock, Jr., and Blalock, Ann B., eds., pp. 60–111. New York: McGraw-Hill.

Vidich, Arthur Jr., and Bensman, Joseph. 1964. "The Springdale Case: Academic Bureaucrats and Sensitive Townspeople." In *Reflections on Community Studies*, Arthur J. Vidich, Joseph Bensman, and Maurice J. Stein, eds., pp. 313–49. New York: John Wiley.

Vidich, Arthur J., Bensman, Joseph, and Stein, Maurice R. 1964. (Eds.) *Reflections on Community Studies*. New York: John Wiley.

Wallace, Samuel E. 1965. *Skidrow as a Way of Life*. Totawa, N.J.: Bedminster Press.

Wax, Rosalie Hankey. 1960. "Twelve Years Later: An Analysis of Field Experience." In *Human Organization Research: Field Relations and Techniques*, Richard N. Adams and Jack J. Preiss, eds., pp. 166–78. Homewood, Ill.: Dorsey Press.

Webb, Eugene J. 1966. "Unconventionality, Triangulation and Inference." In the *Proceedings* of the 1966 Invitational Conference on Testing Problems, pp. 34–43. Princeton, N.J.: Educational Testing Service.

Webb, Eugene J., Campbell, Donald T., Schwartz, Richard D., and Sechrest, Lee. 1966. *Unobtrusive Measures: Nonreactive Research in the Social Sciences*. Chicago: Rand McNally.

Weber, Max. 1958. *From Max Weber: Essays in Sociology*. H. H. Gerth and C. Wright Mills, trans. and eds. New York: Oxford University Press.

Weinberg, S. Kirson. 1952. "Comment on W. S. Robinson's 'The Logical Structure of Analytic Induction'." *American Sociological Review* 17 (August): 493–94.

Weiss, Robert S. and Jacobson, Eugene. 1955. "A Method for the Analysis of the Structure of Complex Organizations." *American Sociological Review* 20 (December): 661–68.

Westie, Frank R. 1957. "Toward Closer Relations Between Theory and Research: A Procedure and an Example." *American Sociological Review* 22 (April): 149–54.

Whyte, William Foote. 1955. *Street Corner Society*, 2nd ed. Chicago: University of Chicago Press.

Wolff, Kurt H. 1959. (Ed.) *Georg Simmel, 1858–1918*. Columbus, Ohio: Ohio State University Press.

————. 1960. "The Collection and Organization of Field Materials: A Research Report." In *Human Organization Research: Field Relations and Techniques*, Richard N. Adams and Jack J. Preiss, eds., pp. 240–54. Homewood, Ill.: Dorsey Press.

Wolfle, Dael. 1968. "The Use of Human Subjects." *Science* 19 (February), no. 3817.

Wordsworth, William. 1948. *The Prelude, with a Selection from the Shorter Poems and the Sonnets and the 1800 Preface to Lyrical Ballads*. Carlos Baker, ed. New York: Rinehart and Company.

Wuebben, Paul L. 1968. "Experimental Design, Measurement, and Subjects: A Neglected Problem of Control." *Sociometry* 31 (March): 89–101.

Young, Kimball. 1952. *Personality and Problems of Adjustment*. New York: Appleton-Century-Crofts.

Young, Pauline V. 1966. *Scientific Social Surveys and Research*, 4th ed. Englewood Cliffs, N.J.: Prentice-Hall.

Zelditch, Morris J. 1962. "Some Methodological Problems of Field Studies." *American Journal of Sociology* 67 (March): 566–76.

Zetterberg, Hans. 1955. "On Axiomatic Theories." In *The Language of Social Research*, Paul F. Lazarsfeld and Morris Rosenberg, eds., pp. 533–40. Glencoe, Ill.: Free Press.

Zetterberg, Hans. 1965. *On Theory and Verification in Sociology*, 2nd ed. Totawa, N.J.: Bedminster Press.
Znaniecki, Florian. 1934. *The Method of Sociology*. New York: Farrar and Rinehart.

# Name Index

# Subject Index

Made in the USA
Monee, IL
25 January 2024